1,000,000 Books

are available to read at

www.ForgottenBooks.com

Read online
Download PDF
Purchase in print

ISBN 978-0-243-28795-6
PIBN 10791300

This book is a reproduction of an important historical work. Forgotten Books uses state-of-the-art technology to digitally reconstruct the work, preserving the original format whilst repairing imperfections present in the aged copy. In rare cases, an imperfection in the original, such as a blemish or missing page, may be replicated in our edition. We do, however, repair the vast majority of imperfections successfully; any imperfections that remain are intentionally left to preserve the state of such historical works.

Forgotten Books is a registered trademark of FB &c Ltd.
Copyright © 2018 FB &c Ltd.
FB &c Ltd, Dalton House, 60 Windsor Avenue, London, SW19 2RR.
Company number 08720141. Registered in England and Wales.

For support please visit www.forgottenbooks.com

1 MONTH OF
FREE
READING

at
www.ForgottenBooks.com

By purchasing this book you are eligible for one month membership to ForgottenBooks.com, giving you unlimited access to our entire collection of over 1,000,000 titles via our web site and mobile apps.

To claim your free month visit:
www.forgottenbooks.com/free791300

* Offer is valid for 45 days from date of purchase. Terms and conditions apply.

English
Français
Deutsche
Italiano
Español
Português

www.forgottenbooks.com

Mythology Photography **Fiction**
Fishing Christianity **Art** Cooking
Essays Buddhism Freemasonry
Medicine **Biology** Music **Ancient Egypt** Evolution Carpentry Physics
Dance Geology **Mathematics** Fitness
Shakespeare **Folklore** Yoga Marketing
Confidence Immortality Biographies
Poetry **Psychology** Witchcraft
Electronics Chemistry History **Law**
Accounting **Philosophy** Anthropology
Alchemy Drama Quantum Mechanics
Atheism Sexual Health **Ancient History**
Entrepreneurship Languages Sport
Paleontology Needlework Islam
Metaphysics Investment Archaeology
Parenting Statistics Criminology
Motivational

CHARLES DE FOUCAULD

HERMIT AND EXPLORER

BY

RENÉ BAZIN

TRANSLATED BY PETER KEELAN

NEW YORK, CINCINNATI, CHICAGO
BENZIGER BROTHERS
PRINTERS TO THE | PUBLISHERS OF
HOLY APOSTOLIC SEE | BENZIGER'S MAGAZINE

1923

Made and printed in Great Britain

CONTENTS

	PAGE
GLOSSARY	vii

CHAPTER
I. HIS YOUTH	1
II. THE PRELIMINARIES OF THE JOURNEY	16
1. THE DISGUISE AND THE FIRST STEPS	17
2. THE STORY OF MARDOCHÉE ABI SERVUR	23
III. THE EXPLORER	35
IV. HIS CONVERSION	61
V. THE TRAPPIST	77
VI. NAZARETH AND JERUSALEM	110
VII. CHARLES DE FOUCAULD A PRIEST—THE DESERT ROAD	136
VIII. BENI-ABBES	150
IX. TRAINING TOURS	211
X. THE SETTLEMENT IN HOGGAR	231
XI. POETRY AND PROVERBS	273
XII. TAMANRASSET	280
APPENDIX	355

GLOSSARY

ABD ENNEBI, servant of the Prophet.
ABDJESU, servant of Jesus.
AHAL, social gathering among the Tuaregs.
AMAN, armistice.
AMENOKAL, a noble elected chief over a confederation of tribes.
AMRAR, a subordinate chief under an Amenokal.
ANAIA, the pledged perpetual protection of a man or tribe.
BARAQUER, to kneel down (of camels).
BELRAS, Turkish slippers.
BEN, son.
BERDIS, reeds or rushes.
BLED, country, but especially used of the back-country or hinterland, the Saharan desert.
BORJ, blockhouse or fortified post.
BURNOUS, an Arab cloak.
CAÏD, judge of a town or village: see Khalifa.
CASBAH, chapel or citadel.
CHAMBI, CHAMBAA, warlike plundering tribes like the Cossacks.
CHEGGAR, cloth or linen.
DEBIHA, the act of putting oneself under *anaia.*
DISS, a reed or rush like an alfa.
DOUAR, a village of tents, arranged in streets.
ETHEL, an atlee—a kind of tree.
FELLAGAS, outlawed native factions hostile to the friendly natives under French protection.
GAILA, midday heat, time of siesta.
GANDOURAH, an Oriental sleeveless shirt-like garment.
GUETTAF, a whitish saltwort.
GUM, band or troop; escort of Arab chiefs; also French commanders in Africa.
HAJJ, a Musulman who has made the pilgrimage to Mecca.
HARKA, an expeditionary column.
HARRATINS, a crossbreed of Arabs and negroes, between slaves and freemen, who work as labourers, without political status.
HARTANI, singular of Harratin.
IMRAD, equality, also a clan.
IMZAD, violin, with only one string.
JELABIA, a cowl or hood.
JERJIR, a flower, the stems of which are blown away by the winds of the desert.
KAFER, infidel.
KHALIFA, Arab chief: the order is as follows: Caïd, Khalifa, Cadi, Adel, Bachadel.
KHAUA, brotherhood or confraternity.

GLOSSARY

KHEFIS, a very composite food liked by Father de Foucauld (*see* p. 382).
KHENIF, a black *burnous* with a yellow moon.
KHOJA, a Mohammedan schoolmaster or teacher.
KSAR, settled village, not movable like a *douar*.
KSUR, same as above.
LITHAM, a blue bandage fastening the veils of the *Multimin* and other Tuaregs in place.
MAKHZEN, an administrative district, or a troop recruited from such a district.
MARABOUT, a Mohammedan name for a holy man or saint.
MEHARI, a racing camel or express camel.
MELLAH, a quarter set apart, as the Jewish quarter of a town.
MOKHAZENI, a territorial coming from a makhzen.
MULTIMIN, veiled men of the time of the Crusades, probably ancestors of the Tuaregs.
NOUADER, locks (of hair).
RAHLA, a pack-saddle for camels.
RAZZIA, a raid.
REZZU, an expedition, or band of a tribal faction.
RUMIS, "Romans," a general name applied by Moslems to European Christians.
SBAOT, Feast of Weeks, corresponding with Pentecost.
SHEHADA, the Musulman form of prayer.
SHERIF, a noble, a title of honour, a local governor.
SHOTT, a shallow saline lake.
SIDI, an African title of respect given by Musulmans to one in authority.
SISIT, a long garment.
TAMAHAK or TAMACHEK, the spoken Tuareg language.
TEBBEL, a war-drum.
THALEBS, religious teachers of Islam.
THOLBA, same as Thalebs.
TIFINAR, the written Tuareg language.
WADY, river or dry watercourse.
ZAPTIE, a Turkish policeman.
ZAUIA, house of an Arab chief and his dependents.
ZERIBA, an improvised stockade, usually of thorn-bushes.
ZETTET, a protector who gives *anaia*.

CHARLES DE FOUCAULD

CHAPTER I

His Youth

CHARLES *EUGÈNE* DE FOUCAULD, whose history I shall try to relate, was born at Strasbourg on September 15, 1858.

He was not of Alsatian origin. His father, François Édouard, Viscount de Foucauld de Pontbriand, Deputy-Inspector of Forests, belonged to an ancient and noble family of Périgord, which gave saints to the Church and very good servants to France, and of which it is important that I should here say something, because the merit of ancestors, even unknown, even forgotten, continues to live in our blood and urges us to imitation.

According to the genealogist Chabault, the name of Foucauld has been known since 970, an epoch in which Hugues de Foucauld, having given a part of his wealth to the Abbeys of Chancelade and of Saint-Pierre d'Uzerches, retired from the world, and, in order to prepare better for death, entered the monastery. One Bertrand de Foucauld, who set out for the Crusade with St. Louis, fell in the battle of Mansurah defending his King against the Musulmans. Another, Gabriel, was delegated by François II to espouse Mary Stuart by proxy.

Jean, chamberlain to the Dauphin, assisted, near Jeanne d'Arc, at the coronation of Rheims. In several letters Henry IV called Jean III de Foucauld " his good and very trusty friend." In order to express still better his friendship for him he named him Governor of the Comté of Périgord and Vicomté of Limoges : " I can assure you, Monsieur de Lardimalie," he wrote to him, " I esteem you and your virtue, and I am as satisfied with you as you could desire "—a fine testimonial, which was worth a government and would last longer.

Numerous other Foucaulds, in the course of time, were killed at the head of their company or their regiment, in France, Italy, Spain, or Germany, always in the service of France. But one of its greatest glories came to this family from Armand de Foucauld de Pontbriand,[1] Canon of Meaux,[2] Vicar-General to his cousin Jean-Marie du Lau, Prince Archbishop of Arles. He was a man whose charity was very great, who distributed to the poor the larger part of his income, and "frequented only his church and the hospitals."[3] Now this income was considerable—not that he had inherited it, he a son of a younger son and fifth of eleven children; but two years before the Revolution he had been endowed by the King with the usufruct of the Abbey of Solignac in Limoges.

In 1790 the Archbishop of Arles addressed to his clergy the celebrated *Exposition des principes de la Constitution civile du clergé*, a document in which he denounced the attempt at schism decided by the men of the Revolution. It was signed by one hundred and twenty-nine bishops of France, defenders of the Roman Catholic and Apostolic Faith. The Chapter of Arles replied by an address of the soundest doctrine, at the bottom of which is found, among those of the other canons, the signature of Armand de Foucauld. Having become suspected through their attachment to the Church, the refractory priests were soon condemned to transportation by the *décret* of May 26, 1792. Armand de Foucauld then set out from Arles for Paris to join Mgr. du Lau, who said: "They want to inoculate the Church with schism and heresy; we can only die." This was giving himself up to death. On August 11 he was arrested with his bishop, and led into the confiscated church of the Carmelites, in which numerous priests were already shut up. Many of these confessors of the Faith were about to become martyrs. They knew it. They were all preparing for it, trembling and staunch, depending on the grace of God for the courage of which none are sure.

On September 2 the prisoners received the order to walk in the garden of the Carmelites; even the sick and infirm must go out. They understood that they were going to the torture. M. de Foucauld and the other Vicar-General of Arles, gathering round their Archbishop, directed their steps towards an oratory, at the bottom of the garden, dedicated to the Blessed Virgin. The windows of the convent were full of red caps, brandishing their arms and insulting the penned-up victims. "Let us thank God, gentlemen," said the prelate, "that He calls us to seal with our

[1] His mother was Marie Sibylle de Lau.
[2] Where he was ordained priest in 1774.
[3] *Armand de Foucauld de Pontbriand*, 1751-1792 (H. Oudin, Paris, 1902).

blood the faith which we profess." He was the first to be struck down by sabres and pikes. A moment after, M. de Foucauld fell near the body of his cousin. He was forty-one. To the old nobility another of the highest was added.

In his race little Charles found by the score fine examples to follow.

He did not, as will be seen, at first follow them, but he was brought back to them; and none, since then, among the soldiers, the sailors, or priests of his house, could be named who had surpassed this Charles de Foucauld in self-sacrifice, austerity, bravery, and pity.

He was pious during the days of his childhood. Many are the same in France, where there are so many pre-destined mothers. Madame de Foucauld had two children, Charles and Mary.[1] She had barely the time to teach them to join their hands and say their prayers; she hardly saw the first dawn of the passionate soul of her son Charles, over which she would have wept, if death had not prematurely carried off that Monica from this Augustine. In order to train her children in piety, but quite as much to obey a divine attraction and habit, she used to visit various churches in turn, loving them all on account of Him who inhabits them all. In the same way, at home, with her children she used to decorate the crib at Christmastide, a statue of the Virgin in the month of May. She gave Charles a little altar which was placed on a chest of drawers, before which he used to kneel morning and evening, a relic of his first years, of presage still obscure, which he mentions later on: "I kept it as long as I had a room to myself in my family, and it outlived my faith." When they went for a walk on the sloping woods of Saverne or spent the holidays together, she recommended her children to gather bunches of flowers and to place them at the foot of the calvaries at the cross-roads, betraying a French mother's tender love, more educationist in acts than in words, the memory of which is never effaced.

Madame de Foucauld died on March 13, 1864, at the age of thirty-four; her husband on August 9 of the same year. The orphans were then confided to their maternal grandfather, M. Charles-Gabriel de Morlet, a retired colonel of Engineers, who was nearly seventy years of age.[2] Men do not often have that passionate application to the duties of primary education, nor that gift of divination which

[1] A first child named Charles had not lived.
[2] His first wife was Mlle. La Quiante, and his second Mlle. de Labouche; the latter had no children.

teaches mothers and prompts them to take alarm at the faults of their children and to correct them. Affectionate, passionately fond of play, with a great gift for drawing, quick-witted, a pretty child and with a bold expression, Charles pleased the old soldier. He was spoiled; M. de Morlet could not resist the tears of this little Charles : " When he cries," he used to say, " he reminds me of my daughter." Even Charles's fits of anger met with a secret indulgence, and were passed over as a sign of character. He was violent. The most innocent mockery put him into a rage. He had once cut out and modelled a fort in a heap of sand, an elaborate construction of moats and towers, of bridges and approaches. One of his relations, thinking to please him, took it into his head to put lighted candles on the summit, and potatoes for cannon-balls in the moats. Charles thought that they were making fun of him and flew into a violent fury. He trampled on his work till no trace of it remained; then, in revenge, after dark he threw the very sandy potatoes into every bed in the house.

We know by his letters that he made his first communion with fervour. He was sent to the episcopal school of Saint-Arbogast, under the management of the priests of the Diocese of Strasbourg, then to the Lycée.[1] The war came on, and the grandfather and the two children were driven from Alsace and took refuge in Berne.

In 1872 M. de Morlet, not being able to go back to Strasbourg, went to live in Nancy. It was in the Lycée of this town that Charles commenced to lose the habit of regular ordered work, and soon lost the Faith.

When one goes through all the correspondence of Charles de Foucauld, one understands the bitterness of his memories of his years of study at Nancy. These years were the beginning of a life of frailty, the period which in penance he goes over again and again till the end, to efface the faults of mind and body.

[1] One of the former professors of the Lycée de Strasbourg has been good enough to write to me on this subject : " I had Charles de Foucauld as pupil, 1868-1869, in my sixth form. He was an intelligent and studious child, but was far from giving any indication of the passionate and quick-witted nature that he was to manifest later on. Besides, his delicate health did not allow him to attend the classes regularly enough to get always into the first places. I find, however, to his credit, that he was fourth and third for Latin translation, in a class of fifty-five pupils. He was under the care of his grandfather, M. de Morlet, an old gentleman with distinguished manners and language, who occupied himself with archæology and was passionately fond of the classics."

I ought, indeed, to quote here some of his confessions after he had returned to God and judged his past.

He wrote to a friend: " If I worked little at Nancy, it is because I was allowed to mix with my studies a quantity of reading which gave me the taste for study, but did me the harm of which you know."

He again wrote to him that it was during his course of rhetoric that he lost all faith, "and that is not the only evil."

The year of philosophy was worse: "If you knew how all the objections which tormented me, and which lead young men astray, are luminously and simply solved by a good Christian philosophy! It meant a real revolution when I saw that. . . . But children are thrown on the world without giving them the arms that are indispensable to combat the enemies they find in and outside themselves, lying in wait for them in hosts on the threshold of youth. The Christian philosophers have long since and very clearly solved so many questions that each young man puts feverishly to himself, without even suspecting that an answer, luminous and clear, lies close at hand."

Still later on, in a letter to his brother-in-law, he earnestly begs that his nephews be brought up by Christian masters: "I had no bad master; all, on the contrary, were full of reverence; but even those are harmful, because they are neutral, and youth needs to be educated not by neutrals but by men of faith and sanctity, learned in religion, knowing how to give reasons for their beliefs and inspiring young men with a firm confidence in the truth of their Faith. . . .

"Let my experience, I pray you, do for the family."[1]

This collegian left the Lycée a bachelor (B.A.), like others, inquisitive about everything and determined to enjoy himself; and sad M. de Morlet wanted his grandson to enter the École Polytechnique. But Charles chose to lead an easy life. He declared, with that frankness which was one of the unchangeable features of his moral life, that he would prefer to go to the École de Saint-Cyr, because the competition demanded less work; and he set out for Paris.

From memory he depicts himself as he was when he was attending the preparatory classes of the École de Saint-Geneviève.

" At seventeen I was beginning my second year at the Rue des Postes. I believe I had never been in such a lament-

[1] Letter of March 5, 1901.

able state of mind. In a way I have done more harm at other times, but then there was some good mingled with the evil. At seventeen I was all egotism, vanity, impiety, with every desire for evil; I was, as it were, mad. As for my laziness, at the Rue des Postes it was such that they would not keep me there, and I have told you that in spite of the form used so as not to grieve my grandfather, I considered my departure a dismissal, a dismissal of which idleness was not the sole cause. . . . I was so free, so young! What I wish above all to say is that, for me and for many others, the age of X . . . was the worst period. . . . At seventeen I had made my poor grandfather suffer so much, refusing work to such an extent that in the month of February, I had not, I believe, yet cut the pages of Euclid which I ought to have studied every day since November; writing to him nearly every other day, sometimes letters forty pages long, to ask him to bring me back to Nancy, and all else that you can suppose such folly must suggest. . . ."[1]

"Of faith, not a trace remained in my soul."[2] Elsewhere he says and repeats that for thirteen years he did not believe in God.

The confession, though not developed, is clear. It appears to me that it calls for an observation, and sets a problem.

No doubt faith in the Church and her morality had been cast aside. Had it disappeared? That is another question. I rather think it was kept far in the distant background, invisible, like a land that a navigator has abandoned and means never to revisit, but the existence of which he knows; a land which he still loves, and, if not the days that he spent there, at least several of the inhabitants who live there and belong to his quondam home. As long as one loves a Christian, one still has a little love for Christ who formed him. General hatred alone is a sign of atheism. This young man read everything with the superb imprudence of his age, and saturated his mind with objections against a doctrine which he did not know well, but in him two sentiments which might call the past to life survived—respect for the priest and most tender attachment to the family. Nay, more, he had a taste for reading, giving strong grounds for hoping he might return to the Faith, and, further, he knew how to read. The true name for his idleness was fantasy, imprudence, and sensual curiosity. But his ardent mind,

[1] Letters to a friend, April 17, 1892, and November 8, 1893.
[2] Letter to a friend, February 24, 1893.

capable of reflection, would not look upon life without understanding its lessons, would not read what pleased without paying attention to that which condemned him, save to reject the conclusion. Foucauld was an intellectual given up to the senses, but capable of dominating them, if some great event, hidden in the heart—the grace of God— showed him his error.

I have just said that he much esteemed his religious masters. They first warned him, and then threatened him with dismissal, and soon even requested him to leave the school of the Rue des Postes.[1] Here is what he says of them : "You know what I think of the boarding-school; good for many, it was detestable to me. Liberty at the same age might perhaps have been worse, and, in any case, I must say that I brought away with me from this boarding-school such deep esteem for the Jesuits that, even when I least respected our holy religion, I always very highly respected the Fathers, and that is no small blessing."[2]

When the hour of return came, Charles de Foucauld had no fear of priests. Remembering the good Fathers he knew, he went to one of them with confidence.

The affections of his childhood helped him still more powerfully. Those who loved, petted, and even spoiled him, he continued to cherish, and, as he came to understand better what they had done for him, to admire. In them, he came to see, not only his mother, sister, grandfather, aunts, and cousins, but the united members of a very Christian family, very devoted to their brother, son, nephew, cousin Charles, exercising a great silent pity towards him, and not abandoning him; for to that pity he was the child of silent prayer, the wordless prayer that proceeds from the depths of the soul at night, when they are all together still on their knees, and about to rise.

I have also said that a question presents itself. This is it. This child of a bold race was endowed with a strong will. It will be seen by the sequel. How could he thus give himself up to idleness, and afterwards live a loose life for many years? One could understand violent passions, storms, occasional adventures, but this insipid commonplace life with no relief? What was his will doing then, and where was it hiding? It was on the watch that nothing should disturb a life of pleasure. It is not a faculty which

[1] As Charles was poorly, his status was changed from a boarder's to a day-boy's.
[2] To a friend, Easter Monday, 1890.

remains unemployed. It is at the service of that high centre of the mind which chooses one's abode and friends, one's habits and occupations. And if the misled, perverted mind, detached from all restraining morals, perceives its weal in the disorder of the imagination and the satisfaction of the body, it is wonderfully quick in walling up the windows even in the garrets through which we might see any sky; in driving away intruding recollections; in protecting our inner selves from any words and examples involving a reproach.

Charles de Foucauld sat for the competitive examination of the Military School in 1876. He just scraped through, and was then on the point of being rejected for premature corpulency at the medical examination. Colonel de Morlet was sad that his grandson was one of the last to be admitted. "On the contrary," replied Charles, "it is very jolly; I shall have a chance of many a rise in rank." He did not rise at all, and came out as he had gone in. General Laperrine wrote, in an account which he called *Stages in the Conversion of a Hussar*,[1] these lines, full both of meaning and reserve: "Very clever indeed would be the man who could have foreseen in the gluttonous and sceptical young fellow of Saint-Cyr the ascetic and apostle of to-day. A scholar and artist, he employed the leisure which the military exercises left him to stroll about, pencil in hand, or to plunge into the reading of the Latin and Greek authors. As to his theories and lectures, he did not look at them, trusting to his lucky star not to be *plucked*."

He told the truth; the portraits of the pupil of Saint-Cyr are a proof of that. Above a too thick bust and neck the photographs of this period represent a round puffy face without distinction, which has nothing fine but the straight broad forehead, and the scarcely curved line of the eyebrows. Deep set in their orbits, the brilliant and forbidding eyes appeared smaller on account of the fat which surrounded them. As to the almost formless and indolent lips, they were such as taste, talk but little, and do not command. Flesh predominated. How is this face hereafter to become, with the tense energy of all the features, the splendour of the eyes and the celestial charity of its smile, almost like that of St. Francis of Assisi? It is the miracle of the soul, which models the body and sets its stamp upon it.

From Saint-Cyr, Foucauld passed, in 1878, to the

---

[1] *Revue de cavalerie*, October, 1913.

Cavalry School of Saumur.[1] He shared the room of a comrade with whom he had contracted a friendship at Saint-Cyr, Antoine de Vallombrosa, afterwards Marquis de Morès, destined to display a dazzling and brief career, and who was also to perish assassinated in the desert. This room "became celebrated on account of the excellent dinners and long card parties which were held there, to keep company with the one under punishment, for it was very rare that one of the two occupants was not under arrest."[2] The contrast was very great between Vallombrosa, always on the go, a fine horseman, a sportsman, and Foucauld the stay-at-home, apathetic, and dreamer. However, for common or different reasons they were both in favour with the officer students: Foucauld, for instance, as much as his comrade, was liked for his generosity, his quick-witted intelligence and frankness. His pranks and whims were laughed at. He dressed with extreme elegance, only smoked cigars of a certain brand, never took the change of a louis from a waiter or jarvey, played for high stakes, and spent so foolishly, that his uncle, M. Moitessier, was soon obliged, to the great fury of Charles, to provide him with a legal guardian. One surmises that others besides innkeepers, bootmakers, tailors, and croupiers, were sharp enough to make holes in the fortune of this young nobleman. The life he led at Pont-à-Mousson, on leaving the Cavalry School, was no more staid. It is even said that he was obliged to leave several lodgings because the other tenants complained of the racket he made and the disagreeable company which he brought in, and he finished by having some difficulty in finding a lodging in that little town. Fortunately, in 1880, the Fourth Hussars, of which he was a lieutenant, were sent to Algeria.

It was a day of decision: the passion for Africa—in a word, the colonial passion—was to take possession of the young officer, and grow till it gave a fresh direction to a badly begun life.

The Fourth Hussars, afterwards the Fourth Chasseurs d'Afrique, garrisoned Bône and Setif. Pronounce the word Setif before one of those who know the legend, if not the history of Father de Foucauld, you will almost surely hear one or two anecdotes of which the famous lieutenant was the principal personage. They are amusing; are they true? I doubt it. In my presence many of the tellers of

---

[1] From October, 1878, to November, 1879.
[2] General Laperrine, *op. cit.*

these regimental tales would change the hero's name. He was no longer Charles de Foucauld, but one of his comrades; and the dates changed. I prefer to keep to well-established facts. Here they are. The lieutenant had hardly landed than he set out for the manœuvres. A few weeks passed; he came back to Setif and settled down. Soon remonstrances were made to him, friendly at first, then stiffer; he was reproached with giving scandal by living with a young woman who had come from France at the same time as he and was making a parade of the liaison. He took his colonel's counsels, and afterwards his orders, very badly. His retorts and absolute refusal as lieutenant to obey his superior officer injured discipline. The issue was a foregone conclusion—he must break with his mistress or leave the regiment. What will Foucauld do? He will not give in. I do not believe it can be said in this case that passion swayed him; no, it was the will, terrible and still without a master, which refused to bend. He left his comrades, half broke his career, got the Minister to put him on temporary leave, and returned to Évian.

He was there, far from his relations, useless, when in the spring of 1881 the news reached him of the insurrection of Bu-Amama, in South Oranais. The Fourth Chasseurs were going to begin the campaign, his comrades were going to fight. When the blood of France cries aloud, nothing can silence it. Lieutenant de Foucauld wrote at once to the Minister of War. The letter urged that he could not bear the thought that his comrades would be at the post of honour and danger, whereas he would not, and that, in order to rejoin his regiment, he accepted any and every condition that would be imposed on him.

His request was granted. Foucauld set out again for Algeria. An unexpected event had aroused him. The thought of sacrifice had come home to his soul. It begets all sorts of nobility. Charles de Foucauld was no more a believer than he had been of late, but the force which makes Christians asserted itself in him. Since he had offered himself for France, he had drawn nearer to God, who sees his Son in man's self-sacrifice, and is moved at the sight.

A native marabout, Bu-Amama, of the Ulad-Sidi-Sheikh-Gharaba, was stirring up the tribes, and preaching a holy war in South Oranais. The campaign against the fanatic brought out the first indications of the final personality of Charles de Foucauld. General Laperrine, who was with the expedition and could judge his comrade, writes in the *Étapes de la conversion d'un hussard* as follows :

"In the midst of the dangers and privations of the expeditionary columns, this literary *viveur* showed himself to be a soldier and a leader, gaily enduring the hardest trials, constantly exposing himself to danger, devoting all his time to his men. He was the admiration of the old Mexicans of the regiment, who were connoisseurs.

"Of the Foucauld of Saumur and Pont-à-Mousson nothing was left except a tiny pet edition of Aristophanes which was always with him, and just a touch of snobbery which made him give up smoking from the day that he could no longer procure cigars of his favourite brand."

One of the old soldiers who had chased Bu-Amama told me that one day, after a long march, when Lieutenant de Foucauld saw his men, exhausted by the heat, rush to a well, he went back quickly and bought a bottle of rum from the canteen-woman, and returned saying, "How glad I am to have my bottle to give you!" And the soldiers mixed a little of the rum with the brackish water. "He made the men love him," added the narrator, "but he, too, loved the privates! Many years after our fights with Bu-Amama, I saw my old commander, and he said to me these very words: 'The African army is still better than the European; half of the men in my company would have made excellent monks.' Perhaps he exaggerated a little; but that proves the friendship which he still felt for us.[1]

"The Arabs made a deep impression upon him. When the insurrection was over, he asked for leave in order to go on a journey in the South and study them. As he could not get this leave, he sent in his resignation, and went and settled down in Algiers to prepare for his great journey in Morocco."[2]

He was twenty-four. If the unknown bulked largely in the future of this very young ex-officer, one thing was from that time certain : he was born to inhabit the East. He had in him that vocation which is not born, as some fancy, of the love of light, but rather of the love of habitual silence, of space, of the unforeseen and the primitive in life, and of the mystery one suspects of being concealed in the very reserved.

When this vocation speaks and issues orders within a

---

[1] It was in that expedition that Lieutenant de Foucauld got to know the Officer-Interpreter Motylinski, whom he was to meet again later on in the Tuareg country.

[2] General Laperrine, *Les étapes de la conversion d'un hussard*.

man, he can do nothing but follow it. He fights against it, and cannot get over it. Ask the veterans of the Sahara who have tried service in France, and find that the best garrison is not worth the desert, and that no colonel at the head of his regiment experiences the sensation of free power, or the slight thrill of loneliness and possible adventure which keeps the little lieutenant on the alert and in fidgety joy. He, too, is a company commander with his twenty-five *meharistes* marching in Indian file under the stars, making the sand of the dunes give way under the feet of the camels, following a wandering and often uncertain trail, in search of a well or of some plundering band. Ask those who have imprudently retired to the seaside in Brittany or on the shores of Nice; above all, those, too old for a wandering life, hence feeling too deeply uprooted in their native land, whose homes are hidden in the neighbourhood of Algiers or Oran, in a villa under the pines, where they still hear the noise of the wind which comes from the South, and receive the visits of their young successors, the happy ones who knock at the door, saying, "Good-morning, Captain, I'm back from the *bled*."

After handing in his resignation, Charles de Foucauld followed the first call of his vocation, which the manœuvres around Setif, the tales of the old Africans, the discovery of a new people, lastly the war against the fanatic, had settled. He would not leave Africa without having studied it, he would be a man of action. What then would he do? One of the most difficult things there is: he would undertake to explore Morocco, a closed country, mistrustful of the foreigner, cruel in its vengeance, but so near our coasts, that one was sure, in travelling over it, to help the France of to-morrow. He went to Algiers. Seized by the thirst for knowledge which he had so far slaked at haphazard, he shut himself up in libraries, took lessons in Arabic, and got into contact with men who could prepare him for the daring enterprise.

One of these, the most useful perhaps, one of the best known figures in old Algiers, was called Oscar MacCarthy. He was quite a little man, "as brown as a white man could be, as lean as a man in health could be,"[1] who wore his hair close cropped and a long beard, and whom the Arabs sometimes called "the big-headed man," or "the gun man." He got this second nickname from the custom he had while travelling of suspending over his shoulder a big

[1] Eugène Fromentin, in *Un été dans le Sahel*, often speaks of his friend Louis Vandell, who is none but this MacCarthy.

barometer shut up in a leather case. MacCarthy had once planned crossing the Sahara and reaching Timbuctoo. He never set out, but the biscuit prepared for that expedition still existed twenty years after, and MacCarthy used always to speak of starting soon.[1]

He had visited the least important villages, stayed in the douars of all the tribes, collected thousands of notes which he confided to friends here and there; he had read all that had been written by travellers, historians, and archæologists about the things and people of Africa, and remembered it all. "The land of Africa was his mind's possession."[2]

In his frail body lived an intrepid and learned soul. A sure guide, with methods of exploration always very much his own, his advice to the young officer who put himself into his hands is easily conjectured. To be safe everywhere, he had become insensible to heat or cold, travelled without escort or baggage, his pockets stuffed with notebooks and manuscript cards, heedless of all the conveniences of material life, protected by his destitution itself, according to the Oriental proverb which says: "A thousand horsemen could not strip a naked man."

Oscar MacCarthy was the keeper of the library of Mustapha Pasha's palace in the Rue de l'Etat Major. "Both the old scholar and the young officer used to spend long hours, leaning on the balustrade of the Moorish courtyard, bent over ancient maps and dusty folios, turning over the pages of old geographers, whom Foucauld was to leave far behind him."[3]

Most important for the success of a journey in Morocco was the choice of the disguise. It was impossible to go through this hostile country without concealing the fact that he was a Christian. Only the representatives of European Powers could do it, if they kept to the "Ambassadors' road," which ran from the coast to Fez or to Marrakesh, and did not wander from the traditional track where they are constantly spied upon, and obliged to know no more of Morocco than the functionaries and intimates of the Sultan, always haunted by the fear of conquest, are willing to show them. With only two costumes could anyone pass among the tribes and be received in villages where no European had ever put his foot, and converse with the Moroccans: the costume of the Arab, and that of the Jew,

---

[1] *Un saint français, le Père de Foucauld,* by Augustin Bernard, Paris, Plon, 1917.
[2] Fromentin, *loc. cit.*   [3] Augustin Bernard, *op. cit.*

a dealer who is tolerated and watched. But what a knowledge must he possess of Musulman or Jewish ways, so as not to betray himself!

MacCarthy advised, and Charles de Foucauld accepted, the second solution. He has told us why:

" There are only two religions in Morocco. It is necessary, at no matter what cost, to be of one of them. Would I be a Musulman or a Jew? Should I put on the turban or the black cap? René Caillie, Rohlfs, and Lenz had all chosen the turban. I, on the contrary, decided for the cap. What, above all, induced me to do so was the thought of the difficulties which these travellers had met with in their costumes—the obligation of leading the same life as their co-religionists, the continual presence of real Musulmans around them. The very suspicion and watchfulness of which they found themselves often the object, were a great obstacle to their work. I was afraid of a disguise which, far from favouring my investigations, might put many hindrances in the way; I cast my eyes on the Jewish costume. It seemed to me that its lowliness would help me to pass more unnoticed and give me more liberty. I was not mistaken. During all my journey I kept this disguise, and had only reason to congratulate myself. If I sometimes incurred a little ill-treatment, I was indemnified for it, always finding facilities for work: during the stops, it was easy for me to make my astronomical observations in the shade of the *mellahs,* and to spend whole nights in writing and finishing my notes. On the march no one paid attention or deigned to speak to the poor Jew who was just then consulting compass, watch, barometer, one after the other, and taking the bearings of the road we were following: besides, in every place I obtained from my cousins, as the Jews of Morocco call each other among themselves, sincere and full particulars of the region in which I found myself. Lastly, I excited little suspicion. My bad accent might cause some, but one knows that there are Jews of all countries. My disguise was further completed by the presence of a real Jew at my side. His first business everywhere was to swear that I was a Rabbi, then so to put himself forward in all dealings with the natives as to leave me as much as possible in the shade; lastly, he always had to find me lodgings by myself in which I could conveniently take my observations, and, if that could not be done, he had to forge the most fantastic stories to explain the exhibition of my instruments."[1]

[1] *Reconnaissance au Maroc,* Preface.

This decision to travel disguised as a Jew forced the explorer to learn Hebrew at the same time as Arabic, and also to study Jewish customs.

It was again MacCarthy who, at the library of Algiers, introduced to Charles de Foucauld the Rabbi Mardochée, his future guide.

CHAPTER II

The Preliminaries of the Journey

THE account of his exploration in Morocco, published by the Vicomte de Foucauld, begins at Tangier on June 20, 1883. Now, the traveller had left Algiers on June 10, and, according to his plans, he was not to penetrate into the forbidden empire by the north, but to seek his route by the Rif, crossing the frontier of Algiers and Morocco. What reasons prevented him? What happened between June 10 and 20? We should not have known very much about it, unless, luckily, on returning to his family in Paris, the explorer had written for the benefit of one of his nephews, in a fair hand on fine sheets of vellum bound up with the printed pages, three important fragments, the first of which relates precisely the preparations for the journey and the incidents of the start. I shall publish first this sort of unedited preface of the *Reconnaissance au Maroc*. Likewise I shall cite at length the story of the guide Mardochée, not so much because it is amusing, dramatic, a little extravagant, like so many Oriental stories, but because it shows admirably to what sort of a man Charles de Foucauld had confided himself. In short, when in rapidly and boldly analyzing the book, I come to where the author relates his stay at Ab-el-Jad, I shall publish the third fragment, at the head of which he wrote these lines

" I had to do with several members of the family of Sidi ben Daud. I suppressed this in my work, because if the knowledge of it had reached the Sultan that would have created dangers for my friends of Abu-el-Jad. I am going to tell you about it, my dear nephew."

To-day the public may be told of these interviews, in the course of which the young French officer, cleverly questioned and feeling himself found out, confessed to being a Christian, and confided in the honour of his host. Time has flown. What might have been a cause of annoyances —even death might have been one of them—under the reign of the former Sultans has assumed its true character of rare generosity and chivalry. The treaty of 1912 makes the printing of it possible.

1. THE DISGUISE AND THE FIRST STEPS

"On June 10, 1883, at 5 o'clock in the morning, I enter an old house in the Jewish quarter of Algiers: it is the home of Rabbi Mardochée. My companion lives there in a single room with his wife and four children; he expects me: I am to get out of my European clothes and put on a Jewish costume: a long shirt with flowing sleeves, linen trousers reaching to the knees, a Turkish waistcoat of dark cloth, a white robe with short sleeves and hood (*jelabia*), white stockings, open shoes, a red cap, and a black silk turban are prepared for me. This makes up a Jewish costume half Algerian, half Syrian, which suits the various rôles I may have to play.

"I dress up; and Mardochée, his wife, children, and myself, go out and down the steps of the little narrow streets that lead to the harbour, where the Oran station is. We shall start for Oran in the morning by the 7 o'clock train. To be in keeping with my costume, I asked for two tickets, in bad French; Mardochée bade farewell to his family, and behold both of us seated in a third-class carriage. The weather is splendid, the carriage full of Arab workmen; we set out surrounded by gaiety and flooded with sunshine.

"I am called Rabbi Joseph Aliman. I was born in Muscovy, whence recent persecutions have driven me. I fled first to Jerusalem. After piously spending some time there I have reached the North of Africa, and now I am travelling at random, poor but trusting in God. Mutual esteem binds me to Mardochée Abi Servur—like me, a learned Rabbi who has spent long years in Jerusalem. Mardochée wears a costume similar to mine, that gives us a family appearance. He declares, too, that I am like him, and if necessary he will pass me off as his son. We have little luggage—a sack and two boxes. The boxes hold: the first one a medicine chest, which will enable me in case of need to call myself a doctor; the other a sextant, compasses, barometers, thermometers, paper, and cards. The sack contains a change of costume and a blanket for each of us, cooking utensils, and provisions. As money, I brought 3,000 francs, partly in gold and partly coral. It was in this equipment that we dragged along towards Oran. I am going to Oran because I wish to enter Morocco by land; my project is to go from Tlemcen to Tetuan by crossing the region of the Rif, which makes all the coast-line between the Algerian frontier and Tetuan. From Oran, I shall go to Tlemcen; there, I shall find out how to travel in the Rif."

" We arrived at Oran at 6 o'clock in the evening. The station is outside the town. Going halves with two Jews who were in the train, we took a cab which brought us to an hotel frequented by Israelites. We hired a room at two francs a day, and drawing on our provisions we took our first evening meal *tête-à-tête*. A strange house, the hotel in which we are! I was surprised for a moment on hearing myself addressed in the second person singular by the servant. In Algeria the Jews are all addressed thus."

"*June* 11.—This day is the first of the feast of Sbaot (Pentecost), on which the gift of the faith to Moses on Mt. Sinai is celebrated; the Jews are forbidden to travel to-day or to-morrow. I remain in my room; Mardochée went to the synagogue and came back at night with his co-religionists. They began to chat. I learn that my companion applies himself to seeking the philosopher's stone, the other Jew is a fellow-alchemist. For a long time I see them argue, feebly lit by a candle, their shadows making enormous silhouettes on the walls. I fall asleep on my straw mattress, lulled by this strange talk."

"*June* 12.—Towards 5 o'clock in the evening, we board the diligence, and set out for Tlemcen. In going to the coach, I hear a passer-by saying to his neighbour, pointing to me, ' Do you know where we get that from ? That's what comes to us straight from Jerusalem.' "

"*June* 13.—Reaching Tlemcen at 9 in the morning, we at once set out in quest of the Jews of the Rif. At 1 o'clock we had not found one who could give us any useful information. Being tired, we bought some bread and olives, and we began breakfast seated on the ground in a square. Whilst we were thus, a band of officers of the Chasseurs d'Afrique, coming out of the club, passed at two paces from me. I know nearly all of them; they looked at me without suspecting who I was.[1] Our afternoon was more fortunate than the morning : we discovered a certain number of Jews of the Rif; they were to come and see us at

[1] Captain René de Segonzac, in an article dated from Rabat January 15, 1917, confirming the account of Charles de Foucauld, writes : "The officers filed off, heedless or contemptuous ; one of them, with a sneer, remarked to his comrades, that that little squatting Jew, eating olives, looked like a monkey. None recognized him" (*L'Afrique français*, Janvier-Février, 1917).

eight o'clock in the evening in a hired room, where we were to meet and discuss the means of crossing the Rif. No more Jewish hotels here; so we hire a room in a Jewish family.

"At 8 o'clock all is ready to receive our guests: in a room 2 metres wide by 5 long, of which the walls, floor, and ceiling are painted in grey, a candle, a bottle of aniseed and a glass were placed on a stool. One after the other a dozen Jews, the greater number with white beards, come discreetly in, and here we are all seated on the ground in a circle round the candle. Mardochée fills his glass of aniseed, raises it and says, 'To the health of the Law! to the health of Israel! to the health of Jerusalem! to the health of the Holy Land! to the health of the Sbaot! to all your healths, O Doctors! to the health of the Rabbi Joseph (me)!' He touches the glass with his lips, and passes it to his neighbour, who empties it: then the glass goes the round, and each of the Jews, at one draught, empties it. Mardochée begins to speak. . . .

"He tells his tale, and winds up with this wholly fancy incident: it is now two years since Mardochée had a discussion with his wife's brother, and the young man left Algiers and was seen no more. Since then, Mardochée's wife cannot be consoled. She does nothing but weep.

"Now, a few days ago, she was told, without being able to specify the town, that her brother was in the Rif, carrying on the trade of jeweller. At once she prayed her husband to go and seek out the fugitive, and he, good man, in order to restore health and peace to his wife, decided upon this journey; he has therefore resolved to explore the Rif, village by village, if necessary, to find his brother-in-law again. That is what brings him to-day to Tlemcen. As to this young Israelite who accompanies him, and whom they hear him call Rabbi Joseph, he is a poor Muscovy Rabbi who is going to Morocco, the land of pious Jews, to collect alms; Mardochée brought him with him through pure pity, and paid for his journey as far as Nemours. Now he begs these doctors, who all have lived in the Rif, to consider and let him know if they had not seen the man he is seeking, a fair and pale Jew, about twenty-two years of age, called Juda Safertani. What present will he not give to anyone who will tell him where to find him? The company reflected, inquired and debated, but in vain; none of them knew Juda Safertani. Mardochée sighs, and begs them to give him at least some information about the Rif: Where to get into it? How to travel there? And in what places are there Jews? Who are the influential men of the country? The conversation on the subject is taken up again, the glass goes round and round and round. Voices grow louder, and the discussion as to the best means of travelling through the Rif gets animated. When our cousins retire, it is agreed that we shall start the next morning for Lalla-Marnia; from there we shall get to Nemours; thence we shall, if it pleases God, enter the Rif."

"*June* 14.—A diligence brings us from Tlemcen at 9 o'clock in the morning, and we stop at 6 o'clock in the evening at the village of Lalla-Marnia. We settle down for the night in the synagogue : it is just like all the Jewish temples I saw in Morocco : a rectangular hall, with a sort of desk in the centre, and, in the wall, a cupboard. The desk serves to rest the book of the Law on, for the public readings which are given twice a week : in rich communities it is on a raised platform and under a canopy; in poor villages, it consists of a horizontal piece of wood resting on two posts. The cupboard contains one or several copies of the Law (Sepher Torah), written on parchment and rolled on wooden cylinders (like Roman books, except that it is rolled on two cylinders instead of one); these double rolls are about 18 inches high and are covered three or four times deep with the richest materials. Such is the synagogue ; a bench resting against the wall goes all round and completes it. We were finishing dinner when, one after another, thirty or forty men entered and sat down on the benches and chatted in a low voice. They are the Israelites of the place, who come to say their evening prayer in common. At a signal all stand up, turn towards the east, and begin to pray in a low or subdued voice. In perplexity I look at them to do as they do. Trying to imitate them, I sway rhythmically backward and forward like a schoolboy saying his lesson, now dumb, now mumbling through my nose. At the end of eight or ten minutes everyone makes a great bow simultaneously, and all is over. The Jews are just moving off when, to my great surprise, Mardochée begs them to remain and listen to him. He is, he says, a poor Rabbi living in Algiers, whom a misfortune obliged to leave his wife and children, and, though old and ill, to undertake the long journey of the Rif. He is going to explore this province in search of his brother-in-law; he tells the tale of yesterday, of the despair and illness of his wife ; . . . lastly, and here is the crown of all ills : he believed the journey easier than it is, and, though so far from the end, he already lacks money. . . . Now he begins to shed tears, and, in a broken voice, beseeches his brother of Lalla-Marnia to have pity on him and give him some alms. They drily tell him to apply to the Consistory of Oran. As much astonished as displeased at this comedy, I ask Mardochée for an explanation as soon as we are alone, ' It was to get used to lying,' he replies."

"*June* 15.—Left Lalla-Marnia by diligence at 4 in the morning. Arrived at the little harbour of Nemours at 10 a.m. We take a room in a Jew's house and begin collecting information about the Rif.

"Here we change our tales, especially mine. Mardochée tells the same yarn as at Tlemcen, adding that the people of that town assured him they knew his brother-in-law in the Rif. As for me, I am a great doctor and a learned astrologer; I have wrought wonderful cures; I am invincible with diseases of the eyes, curing the worst cases; I have restored sight to the born blind. This great science, this wonderful success, has so drawn down on me the envy of Christian doctors, that they would have done me bodily harm if I had stayed in my own country. I was obliged to flee, and I decided to go and exercise my profession in Morocco, where, according to Mardochée, I hope to make great profits. Such was his tale on our arrival. I forbade him to spread the story in that form; he told it the next few days, leaving out the envy of the Christian doctors and the danger caused by their hatred."

"*June* 16 *and* 17.—In vain do we try to find a way of entering into the Rif : many of the Jews whom we consulted declare that one can only enter by Nemours with the protection of a certain Moroccan sheikh who will perhaps come here in a fortnight or a month, perhaps later; and even this means would be uncertain; they add that it is as difficult in starting from here to cross the Rif as it is easy in setting out from Tetuan, where men of influence can give efficacious recommendations. I do not wish to wait a fortnight or month at Nemours; much better reach Tetuan by sea and begin my journey from there."

"*June* 18.—A steamer appears in the roadstead. It is going to Tangier via Gibraltar. I embark on it with Mardochée. Being Jews, we take the lowest class and cross on deck in the company of Israelites and Musulmans. Start at 9 a.m. : pretty bad weather."

"*June* 19.—Wake up in the roadstead of Gibraltar. The packet-boat will lie at anchor all day. I land and visit the town; Mardochée remains on board. A young Jew of eighteen who knows Spanish accompanies me; as for me, I know nothing but Arabic. My excursion has a practical aim. On board, the water we are given is filthy; took a large iron pot and brought it back full of water. I walk about for five hours in Gibraltar, pot in hand; I push on to a Spanish village under a mile from the town. Cross the frontier and note the English and Spanish sentinels mount guard only 60 yards apart, the former as well as the latter badly dressed."

"*June* 20.—Left Gibraltar at midday; arrived at Tangier at 2.45."

"On *June* 20, 1883, my journey really began, lasting till May 23, 1884. During this time my made-up tale altered but little. I was a Rabbi of Algiers going, as the Musulmans thought, to collect alms, to inquire about the conditions and wants of my brethren; while Jews believed Mardochée was from Jerusalem: for the Musulmans he was asking for charity, for the Jews he was fulfilling the same mission as I. It was no longer a question of Juda Safertani nor of medicine. The latter had a double inconvenience: the Moroccans, for whom every Christian is a born doctor, were disposed to suspect my race on account of this profession; then the box of medicine inspired covetousness: a box suggests a treasure, and they said I had two cases of gold with me. At Fas, in the course of the month of August, taught by the experience of the first days on the road, I distrusted my remedies, and changed my baggage and dress. The boxes were replaced by a goat-skin sack; in my dress I left out what recalled the Eastern Jew—that is to say, the red cap, the black turban, the shoes and stockings, and I adopted the black cap, the blue handkerchief, and black *belras* (Turkish slippers) of the Moroccan Rabbis. I let grow *nuader*—locks of hair, placed on the side of the temples, which fall down on to the shoulders. My costume was henceforth that of all the Jews of Morocco; nor was it further altered except that at the beginning of winter I added a *khenif* (black burnous with yellow crescents or moons). At Fas I definitely organized my means of transport. Up to then I had hired mules; I bought two that carried Mardochée and me with our baggage for ten months, until our return to the Algerian frontier.

"In the first days of my journey, I had found lodgings, sometimes in hired rooms in Jews' houses, sometimes in synagogues. At Tangier and at Tetuan, I hired rooms; beyond Fas, that never happened again. From there, in the desert I spent my nights in the open air, in inhabited places, under the shelter of Jewish or Musulman hospitality. When we halted in an inhabited place, a group of tents or village, if no Jews resided there, my escort kept me with them, and got me hospitality from the family from whom they had asked it for themselves; when there was a Jewish community, the escort conducted me to the synagogue, where Mardochée and I unloaded our mules and took up our quarters provisionally, whilst waiting till the Rabbi and the Jews of the place came and offered us full hospitality, shelter, and food. The maintenance of travelling doctors falls upon all the families, a rota regulates the order in which they take their turn: in poor places the Rabbis keep the synagogue for putting them up, and hospitality has only to do with food, and the list makes each family give one day or one meal, so that one goes successively to all the inhabitants; in rich localities, the hospitality includes lodgings and lasts two, four, or eight days. The rota obliges one to feed a Rabbi, so that at the Jews' houses Mardochée and I were generally separated for meals, but we were allowed to lodge together with one of our two hosts. In rare places, we were received together outside of the rota, and for an unlimited time by rich families. In some miserable places, the Jews turned their backs on us, and knowing that we were in the synagogue, they did not come there, and went without saying their prayers in order to dispense with receiving us. We were obliged to return to our escort and ask a shelter from the Musulmans. With the Musulmans as well as the Jews hospitality is gratuitous: I used to return thanks by a present of sugar or tea, sometimes of coral or a sheep."

2. The Story of Mardochée Abi Servur.

"Mardochée Abi Servur, son of Iais Abi Servur, a native of Mhamid-el-Rozlân, was born in the South of Morocco, in the oasis of Akka, towards 1830. Before he was fourteen, he left his country to complete his theological studies. He studied at Marrakesh, Mogador, and Tangier, whence he embarked for Palestine. After having resided a year or two in the Holy Land and having there become an acting Rabbi, he gained Algeria, where he spent some months at Philippeville as officiating Rabbi; then, remembering his native place, set sail for Morocco and returned to Akka. He was not twenty-five. Enticed by the prospect of a rapid fortune, he threw himself into an audacious enterprise; he was the first of his race to enter Timbuctoo. His arrival in the Sudan and the beginning of his stay there were surrounded with a hundred dangers; by dint of courage and cunning he maintained his position; his business soon assumed great prosperity; and with fortune came security, credit, and even power.

"In a short time, he was the most notable merchant in Timbuctoo. He then had ten or twelve years of prosperity and happiness. His business consisted in the exchange of the produce of Morocco and the Sudan; the desert was crossed in every direction by caravans bearing his merchandise. His fortune reached 200,000 or 300,000 francs. His name was honoured at Timbuctoo and Mogador, and known to all the tribes of the Sahara. Every year he used to spend two or three months in Morocco. Towards 1865 he married. He contemplated bringing his wife to the Sudan and founding a colony of Israelites there, when his brilliant star suddenly became dim. In returning from the vicinity of Mogador, where his marriage was celebrated, he received at Akka the news that several caravans belonging to him had just been carried off by plunderers. A few days after some Musulmans arriving from Timbuctoo reported to him that during his absence one of his brothers, left at the head of the firm, had died, and that the leading man in the town had at once confiscated the contents of the deceased's house on the pretext of debts. Foreseeing grave difficulties, Mardochée left his wife at his father's in Akka, and hastened to set out alone for the Sudan. All sorts of troubles were lying in wait for him. The chief refused to give back what he had confiscated and became unfriendly; the pent-up envy of his competitors broke loose at the sight of his adversity and misfortune, and displayed itself in noisy hostility. Mardochée felt that, for the moment, his residence in Timbuctoo was impossible; he gathered together the remains of his fortune—40,000 francs—and left the Sudan.

"Sad and discouraged, he again took the road to Morocco, which he had so often followed full of joy and hope; only a Jew, a black slave, and a very trusty Arab guide, called El Mokhtar, accompanied him. All four were mounted with luggage on swift camels and marched quickly. Mardochée had converted all his wealth into gold-dust; two little goat-skins contained the treasure; he carried one of them, the Jew the other. It is not without danger that so feeble a troop enters the Sahara; generally it is crossed in a numerous caravan, but the caravans take thirty days to do the journey, and Mardochée, mounted as he was, hoped to do it in twenty-one. He had thus crossed the desert often, and always successfully. The first eighteen days on the road were passed in safety; the travellers did not meet a human being. El Mokhtar led them outside the beaten tracks, and stopped for water at places known to him alone. They had just halted at one of them, which Mardochée saw for the first time. It was a little grass-bordered marsh, hidden at the bottom of a circle of sandy downs. The two Jews were there with hearts full of joy and thanksgiving, beginning to rest, for they thought their dangers were at an end: three days separated them from Aqqa, and they were watering for the last time.

" Suddenly El Mokhtar, who had set out to go round the marsh, came running back looking very disturbed. He had just perceived fresh traces of numerous camels on the other side; more than twenty had quenched their thirst here a few hours ago. Would they come back? What direction had they taken? Their lives depended upon knowing. El Mokhtar jumped on to his *méhari* and flew to reconnoitre in the direction of the tracks. Mardochée looked after him, and saw him go into the downs, appearing or disappearing between the sand-dunes. As for him, he hastily takes his measures in case of a surprise; for safety's sake they had taken Musulman clothes and a small stock of perfumery with them. In a twinkling the two Jews undressed, disguised themselves as Musulmans, and buried the gold dust at the foot of a gum-tree. 'You are called Muley Ali, and I Muley Ibrahim,' said Mardochée to his companion; 'we are two sheriffs from Tafelelt going to Sahel to deal in perfumes.' A question arises: if they are plundered, their slave will tell from where they come and confess the presence of the gold: they must kill him, but the unfortunate man is only twenty-one and since his childhood has been brought up in Mardochée's house. After some hesitation, pity gains the day; he is not to be killed. They begin to scrutinize the horizon again, but do not see El Mokhtar. Suddenly, he appears on a near ridge, arriving at full speed and, with the skirt of his burnous, making signs of despair to them. They run to their mounts; it was too late. El Mokhtar had not advanced a hundred yards when amidst a violent dust appears a numerous troop of *meharis* in full cry after the guide. Shots ring out. El Mokhtar falls dead with a bullet in his skull. Next moment Mardochée was surrounded by sixty Arabs. Without saying a word they cut open the sacks which contain the goods. Finding nothing of any value, they seize the two Jews and strip them; Mardochée scolds them in vain, calls them miscreants, and says that his name is Muley Ibrahim. Turban, burnous, and shirt are off in an instant: ' Ungodly fellows ! will you take away the trousers of a child of the Prophet?' He had hardly finished when off came his trousers, too. The filched clothes are searched, turned inside out, and thoroughly examined; nothing is found. Furious, the plunderers turn towards the two men who are naked on the grass. 'From where do you come? Who are you?' they all ask at the same time. 'They are not here for nothing ! They have merchandise ! They must come from the Sudan ! They have gold ! Where is it ? Let them confess, or, by God, they shall be killed on the spot !' They shout and push and pull them about, and brandish their arms. . . . Now, by their language, Mardochée recognized Arabs of the Sahil, a region not far from his native place. In an instant he changed his plan and says, with a laugh : ' Ha ! why did you not say you are Regibats ? I am one of your party. May God curse Muley Ibrahim and Muley Ali ! We are called Mardochée and Isaac, and are Jews of Akka ! You will not injure poor Jews, your servants ! How could we have gold ? We come from Akka, and we are going to your tribe itself to sell perfumes : do you not see our stock ?'

"This speech throws doubt into the minds of the robbers : the accent and faces of the two men are those of Israelites, the box of perfumery seems to indicate that they are telling the truth; they search the baggage a second time. Mardochée had changed his plan because he felt that if he persisted in calling himself a shereef they would take what he had, and kill him to avoid reprisals; a Jew, they would take everything from him, but they would perhaps spare his life, not having to fear any vengeance from him. Nothing would make him own to having gold, which would increase his peril. The Arabs, in fact, found nothing, and everything indicated Mardochée's sincerity; they were getting ready to lead the *meharis,* slave, and baggage away, and leave the two Jews to extricate themselves as best they could. Naked, without food or guide, they would get back to Akka or die on the way, please God. Mardochée sighed, wept, begged that they would at least leave him a camel

THE PRELIMINARIES OF THE JOURNEY 27

and goat-skin, but was unfeelingly spurned. He expected this refusal. His demand was just a comedy; really, he was pleased; he saved his life and his gold, and, knowing the country well, he would easily reach Akka. In less than an hour, when the Arabs had disappeared, he would set out. His despoilers are loading his *méharis,* and a few are already starting. Suddenly, one of them, in consolidating the pack-saddle of one of the four animals, perceives, through a tear, some bits of the straw stuffing; he pulls out one: ' Ha ! come back ! Ha ! come back !' he shouts. ' Sudan straw ! The Jew lies : he comes from the Sudan !' In less than two minutes all the Arabs throng round Mardochée: ' Gold ! Gold ! ' is the only cry that is heard. ' By God ! I have none. By our Lord Moses, I have none. O gentlemen, I have none, I have none !' No more stories. A dagger is pressed to his throat. " Where is it ?'—' I have none.' The point is thrust in a little; blood flows. ' I have none !' he murmurs, having half fainted. The question will be renewed when he comes to; while he is recovering his senses, they go on to the other Jew : he sees the blood flow without confessing. They leave him swooning and run to the slave. ' Where do you come from ?'— ' From Timbuctoo.' ' Have your masters any gold?' —' No.' In his turn he feels the point of the blade press against his throat; the poor negro trembles : ' I do not know whether they have gold or not,' he groaned; ' a while ago they dug at the foot of that tree, look.' . . . It was useless for Mardochée and his companion to allow themselves to be wounded and their throats almost cut—their secret was discovered; Mardochée was ruined and would probably be killed to prevent any vengeance after so considerable a robbery. For the second time that day safety had given place to the greatest danger. . . . It did not take long to dig up the treasure. Who will describe the joy of the Arabs at the sight of so much gold? There was no longer any question of starting. They killed a camel and thought of nothing but eating to celebrate their prize. The two Jews spent this day and night in the midst of a circle of Arabs, witnessing their rejoicing without knowing what was to become of them.

" The next day the Arabs wished to divide the gold between them. . . . They were sixty troopers; not knowing how to make sixty equal parts, they ordered Mardochée to do the sharing. The little scales found among his baggage were put into his hands, and for two days he was, under the eyes of his ravishers, obliged to weigh out his own gold and tax his wits in allotting sixty equal parts to them. The unfortunate man looked upon that as a respite; he expected to be butchered as soon as he had completed his work. Besides, was he not going to perish of hunger? All food was refused him, and since his captivity he fed on grass.

"Most of the robbers were Regibats, some Ulad Delim accompanied them. On the second day of the sharing Mardochée heard one of the men who surrounded him speak of the Shgarna tribe as being of the party: 'Are there any Shgarnas among you?' Mardochée asked. 'Yes, we are five Shgarnas here, such and such and such a one.' . . . A few hours afterwards, the Arabs having scattered to take their siesta, Mardochée went towards the Shgarni who had spoken to him, and falling at his feet, holding on to his burnous, exclaimed: ' By God and your honour! God put me under your protection, do not take it away from me. I have a *debiha*[1] on the Shgarnas. I am called Mardochée Abi Servur, such a one amongst you is my lord. By God and your honour! save me, show that the Shgarnas defend their clients, and that their protection is not vain.'

"The Shgarni was a relation of Mardochée's lord; he replied that as for the gold, he could not get it given back, the more so as it had been taken before the knowledge of the *debiha,* but he guaranteed the life of the two Jews; he could give no other pledge on account of the small number of Shgarnas present at the *rezzu*.[2] On the evening of the same day, when the sharing was over, the Arabs held council; they discussed what they would do. It was decided that they would scour the desert in the same region. Then they spoke about Mardochée; the greater number were for killing him and his companion. The five Shgarnas opposed this, acknowledging Mardochée as a client of their tribe. Hence, they declared, he was under their protection. A violent discussion arose, the chief of the *rezzu*, a Regibi,[3] wished for the death of the Jews, and his Regibats applauded him loudly. The Shgarnas were firm, and, when it was seen that they were ready to fight rather than abandon the suppliants, they gave way to them.

"Mardochée led a sad life during the week which followed: the *rezzu* had resumed its incursions; 50 kilometres a day were often covered at a rapid pace; the two

[1] The act by which one places oneself under the perpetual protection of a man or a tribe. It is a prolonged *anaïa*.
[2] An expedition, or band of adherents.
[3] Singular of Regibat.

Jews ran naked by the sides of the mounts of the Shgarnas, from whom they dared not get separated. They were tormented by hunger, for their protectors only had what was strictly necessary, and could give them nothing. Herbs, filthy bones flung away by the Musulmans, and a pinch of tea obtained through charity—such was the only food of Mardochée and his companion during this period. How long would this existence be prolonged? Mardochée, squatting near a well at which they camped on the eighth day, asked himself. In vain he begged the Shgarnas to bring him to Akka; they replied that if they separated themselves from the *rezzu* the pact of union would be broken, and the latter would pursue and attack them after their departure. As the objection was sound, Mardochée did not insist. Whence, then, would deliverance come? Would it arrive in time? All at once a whirlwind of dust appeared at the end of the valley; it approached like a hurricane. A few Arabs jump up in a scare, but not one has, so far, seized his arms. The cloud is upon them, and shows two hundred horsemen mounted on *méharis*. A man comes out of it and rides towards the Regibats; his white camel lies down, he places his feet, on which he is wearing high top boots, on the animal's head, levels his rifle at the Regibi chief. ' May God curse the Regibats and Sidi Hamed the Regibi their patron! May God burn your fathers and your ancestors! You have oppressed our brothers and wish to put our clients to death; at this moment you are at our mercy. Ha, women! you are only courageous against Jews; you are about to learn what a man's word of honour means!' It was the Shgarna chief who spoke thus; celebrated in the Sahara for his famous courage, he was recognized from a distance by his white mount, better trained than the best horse and taught to obey his master's voice. The man who had taken Mardochée under his protection had sent a trusty servant to warn him of the danger which the Shgarnas and their protégés ran, and he came to deliver his brothers out of the Regibats' hands.

"The Shgarnas only made use of their advantage to bring away their men and the two Jews. Mardochée, sent back to Akka under a good escort, at length regained his home. As to the *rezzu*, this adventure brought it bad luck. They went to attack a Berber band, and were so vigorously received, that their chief and the greater part of the horsemen were killed and but very few returned. The Sahara, after twenty years, still remembers the disaster of this *rezzu*.

"Mardochée was back in Akka, which he had never expected to see again, but he returned ruined, and a still greater grief awaited him. During his absence, his father and mother had quitted this world. Their legacy ought to have been considerable; it was a trifle. Mardochée, coldly received by his brothers, who had undoubtedly purloined a part of the inheritance, decided to leave a country in which he had found so much sadness. Selling what remained to him, he went for the last time to his parents' grave, taking away a little scrap of it—a relic which was never to quit him—and set out with his wife for Mogador.

"There a new period in Mardochée's life began, a period of constant relations with Europeans, which includes the remainder of his existence. At Mogador, he was found by M. Beaumier, the French Consul, a conscientious Orientalist and zealous member of the Société de Géographie. M. Beaumier put him into touch with this society, which brought him twice to Paris, and entrusted him with missions in Southern Morocco. In his journeys to France, Mardochée entered into relations with the general Union of the Israelites, and with several scholars such as Dr. Cosson, who, by the help which they gave him and the paid missions with which they entrusted him, helped him to earn a living for some years. Mardochée thus made, from 1870 to 1878, two or three expeditions in the interest of the Société de Géographie, and several collections of plants for Dr. Cosson. His work fell short of what was expected, for at the end of this time they ceased to give him any. Meanwhile M. Beaumier died. His means of subsistence and patron disappeared at the same time. Without means of existence at Mogador, where he was in bad odour with his co-religionists, Mardochée, with his wife and children, embarked for Algeria, and, supported by the Société de Géographie, asked the French Government for a post which would enable him to get a living. He was appointed Rabbi tutor at Oran, then at Algiers.

"One day in February, 1883, I was in the library of this latter town, chatting with the keeper, M. MacCarthy, when we saw a Jew, fifty or sixty years old, tall, strong, but bent and walking with the hesitation of those who have bad sight, come in. When he was near, I saw that his eyes were red and sore; he wore a long black beard mixed with white hairs; his face expressed rather simplicity and peace than anything else. He was dressed in Syrian fashion; a crimson caftan tightened at the waist fell down to his feet; over this hung a blue cloth mantle of the same length; his head-dress was a red cap surrounded by a black turban; in his hand he had a snuff-box, out of which he was continually taking pinches; his clothes, formerly rich, were old and dirty, and his whole person revealed a poor and negligent man. 'Who is that Jew?' I asked. 'He is just what you want; a man who has spent all his life in Morocco, was born at Akka, has travelled very much and been several times to Timbuctoo, and can give you precious information; he is the Rabbi Mardochée mentioned in the bulletins of the Société de Géographie.' I went to Mardochée and questioned him, judging that he could furnish me with good information. I took his address and went to see him. A Musulman of Mascara, with whom I was to set out for Morocco, having in the meantime written to me that he could not accompany me for family reasons, I proposed to Mardochée to take him in his place; he consented, on condition that I should put on a Jewish costume. I saw nothing but advantage in such disguise. All that remained was to make my agreement with Mardochée. With my authority, M. MacCarthy took the negotiations upon himself, and, after long debates, drew up an agreement which Mardochée and I signed, and it is now in the library of Algiers. Here is a summary of it:

"'Mardochée will leave his wife and children at Algiers during the whole of my journey. He is to accompany me and second me faithfully in all the places in Morocco to which I please to go. On my side I shall give him 270 francs a month; 600 francs will be handed to him before we start, the remainder on our return; if my absence lasts less than six months, he is nevertheless to receive six months' salary. The maintenance of Mardochée during the journey will be at my charge. If Mardochée should, without my permission, abandon me in the course of the journey, he will thereby lose his rights to all remuneration, however long may have been the time spent with me, and he himself will owe me the 600 francs he has received beforehand.'

"My companion's obligation to leave his family at Algiers guaranteed me against all thought of treason on his part. The article by which he was to lose his pay, if he left me against my will, assured me that he would not abandon me. These two clauses, inspired by M. MacCarthy through his knowledge of the Algerian Jews, ensured the success of my journey and probably saved my life; how often did Mardochée wish to leave me, and how often did the signed conditions alone prevent him.

"These agreements were signed in May, 1883; a few days after, on June 10, Mardochée and I set out together for Morocco.

"I have spoken little of Mardochée in the account of my journey, I have hardly mentioned him. His part was, however, great, for he was entrusted with our relations with the natives, and all material cares fell upon him; speeches to the Jews and Musulmans, explanations on the object of the journey, organization of the escorts, the search after lodgings and food—he undertook all that; I intervened only to approve or say no. Intelligent, very prudent, and too much so, infinitely cunning, a fine and even eloquent talker, a Rabbi educated enough to inspire the Israelites with consideration, he rendered me great services; I ought to add that he always showed himself vigilant and devoted in looking after my safety. If I have kept silence about his many services, it is because his ill-will was a constant and considerable obstacle to the execution of my journey. While contributing to the success of my enterprise, from the first day to the last he did all he could to make it fail. In leaving Algiers, Mardochée, knowing only the environs of Akka and the coast of Morocco, thought he was setting out on an easy and dangerless journey. I had given him details of the places which I wished to visit, but as he did not even know the names of most of them, this enumeration awoke no idea in his mind. Besides, he undoubtedly said to himself, that once in Morocco, he would do what he liked with so young a companion, and change my plans at his pleasure. Now, the journey was full of perils, and he could not change my designs at all. This was doubly unlucky for him; the conditions of the journey were, in fact, very different from what he had thought them. From Nemours, we had serious disputes, and he spoke of returning to Algiers; the Rif was the cause. At the first word about the dangers of this region, he declared he would not enter it; I ordered him to seek the means of going into it, and I sought them myself. At Tetuan, the same quarrel lasted for a fortnight; at Fas, it began again with extreme violence, and there, so much did Mardochée dread the route which led to Abu-el-Jad, that he was on the point of leaving me. After Fas, the dispute did not cease; two causes stirred it up afresh each day. Mardochée did not want to follow the route I had fixed, and wished to travel slowly; I, on the contrary, was determined to execute my original plan exactly, and I held to travelling without loss of time. On the first point, after Fas, I never yielded, and my route was followed according to my will. On the second point, I was not so successful, and, in spite of my reproaches, our progress was extremely slow until my departure from Tisint for Mogador. If my journey was quicker towards the end, it was that I promised Mardochée a gratuity, if we were at Lalla-Marnia on May 25. Between these two parts of my journey I was on the point of breaking with Mardochée. When I went to Mogador, I left him at Tisint, and set out with a Musulman, the Hajj Bu Rhim, an excellent man whom I can hardly praise enough. I travelled with him from January 9 to March 31, 1884. Once again in Tisint, I proposed to him to replace Mardochée and to accompany me to Algeria; he accepted, and I had already given Mardochée his testimonial and the sum necessary to get back to Algiers, when an obstacle prevented the Hajj Bu Rhim from starting. I took back Mardochée, who was only too pleased.

"If I had to complain of Mardochée's disagreeableness, it is fair to say that it was not inspired by any desire to be disobliging to me personally: his fear of danger caused his opposition to my route; his love of ease and his interest in prolonging services paid for by the month kept his slowness alive.

"After my return from Morocco in 1884, Mardochée left Algiers no more. Retired in his house, his old passion for alchemy again took hold of him. To find gold! With the gold of his pay he bought mercury for experiments in the transmutation of metals. And as he hung all day over his crucibles, the vapour of mercury did not take long to poison the last of alchemists."

If the *Reconnaissance au Maroc* is almost silent as regards Mardochée, the intimate letters written by the explorer are not. I must say they speak of the Rabbi without great consideration, and that the notes go *decrescendo*. Their descent is curious. Foucauld writes on June 17, 1883, a few hours after starting: "I am very satisfied with Mardochée. He has but one fault; it is excessive prudence."

On June 24, having already travelled a few days in Moroccan country, he writes to his sister: "I am fairly pleased with Mardochée; he goes on all right, but he has to be vigorously shaken. I am obliged to give him a pulling up nearly every day." July 2: "I am not pleased with Mardochée. He is lazy and cowardly, he is only good for cooking." July 23: "As for Mardochée, I am not satisfied with him; you could not find a lazier creature. Besides, he is cowardly beyond all expression, awkward, and knows nothing about travelling." Lastly, January 30, 1884, he wrote: "Mardochée is a brute."

It is only quite at the end that a little pity, as we have just seen, brings back what he has to say towards indulgence and excuse. When the journey is over, the route becomes more beautiful, and so does his companion.

CHAPTER III
The Explorer

LA RECONNAISSANCE AU MAROC is, above all, a scientific work, at once geographical, military, and political. The qualities of order and precision which one observes in each page are quite astonishing, and still more so if one thinks of all the difficulties, even dangers, which the explorer ran, if he wished to take notes. He was surrounded by people who suspected, and sometimes divined, his being a Christian, and therefore always in peril. In the *Itinéraires au Maroc* he explains how he was able to beguile the watchfulness of witnesses or to get them out of the way.

"The position of an Israelite did not lack unpleasantness; to walk barefooted in the towns, and sometimes in the gardens, to receive insults and stones was nothing; but to live constantly with Moroccan Jews—people, apart from rare exceptions, despicable and repugnant among all others—was utterly intolerable. They spoke openly to me as a brother, boasting of their crimes, disclosing their base feelings. How often I regretted my hypocrisy! All this annoyance and disgust were recompensed by the facility for work which my disguise gave me. As a Musulman it would have been necessary to live the common life unceasingly in broad daylight, unceasingly in company; never a moment of solitude; with eyes constantly fixed upon one; difficult to obtain any information; more difficult to write; impossible to make use of my instruments. As a Jew these things did not become easy, but were generally possible.

"My instruments were: a compass, a watch, and a pocket barometer, to take the bearings of the route; a sextant, a chronometer, and a false horizon, for observations of longitudes and latitudes; two holosteric barometers, some hygrometers and maximum and minimum thermometers, for meteorological observations.

"My route was mapped out with the compass and barometer. On the tramp, I always had a notebook 2 inches square hidden in my left hand; and a pencil less than an inch long, never out of the other hand, recorded anything remarkable on the right or left of the road. I noted the changes of direction by referring to the compass, the rise and fall of the ground by reading the barometer, the exact time of each observation, the stops, my rate of progress, and so on. Thus I was writing almost all the time I was on the road, and all the time in the hilly regions. Even in the most numerous caravan, no one ever perceived it; I took care to walk in front of or behind my companions, in order that the amplitude of my garments might prevent them from seeing the slight movement of my hands. The contempt felt for the Jews favoured my isolation. The description and survey of my itinerary thus filled a certain number of little notebooks. As soon as I reached a village where I could have a room to myself, I completed them, and recopied them into memorandum-books which formed the diary of my journey. I devoted my nights to this work; in the day I always had the Jews around me; to write for long before them would have filled them with suspicion. Night brought solitude and work.

"To make astronomical observations was more difficult than to map out the route. A sextant cannot be disguised like a compass. It takes time to use it. I took most of the elevations of the sun and stars in the villages. In the daytime I used to watch for the moment when nobody was on the terrace of the house. I carried my instruments wrapped in clothes which I said I wanted to put out to air. Rabbi Mardochée remained on guard on the stairs and had to stop all who tried to get at me with interminable stories. I began my observation, choosing the moment when nobody was looking from the nearest terraces; I was often obliged to break off; it took me very long. Sometimes it was impossible to be alone. What stories were not invented to explain setting up the sextant? Sometimes it was for reading the future in the sky, sometimes for getting news of the absent. At Tasa, it was a preventative against cholera, in the Tadla it showed the sins of the Jews, elsewhere it told me the time of the day, what the weather would be; it warned me of the dangers of the road and I don't know what else. At night I operated more easily: I could nearly always work in secret. Few observations were made in the country; it was difficult to isolate oneself there. I sometimes succeeded, pretending to pray; as if for meditation, I went to some distance, covered from head to foot in a long *sisit;* the folds hid my instruments; a bush, a rock, an undulation of the ground hid me for a few moments; I returned when I had finished praying.

"To draw mountain contours and make topographical

sketches, more mystery still was necessary. The sextant was an enigma which revealed nothing, French writing kept its secret; any drawing would have betrayed me. On the terraces, as in the country, I only worked alone with paper hidden and ready to disappear under the folds of my burnous."

His *Reconnaissance* is also a diary. Usually there are as many chapters as there were days in it. Charles de Foucauld rarely dallies for descriptions. He does it in few words, and as an artist; his simple landscapes, his choice of expression and discreet and harmonious elegance reveal a remarkably gifted man, and he might have been counted among the writers who have given us a picture of new countries. But he did not allow himself to yield to such inclinations. He wrote with the fixed intention, not to get himself admired, but to help France, the probable heir to Morocco, to prepare the way for her, for the benefit of comrades who, as he feels, will one day have the mission of conquering this empire, in which he often met chiefs secretly desirous of the coming of the French. In a word, he is already *the forerunner*. This mark distinguishes his whole life. Later on, when he reappears in Africa, Foucauld sets himself the mission of " taming " the Musulmans, of bringing them nearer to us and to the law of Christ. All his efforts, all his sacrifices to the very last, tend only to that : they make the preaching of the Gospel possible for the missionaries who come after him; he will also be the precursor, the quartermaster, the leader in religion.

Viscount de Foucauld and Mardochée leave Tangier on June 21, 1883, at 3 p.m. They form part of a small caravan; they are mounted on mules, thanks to which the long journey undertaken in Morocco is accomplished quickly enough. They ride until 9 in the evening, part of the time amidst splendid wheatfields. Next day the caravan starts at 4 a.m. There were then no roads in Morocco, but only tracks of men and beasts. Each day Charles de Foucauld notes the quality of the land, the principal properties of the trees which cover the ground in places, the colour of the rocks; he tells of meetings with other travellers, whether many partridges and doves rose on his way, if many hares started. At the outset of his journey he is struck by the multitude of brooks and little rivers that he crosses or walks by the side of, the vigour of the vegetation, the beauty of the tillage, and already he pities the poor Moroccan peasant from whom the pillager on one hand, the treasury on the other, carry off the best part of the crops.

Almost at once the travellers make a loop to the east, and spend a few days at Tetuan. They set out again from there on July 2 in the direction of the south, for Sheshuan. One is surprised, in reading the *Reconnaissance au Maroc,* at the frequency of the idyllic tone. The freshness of the gardens, the abundance of the crops, the mildness of the air, are expressions which come again and again under the pen of the explorer when he describes certain regions, as that of the Sheshuan. In the first place, it is not doubtful that he saw accurately, but also a kind of natural sympathy puts him in harmony with this landscape, and makes him enjoy its beauty.

Reaching the mountains on July 2, he writes: "The Jebel beni Hasan now affords an enchanting view; fields of wheat rising one above another form an amphitheatre on its slopes, and, from the rocks which crown it down to the bottom of the valley, cover it with a carpet of gold; among the wheatfields shine a multitude of villages surrounded by gardens. Springs gush out on every side; at every step one crosses brooks; they flow in cascades amongst ferns, laurels, fig-trees, and vines, which themselves grow on the edges. Nowhere have I seen a more smiling landscape, nowhere such an air of prosperity, nowhere so generous a land, nor more laborious inhabitants. From here to Sheshuan, the country is just the same; the names of the valleys change, but there are the same riches everywhere; indeed, it increases as one goes on."

From the beginning of the journey, ten days after he left Tangier, the explorer is right in the unknown. Into this little village of Sheshuan a single Christian had entered, a Spaniard, about 1863; he did not return. Charles de Foucauld, twenty years later, on July 2, stopped on the neighbouring heights to take a sketch, from which Viscount de Bondy was able to produce the large and accurate drawing published in the *Reconnaissance au Maroc.* He even went into the Jewish quarter, and on the way met people of Beni-Zejel, who shouted at him: " May God eternally burn the father that begot thee, Jew." He spent the night between the 2nd and the 3rd in the *mellah.* He does not seem to have visited the town itself. But he went as far as he could go, and alone. Into this Morocco he enters in a sorry garb, but with a strong and magnificent ambition—on the look-out for the unknown, above all. All his preferences are for the forbidden and wilder countries. From one point on the map to another equally settled on, he at any rate tries to go by a route over which nobody has been. Must he wait? He waits. Pay guides more? He pays up. Dangers, he never thinks about them. On the word of many of his intimate friends, I believe that fear and he were strangers.

The traveller who thus describes and sketches the landscape, also points out all the characteristics of the habits and customs that he observes. In this excursion, he meets a *Hajj*—that is to say, a Musulman who has made the pilgrimage to Mecca, and he at once notes that these pilgrims, who have some idea of what Europeans are, in general are less fanatic, more polished and affable than their co-religionists. Ten pages further on, he analyzes the different political position and the similar misery of the two parts of Morocco, the *bled el Makhzen* under the Sultan, and the free or revolted country, the *bled es Siba;* everywhere he collects and with an extreme care records information which may be of service to a geographer, sociologist, colonist, or soldier. Even had he been quite free to travel about in Morocco, one would be astonished that he had been able to become so completely acquainted with it.

Sometimes he ceases to make notes, and judges. His judgments have a contour as firm as his topographical details or his pen sketches. He has a certain sympathy for the Moroccans. I made allusion, for instance, to what he said about the pilgrims to Mecca. But he saw too closely, though enclosed in the crowd, what the inhabitants of the towns and villages were morally worth; he cannot pass over in silence the vices which consume the Musulman populations. And it is curious to read the lines I have just cited, when above all one remembers that the man who wrote them was to give a great part of his life to the conversion of these peoples of North Africa, as to whom he had few illusions even when quite young.

He says: "Extreme cupidity and, as companions, robbery and lying in all their forms reign almost everywhere. Brigandage, armed attacks are, in general, considered as honourable actions. Morals are dissolute. The condition of woman, in Morocco, is what it is in Algeria. The Moroccans are ordinarily but little attached to their wives, and yet have a great love for their children. The finest quality they show is devotion to their friends; they push it to the last limits. This noble feeling daily produces the finest actions. With the exception of the towns and some isolated districts, Morocco is very ignorant. They are, nearly everywhere, superstitious, and accord an unbounded respect and confidence to the local marabouts, the extent of whose influence varies. Even external religious duties are nowhere regularly carried out, save in the towns and districts above excepted. There are Mosques in every village or important douar; they are more frequented by poor travellers who use them as shelters, than by the inhabitants."

He is harder upon the Moroccan Jews. On July 7 he was detained at El Ksar for twenty-four hours because of the Sabbath, and writes: "If I could only take advantage of this delay to write out my notes! But it is almost impossible. In Morocco, has a Jew ever been seen writing on the Sabbath? It is forbidden just like travelling, lighting a fire, selling, counting money, talking business, and what not? And all these precepts are observed with equal care! For the Jews of Morocco, all religion consists in that: moral precepts they deny. The ten commandments are bygone tales, at most good for children; but as for the three daily prayers and lengthy graces before and after meals, keeping the Sabbath and feasts, I believe nothing in the world would make them miss them. Endowed with a very lively faith, they scrupulously fulfil their duties towards God, and indemnify themselves at the expense of His creatures."

To visit Tetuan, and above all Mt. Beni-Hasan and Mt. Sheshuan, Foucauld had left the road from Tangier to Fez. He took it up again, and, going on a line from nearly north to south, he reached Fez on July 11.

He hoped not to remain long in that well-known town, but a man with no time to waste should not venture into sunny lands. A man in a hurry, chooser of the most dangerous roads! A man—a Jew, it is true—who seems to forget dates and not to remember the great Musulman fast! What insolence! He was made to feel it. From Fez, on August 14, he wrote this letter, addressed to his cousin M. Georges de Latouche:

"You see I am still at Fez, and you must think that I have hardly made a start; it is but too true. It is because I always wished to go by the least known roads, and it is sometimes a long job to find the means of travelling by them.

"From Fez, I wished to go to Tadla; there are two roads; one by Rabat, easy and safe; the other very little frequented, very difficult, and crossing a completely unexplored country; naturally I had it very much at heart to take the second. From what I learn there is nobody here who can guide us safely along it. We are sending inquiries to Mekinez; from there they reply that there is an influential shereef, who knows the road, takes it sometimes, knows the tribes we shall come across, and who can, in a word, bring us safely to Bu Jaad, the capital of Tadla. (Tadla is a province, and not a town as shown on the maps.) We get him to come here; he consents to accompany us, but declares he will only start after the fêtes which finish Ramadan. We have been obliged to wait, and that is why we have remained so long at Fez. The Ramadan festival will be over the day after to-morrow; so to-morrow we set out for Mekinez, and from there, immediately, for Tadla. During the three weeks that I knew I should be obliged to remain in Fez, so as not to lose my time, I went from Fez to Tasa (three days' distance). I went there by one road and came back by another. The position of the town was known, but the roads which converge to it had not been marked; I mapped them as exactly as possible.

"I there unexpectedly discovered a town where all the inhabitants, Musulmans and Jews, think but of one thing —the coming of the French before long. These poor devils are in a country in which the authority of the Sultan is nil, and they are a constant prey to the violence and robbery of the powerful Kabyle tribe of the Riatas; so they do not cease praying to Allah to send them the French, in order to rid them of the Riatas. I remained a week at Tasa, because I could not find anyone with whom to get out of it safely. We are at last back from it, and are going to set out for Tadla.

"Up to the present I am not at all satisfied with Mardochée: he is inexpressibly cowardly and lazy. As in the case of Figaro, it cannot be said that these two failings divide him up between them; they reign within him together in the most perfect harmony. He is unspeakably downhearted into the bargain: he spends his time whining, and sometimes even sheds floods of tears. At first it was only ridiculous; in the end it gets very tiresome. If we are riding, it is the sun and the jolting of the mule; when we are in town, there are the fleas and bugs. And then there is the water, that is hot; and next the food is poor. All these little things may sometimes be hard to endure; but all he had to do was not to worry me in Algiers to travel with me. I confess to you that if I had not the accomplishment of my itinerary very much at heart, and not to return without having done anything, I should have dismissed him more than a month ago, and should have returned to Algiers to seek someone more active, enterprising, and manly. But I won't come back at any price without seeing what I said I would see; without going where I said I would go.

"I think that my journey will cost me all that I brought with me, or little less; up to the present I have spent 1,500 francs, and I have not gone far; it is true I have to the good two mules worth 250 francs each. . . . It is the travelling that is dear. If you want to go from one point to another, here is what you must do; you go to some local notability, who can certainly bring you safely to the point you wish to reach. You say to him : 'I want to go to that place: give me your *anaia*, and be my *zettet*.' *Anaia* means protection, and the *zettet* is the protector. He replies, very willingly, it is so much. We bargain for a good hour, finally the price is agreed. The said sum is given to him on condition that he accompanies you himself or gets one of his relations or servants to accompany you as far as your destination. This is the only way to travel among the Berber and Kabyle tribes. Without this precaution, even the people of the place you are leaving run after you, to rob you within a mile of the town or village from which you come.

"This *zettet* is the real costly thing in our journey; it costs more or less, according to the danger of the tribes one has to pass through. Sometimes it is excessively dear; thus, in leaving Tasa for another point on the Fez route, only six hours' distance by road from the town, I paid sixty francs (it was a question of crossing the territory of the terrible Riatas). You understand that with such difficulties in communication, trade in Morocco is not brisk; although the country is marvellously fertile, the inhabitants are not rich; they cultivate just the necessaries of life, not being able to sell their surplus. There is no comparison between this country and Algeria, which is a desert compared to it. In Algeria, even in winter, there is no water anywhere. Here at this season there is water everywhere; there are running rivers, brooks, torrents, and springs. And note that since I set foot in Morocco I have not seen a drop of water fall. But there are high wooded mountains, and, in the direction of the south-east, from the terrace of this house, threads of snow can be seen on the distant tops of the Jebel."

A month's halt! Charles de Foucauld employs it to make two great excursions—one to Tasa, as he said, in the east, the other to Safra. The very detailed account which he gives of these two excursions seems to me to be the best part of the *Reconnaissance au Maroc*. Here, also, picturesque phrases abound; for instance, this one : " At half-past three, we reached a pass : Tasa appeared, a high cliff standing out in relief from the mountain and advancing, like a cape, into the plain. On its summit the town dominated by an old minaret : at its feet vast gardens." Foucauld reaches the gate of the outer walls, takes off his shoes, and enters the town.

The most miserable town in Morocco ! The Riata tribe pillage it perpetually. Always in arms, filling the narrow streets and squares, if they find any object or beast of burden which suits them, they seize it, and there is no hope of justice against them. " It is difficult to express the terror in which the population live; so they think only of one thing—the coming of the French. How many times have I heard the Musulmans exclaim : ' When will the French come ? When will they at last rid us of the Riatas ? When shall we live in peace, like the people of Tlemcen ?' And then they pray for the hastening of that day; they have no doubt of its arrival : in this respect they share the common opinion of a great part of Eastern Morocco, and of nearly all the upper class in the Empire. . . ."

Safra, on the contrary, is flourishing, full of well-built white brick houses; there the traveller walks about in " endless and wonderful gardens . . . big bushy woods whose thick foliage spreads an impenetrable shade and delightful coolness on the ground."

When these excursions were over, the terrible road was at last open, and the explorer was able to reach Mekinez, and from there Abu-el-Jad, where he arrived on September 6.

" Here was neither Sultan nor *makhzen*: nothing but Allah and Sidi Ben Daud." This great personage has hardly seen Rabbi Joseph Aleman than he gives evidence of the most singular respect towards him. The *Reconnaissance au Maroc* does not make any allusion to this, but in the third manuscript note already mentioned, Charles Foucauld tells at length the exciting adventure which befell him in the town of Abu-el-Jad :

" I arrive in Abu-el-Jad escorted by a grandson of Sidi Ben Daud : the Sid had sent me this distinguished protector after having received a letter from a great lord of Fas, his friend, Hajj Tib Ksous. To do complete honour to this recommendation, he gave me audience immediately on my arrival in his town. Mardochée and I were received and questioned separately; we presented ourselves as two Rabbis from Jerusalem who had been settled in Algiers for seven years. We had hardly come out of the Sid's house than we saw a Musulman, seated in the middle of a group, make us a sign to approach. He who called us was the second son of Sidi Ben Daud, Sidi Omar. He brought us into his house, and began to put questions about Algeria. Meanwhile, the Sid sent for the principal Jews of the town, ordered them to receive us well, and appointed one of them to give us hospitality in his name. These two audiences and such care for putting us up were extraordinary favours.

"The day after my arrival, I received the visit of a son of Sidi Omar, Sidi El Hajj Edris; although a mulatto, he is a very fine young man of twenty-five; tall, well-proportioned, supple and graceful in movement, intelligent-looking, lively and gay. His title of Hajj, intelligence, education, and a fine appearance made him one of the most highly esteemed members of Sidi Ben Daud's family. He comes, he says, to see that we want for nothing; three or four Musulmans accompany him; for half an hour we chat of one thing and another, our visitors showing an extreme affability. In taking leave of us S. Edris asks whether we have seen the Rabbis of Abu-el-Jad. 'Not yet.'—'Whether they come or do not come, whether you remain several days or months, you are a thousand times welcome!' What is the meaning of such unparalleled attentions to the Jews?

"It was not long before I understood. Two things were remarkable during the four following days: on the one hand, the frequent visits, the excessive amiability of Sid's relations, who endeavoured to give me confidence and to make me speak; on the other, the open spying of the Jews who watched my least act, thrust their noses into my notebook as soon as I wanted to write, rushed on my thermometer, as soon as I touched it, and were rude and insufferable. . . . These two lines of conduct were too accentuated not to betray their cause. Something must have made Sidi Ben Daud, or his son Sidi Omar, suspect my being a Christian. The marabouts had resolved to enlighten themselves by having me spied upon by the Jews, while making their own examination of me; for the last four days they were plainly following up this investigation.

On September 11, in the morning of the sixth day after my arrival, one of Sidi Edris's slaves came into my room, and told me to follow him with Mardochée to his master's. He showed us into a house of the *zauïa*. We expect fresh questions. No! as soon as we are seated, breakfast is brought in. Tea, pastries, butter, eggs, coffee, almonds, grapes, and figs are placed on dazzling dishes. S. Edris offers me lemonade, and makes excuses for having neither knives nor forks; he eats with us, which is an unheard-of favour, and, keeping up a long conversation, tells us that he knows Tunis, Algiers, Bône, Bougie, Philippeville, and Oran, which he visited in coming back from Mecca. At the end of two hours, we are dismissed, and a slave conducts us back to our house.

"My relations with S. Edris and his father become more intimate from day to day. On the 13th at noon, I am called with Mardochée to the house of the former. Again a breakfast is waiting for us: S. Edris shares it with us. As I speak to him of my desire to leave Abu-el-Jad, he replies that he will escort me himself. He is one of the most exhalted personages of his family, and puts himself out only for caravans of two or three hundred camels; but for my companion and me, there is nothing that he will not do. All three of us are to set out alone in a few days; he wants to make friends of us; we are to write to him on our return to Algiers, and he will come and see us there. When the meal was over, he led me to a window, and showed me the chain of the Middle Atlas which extends along the horizon towards the south. He begins describing and giving me a host of details about its inhabitants. For me the better to enjoy this fine sight, he has a chair and a small telescope brought me.

"So many favours cannot possibly be disinterested. What are S. Edris and his father driving at? I do not know; however, they have promised to escort me on my departure from Abu-el-Jad; so their good intentions must be cultivated. The same day, I send S. Edris twenty francs and three or four sugar-loaves—a suitable present for the country. Next day, the 14th, S. Edris sends for us towards evening to dine with him on his terrace. As we are talking he repeats that he would like to go to Algiers, and from there to the Christians' continent; would it be possible? Nothing easier, I tell him, the French minister at Tangier will enable him to reach Algiers, where I shall be altogether at his service. And could he bring a Christian to Abu-el-Jad? He would be delighted to do so, provided that the Christian were disguised as a Musulman, or a Jew, and that the Sultan knew nothing about it. The affair would have to be negotiated secretly between him and the French minister. In that case, added Mardochée, the French authorities would give him the best of receptions, for they would be very pleased to send a Frenchman to explore Abu-el-Jad, which no Christian has ever seen. S. Edris smilingly replies that Christians have visited it. 'In Musulman costume?'—'No! In Jewish costume no one knew who they were; but we recognized them.'

"Next morning, a fresh visit to S. Edris: the conversation became quite intimate. After what he said to us yesterday, would he write a letter to the French minister, and enter into an engagement to receive and protect any Frenchman in his town? Willingly, he said, and he was ready to visit the functionary, to assure him of his goodwill towards France.

"The same day, we were called to Sidi Ben Daud's house. We were shown into a beautiful hall, in which seven or eight marabouts of the Sid's family were seated on carpets around him. We were invited to sit down, and little negresses from eight to ten years old brought us cups of tea and *palmers*. When we had enjoyed looking at the saint for half an hour, we were dismissed with kind words, and he himself said to us: 'May God aid you!' In coming out, we were rejoined by S. Omar, who led us away to his house; it was he, he said, who had got us invited to his father's, with the thought that that visit might interest us. He questioned me on astronomy. The Jews had told him I was a great astronomer. I am said to spend my nights in looking at the stars. Thus the Jews spy upon me for the benefit of the Musulmans. On the 16th, Sidi Edris sends for me early; first of all he puts into my hand two letters recommending Mardochée and me to the Jews of Kasba and to those of Kasba-Beni-Mellal, signed by the Rabbis of Abu-el-Jad. They were not written willingly; Sidi Edris makes the Rabbis come to his house and orders them to sign the letters under his eyes. Sidi Edris afterwards gives me a word of recommendation for a friend of his who lives at Bezzu, a place to which I shall go later on. Lastly he composes a letter to the French Minister: he reads it to me before closing it; it is couched somewhat thus: 'To the Ambassador of the French Government. I inform you that two men of your country have come to me, and that, for love of you, I have given them the best of receptions and have taken them where they wished. In like manner I will receive all those who come in your name; the bearers of this letter will give you more complete information. If you wish to see me, let me know through the French Consul at *D*ar-Beida. I shall at once proceed to Tangier.' Şidi *E*dris signs this document, folds it, seals it with his seal, and hands it over to me, recommending secrecy and prudence: he is putting his head into my hands; a great risk to run, if the letter gets lost and comes to the eyes of the Sultan.

"This business done, S. *E*dris told me we should start the next day for Kasba-Tadla. Not only would he be my guide, but my companion as far as Kasba-Beni-Mellal, where I should leave the Tádla. I was to be as a brother to him, and he would go to the end of the world to please me, but he could no longer bear my living in the town with the Jews, who were savages. He would have my mules and baggage fetched, and henceforth I was to be his guest. An hour later, I was put up in his house.

"From this moment, my relations with S. *E*dris assumed a new character: up to then his excessive attention had made me distrustful, the gift of the letter for the French minister was such a mark of confidence, that I could no longer doubt of his present good intentions: besides, this letter explained his advances, showing that the cause of them was his desire of entering into relations with the French Government. Sure of S. *E*dris, henceforth I was on the same footing with him as a friend. I returned his confidence and, as he had put himself into my hands, I put myself into his. I told him unreservedly who I was, who Mardochée was, and what I came to do. This only increased his fidelity. He was overwhelmed with regret at not knowing the truth sooner. From the first day I should have lodged in his house; I should have worked there, drawn and made my observations at my ease; if I would postpone my departure, he would bring me to visit the *qoubbas* and mosques, put at my disposal the library of the *zauïa,* which is rich in historical works, and take me for walks in the neighbourhood. . . . What would he not do?

"Then he offered me a hundred things, Musulman costumes, a slave; . . . as the waiting of the little negresses at Sidi Ben *D*aud's seemed to me so charming, he offered me one of them. Upon my arrival, he said, my face made him suspect that I was a Christian, and the Jews had confirmed that opinion. Let me beware of the Jews! they were untrustworthy people, rascals to be unceasingly on one's guard against. The day after my arrival the local Jews told him that I was busy with astronomy, that I did not speak their language, did not write as they did, never went to the synagogue; in a word, that they believed I was a Christian. He told them they were asses, and that the Jews of Algiers and France were different from the Jews of that country.[1]

" On September 17, Sidi Edris, Mardochée, and I quitted Abu-el-Jad. On the 20th we arrived at Kasba-Beni-Mellal. On the 23rd Sidi Edris bade us adieu and again took the road to his *zauïa*. I cannot express what he was to me while we travelled together. As we rode, he would ride close beside me, and give me explanations about all we passed through, met, or saw. If I wished to draw, he stopped. On his own initiative he always chose the most interesting and not the shortest roads. If we stopped anywhere he took me by the hand to see anything curious. He used to do more; as the house in which he received hospitality filled on his arrival, and a crowd came to kiss his hand, this great marabout used to hide a part of my instruments in his ample garments, whilst I carried the other, and lead me to a retired place to make my observations; he would mount guard over me, to prevent me from being surprised. How many excursions we made together near Kasba-Beni-Mellal. If I stopped to draw, he used to sit down beside me, and his talk taught me a host of things. All I know about the *zauïa* of Abu-el-Jad, Sidi Ben Daud's family, the population of the Tadla, came from him. From him I got nearly all the information printed in this volume from page 259 to 267, about the Wady-Um-er-Rebia basin. He also dictated what one reads from page 65 to 67, on the campaign of the Sultan in the Tadla in 1883; he had followed the expedition of Marrakesh to Meris-el-Biod as Sidi Ben Daud's representative to Muley el Hasen. On the subject of the relations of his family with the Sultan, he said to me : ' We do not fear

---

[1] I found, in Charles de Foucauld's papers, this note about the incident here related :

"Mardochée never knew that I had disclosed my Christianity and the plan of my journey to Sidi Edris : an instinctive hatred rather than a reasoned prudence made him distrust every Musulman, and he would have thought himself lost if he had believed me guilty of confiding in a Musulman. I revealed who I was and what I was doing to four persons only in Morocco : Samuel Ben Semhoun, a Jew of Fas ; the Hajj Bu Rhim, a Musulman of Tisint, who was a real friend to me ; Sidi Edris ; and a Jew of Debdu. To the two Jews, Mardochée and I agreed to make our disclosures together. To the two Musulmans I alone made it, and Mardochée was always ignorant of it. All four religiously kept my secret, rendered me a thousand services, and it only remains for me to congratulate myself for having trusted them and to feel a lively gratitude towards them."

him, and he does not fear us; he can do us no harm, and we can do him none.' Having asked him whether Muley el Hasen was loved : ' No, he is grasping and avaricious.' (this was, word for word, what was told me at Fas). Sidi Edris intends to come and see me at Algiers and in France, and makes me promise to return later on to Abu-el-Jad; that if I come back as a Turk, he will put me up in his house, and we shall spend pleasant weeks there, and I shall travel about as much as I wish. He entrusts me with the letter he has given me : ' If the Sultan had any knowledge of it, he would have my tongue cut out and my hand cut off.' I ask him if his father S. Omar knows that he has written it. Yes, it was S. Omar who inspired it, and it was he who told his son to behave to me as he had done; but the secret remains between S. Omar and S. Edris : they had not confided it to Sidi Ben Daud, ' because he is rather old.' ' How rich this country would be if the French were governing it!' my companion was always saying, as he gazed on the fertile plains which spread out at our feet. ' If the French come here, will they make me Kaïd,' he once added.

"The belief in a coming invasion by the French was the cause of the reception I had at Abu-el-Jad. The marabouts received me well because they took me for a spy. In the greater part of Morocco, it is believed that before long France will seize Muley el Hasan's empire, and they are preparing for this event, and already the great are seeking to assure themselves of our favour. The favours with which Sidi Ben Daud's family loaded me and the letter entrusted to me, are a proof of the state of mind of the highest persons in Morocco.

" Do they dread this expected French domination? The great lords, the traders, the groups oppressed by the Sultan or by powerful neighbours would accept it without displeasure. To them it represents an increase of riches, the establishment of railways (a thing very much desired), peace, security; in a word, a regular and protective government."

Eleven years later, Charles de Foucauld, who had become a priest travelling in the Sahara, to his great astonishment received the following letter, signed by a young marabout, who had become chief of the *zauïa*:

"CASABLANCA,
"*August* 16, 1904.

"I desire excessively to hear from you, for I have no good news of you for a long while, though I am very interested in hearing of you. Lately, I asked the French Consul here about you. He told me that you are in Jerusalem in the Holy Land in the honest service of God, and that you have sacrificed your time to the Eternal.

"I congratulate you, and I am certain that the world no longer interests you: and this is essential for the present and the future. Be good enough to write to the French Ambassador at Tangier, to tell him of my work and endeavours with you during your stay here. This is to get the Ambassador to write to the French Consul to let him know of my fidelity towards you.

"Thanking you sincerely in anticipation, and again congratulating you on the good state to which you have attained.

"For ever your devoted servant,
"H$_{\text{AJJ}}$-D$_{\text{RISS}}$-E$_{\text{L}}$-S$_{\text{HERKAUI}}$.

"Abu-el-Jad, where I was with you in the Kabil Tadla journey."

The letter was addressed "à l'officier Foukou," and handed, at Algiers, to Commandant Lacroix, who filled in the address.

After leaving Abu-el-Jad, Charles de Foucauld was escorted by one of the grandsons of Sidi Ben Daud, and that for as long as the travellers were in the Tadla. They kept going to the south and through dangerous regions. During a stay at Tikirt, he studied the very different political régimes of the tribes dwelling in the independent countries to the north of the Great Atlas range, or to the south of the mountains. In the former, the government was democratic, each section of the tribe governed by an assembly in which each family was represented. In general there were no laws, and, when the clans of the same tribe were not agreed, each followed its own will or caprice, and the dispute was sometimes settled by shooting. To the south of Mt. Atlas, there was also a kind of democratic State, but the tribes were not always isolated, and between them, there were bonds of seigniory and vassalage. All these kinds of local polities are explained in the *Reconnaissance au Maroc,* with an abundance of details and nice distinctions which prove the cleverness of the inquirer and the richness of his notebooks.

A little farther on he describes the three mountain-chains of the Great, Middle, and Lesser Atlas. After these dry pages, and when he leaves Tikirt to go to Tisint, the poet reappears, always keeping himself well in hand, but taking pleasure in painting in a few lines these gardens of the oasis, and, beneath the shade of the palm-trees, the land divided in squares, watered by a thick tangle of canals, and covered with maize, millet, and vegetables. They are spots of happiness between the most wild, bare, and desolate of landscapes. He goes as far as to write: " A charming spot, and made for none but the happy."

In his journey to the south, he reaches the region of the Saharan Morocco, via Tanzida and Tisint. The description which he gives of the southern landscape, as seen from the Tisint oasis, is, I think, the most finished picture that he brought back from his exploratory journey: " On entering Tisint, one steps into a New World. Here, for the first time, the eye looks to the south without seeing a single mountain. The region to the south of Bani is one immense plain, now white, now brown, with its stony solitudes stretching far away out of sight; an azure streak limits it on the horizon and separates it from the sky: it is the slope of the left bank of the Dra. Beyond commences the Hammada. This scorched plain has no other vegetation than a few stunted gum-trees, no other relief than the narrow chains of rocky and broken hills twisting about like fragments of serpents. Alongside of the dismal desert are the oases, with their wonderful vegetation, their forests of evergreen palm-trees, their *ksars* full of comfort and riches. Working in the gardens, stretched nonchalantly in the shadow of the walls, squatting at the house-doors, chatting and smoking, are seen a numerous population of black-faced men, very dark *harratin*. First I am struck by their garments; all are dressed in indigo cottons, Sudan materials. I am in a new climate; there is no winter. They sow in winter, reap in March; the air is never cold; above my head the sky is ever blue."

Charles de Foucauld stops only two days at Tisint. He is the object of the most lively curiosity. " All the *Hajjs*, familiar with the things and peoples of distant countries, wished to see me. Once more, I recognized the excellent effects of the pilgrimage (of Mecca). From the fact alone that I came from Algeria, where they had been received well, all gave me the best welcome. Several, I knew later on, suspected that I was a Christian; they did not say a word, understanding better perhaps than I the dangers into which their talk might throw me. One amongst them, the Hajj Bu Rhim, eventually became my true friend, and rendered me the most signal services, saving me from the greatest perils." Long excursions in the south, to Tatta, to the Mader and to Akka, filled the following month.

Home from these two excursions, Foucauld thought of regaining Algeria, recrossing the inhospitable Rif, the western approach of which had been forbidden him at the start. He could not undertake such an adventure without powerful protection, and once more he turned southwards to pay a visit to Sidi Abd Allah, a person of mark, living at Mrimima. No doubt this man would provide him with the necessary guides.

But the stranger had no sooner entered Sidi Abd Allah's house than the report spread that he was a Christian and laden with gold. Immediately two bands of robbers lay in ambush in the mountains, and set about watching for this excellent and easy prey. Foucauld was kept in sight by the sons of his host. In this danger, he wrote a letter to his friend the Hajj Bu Rhim, and gave it to a beggar.

"At 7 a.m. next day there is a great stir in the village. A troop of twenty-five foot soldiers and two troopers arrive suddenly, and go straight into the courtyard. It is the *Hajj* coming to take me. He received my note that night. He got up at once and ran to his brothers and relations; each armed himself and joined him with his servants; they set out on march, and here they are."

Half an hour later he was delivered and left Mrimima. But the unreasonable demands and successive robberies of which he had been the victim had so reduced his resources that, when he had got back in Tisint and made up his accounts, he recognized that it was impossible for him to undertake the return journey without renewing his supply of money. Mogador, to the north-west on the Atlantic coast, was the nearest town, in which there were Europeans. There he must go. Foucauld confided his project to his friend the *Hajj*. The latter agreed to accompany the traveller to Mogador, wait for him there, and bring him back to Tisint. Mardochée, on the contrary, was to remain in that village. They were to join him later on.

They had to start at night with the greatest secrecy, so as not to be attacked and robbed. This departure from Tisint for the Atlantic coast took place on January 9, 1884.

From Mrimima, and just at one of the really perilous hours of his journey, Charles de Foucauld had written to his sister Mary. It was not the first time he had written to her. How, by whom, was this note brought? It was written on a little square of paper, folded and refolded, so as not to show more surface than a receipt stamp. I do not know. Some caravan must have taken charge of it. The letter was received; it was dated from the *zauia* of Sidi Abd Allah Umbarek, January 1.

"A Happy New Year, my good Mimi; if only I could let you know this day that I am well and in no danger! If you knew how sad I am at the thought of your probably not having heard from me for so long, and being uneasy about my fate, so that this day, which is a holiday for so many, is sadder for you than other days! At this time, when everyone receives letters from relations and friends, you alone receive none from the only very near one you have in the world. I know how sad you must be, and how full your heart must be. But perhaps I am mistaken: God grant it! Perhaps some of my letters have reached you. If you get this letter, my good Mimi, be of good cheer, don't be anxious. I run no risk and shall run none until my arrival. The road is long, but it is not at all dangerous. If the bad weather, which has delayed my going for the last month and a half, continues, I shall take three good months to get back. If I find the roads easy, two will be enough. God grant that it may be so, and that I shall soon be again with you. . . ."

At Mogador, where he arrived on January 28, after having, for three and a half hours, travelled through "a vast forest overshadowing immense grazing fields," he went straight to the French Consulate, where he found himself in presence of a Jewish secretary and translator, called Zerbib, who was working in the offices.

"I should like to see the French Consul, to cash a cheque on the Bank of England. I am the Vicomte de Foucauld, officer of the French Cavalry."

The other, eyeing this dirty and tattered pedestrian from head to foot, and knowing the dodges of such cadgers received him very badly.

"Go and sit outside with your back to the wall: you can't see the consul in that rig."

Charles de Foucauld went and lay down near the wall, and remained there some time. Then he came back to Zerbib:

"Give me a little water, and please show me a spot to undress and wash in."

While he was stripping in a shed close by, someone looked through the keyhole. It was Zerbib. To his great astonishment, he saw this tramp was the bearer of a number of surveying instruments hidden in the pockets or folds of his clothes, deposited one after the other on the ground.

"After all," he said to himself, "I may be mistaken, and he may be telling the truth."

He goes at once and informs his superior. The Vicomte de Foucauld is shown in to M. Moutel, chancellor of the Consulate. The first question he puts to the latter is this: "Have you received the letters for my family which I addressed here?" Alas! of all the letters that he had written, the last eight months, not one had yet come to hand. He therefore writes without further delay to his sister Marie, telling her first that he has never been a minute ill, and has never risked the least danger. This assertion was not quite true. He added that of the 6,000 francs which he had at his disposal for the journey, 4,000 were spent, and that he had left in reserve 2,000 francs, which he now comes for.

"In setting out, I told you I shall remain a year. At the bottom of my heart, I thought of remaining at most six months. I told you double so that you might not be anxious in case my absence was prolonged; and you see the time I gave you turns out right. My journey has lasted very nearly a year. It is now eight months since I set out. I am going to spend about a month here, waiting for news from you and money, then I shall again set out for the south, and return to Algeria, if it please God, by the following route: Mezquita, Dadis, Todra, Ferkla, Ksabi-esh-Sheurfa, the course of the Wady-Muluya, Debdu, Ujda, from where I shall re-enter French territory by Lalla-Marnia; all that will take me two months and a half. As soon as I get back to Algeria, how happy, my dear Mimi, shall I be to take the steamer and hasten to you!

"From the geographical point of view, my journey goes on very well: my instruments are in good condition; none of them got out of order; I have visited new countries, and bring back, I believe, some useful information. From the moral point of view, it is very sad; always alone, never a friend, never a Christian to speak to. . . . If you knew how much I am thinking of you, of our happy days of the past with grandfather, and of those we spent together with my aunt; and how all these thoughts absorb one when one is as isolated as I have just been. It is, above all, Christmas and New Year's Day which seemed to me so sad. I remembered grandfather and the Christmas-tree, and all the good times of our childhood. And on New Year's Day, it is for you I was sorry. . . . And yet I did not know that none of my letters had reached you! I sent you some by special messenger, I sent you some by caravans:

each time I found an opportunity to send off a word, I seized it eagerly; and nothing got through. My poor Mimi, how pleased you will be to hear from me, and how happy I shall be to hear from you! I fear but one thing: it is that you will beg me to end my journey and return immediately. I pray you to be sensible: relatively I shall want only a very little time to end it, and then I shall have made a fine journey, and finished what I meant to do. When you start with saying what you are going to do you must not come back without having done it. . . ." At the end of the letter, Charles de Foucauld explains how the money is to be sent to Tangier, where a banker will write to one of his colleagues in Mogador, and the traveller will be able to set out again.

Other letters to his sister relate, with charm and vivacity, the life he is leading at Mogador; it is not an idle life or simply repose. "I am up to my neck in my longitudes," he writes on February 8. " I work from morning to night, and a part of the night. This is a hundred times more thrilling than the journey itself, for there lies the result. If it is not good, then eight months of toil and trouble have been thrown away; but I hope it will be presentable. Here I am marvellously placed for work. I lodge in a boarding hotel arranged in European fashion, but kept by Spanish Jews; I have a suitable room, in which I stay all day long, and in the evening dine in it. I go out only once a day, to lunch at the house of the only Frenchman in Mogador, M. Moutel, chancellor of the Consulate (the consul is absent). . . . Every day I am very pleased to find myself once more, for two or three hours, in a French home. . . ."

"*February* 14.—I spend my time in the most routine manner in the world: From 7 o'clock to 11 in the morning I work: from 11 to 1 o'clock, I go and lunch at the Chancellor's; at 1 I get back to work; at 7 o'clock I dine at my hotel. Then I go back and work till 1 o'clock in the morning. As to visits, I pay none, since there is nobody to see; I receive one each day from the negro who commands the escort which accompanied me. Don't fancy this is enormous. At the start it was three men, and now is no more than two; the third, who was a slave of the said negro, was latterly sold by his master. Those that remain are patiently, or rather a little impatiently, waiting for the time of my starting again. Every day the chief, the negro, a Sheikh of Tisint, comes to report the condition of the men and mules, and what he has done, and to take his money for the day: it means a chat and a lesson in Arabic. . . . I am very anxious not to be too much noticed, so that the Moroccan Government may not get wind of my projects, and seek to put obstacles in my way: its policy has long been to prevent Europeans by every possible means from travelling in the interior of the empire. . . ."

" *March* 7, 1884.—Letters are very behindhand, my good Mimi. Every minute I fancy I see a mail arrive; but nothing comes, always nothing. However, it is thirty-five days to-day since my first letters left. . . . I am still staying at the same Jewish hotel. . . . The French Colony is not very numerous here: the consul, the chancellor and his wife, a merchant and his wife, an Anglican missionary, nationalized French, and an Alsatian doctor. The missionary is a very agreeable and well-bred man. He is married and has almost always European friends in his house. At present a very handsome young English lady is there, who speaks French perfectly. I find it very pleasant to go from time to time and spend the evening in this house, where I hear the *Lac* and *l'Envoi de Fleurs* sung, which reminds me of a very happy time: but it is already far away. . . . However, as soon as your letters arrive, I shall be off at a gallop towards the South."

In a letter Charles de Foucauld pretends that he cannot draw. If you open the *Reconnaissance au Maroc,* you will find on the title-page: *With Four full-page and a Hundred-and-one other Illustrations from the Author's Sketches.* These sketches, a few pen-strokes, but composed with a very sure feeling for landscape, and drawn with an evident scruple for exactitude, add singularly to the beauty of the work, and afford play to the imagination. Doubtless, we would like to see the colour of these rocks, mountains, this desert and those palm-trees on the bank of a *wady,* but, however imperfect a simple line illustration may be, it helps to guide our eyes, which arouse memory and fill it with light.

The money having come, Foucauld sets off again with the Hajj Bu Rhim from Mogador for Tisint on March 14, 1884, by a different way to that which he had taken in going there. Reaching the Wady-Sus to the south of Agadir, he follows the right bank of the river some way off:

" I shall see it all day long, winding among tamarisks, surrounded by cultivation, with tall olive-trees shading its course, and two rows of villages arranged in a zig-zag along its banks. The river, with its border of fields, trees, and houses, forms a wide green band unwinding through the middle of the plain, about 35 feet below the general level. A slope with an angle of 45° unites the hollow to the surrounding land. I go to the north of the slope, in the Sus Plain. It is an immense surface, smooth as a mirror, of red earth without a stone. It spreads between the Great and Lesser Atlas. . . . Here its width is 40 kilometres. . . . The valley of the Sus does not vary during the three days that I go up it; a plain of marvellous fertility, enclosed between two long chains, one of which, less lofty and with uniform ridges, borders the horizon on the south by a brown line, whilst the other, shooting into the clouds, raises above the country the bluish flanks and white tops of its gigantic masses perpendicularly. . . ."

On March 31, the traveller was back in the Tisint region, where Rabbi Mardochée was waiting for him.

He did not immediately proceed to the North-East. No one would agree to accompany him into the country which he first sought to enter: he was obliged to go back by Tazendakht.

We know henceforth what was Charles de Foucauld's manner of travelling, the endurance and courage he showed, and how fine a mind as scholar and poet he showed in writing his memoranda. I have therefore only to note a few names, on this return journey, so soon finished.

From Tazendakht, he went to Mezquita, then to Dadis, then to Ksabi-esh-Sheurfa. On the way, he was detained for two days by heavy rains. On May 8 he forded the Muluya, apparently the widest stream that he crossed, since the *Reconnaissance au Maroc* notes here a width of over 100 feet and a depth of 4 feet.

The last stages brought him to Debdu, the first place carrying on regular trade with Algeria. The traveller had not a centime. Fortunately he was only a four days' ride from Lalla-Marnia. He sold his mules, thus procuring the wherewithal to hire others, and, starting from Ujda at 7 a.m. on May 23, arrived on French territory at 10, and soon after in Lalla-Marnia, where he left Mardochée.

After the *Reconnaissance au Maroc*, Charles de Foucauld wrote a second part, which he entitled "Information," with the methodical mind that is so striking in the actual telling of his travels. In this wholly scientific part are assembled the details that the traveller was able to observe or collect about the rivers and their tributaries; the tribes and their divisions; the number of guns and horses at their disposal; the routes, those which he had followed and those which he was told about, with notes of the duration of the stages : a sort of guide-book used, and still in use, by the leaders of our troops operating in Morocco. Towards the end is an appendix on the Jews of Morocco, a social and statistical study; then the list of astronomical observations made in the course of the journey, the table of latitudes and longitudes, the meteorological observations, and an index of the geographical names contained in the volume and the atlas.

A year after the return of Charles de Foucauld to French territory, on April 24, 1885, at the Paris Société de Géographie a report was read by Duveyrier on the *Reconnaissance au Maroc*, of which he had studied the manuscript. " In eleven months, from the 20th of June, 1883, to the 23rd of May, 1884, a single man, the Vicomte de Foucauld, has doubled, at least, the length of carefully surveyed itineraries in Morocco. He went over again and perfected 689 kilometres of the works of his predecessors, and added 2,250 other kilometres to them. As to astronomic geography, he has determined 45 longitudes and 40 latitudes; and where we only possessed a few dozen altitudes, he has brought back 3,000. You must see that we have to thank M. de Foucauld for opening what is indeed a new era, and one does not know which is to be most admired, these fine and useful results, or the self-sacrifice, courage, and ascetic abnegation, thanks to which this young French officer has obtained them." Duveyrier indicates afterwards which are the parts of the journey that may justly bear the name of discoveries; they are numerous and important. He proves that the Vicomte de Foucauld's observations have corrected by a full degree to the west the direction of the course of the Dra, as shown on the map of the German doctor Rohlfs. Lastly, he announced, in finishing his report, that the Société de Géographie conferred the first of its gold medals on the young explorer.

In our curtailed account of it the journey may appear to be comparatively easy. In reality, it presented all sorts of difficulties and dangers. Although, on this last point, Charles de Foucauld has been very sparing in details, and has elsewhere voluntarily omitted many troublesome incidents which delayed or hastened his journey, it is easy, in going through the *Reconnaissance au Maroc*, to point out numerous occasions where the energy, endurance, and skill of the French officer were put to proof. For instance, on October 26, 1883, the chief of a caravan met on the road proposes to the escort to help him to loot the traveller and share the booty. On April 7, 1884, Charles de Foucauld's host tells him that he receives him willingly on the recommendation of a friend, but that if he, Abd Allah, or his sons, had found this Jew in the country, with so feeble an escort, they would undoubtedly have robbed him. On May 12, the traveller, who was taking notes and riding at the head of the caravan, is suddenly shot at from behind, thrown off his mount by two of his guides, who rob him of his money and all the objects which appear to them of any value. Still more, for a day and a half these robbers pressed the third guide to let them kill Charles de Foucauld, who did not miss a word they said. It must be added, to the honour of the Rabbi Mardochée, that he there and then went to the help of his companion; but he was quickly thrust aside.

These few incidents, others that I have cited, and others that may be guessed between the lines; but, above all, his tenacity in following up his route, in spite of all kinds of obstacles; his refusal to interrupt his journey at Mogador and return directly to France; his patience in presence of insults; his fidelity to take daily, on march or in repose, always at the risk of his life, notes and sketches; his quickness in discerning the secret dispositions of minds so different from his own; such strength of will in moral solitude, so austere a diet, such unremitting work—reveal in this young man a mastery over self, such as the past hardly foretold. He, himself, recognized it later on, and said that the eight months' campaign against Bu Amama had changed him very much.

The great exploration of Morocco will, as we shall see, change him still more deeply.

What must be said in finishing this chapter is that Charles de Foucauld will never forget Morocco. Once, he will seem on the point of returning there: he will rejoice in his heart at the thought of going freely over this country to which France has at last come, and, along with her, a hope of improvement, of justice and friendship for the people "seated in the shadow of death." Soon the project of a mission that he had neither inspired nor hastened was abandoned, and fell along with the good political intentions which have found no man strong enough to defend them. But all his life, the officer, become a priest, will remain "at the disposal of Morocco"; in 1901 he will settle down, almost on the frontier of this State; he will note in his memorandum-book, with a happiness that may be guessed, the visits he has received from Moroccans; in his conversations, in his letters, above all in his prayers in which the unfortunates of so many nations will find a place, he will not cease to name Morocco. He will feel for the tribes which he visited, for the known and unknown of this land of his youth, renewed and increasing friendship. For it is not only the geographer, the clear-eyed artist, the Frenchman always thinking of the call of France, who will love the Maghreb Empire; it will be the priest moved by a fraternal compassion, and who will write on a December evening: "For some time I have been thinking so much about Morocco, of that Morocco where ten million inhabitants have neither priest nor altar; where Christmas night will pass without Mass and without prayers."[1]

[1] Foreign geographers, and specially the English, have appreciated, in a suitable manner, the exploration undertaken by Vicomte de Foucauld and the account which he has given of it. I would give many quotations. I reproduce only these lines written by one of the most competent judges, Mr. Budgett Meakin :

"It is a real satisfaction to have these magnificent volumes in one's hands. They relate the most important and most remarkable journey that a European has for a century or more undertaken to Morocco. . . . No modern traveller has approached M. de Foucauld, from the double point of view of the precision of the observations and the preparation for the journey. Besides the work accomplished by him, the attempts of other travellers have been but child's play" (extract from the *Compte rendu du Congrès de géographie d'Oran*, April, 1902). The Paris Société de Géographie possesses three books of drawings by Vicomte de Foucauld, lead-pencil drawings, done during the journey in Morocco. These number 135. The day on which the gold medal was awarded to him by this Society, the explorer was in Algiers, and the reporter, Duveyrier, was travelling in Morocco. The medal was handed to Vicomte de Bondy, Charles de Foucauld's cousin.

CHAPTER IV

His Conversion

THE first months, after the return from Morocco, were almost entirely spent in Algeria. Charles de Foucauld did not at once begin to compile and write the book for which he brought back the materials: he verified his notes, deciphered them if necessary, consulted his friends—in a word, prepared the work that he was to do a little later in Paris. He made a few stops in France, some visiting tours and looking people up, but his "headquarters," his papers, library, and habits continued to be what they were before the great journey. At one moment, it might even be thought that the explorer was going to get married in Algeria. A young girl had taken his fancy. She was of a good family, and he came from far. He wrote to Paris, where he found little encouragement. I don't know whether he was badly smitten and what opposition he had. But when he had made another excursion to France, in the summer of 1885, and lived some time near Bordeaux, at his aunt's, Madame Moitessier, in the Château du Tuguet, he gave up the idea. He was called to quite other destinies; he thus helped them forward without knowing it.

A higher will has him in its grip. It urges him on to action, lashes him, and leads him on towards a hidden goal. The call of the desert makes itself heard once more. From the beginning of September, Charles has been at Nice, at his brother-in-law's, M. de Blic, the confidant of his thoughts. What are they? Do you not guess? He is going to set out again: naturally, he is going South. He wants to visit the oases and the *shotts* of Algeria and Tunis. It may be only the prelude to a greater journey. I know an intimate friend of his who believes that the explorer's secret intention was to investigate the means and find the best starting-point for crossing the Sahara. Henceforth who can tell? Foucauld hardly gave any intimation of his plans and did not talk about his recollections. On the eve of undertaking this "excursion," as he used to say, in the regions of the *shotts*, he now and then saw his sister's uneasy looks directed towards him. "Fear nothing," he used to reply, "no harm will happen to me: with care one can go anywhere."

On September 14, he embarked at Port-Vendres for Algiers. A few weeks earlier he had written to his friend de Vassal, who was at El-Golea, begging him to get two camels and two horses, and to engage an Arab servant for the expedition.

The route in all its parts is not known to us. We only know that Foucauld, passing through the south of the province of Oran, visited Laghuat, then, going still more to the south, the oasis of Ghardaïa and the inhospitable Mzab, where he was one day to return in the habit of a monk, and to win the sympathy of a people hostile beyond all others to Christians: then El-Golea, Wargla, where Lieutenant Cauvet was officer in charge (at the end of November, 1885); Tuggurt: the region of Jerid, between the *shott* El-Gharsa and the *shott* El-Jerid. An immense journey through desolate countries, where one must travel many days and sleep many nights, before perceiving, paled by the blinding light, a palm-grove's dash of green. If you try to follow it on the atlas, you will find few names printed between the above-mentioned. But what do they indicate? Not villages, as in Europe, or running rivers, but dunes, stony expanses, fossil rivers, dried-up quagmires where, among the salt deposits of the evaporated waters, a few tufts of reddened or grey grass live with difficulty; a well; the uncertain habitat of a wandering tribe. We know, moreover, that Charles de Foucauld, in love with solitude, already affianced to her, often leaves his native servant and baggage behind, and steals off, until he no longer sees anything around him but the desert. He thus more than once went two days ahead. He used to eat what he had in his pockets. At night he lay down on the ground, and gazed for a long time at the stars. Perhaps training himself to do without sleep. Perhaps the religious crisis which I am going to relate kept him awake, questioning, waiting for the breath of God, which fills the heart better in darkness and silence. He loved scenery, and therefore the starry heavens, the grandest of all. In the morning he saddled his tethered horse, joined his Arab servant, took food enough for a day or two, and went off again.

Having crossed Southern Algeria, from west to east, he must naturally end on the Tunisian coast. The last oasis he visited was, in fact, the warm and hidden oasis of Gabes, quite close to the shore, where barley and vegetables grow under the bushes, and the bushes beneath the shade of high palms. From there he embarked for France.

Back in Nice, on January 23, 1886, after more than four months' absence, Charles rested until February 19. At that date he left his brother-in-law and sister, came and settled down in Paris, where he took a small apartment at No. 50, Rue de Miromesnil. The period which opens belongs to work and the family circle. The family, far from which he had lived for a long time, received him intelligently and delightfully. There was nothing but joy: no sermons or reproaches, and no wish put forward. He was fêted and they were proud of him; he saw the most select and thoughtful society of Paris. Men, whose ascent to power had made them famous without compromising them, conversed in his presence of the religious and political affairs of France. They were Christians who made no mystery of their Faith. Charles met them every week. Gentle feminine influences were all about him; he lived in the intimacy of relations who reminded him of his mother, and from whom he received, without their knowing it, a perpetual example of wit, grace, and wholesome gaiety and piety. They were the Countess Armand de Foucauld, mother of Louis de Foucauld, the future military attaché in Berlin; and Madame Moitessier and her two daughters, the Countess de Flavigny and the Countess de Bondy.

Inés de Foucauld, Charles's aunt, a person of great beauty, painted twice by Ingres,[1] had married M. Moitessier, a native of Mirecourt, who had made a considerable fortune as an importer of tobacco. She lived in a fine mansion, 42, Rue d'Anjou, at the corner of Boulevard Malesherbes, where she received a great deal of company. Very intelligent, endowed with a will of the Foucaulds, which goes where it wants to go; very much a woman of the world; marvellously skilled in the art of making others appreciated and desired, of appearing interested in discussions she did not quite understand, of starting them again if they languished, marking by a word or smile what she did not approve, without ever offending—she had held the political salon of one of the youngest ministers we have had, Louis Buffet, her husband's nephew, who was minister at the age of thirty. Louis Buffet; Aimé Buffet his brother, an inspector of bridges and roads; Estancelin, duc de Broglie, had remained the intimates of the house. Some were invited of right, and there were others. Charles was one of those at all Madame Moitessier's "Sunday at homes." In addition to that, he used to go to the Rue

[1] These two fine portraits were exhibited in Paris among others of Ingres in May, 1921. One of them is dated 1851, the other 1856.

d'Anjou several times a week to dine at 6 o'clock, of course always in evening-dress. When he got home to the Rue de Miromesnil, he undressed, put on a *gandourah*, soft leather slippers, enfolded himself in a burnous, put a cushion under his head, and lay on a carpet. One of the remarkable particularities of Charles de Foucauld's room was that no bed was seen there. There was none. The furniture was that of a man of taste, who had had ancestors in the history of France, and who dreams of the East. On the walls water-colours and pen sketches of landscapes in Morocco hung beside family portraits painted by Largillière; here and there were suspended arms and stuffs, brought back from Algeria. The book-case did not contain a great number of books, but the greater number were rare ones or elegant editions. Shut up all day, Charles used to write, delete or correct, consult his notes and put together the solid and magnificent book which was to make his name known to all the geographers in the world and even in other circles. If he was puzzled or had to look up something, he left his work-table and went to a public library, or to Duveyrier's. Duveyrier was celebrated at the age of twenty : since then he had lived in the glory of his past, incapable of renewing it. In 1860, when young men are still but B.A.'s, uncertain of the road to choose, already a botanist, geologist, versed in Oriental languages, thoroughly civilized, marvellously endowed for meeting and winning barbarians, he made the then perilous journey from Laghuat to El-Golea. Imprisoned by the inhabitants of El-Golèa, then delivered, he only made use of his liberty to plunge into the dread unknown of the Sahara, to visit the South of Tunis, a part of Tripoli and the territory of the Azjers, the most Oriental, and also the most hostile of all the Tuareg tribes. The book he then wrote very justly made him famous ; but prostrated by illness, and hence condemned to be no more than an adviser on the Sahara, Duveyrier suffered, not only from being unable to start afresh and make new discoveries and increase his reputation, but from seeing France lessened in 1871, and as it were diffident of her powers. He never lost his recollection of the work he had done, but could not continue it. He received his rival, the explorer of Morocco, affectionately, and began to travel again, but in a way he did not like : on maps, in books, in his own memories, and in those of others.

Slowly, the innumerable documents brought back by Foucauld turned into science and life. Not without some astonishment can one witness this transformation in the habits of the former lieutenant of Pont-à-Mousson and Sétif. Whence does it come? Principally from an ambition that had taken possession of him, and which he served with that tense and restless will which was the original mark of Charles de Foucauld, and, it may be said, of his race.

After the publication of the book which he wrote after the excursion to the *shotts,* he had resolved to undertake other great journeys. He did not speak of his plans to anybody, but his mind was often busy with them. Another thought haunted and disturbed it.

I said that Charles de Foucauld had been deeply moved, during his sojourn in Algeria and Morocco, by the perpetual invocation of God among those around him. Their calls to prayer, the prostrations five times a day towards the East, the name of Allah unceasingly repeated in conversations or writings, all the religious pomp of Musulman life, led him to say to himself: "And here am I without religion!" For the Jews prayed also, and to the same God as the Arabs or the Moroccans. The vices which had corrupted the mind or heart of these men had not prevented their meditative witness from feeling the grandeur of faith. Again in Algeria, he had even said to a few of his friends: "I am thinking of becoming a Musulman." Words of feeling, which reason had not ratified. On the first examination, it appeared to him, as he confided to one of his intimate friends, that the religion of Mahomet could not be the true one, "being too material." But the uneasiness remained. Blessed be it! For it is a proof of superiority in him who experiences it, a great event in the order of grace, the blessed sign that a soul is going to find the way again. This young man, born in Catholicism, lacked a good understanding of this magnificent, divine and sound religion, and any such sense of its transcendence to return to it without hesitation as soon as the tyranny of matter weighed too heavily upon him. He was, in truth, sad at the bottom of his heart, with an old sadness. Live a life of pleasure as he would, it had only increased. It had held him, as he confessed when he wrote: "silent and overwhelmed at so-called fêtes." Since then, it had neither been dispelled by man's science, nor by action, nor by success and fame. Now he had certainly submitted to the discipline of work, and hence felt better than in the past, but not disburdened of his faults, not what he ought to be, morally very far from those dear ones whom he saw living in his own united and happy family.

He read a great deal. But a great secret cowardice is in us when it is a question of taking up a rule of life which we know to be strict and repressive. We seek approximations in order not to have to come to the ideal of perfection, and trembling nature makes us take counsel with men rather than with God, because we know that God is exacting. It was thus that Charles de Foucauld, in the intervals of writing the *Reconnaissance au Maroc,* used to consult pagan philosophers, and question them upon duty, the soul, and the life to come. He thought their answers were poor. They are necessarily so. Unguided reason does not go far in the problem of creation and destiny. Charles's mind was too clear to be satisfied with the noise of words and the brilliancy of images. He also knew that the philosophy of ancient times had purified nothing, softened nothing, brought no consolation, and doubtless he would have returned to the maxim of absolute scepticism he had learnt at college : " Man cannot know the truth," if the sight of the chosen little society in which he again found himself had not each day shaken the fragile authority of this inference.

The probity, delicacy, and charity which had become habitual and in a manner natural, the joy also of the consciences around him which were not hidden from him, but which he could read, constantly forced him to return to himself. " Here are," he said to himself, " men and women, all cultivated, some of quite superior intelligence, and since they entirely accept the Catholic Faith, may it not be true ? They have studied it, they live it fully. And what do I, indeed, know of it ? Honestly, do I know Catholicism ?"

Mere anxiety about such things is itself a prayer, and God was hearkening to it. A few pages of a Christian book which he had opened after so many others, in a moment of anguish—I do not know what it was—began to enlighten this unbeliever, who had sought perfect beauty and infinite tenderness wherever they were not.

Probably his aunt, cousins, and sister, who came several times to see him in Paris, and whom he loved tenderly, had some suspicion of the interior work which was leading a stray heart and mind to the truth. They did not hurry it on by any human means. They were good and kind, they followed the straight path, they prayed. It was by chance that one evening, at Madame Moitessier's, Charles met Abbé Huvelin, who had long been a friend of many of the de Foucaulds. Being very humble, very simple, very much a man of prayer and mysticism, this old Normal scholar made a great impression on the man who was one day to resemble him. What did he say that evening?

It is quite certain he did not try to be smart. If he had wit, it was because he could not help having it. Friendships like that about to spring up between Charles de Foucauld and him have not their origin in words, nor in the brilliancy of talent, nor in the will to conquer. An unbeliever, who had also lived badly, finds himself in presence of another man, not only believing and chaste, but now a man of prayer, and the essence of pity for man's immense frailty and suffering; perhaps even more, perhaps one of the victims who are said to offer themselves in secret to God for suffering to make reparation for the evil, and to alleviate the punishment of others.[1] These two men may only have exchanged commonplace remarks; may only have bowed, then looked at each other five or six times that evening. That was enough: they recognized and waited for one another; in their hearts henceforth they called this meeting a great event. The one thought: "You are religion itself"; the other: "Brother, unhappy brother, I am but a poor man, but God is very kind. He is seeking your soul's salvation." They never forgot one another.

Abbé Huvelin, born in 1838, was therefore, in 1886, still a young man, although he hardly appeared so; the penitent life which he led from his youth, and which had made his comrades of the École Normale smile or stirred them; the fatigue of being and of having been at the mercy of all sorrows in quest of easing, of all human restlessness seeking a decision; illness also, a sort of general rheumatism which already afflicted him, left him little but the youth of a quick mind and a very tender heart. His head leant upon his shoulder, and his face was full of wrinkles; walking was often a torture to him. In Paris, this curate at Saint Augustine's had a tremendous clientèle of penitents, innumerable friends, and, what further singularly added to the complications of his life, a reputation for sanctity.

Holiness is the most powerful attraction for drawing souls together. His had promptly revealed itself in the conferences which he gave to young men, from 1875, on the History of the Church. In spite of his protestations, he had seen women in great numbers, and men whose youth

---

[1] One of his maxims was this: "One does good much less by what one does or says, than by what one is." See *L'Enseignement catholique dans la France contemporaine*, by Mgr. Baudrillart, Bloud et Cie., 1918.

was over, mix with the public for which his conferences in the crypt were first arranged. He spoke also in the parish pulpit, and they thronged to hear the talks of one who did not make a recitation, did not seek to astonish, but improvised on a theme always thoroughly prepared, pouring forth an exuberant wit in living and natural language, prudent in doctrine, bold in what he had to say, abundant in reminiscences of literature or history, a man of digressions, parentheses, exclamations, and unexpected flashes—above all, a man with a long experience of the world and of mercy. Hence he was near each of his hearers: hence he was their sure and wished-for friend. His pity for sinners, one may say his tenderness for them, touched the most indifferent. They felt that he wished them better so that they might be happier, and that he was always thinking, for those who hardly reflected about it, of the definite hour at which they would appear before God, when they would be judged, condemned in their unhappiness without hope of dying, for death does not exist, even for a moment; all we have is two lives.

The extreme zeal of Abbé Huvelin, the steps he took, the visits he paid and those he received, his immense correspondence — short, affectionate, and clear notes — the increase of austerity, proof of which is forthcoming at certain periods, though we cannot exactly tell why: all this is explained by his love for souls in danger.

For yet another reason, and a very powerful one, he was a counsellor to whom people resorted at once: he understood human suffering. He sympathized with it; whatever it was, he had already met and heard and helped it. For him no aspect of it was unknown. Of it he said, simplifying a phrase of Bossuet's and stripping off its seventeenth-century majesty: "We get a charm from sorrow." In the same spirit he thus defined the Church: "The Church is a widow." This saying to a society woman is also his:

"Long ago I found out how to be happy."
"How?"
"By abstaining from pleasures."

But to give a better understanding of how far such words go, I must quote others, and shall do so from one of his hearers. At the same time we shall hear the orator speak. It will be no *hors-d'œuvre*, since we are speaking with the priest who is to convert Charles de Foucauld and turn him into Father de Foucauld.[1]

[1] I owe this inestimable passage to Vicomte de Montmorand.

"Jesus is the Man of Sorrows, because He is the Son of Man, and man is but sorrow. Sorrow accompanies us from birth to death; it purifies and ennobles us, it gives us charm. It is because it is our inseparable companion that Jesus wished it to be His.

"Great souls—for the honour of humanity, we must have some to follow in the footsteps of Christ—have called for and desired sorrow. They have said the *Fac me tecum plangere* of the *Stabat Mater*. We have no such ambition; we only ask to accept sorrow with compunction and resignation, when it is offered.

"Far from us, above all, be those little sorrows, less easy to endure than the great ones, those wounds so paltry, so peevish, so venomous, wrought by the passions, and by self-love! It is the shame of mankind to suffer so much for so little.

"*Jesus in the Garden of Olives.* He is sorrowful even unto death. The apostles do not understand His sorrow; this divine sorrow is too far beyond them. To understand it, one must know what sin is. They knew it not, nor can we know it.

"His attitude is not a *Greek* attitude. He does not dominate His sadness, does not say, as a stoic would: 'Sorrow, thou art but a word!' Far from it! Sorrow invaded Him through every pore; it inundated His soul; it rose like a tide and submerged all the heights.

"He prays, but His prayer is not the natural movement, the happy breathing of His soul; nor is it a flow of beautiful thoughts; it is a sob, a sob dying down into an *amen.* 'So be it!' is His whole prayer. His will, united, identified hitherto with that of the Father, now for the first time seems something distinct. The load is too heavy: 'Thou canst do all things: take away this chalice from Me.'

"He seeks help from the Apostles and finds them asleep. One is alone in sadness when yearning for a word from the heart. Friends come only in our hours of calm, or if they drop in during the storm, they don't say what should be said, or they wound by their want of tact or silliness. Such were Job's friends.

"At last an angel comes to strengthen Him: *Angelus confortavit eum.* To *strengthen,* not to console Him. Grace is essentially strengthening, not consoling. . . ."

I cannot quote more at length without going beyond my purpose. The above quotation and what I have said are enough to make us understand why all human miseries, all doubts, and all repentance went naturally to Abbé Huvelin.

He heard confessions at Saint Augustine's, he received many people at home. What a robust and agile mind must this invalid and cripple have had, to form one idea after another of all the moral problems submitted to him, so as to study and solve them in a moment! But he was gifted with so sure a judgment that he unravelled all the cases, and with a vision so penetrating of the intimate dispositions of the persons who consulted him, that several attributed it to a singular grace of God. Even circumstances are quoted in which he alluded to past and secret events in the life of his penitents. His advice was clear, simple, full of good sense, and he did not change it. He varied it according to persons. He did not treat bears as if they were swallows. More than once he was heard to say : "To some one has to say : 'You must submit to that!' In canonical decisions there is a force with which those who despise them have to reckon more fully than they think." This great specialist in spiritual direction was generally at home in the afternoon. People of all ages and classes, Parisians and passing travellers, were to be met in his little antechamber. By turns they entered the next room, filled with books and papers, in which M. Huvelin was sitting with a cat on his knees, and as resigned to the crowd as to illness. The visitors who had been introduced to him, even in the distant past, were sure to be recognized. He listened with all his faculties. As he was brief, he required them to be the same. His office was a hard one. He, though naturally gay, was very often seen to weep; he suffered with all the sorrows brought to him, with all the sins acknowledged to him, or that he divined in men's hearts.

Such was the priest eminent in holiness—that is to say, in the science of God and man—whom Charles de Foucauld had met late one summer's evening. They did not immediately see each other again. But in Charles's soul the tide of grace was rising. One does not know whence it first comes. It is promised to men of good-will, or rather it is already given to them, and their good-will itself is its work. Just when it looked a long way off, it has already covered the muddy background; it is cool; it brings the birds with it, and its waves, breaking one after another, all say: "You must believe, be pure, be joyous with the great joy of God, and get the light on the living waters." This dim stirring, this desire for illumination, he felt more and more strongly within him. Between two walks or at nightfall, he might now be seen to go into a church; he would sit far from the altar, understanding neither what had drawn him in, nor what held him there; and he would say none of his prayers of former days, but this, which went straight up to heaven: "My God, if You exist, make me know it!"

One October evening, in one of those family talks, in which the mind and heart speak freely and without trying to find the way, when the children were playing round the table before going to bed, one of his cousins said to Charles:

"It appears that Abbé Huvelin will not go on with his conferences again; I regret it very much."

"So do I," replied Charles, "for I intended to follow them."

The reply was not noticed. Some days later he gravely said to his cousin:

"You are fortunate to believe; I am seeking the light, and do not find it."

Between October 27 and 30, the next day after this conversation, Abbé Huvelin saw a young man enter his confessional without kneeling down. He simply bent forward and said:

"Abbé, I have not the faith, I have come to ask you to instruct me."

M. Huvelin looked at him.

"Kneel down, confess to God; you will believe."

"But I did not come for that."

"Confess."

The man who wanted to believe felt that pardon was for him the condition of light. He knelt down, and made a confession of all his life.

When he saw the absolved penitent get up, the Abbé added:

"Are you fasting?"

"Yes."

"Go to communion!"

And Charles de Foucauld at once approached the holy table, and made his "second first communion."

He did not speak of his conversion. It was by certain acts that it was gradually seen that the depths of his soul were changed. His life continued to be laborious; peace had returned to it, and was always transparently visible in his eyes, smile, voice or words. His letters, which never had ceased being affectionate, became grateful. The name of God often occurs in them. His life is silently remoulded on the recovered ideal. In this renewal all is profound, discreet, and simple.

For instance, Charles soon heard of the birth of a nephew,

who became his godson : he set out for Dijon, spent a few days with his sister and brother-in-law, and was no sooner back in Paris than he sent them the thanks of a rejuvenated heart :

"Visits to you are very pleasant. They only have one fault : that one is surrounded with so much kindness and affection that one feels one's heart too poor to give back as much as one has received, and one fears never to love enough, never to show enough appreciation and gratitude. Living in your home is not only most delightful, but also one gets better from inhaling its atmosphere of affection and calm. I hope soon to be able to return. In leaving you, I am thinking of nothing but the time of my return. I do not believe much in acting according to plans, but if I do not rely on my foresight, I preserve the hope that some unforeseen thing will bring me to you before long.

"You know my work and ideas, and my vague thoughts as to the future : we spoke of them yesterday : you will easily follow me from now until we see each other again. In leaving you, it is a very great joy for me to know all the places between which you will divide your time. In writing to you, I am near you in Dijon : the day after to-morrow, I shall follow you to Echalot ; I shall hunt with you, I shall drag the wheelbarrow with Maurice ; I shall admire M. de Blic's library ; I shall warm myself *en famille* by the fireside. Now that I know all your retreats, I am going to be very often and pleasantly with you."

The manuscript of the *Reconnaissance au Maroc* was finished at the beginning of 1887, and, immediately, the printed proofs began to come in abundance to the rooms in Rue de Miromesnil : very laborious work for a scholar so careful about details, who wished his work to be in full-dress, as he was himself at the time of the Cavalry School : a heavy expense for a budget which the journey to the *shotts*, ten excursions in France, and setting up in Paris, had already burdened him. "My income is enough for these unusual expenses, but only just ; also, since my return from Morocco, I have borrowed nothing whatever, but I have saved nothing. I desire to get rid of my legal guardian, whom I have had now for seven years. With this guardianship going on, I cannot think of any other journeys, and as my book is coming out, it is time to consider fresh expeditions."[1]

At the end of 1887 and beginning of 1888, Vicomte

[1] Letter to a friend, April 9, 1887. The guardian was removed in October, 1888.

de Foucauld's works, *Itinéraires au Maroc, Reconnaissance au Maroc,* appeared among the booksellers. Their success, as I have said, in the restricted circle of geographers, scholars, and colonials, either in France or foreign countries, was very great. But, when a great book appears, the people who speak of it are of two sorts, and are like the moon with its halo: some read the famous pages and carry away with them fresh information and ideas; others get some brightness at any rate. They run through a few pages; they pick out some quotations; they rehearse the title and extol the author on the strength of the nearest newspaper, review, or drawing-room talker. This was immediately the case with the *Reconnaissance au Maroc.* The young explorer was celebrated on all sides: his renown spread: letters of congratulation poured in to the Rue de Miromesnil; friends climbed the stairs, and each recalling his claim upon the memory of his glorious comrade called out: " Well, old man, there is a success for you. And well deserved, too! What untold dangers you ran! Where are you going to now? For you owe it to us and to yourself to start on fresh explorations !"

Our friend, as we know, was not a man to discuss his plans in public. He preferred to think over them with a few rare initiates. Before setting out for Morocco he had consulted MacCarthy, books and atlases. Now he takes counsel of God, who has determined to take the explorer into His service. Nature was not destroyed by de Foucauld's conversion, but improved and renewed. Henceforth his courage, strength of will, and extraordinary faculty of endurance were to be exercised for the good of souls.

One of the men of our times, best endowed for colonial adventure and the study of unknown tongues and customs, was not lost to science; but its disciple, who was never to deny it, now perceived that the finest employment of the gifts which he had received was called charity, consisting in the total oblation of oneself, one's work, one's thoughts, one's patience, and one's blood, if necessary, in order that men may at last recognize their Creator through such self-sacrifice. He wished to prepare himself for this mission by a journey to the Holy Land. He would visit the earthly home of Jesus Christ: he would go and pray in the solitude which had never ceased to attract him.

On November 2, 1888, he went to Le Tuquet, in the Bordeaux country: from there he reached Nancy. He said farewell to the family. He said that his plan was to stay only a few weeks in the Holy Land. And he embarked at Marseilles.

In the middle of December he was in Jerusalem, which he found covered with snow: he lingered to walk through the streets, to visit the churches, to go up and come down the Mount of Olives: he spent Christmas at Bethlehem, then made a great excursion into Galilee on horseback, accompanied by a guide on a pack-horse. In his letters he shows a lively devotion for Nazareth. After leaving the town, he returned to it. There he meditated more feelingly than elsewhere. And if you wish to know the main theme of his meditation, I can tell you. This white town with steep and winding streets on the flanks of Nebi-Saïn, touched the penitent heart of Charles de Foucauld. It inspired him with an unquenchable love for the hidden life, and for obedience, the state of voluntary humility. It re-echoed to him Abbé Huvelin's magnificent saying: "Our Lord took the last place in such a way that nobody can ever rob Him of it." I think I may affirm that all the rest of de Foucauld's life was worked and modelled by the recollection of Nazareth.

It was clearly seen at the beginning of March, 1889, as soon as the traveller was back in Paris. This is the year of resolutions, or—to use the language of spirituality—of election. What was he going to do?

Since his conversion he read still more than befote, but other books, and his reading made him enter into the world of doctrine, morals, and religious history. He marvelled to see how simple and how reasonable truth is; he wondered how he could formerly have been so upset as to doubt religion, as to cast it away for objections so long ago answered and so easy to clear up. He learned the first of the sciences—that of the conduct of life. On the advice of Abbé Huvelin, he went to Mass every morning, and after beginning with frequent communion, it became his daily bread.

We know the care he had given to the preparation of his main journey. He wished all the more to prepare for the vocation which increasingly attracted him. From the very moment of his conversion, he felt himself called to the religious life. But there are numerous Orders. If they are all meant to lead to heaven, the men who enrol themselves in them are different; each has his own temperament, even in the service of God, and ought to have a road of his own. Which should he take?

In order to find out, in that same year Charles made no

less than four retreats. He approached in succession the living Rule of three great Orders. At Easter he was with the Benedictines at Solesmes; at Trinity he started for the Grande-Trappe; on October 20 he went up to Notre-Dame-des-Neiges and spent a whole week in meditation, after which he came to no decision. At last, in the second half of November, under the direction of a Jesuit at Clamart, having again taken up the examination of the first truths and the study of his religious vocation, the former lieutenant of Chasseurs d'Afrique, the explorer of yesterday, wrote to his sister:

"I returned from Clamart yesterday, and I have at last, in great security and great peace, on the formal counsel of the Father who directed me, taken entire and without reserve the resolution of which I have been thinking for a long time; it is to enter La Trappe. It is now a settled thing: I have been thinking of it for a long time. I have been in four monasteries: in the four retreats, I was told that God called me, and that he called me to La Trappe. Inwardly I feel drawn to the same place, my director is of the same opinion. . . . It is something determined, and I tell you of it as such. I shall enter the monastery of Notre-Dame-des-Neiges, where I was some time ago. . . . When? It is not yet settled; I have several things to put straight; I have, above all, to go and bid you farewell. . . . But, indeed, that will not take very long.

"When I start, I shall say I am off on some journey, and not at all that I am entering, or thinking in the least of entering, the religious life."

He had obtained the consent of the Abbot of Notre-Dame-des-Neiges. But in his letter of application, he had named La Trappe at Akbes, in Syria, and begged that after some months of probation and novitiate, he might be sent to that distant house, "if that is, as I think it is, the holy will of our Father who is in heaven."

Alone, the nearest relations were advised of the great decision. The days were henceforth counted. Charles started on December 11 for Dijon: with his sister and M. de Blic he spent a week, the last he could give them before his retirement, solitude, and silence. Then he returned to Paris to settle some business, notably the leaving of his property to his sister.

He went away poor, the world was to see him no more. One of his friends saw him on the top of an omnibus and was very much astonished. A few days later the letters of invitation addressed to Vicomte de Foucauld remained without an answer. One of his cousins asked him to come and partake of some Alsatian venison, venison from Saverne, and Charles, habitually punctilious, gave no sign of life. They made inquiries, and learnt that he had left Paris.

On January 14, 1890, he sent his sister a farewell letter:

"*Au revoir,* my good Mimi. I leave Paris to-morrow. About 2 p.m. I shall be at Notre-Dame-des-Neiges. Pray for me. I shall pray for you and yours. We do not forget one another in drawing nearer to God. . . ."

He had said, at Dijon, a few weeks earlier: "Let us be sad, but let us thank God for our sadness."

CHAPTER V
The Trappist

TO understand the extraordinary life of Father de Foucauld, we must consider two spiritual facts upon which all was built : first, his passion for the East, which was far from a mere love of colour and picturesqueness—it was primarily a preference for solitude and silence, and for such extreme simplicity of dress, food, and lodging as one can adopt without singularity; secondly, the energy, the inward dominance of will, that strove for evangelical perfection with the same ardour, the same tenacity, the same absence of all fear as were seen in the young officer undertaking his journey to Morocco.

The conversion was thorough. Charles de Foucauld abandoned himself entirely to the divine will, to be what it desired. He already knew that he had to serve it in charity and obscurity. Step by step he learnt the rest; he went where the most neglected souls on earth were to call him, and, hard on the flesh which had ruled him in the past, tried by love to bring himself down to the poverty of God made man.

At the time, all that came after was hidden from him; he had only one thing shining clear : the resolve to obey, and his passionate desire for the best. Likewise, around him, nobody suspected into what exceptional ways he was one day to be led. And if we are astonished that so experienced and sagacious a counsellor as Abbé Huvelin foresaw nothing of it, it may be answered that the best endowed of us cannot disclose the future; that just as the world was created in six days, so does God act in transforming a soul, which is also a world; that He exercises consideration for our weakness, and does not at once adapt our circumstances to certain dreams of perfection, which no doubt do not displease, and may even come from Him, but which He wishes us to attain by degrees, when the practice of patience has made us more prudent and stronger.

I decided to visit La Trappe of Notre-Dame-des-Neiges. It is built on the high plateaux of the heights of the Vivarais, in a wild country, which formerly belonged to Languedoc.[1] When you reach the wind-swept, heather-

[1] Situated in the commune of Saint-Laurent les Bains (Ardèche), the Abbey of Notre-Dame-des-Neiges has its station and post-office at the Bastide-Saint-Laurent (Lozère).

clad summits that surround the monastery, you see all around in the far distance only peaks of about the same height, stretching their rocky ridges and meagre verdure upwards into the light, separated from one another by the violet shadows of the ravines. There are, one may say, no farms on the heights; or just one or two, with squat walls and crouching roofs, made to bear six months' snow and storm. I came from afar, by a road which follows the hill-tops. The road descended a little; the motor entered an avenue bordered by two woods of pine and beeches, then, suddenly, coming out of the shade, the wide spaces again stretched out in the sun. Before me, half-way up the slope, stood the monastery of white granite with its barns, cellars, cow-houses, and stables; a forest sown by the monks covered the slopes of the mountain opposite, and the whole valley between the two great woods was but an undulating river of ripe oats and wheat.

The monastery, such as it is to-day, is no longer the one into which Charles de Foucauld was received. The monks' cells, the chapter-house, and the church were destroyed by fire on January 27, 1912, but these monks, the sowers of forests, are also builders. On a more elevated and much more beautiful site than the former one, 3,500 feet up, they have built a new and plain abbey, on sober lines, in which the clock alone speaks, where Cistercian peace and work take shelter.[1]

When Charles de Foucauld presented himself at Notre-Dame-des-Neiges to be admitted among the novices, he was questioned. The rule of St. Benedict orders the Superiors to examine the postulants carefully, and in questioning them to test them, so as to know the character of the future Brother well, and the motives which have brought him to the abbey door. Dom Martin, Abbot of this community of silent workers, knew that the man who speaks willingly of himself thus declares himself inclined to self-satisfaction and boasting. He asked:

" What can you do?"
" Not much."
" Read?"
" A little."

The Abbot saw by this, as well as by many other replies in the same tone, that this lieutenant of Chasseurs d'Afrique

[1] The first inhabitants of this new house were the soldiers wounded in the Great War of 1914. During this war the Trappists of Notre-Dame-des-Neiges had twenty-two of their members in the first line at the front; seven fell for France.

was, on the contrary, no great talker, and so far very modest. Having finished questioning him, he asked him to sweep a little, so as to see. He perceived at the first sweep of the broom that the postulant had had no practice. His education would have to be completed.

It was thus the Vicomte Charles de Foucauld entered the novitiate of La Trappe of Notre-Dame-des-Neiges to become Brother Marie-Albéric.

The Brothers of this great Order afterwards recollected him as a monk ever ready to help, very pious, almost excessive in his austerity, but a man of balanced judgment: in a word, they recollected a personality and a saint. I employ these terms as all those who knew Father de Foucauld do; these monks, soldiers, and travellers knew very well that the Church alone has the right to judge of holiness. Waiting for her decision, if she one day does decide, they followed the custom of the world and said: " I have seen a saint." And how could we express better and more briefly our admiration for a man in whom we think an uncommon virtue lives? Brother Marie-Albéric edified the monastery, above all, by his humility. He was perfectly simple, and he knew what to do, being a man of the best society, whom virtue led to take the lowest place. Education is useful for everything, even for getting oneself forgotten and unnoticed, or for trying to be so. One of these monks, a reaper of wheat, a driver of oxen, whom I questioned, gave me this remarkable reply:

"Sir, I talked to him as I should to a peasant!" He added:

"I saw him every day: he never refused to do anything for anyone: he was as good as a second Francis of Assisi!"

The regimen of La Trappe tested more than one solidly built novice. Brother Albéric had a constitution of iron and a will of the same metal. He declared many times that neither fasting, nor vigils, nor work ever inconvenienced him. The only thing that was difficult for him was obedience, and here again we seize a feature of his proud impetuous nature, made and accustomed to command, which only yielded to grace.[1]

I shall now quote a certain number of letters written from

[1] It is necessary, however, to beware of believing legends which have singularly exaggerated the severities of the Trappist rule. Penance, with the monks, as with all Christians, is but a means of moral perfection; it would exceed its intent if the body became a weak and sickly servant of the soul. A subjugated body; a soul consequently more free: the austerity allowed does not go beyond that point—*i.e.*, equilibrium. It should also be known that in the course of time there was

Notre-Dame-des-Neiges by Brother Albéric, either to his sister or to other members of his family. They will show better than a story the thoughts of the novice in his solitude under the rule of a very capable monk, a worthy son of St. Bernard, Abbot Martin.

He entered the novitiate on January 16, 1890, and the same day wrote in the sorrow of separation :

"I must get strength from my weakness, employ this weakness itself for God, thank Him for this suffering and offer it to Him. . . . I ask Him from the bottom of my heart to increase my suffering if I can bear a heavier load, so that it may afford Him a little more compensation and do His children a little more good : that He may diminish it if it is not for His glory and according to His will, but I am sure it is the will of Him who wept for Lazarus. . . ."

In the second letter he says that he will take the Trappist habit on January 26, the feast of St. Alberic :

"It is probable that I shall send in my resignation as a Reserve officer, giving Akbes as my residence, which will simplify everything.

"I continue to be in the best of health. From the first day I have led the regular life . . . and how goes my soul? Less badly than I expected : the good God let me find unexpected consolation in solitude and silence. I am constantly, absolutely constantly, with Him, and with those whom I love. This continual life with all that is dear to me in heaven and on earth, without filling the void, has afforded me consolation, but, indeed, God has Himself upheld me during these first days. . . . Manual work does not prevent meditation; I am recommended to work steadily so as to be able to meditate.

"I have not suffered at all from cold; up to the present it has not snowed, and it is sunny. No doubt hard moments will come, but as yet there are none; neither have I suffered from hunger,[1] and, thanks to the variety of work and exercises, I did not feel hungry before sitting down to table. This is to tell you that the material side of the life has not cost me the shadow of a sacrifice.

---

some mitigation of the rigour which appeared quite simple to our fathers, undoubtedly more robust than we are. And to quote only the most recent : in 1892 Pope Leo XIII united in a single order —that of the reformed Cistercians—the divers congregations of Trappists, and ordered that fasts were never to be prolonged beyond midday.

[1] The chief meal at La Trappe was then at half-past 2 in the afternoon ; the time of rising 2 in the morning, and of going to bed 7 in the evening.

" Up to now I have carried branches, made wreaths for the perpetual adoration, swept the church, and polished the candlesticks; nothing hard, you see."

"*February* 6, 1890.—In this sad world, we have a real happiness which neither the saints nor the angels have— that of suffering with our Well-Beloved, for our Well-Beloved. However hard this life may be, however long these sad days may be, however consoling the thought of this good valley of Josaphat may be, let us not be more eager than God wishes to quit the foot of the Cross. . . . 'Good Cross,' said St. Andrew. Since our Master has deigned to make us feel, if not always the sweetness of it, at least its beauty and necessity for him who desires to love Him, let us not wish to be freed from it sooner than He wishes. . . . However, God knows that the day when this exile ends will be welcome, for there is more strength in my words than in my heart."[1]

He read St. Bernard, learnt the Psalms by heart, and how to make use of the breviary; he studied the Holy Scriptures for an hour and read Abbé Fouard, Bossuet, the Imitation, the Gospels, the Life of St. Gertrude, and the works of St. Teresa.

"*February* 18, 1890.—About myself, I have little to tell you. No rumour from outside reaches us; here are solitude and silence with God. The time is divided between prayer, readings bringing one nearer to God, manual labour done in imitation of Him and in union with Him. That fills every day, except Sundays and feasts, when work ceases. I could live long thus without having to talk much of myself. . . . They are very good to me, with a charity full of tenderness; a great charity reigns in the convent: I thus, and in many other ways, receive examples which I must beg God to turn to my advantage."

"*Easter Monday*, 1890.—I must not say that I bore the fast and cold well; I did not feel them . . . of the Lenten diet (a single meal a day at half-past four[2]) I can only say one thing: I found it pleasant and comfortable, and I did

---

[1] He expressed this noble feeling for the Cross in another letter of the same period:
"I desired to enter the religious life to keep our Lord company in His sufferings as much as possible."

[2] Now the Trappists take their principal meal in Lent at noon, and partake of a collation in the evening.

not feel hungry a single day. However, I did not *gorge* too much.

" As for my soul, it is absolutely in the same state as at the time of my last letter; the only difference is that the good God upholds me still more; He sustains both my soul and body; I have nothing to bear : He bears all. I should be very ungrateful towards this loving Father, towards our gentle Lord Jesus, if I did not tell you how He holds me in His hand, putting me in His peace, keeping trouble away from me, driving it away, driving off depression as soon as it tries to draw near. . . . This state of things is too unexpected for me to be able to attribute it to any other than Him. What is this peace, this consolation ? It is nothing extraordinary; it is a union of every moment in prayer, reading, work, in all, with our Lord, with the Holy Virgin, with all the Saints who surrounded Him in His life. . . . The offices, holy Mass, prayer in which my dryness was so painful to me, are, in spite of the innumerable distractions of which I am guilty, very sweet to me. . . . Manual labour is a consolation through its likeness to our Lord's, and it is a continual meditation (it ought to be, but I am very apt to idle)."

In this letter and in some other records, we have already been able to note the minute care with which Brother Albéric analyzes the motions of his mind and heart. No doubt, it is more than a first effort and a novelty; it is a habit he had acquired in the solitudes during his great journeys, and which the religious life had perfected. He complains, like all souls given to spirituality, of moments of dryness, and declares that he is unworthy of the consolations which follow.

" *Whit-Sunday,* 1890.—The origin of this dryness is almost always in the slackness with which I resist temptations, especially temptations against obedience in spirit : I find it hard to subject the senses—that will not astonish you; however that is a trifle. I do not accept gladly enough the manual labours assigned me, and this shows a great want of love; if I felt how they bring me near to our Lord, how happy should I be in everything. . . . ' May the will of our Lord be done, not mine '; this I say to Him with my whole heart; I tell Him, at least, that I want to say this to Him with my whole heart, for I fear I only say it to Him with my lips; . . . it is, however, true that I solely desire His will."

Yes, surely, he desired the will of God, and no doubt he wrote these lines to prepare the family at Dijon, and also in Paris, and those still farther away, for the more complete separation which had just been decided upon.

Why did Brother Albéric leave La Trappe of Notre-Dame-des-Neiges? I have said that from the beginning he had asked to be sent to the poorest and most distant monastery in Asia Minor; was it his desire for absolute solitude? To be nothing but a name, one of whom people say, "He is away yonder, we don't know where"? Was it his recollection of the horizons he had loved? No doubt, but the time was past when the East was to him only his favourite land of travel, investigation, and dreams. Other attractions, of an austere and mysterious kind, led him to the monastery of Akbes, now that he had determined to bring under his long dominant body and to do penance. He went to the East to be still poorer there; to feel nearer to the Holy Land, where the Son of God had suffered and worked; he went moved by a compassion for the peoples sunk in error, a feeling which was to carry him much farther away; in short, he went to this new dwelling because it was hard for him to leave France. "I shall not say to you that I am not downcast at this time," he wrote in the month of June; "it will be hard to watch the coast fading away."

Everything is prepared for the departure. A place reserved, for Alexandretta, on a vessel which sails from Marseilles on the 27th. On the eve, Brother Marie-Albéric bids adieu to his Brothers of Notre-Dame-des-Neiges. He writes to his family:

"I find myself on the boat which will carry me away to-morrow; it seems to me that I shall feel each wave, one after the other, taking me farther away. . . . It appears to me that my only help will be to think of each as one step nearer to the end of life. . . .

"From Marseilles to Alexandretta I shall be alone; the Brother who was to leave with me remains. I am satisfied with this solitude; I shall be able to think without check. My address is: Trappe de Notre-Dame-du-Sacré-Cœur, via Alexandretta (Syria). I shall reach Alexandretta on the thirteenth day of the voyage. I set out next day for Notre-Dame-du-Sacré-Cœur, and after two days' travel, get there in the evening of the next day."

And when the voyage is nearly done, he pens these words, a real cry of loving anguish: "To-morrow I shall be at Alexandretta, and I shall say good-bye to this sea, the last link with the country where you all live."

He landed. The journey to the mountains began at once. Brother Marie-Albéric set out from Alexandretta in the afternoon of July 10, with a Father of Notre-Dame-du Sacré-Cœur who had come the night before to fetch him. "Except for a five hours' halt we rode all night and the next day, mounted on mules, escorted by three armed Turks: on Friday at 6 o'clock we arrived at Notre-Dame-du-Sacré-Cœur, a mass of small houses of boards and pisé, covered with thatch, a sort of Jules Verne establishment, a tangle of barns, cattle and little houses crowding quite close to one another for fear of raids and robbers; it is shaded by tall trees and watered by a spring which comes out of the rock; but the outside only is in Jules Verne style, the inside is better: our Lord is within. . . .

" . . . The house is made up of a score of religious and about fifteen orphans from six to twelve years of age, without speaking of birds of passage."

What was this monastery of Notre-Dame-du-Sacré-Cœur, a summary description of which we have just read? An improvised abbey, founded in 1882 as a refuge in the mountains by the Trappists of Notre-Dame-des-Neiges, in case they happened to have to leave France. The domain is called Sheïkhlé (pronounced Shirley) and forms part of the province (vilayet) of Adana. To get there, you leave Alexandretta by the Aleppo road. It ascends a little at first, then the ascent becomes very difficult. Indeed, you must cross the chain of the Amanus. The windings increase. On the road cut out of the rock, and without any parapets, rows of pack-camels, teams, and people riding or walking descend or climb up. In five hours you arrive at the Bailan Pass, a famous spot passed through by all the invaders of this part of Asia: the Assyrians, the armies of Darius, of Alexander, the armies of the Romans, of the Arab Sultans and of the Crusaders, when seeking the plain of Antioch. The ruins of mediæval castles are still used as quarries by the people of the country. You come to a stop at Bailan, the frontier between the vilayets of Aleppo and Adana, for the Turks have placed a Custom-house there. It is here that travellers coming from the interior and intending to go to the coast have to give their arms back to the *zaptiés* (police), or, at least, as the Kurds and Circassians are seldom absent, thrust or hide their pistols or daggers between the folds of their girdles. Beyond the village the descent begins. The bridges over the torrents are not so safe as the fords. The Aleppo road is left only at the foot of the mountain, to take to the left a simple track through the forests, moors or arable land, and it hardly swerves away from the lowest slopes of the Amanus and winds round the spurs of the mountain. After a long march, a very jagged cleft in the mountain is reached.

There is the little town of Akbes with the Lazarist mission. Travellers, like Brother Albéric and his companion, who wish to go on to La Trappe of Sheïkhlé, then enter the ravine, go up it for two hours, and then descend a little to reach the bottom of a high valley quite wonderful in its formation and scenery.

Imagine a circle of mountains surrounding it, all covered with tall parasol pines, under which oaks and other trees and shrubs grow. It is itself cultivated, tilled and sown like the country in France or Italy, since there are monks of St. Bernard in this wild corner of Turkey. Gushing springs water it and form a stream which has ended in cutting through the mountain-side and falls in cascades. In the distance through this cutting stretches away the waving expanse towards Killis and Aleppo. It is the only opening on the world. Outside the gap, there is nothing but verdure and blue sky.

The monastery was built in haste. One really cannot imagine a poorer one. A fence limits and protects it against prowlers, but it is made of dry thorn and stakes. No church is to be seen, with its roof and spire dominating the other buildings as in our Western abbeys. The entrance gate of the Sheïkhlé Trappe opens on to a farmyard. All along the right are the mules' stables and the cowhouses; on the left, a bakery, kitchen, forge, and a shed where the agricultural implements are put up; at the farther end, the chapter-hall, refectory, and the Prior's room. Several other buildings to the left were grouped as required—chapel, joiners' shop, wood-house, rooms for study, library and linen-room; but stone having been reserved for the chapel, the chapter-hall and the stables, the rest were built with cob-walls and roofed with boards or thatch. The appearance had none of the beautiful order that the word "monastery" conveys to us. To live there, men had to be stout in limb and heart. For, not to speak of always possible incursions of bands of brigands tempted by the granaries, or excited by fanaticism, comfort was necessarily lacking and necessaries habitually. For example, in summer the monks slept in a loft over the stables, the worn and badly joined lath floor of which let through the noise and odour of the animals. In winter they had as their dormitory another loft, over the chapter-hall and refectory, but they slept scarcely any better there than in the other one, when the snow covered the sheet-iron roof which was very near their moss-stuffed mattresses. The bed-clothes did not give much protection from the bite of the cold. In addition to this, if the domain sufficed to support those who cultivated it, it did not raise funds enough to build a real abbey. The land had been cleared eight years ago, and produced fine crops of wheat, barley, and cotton; the kitchen-garden furnished an abundance of vegetables; the well-kept and selected varieties of vines, at the end of the summer, promised a delicious white wine, but the distance from the markets rendered the sale almost useless, and carriage ate up the profits.

Such were the place, scene, and material state of life in which Brother Albéric went on with his Trappist novitiate. His time was no longer spent in quite the same way.

"The manual labour here was to gather cotton, carry away stones in the fields and make a heap of them where they are not in the way, to wash and saw wood; we never know beforehand what work we shall have to do. At the hour for work a wooden slab is struck. The choir-monks assemble in a small room where the aprons and sabots are, and the Superior assigns each man his work. Since I have been here, I have spent two, sometimes three days a week, washing, the remainder in working in the fields; there my ordinary work is to clear the soil of the stones which encumber it and to carry them in baskets into heaps. . . . When there is particular work, crops to gather, I am sent to do it. I spent eight or ten days in gathering potatoes, two or three at the vintage, nearly three weeks at the cotton harvest. Besides, novices have the pleasing duty of sweeping the church twice a week. . . .

"Our orphans are Catholic children of Akbes, where three Lazarist missionaries have converted eight hundred schismatics in the last twenty years."

Who are the neighbours of this monastery lost in the mountains of Asia Minor and what may be expected from them? Comte Louis de Foucauld asked his cousin.

"You wish to know," replied Brother Marie-Albéric, "whether I am in contact with the Musulmans: not much. It appears to me that this mixture of Kurds, Syrians, Turks, and Armenians would make a brave, laborious, and honest people if they were educated, governed, and above all converted. For the moment, they are mercilessly overtaxed, profoundly ignorant, and the Musulman religion has its sad influence on morals: our region is a corner of brigands. It is for us to make the future of these peoples. The future, the only true future, is life eternal : this life is but the short trial which prepares for the next. The conversion of these people depends on God, on them, and on us Christians. God always gives grace abundantly : they are free to receive, or not to receive, the Faith : preaching in Musulman countries is difficult, but the missionaries of so many centuries past have overcome many other difficulties. We have to be the successors of the first Apostles, the first evangelists. The Word is much, but example, love, and prayer are a thousand times more. Let us give them the example of a perfect life, of a superior and divine life : let us love them with that all-powerful love which makes itself beloved; let us pray for them with a heart warm enough to draw down on them from God a superabundance of graces, and we shall infallibly convert them. . . ."[1]

"*November* 10, 1890.—The principal difference from Notre-Dame-des-Neiges is that here I am given the order to work with all my strength, though meditation should lose thereby; that is more conformable with poverty, with our Lord's example. But up to the present God has not willed meditation to lose by it; on the contrary, He gives me during work the faithful thought of Him and of those I love, which forms my life."

He adds that he has not taken advantage of any exception.
"It is true," he says, "that I have asked for nothing."[2]
"Our mountains are entirely wooded with tall parasol pines under which grow oak-trees, holm-oaks and wild olives, and amidst which great masses of grey, cavernous rocks rise up in places. They swarm with partridges and deer; in winter, wolves, panthers, bears, and wild boars, which are very numerous in the neighbourhood, venture into them."

"*April.*—Holy Communion is my great support, my all. I dare not ask for it every day : my unworthiness is infinite."

"*Easter Tuesday,* 1890.—We should be joyful, for our Lord is risen; our Well-Beloved, our Betrothed, the divine Spouse of our soul is infinitely happy, and His reign will

---

[1] Letter of November 28, 1892.
[2] He said : "To ask for nothing, unless in great necessity, is a maxim of St. Teresa which I try to put into practice, and each time that I do so, I find myself the better for it."

have no end; . . . this is the true foundation of our joy. . . . However sad I may be when I kneel at the foot of the altar, and say to our Lord, ' Lord, Thou art infinitely happy and dost want for nothing,' I cannot do otherwise than add : ' Then I too am happy, and in want of nothing ; Thy happiness suffices me.' . . ."

July 14, 1890.—The foundation is going on very well : there are many novices, and some come from France, others from this country. . . . I hope that God will bless this monastery, that can do so much good in the midst of a Musulman population among whom there is a certain number of schismatic Christians.

" . . . Exercises follow each other at short intervals, and one can hardly do the same thing long ; it is this that after, and with the grace of God, makes life here so easy materially ; the great diversity of exercises, prayer, reading, and work follow one another. . . . I am coming from church ; I am going, I think, to the fields ; and thus it is all day long. . . . We are now in the season of hard work ; the wheat is being threshed ; for husbandmen, for Trappists, it is a big business.

"*November* 11, 1890.—Here God gives me a novice-master whose knowledge and example are admirable ; he is a retired Abbot. A former Abbot of Notre-Dame-des-Neiges, he has come here to finish his already long religious career ; he is the real founder of this house, and does an immense amount of good in it."[1]

"*January* 3, 1891.—To-day, I write to you particularly to make you a gift of all my flat in Paris contains : henceforth it is yours, do what you please with it, sell, give, order what you like ; it is just yours. . . . Except what is left as a souvenir, which Raymond will give back in my name, you will find most, and even all the things we cared for as coming from grandfather and our parents."[2]

" . . . You ask to hear about me. My soul enjoys a profound peace, which has not ceased since coming here. It grows stronger every day, although I feel how little it comes from myself, how much it is a pure gift from God. It is a peace which increases faith, which calls for gratitude. Give thanks for me, so that I may be less ungrateful. . . .

[1] This monk was called Dom Polycarpe.
[2] In a later letter are these words written to his sister :
"The greatest joy that my little possessions have given me will be to get rid of them and to have them no longer."

I feel more every day that I am where God wishes me to be. In a few days it will be a year since I have been at La Trappe. I am only overwhelmed by the infinite goodness of our Lord Jesus, who has thus called and led and overwhelmed me with so many graces. In a year I shall make my profession. My heart is longing to be bound by vows, but I am already so by all my desires.

"Think much of the poor, my good Mimi, during this hard winter. If you only knew how I regret not having done more for them when I was in the world! I know well you need not have the same regrets, but I think I am right to tell you this, for here in La Trappe, though we don't suffer ourselves, we can imagine what they must suffer when they have not what we have."

"*July* 3, 1881.—You ask me for news of my convent and of our work; we are about a score of Trappists, novices included. We are installed, as you see by the photographs, in a pretty extensive range of huts. There are live-stock; oxen, goats, horses, and asses—all that is required for cultivation on a big scale. In our huts we board from fifteen to twenty Catholic orphans, between five and fifteen years of age; there are at least ten or fifteen lay-workmen also sheltered by us; lastly, guests' whose number varies; you know monks are essentially hospitable. You will also get a very good idea of our life by reading *Les Moines d'Occident* by Montalembert. However, there is a difference: the monks of whom he speaks studied more than we, busied themselves more than we with certain work, such as copying of manuscripts. Our great work is field labour; this distinguishes the Order of St. Bernard, to which we belong, from the old monks. Thus, in autumn there was the vintage and the clearing of the fields; in winter, sawing wood; in spring, working with picks at the vine; in summer, harvesting the hay. The harvest was finished the day before yesterday. It is peasants' work, a toil infinitely salutary for the soul; while employing the body, it leaves the soul free to pray and meditate. Then this work, harder than you think if you have never done it, gives you such compassion for the poor, such charity towards workmen and labourers! You understand the cost of a piece of bread so well, when you see for yourself how much trouble it takes to produce it! You feel so much pity for all who work, when you share in that work! . . .

"You wish me to describe one of our days. We get up at two in the morning, run to church, where we remain two hours reciting the Psalms aloud in the choir; then, for an hour or an hour and a half we are free, we read and pray; and the priests say Mass. Towards half-past five we go back to the choir, we again say some Psalms; it is the first canonical hour; and we assist at Mass in common. From there we go to the chapter and say some prayers; the Superior comments on a passage of the Rule; and if any one has committed a fault, he then confesses it in public, and is given a penance (not generally very hard, far from it). Another three-quarters of an hour free for reading or prayer; again in the choir we say the little office of Terce; then about seven, work begins; the Superior assigns it to each man after Terce. We remain at work till about eleven o'clock; we then say Sext, and go to the refectory at half-past eleven.

"After lunch (the monks' dinner) we go up to the dormitory, where we sleep till half-past one. The office of None is at half-past one. An interval of three-quarters of an hour for privates prayers or reading. At half-past two Vespers. After Vespers, work till a quarter to six. At six o'clock prayer; at a quarter past six, supper; a little free time; at a quarter past seven, reading for the whole community in chapter; then Compline, singing of the *Salve* and to bed. We go to bed at eight.

"Have I spoken enough to you about myself, dear Mimi? I hope you are satisfied."

"*October* 29, 1891.— . . . Thanks for having thought of me on the 15th of September; on that day I was thirty-three; the years pass, may they bring us nearer to God in every way! Let us pray for each other, in order to be faithful to what God desires from us each in our own lives. They appear very different, but it is only in appearance; when God makes the foundation of life as it ought to be, all lives resemble each other, the rest is of little importance."

The ceremony of Brother Marie-Albéric's religious profession took place on Candlemas Day, February 2, 1892. It was presided over by Dom Martin, Abbot of Notre-Dame-des-Neiges, who was in the East for the regular visit.

The newly professed monk wrote next day: "From yesterday I belong entirely to our Lord. About seven o'clock I made my vows; about eleven o'clock a few locks of my hair were cut off in the church, then my head was shaved, leaving the monastic crown. And now I no longer belong to myself in any way. . . . I am in a state I have never experienced, except just a little on my return from Jerusalem . . . It is a craving for meditation and silence, for lying at God's feet and looking at Him almost in silence. One feels, and would like to go on indefinitely feeling, that one belongs all to God, and that He is all our own. The 'Is it, then, nothing to belong all to God?' of St. Teresa, furnishes the prayer. . . ."[1]

Around him, admiration increased. "Our Brother Marie-Albéric appears like an angel amidst us," said the Abbot of Notre-Dame-des-Neiges; "he wants nothing but wings." The Prior of the Sheïkhlé Trappe, Dom Louis de Gonzague, wrote the same way to Madame de Blic, the day after the religious profession: "You know, Madam, what a holy companion on our journey to heaven we have taken to ourselves to-day! His spiritual director, our venerable Father Dom Polycarpe, who will soon have had fifty years of religious profession and has been a Superior more than thirty years, assures me that, in his long life, he has not yet met with a soul so entirely given to God. Allow me to make a little disclosure with regard to this dear and holy soul. . . . I should naturally like to get Father Marie-Albéric to make his theological studies here, so that he may some day be promoted to the priesthood. I have not yet spoken to him of this intention, but I foresee very well that I shall have to maintain a serious struggle against his humility, and finally, it is a thing that, in our Order, we cannot command in virtue of obedience. . . . In spite of his marvellous austerities, his health remains excellent. . . ."[2]

A little later on, when back in France after his journey in Syria, Dom Martin, giving to the General Chapter an account of the visit he had paid to Akbes, named Charles de Foucauld among the monks who might one day be appointed Superiors of that foundation.

Brother Marie-Albéric forbore thinking of the future. But it is so difficult for us to live entirely in the present, that he happened to ask himself: "What will they do with me? If only they don't take me away from the common life of the Brothers who are wood-choppers, weeders of wheat and grass, harvesters, grape-gatherers, according to the seasons!" He disclosed his perplexity to Abbé Huvelin, and, to meet the reply, prepared his defence against dignities and offices: "If they speak to me of studies, I shall show that I have a great liking for being neck-deep in wheat and wood, and a strong repugnance for everything

[1] Letter of January 2, 1892.
[2] Letter of February 4, 1892.

that would take me away from the *lowest place* which I came to find, from the abjection in which I desire to be buried ever deeper and deeper, following our Lord's example, and then, after all, I shall obey. . . . But what I tell you here is a stroll in the forbidden garden; God is with us to-day: is not that enough?"

He was bidden to begin his theological studies a few months after his profession.

"*August* 22, 1892.—This week the Lazarite Father Superior of Akbes comes back. . . . It appears that, over a year ago, it was arranged that he should teach me theology: he was professor of theology at Montpellier and is very learned. He is a Neapolitan (M. Destino). On being told this, I did not conceal my lack of attraction for this new vocation. I also pointed out my great ignorance of monastic things. They replied that it was settled, and that I should soon begin: so I did not persist."

In fact, he became initiated in many other employments, for, having had a slight illness in the course of that year, Brother Marie-Albéric was provisionally exempted from work in the open air, and confided to the linen-Brother, who taught him how to mend and darn.

"*July* 5, 1892.—Why can't I give you a little of my taste for solitude? I, indeed, love it more every day, and think there is never enough of it.

"I am always thinking of our Lord and the Blessed Virgin . . . and I live happy in their dear society. When I am mending the little orphans' clothes, I say to myself, how happy I am in doing this work, so familiar in the house at Nazareth. . . . How unworthy I am of these graces! Fancy me, for three days last week working at a strange job: the orphans' nurse was indisposed, and I was told to take his place by day. Just think how strange it was to find myself all at once in charge of nine little Turks from six to fifteen years old! When I saw myself in the midst of this little family, I could not help thinking of those who say that one enters religion to avoid the cares of life. One has not the same cares, but very happy ones when God wishes it. As for me, on account of my great weakness, He has given me nothing but peace. . . . These poor little ones were as good as possible."

"*May* 21, 1893.—The studies interest me, Holy Scripture above all—it is the Word of our heavenly Father. Dogmatic theology, too; it is the study of what we must believe about the Holy Trinity, our Lord and the Church; that, too, brings us much nearer to God: moral theology less. . . . But these studies . . . have not the same value as the practice of poverty, abjection, mortification, and finally the imitation of our Lord which manual labour provides. However, since I do them through obedience, having resisted as much as I ought, this is evidently what God desires of me now."

Yes, he felt sure of not being mistaken in rejecting the world and becoming a monk, but a long road remained for him to travel, and sometimes his peace was disturbed, and a call came from the heart of God to this man of good-will, splitting wood, patching breeches, or bending over a theological treatise, and a voice said to him: " Go farther into solitude !" The temptations against obedience continued to exercise the virtue of the still young religious; the spirit of mistrust tried him, leading him to think his Superiors were surely making a mistake and did not know how to guide everyone, and that it would be very easy to name a novice whose real inclinations they had overlooked. Brother Marie-Albéric silenced this tempting voice; but the other that said, " Go farther " he always heard. Very resolute not to swerve from obedience, he waited, without knowing where it wished to lead him, for a certain sign of the will which was drawing him outside. It was then that he wrote to his cousin Comte Louis de Foucauld: " I relish the charms of solitude more and more, and I am trying to find out how to enter into a deeper and deeper solitude." Three lines of another intimate letter show even more clearly this extraordinary attraction, which makes him wish for an Order still more strict than the strictest of religious Orders. He told a friend, on June 27, 1893, that the Trappists of Notre-Dame-des-Neiges had received the new constitutions of the Cistercian Order: " It is all very pious," he said, " very austere, very good in every way; however, be it said between you and me, there is not all the poverty I wish for, nor the abjection I long for: my desires in that direction are not satisfied."

Here was a sort of excess and singularity which could not fail to puzzle the most learned and experienced of directors. For the ideal of poverty, humility, mortification and charity has been attained by a great number of holy monks and nuns, in all the recognized Orders, under divers rules. For centuries all religious life has tended that way, even in the world. The obstacles are in ourselves much more than in the exterior circumstances and equipment of life. He was deceived as to the motives which were driving him out of La Trappe : he conceived a project which he was never to accomplish—that of grouping around him "a few souls with which he could form a beginning of a little congregation," answering to the longings of a mind which did not cease to be haunted by the vision of Nazareth. What would be the aim of this new company? What would be its essential rule? From this moment Brother Marie-Albéric sets it forth thus : " To lead the life of our Lord as closely as possible, living solely by the work of their hands, without accepting any gift, either spontaneous or asked for, and following to the letter all His counsels, possessing nothing, giving to all who ask, claiming nothing, stinting themselves as much as possible . . . adding to this work much prayer ; . . . forming small groups only ; . . . scattered, above all, through infidel and neglected lands, in which it would be so pleasing to increase the love and service of Jesus Christ."[1]

Souls chosen, like Charles de Foucauld, for an exceptional life, are led through darkness less and less dense to light. Here the desire of devoting all his forces to the salvation of infidel lands appears, and his often expressed thought of being the most destitute and unknown of men again shows itself. He feels himself urged along by an increasing interior force towards an undefined and dangerous future. For on one point he has no illusions: perhaps he will be long alone. He trembles at the thought, but does not change the desire : " being in a boat, I am afraid of jumping into the sea." But his shrinking does not disquiet him, and his uncertainty does not reach the higher self where peace rules untouched. And the explanation of the wonder was quite simple : Brother Marie-Albéric left the decision of his extreme difficulty to the greatest of all authorities, to the authority which puts God before us in our Order, and self afterwards : obedience. This enabled him to overcome everything and persuade everyone.

Look at this Trappist who has pronounced his first vows. He believes he is called to leave the Order, not to return to secular life, which would not be without precedent, but to follow an entirely personal, and even strange, inspiration, which urges him to disappear still more completely than in a Syrian monastery. He has gained the sympathy and aroused even the admiration of his Superiors and Brothers : and he wants to leave these friends, and theirs is the

[1] Letter of October 4, 1893.

decision he asks for! In France, in Paris, very far away, he had a director who was a curate at Saint Augustine's; and this prudent Parisian with his distrust of the exceptional, a moderate man by temperament and experience, as anxious as a mother, he had to convince and bring to utter this decision: "Yes, my child, go to that wonderful unknown that you long for."

To put one's trust in one who is worthy of it, to speak out freely, not to shirk owning up, to be patient only afterwards, and if one must: men have found no better means of driving away the clouds which uncertainty and conflicting reasons gather within them. It is an honest, prompt, and military method. It was Charles de Foucauld's. He therefore began, about the middle of September, to speak of his trouble to Dom Polycarpe, whom he had chosen as his confessor, and asked him:

"Does this come from God, the devil, or my imagination?"

"Think no more about it," was substantially the prior's reply, "and wait in peace, for the good God, if it comes from Him, will well know how to provide the occasion."

He wrote at the same time to Abbé Huvelin. We have not these letters, but, in a sort of journal addressed to a friend, he summarized them. They showed an entire liberty of procedure and judgment.

Then Abbé Huvelin, who understood his patient very well and was very fond of him, became uneasy. Without retaining the least hope of keeping this man, with his extreme yearnings, a neophyte in whom he observed a sort of agitated seeking after perfection, at La Trappe, he tried to retard the dénouement of the inward crisis. The idea that Charles de Foucauld might be called to follow the vocation of the Fathers of the desert by degrees entered his mind, but before he was persuaded of it, before saying so, he had to oppose a project which appeared to be an adventure, one of those adventures into which he knew the best endowed souls may in good faith throw themselves and perish. Here are a few fragments of the numerous letters that he wrote in the months which follow Brother Marie-Albéric's disclosure. They tell of the suffering brought upon this tender-hearted priest by the event the shadow of which, like that of a storm-cloud, he already felt draw near.

"*January* 29, 1894.—Go on with your theological studies, at least up to the diaconate; cultivate the interior virtues, and above all self-annihilation; as for the exterior virtues, practise them in the perfection of obedience to the rule and to your Superiors; for the rest we shall see later on. Besides, you are not made, *not at all made,* to lead others."

"*July* 29, 1895 (to a third party).—Evidently he will not stay. He will take his idea more and more for the voice of God speaking. The beauty of the end to which he believes himself called will veil all the rest, and above all the unattainable. . . ."

"*July* 30, 1895 (to a third party).—How alarmed I am about the life which he wishes to lead, about Nazareth where he wishes to go and live, about the band which he wants to gather around him! But I do not hope to keep him at La Trappe."

"*September* 30, 1897.—I find that he wishes for too many things, and therein I fear some uneasiness of mind, and that constant striving for the best which upsets a soul."

Thus thought the two advisers to whom Brother Marie-Albéric had appealed. And what was he thinking about during these months of waiting? This, which he had revealed to Abbé Huvelin, and probably to his Trappist confessor: he wished to be a choir-monk no longer, to lead outside of La Trappe what he calls "the life of Nazareth," and, more definitely, to become "a simple inmate, a simple day-labourer in some convent."[1] Besides, he had resolved to undertake nothing, as long as the guides, whose very clear advice we have just seen, would not encourage him to change his condition, rule, domicile, and habit. "As long as my directors refuse their permission, I should think I was disobeying God, whatever I did.[2]

"The Abbé (Huvelin) tells me to find out whether I could not discover what God expects of me, here, in this life where I am. . . . You know with what respect and affection I listen to this word: but everything calls me in an opposite direction. . . . Time or death, and in any case God will arrange the rest. But I always hope He will allow me to follow Him in the way He points out to me."[3]

We shall presently see how these difficulties were unravelled, how, without laying aside all apprehension, men of entire sincerity and men of prayer were led to change their mind and give an authorization that Charles de Foucauld waited for in perfect obedience.

[1] Letter of March 19, 1896.   [2] Letter of January 3, 1894.
[3] Letter of August 30, 1895.

While these things were taking place unknown to the world, two events attracted the attention, not of a great number of men, but of some, to La Trappe of Akbes. In the first place, at the beginning of 1894 it ceased to be attached to the Abbey of Notre-Dame-des-Neiges, and was placed under that of Stauëli, which, having more important farms and vineyards in full produce, could more easily bring help to the very poor Trappe of Syria. The second event was the period of massacres that the Sultan permitted or ordered. Once more Armenia was the victim, Armenia and all the undefined fringe of countries which border upon it.

"It is not the Kurds who stir, it is the Armenian Christians, and the Turks take advantage of this to commit terrible massacres, and to do as much harm as they can, not only to the Armenians, but to all Christians, Catholic or others, who are still so numerous in these countries. . . . Around us there were horrors, a number of massacres, burnings and lootings. Many of the Christians were really martyrs, for they died voluntarily, without defending themselves, rather than deny their Faith. . . . There is frightful misery in this unfortunate country. The winter is very hard; I do not know what these poor unfortunates, all of whose possessions have been seized and their houses burned, will do not to die of hunger and cold. . . . I write to you to ask for alms; not for us, God forbid, for I shall never be poor enough, but for the victims of the persecutions. In the last few months nearly 140,000 Christians were murdered by the Sultan's orders. . . . In the nearest town from here, at Marache, the garrison killed 4,500 Christians in two days. We at Akbes, and all the Christians within two days of us, ought to have perished. I was not worthy. . . . Pray for my conversion, and that next time, in spite of my misery, I shall no longer be thrust back from the already half-open gates of heaven.

"Europeans are protected by the Turkish Government, so that we are in safety: a guard was put at our gate, so that no harm might be done to us. It is miserable to be in such favour with those who slaughter our brethren; it were better to suffer with them than to be protected by their persecutors. . . . It is shameful for Europe; with a word, she could have prevented these horrors, and she did not say it. It is true that the world knew so little about what was happening here, the Turkish Government having bought up the press, having given enormous sums to certain journals not to publish any despatches which did not come from itself. But the Governments know the whole truth through the ambassadors and consuls. What punishments from God are they not preparing for themselves by such ignominies! I come to call you to our help, to aid us to give relief, to prevent several thousand Christians who escaped from the massacres and took refuge in our mountains from perishing of hunger; they do not dare to leave their retreat for fear of being massacred, and they have no means. It is our imperative duty to stint ourselves of everything for them, but whatever we do we cannot satisfy such needs."[1]

Finally, to complete the portrait of Charles de Foucauld during this period so troubled in so many ways; and since our souls are a mystery to ourselves, since they can be happy and suffer at the same time, since they are a vast domain, with the storm below, some mist farther up, and a clear sky over all; I shall quote this note, written by Brother Marie-Albéric to M. de Blic, recently settled in Burgundy, in the castle of Barberey:

"It is the happiness of the country to be able to surround ourselves with all those we love . . . to have always round us those we love, this indeed is sweet. . . . Why did I go so far away, you will say to me, if I feel this happiness so keenly? I have in no wise sought joy, I have sought to follow 'by the odour of His perfumes,' Jesus, who has loved us so much . . . and if I have found my delight in following Him, it is without having sought it. But this delight does not prevent me from feeling profoundly the sorrow of being separated from all those I love."[2]

Days and months went by. The time came when the fifth anniversary of the simple vows would be fulfilled. At this date, February 2, 1897, solemn vows had to be taken, or a dispensation requested, and the Order of St. Bernard must surely be left. Brother Marie-Albéric's heart was always troubled by the same obsession:

"I am very eager, indeed, to follow the life that I have been seeking for seven years . . . which I caught a glimpse of and divined in walking through the streets of Nazareth, where our Lord's feet had trodden, when He was a poor artisan, lost in abjection and obscurity."[3]

Then the consent of Abbé Huvelin, hoped for but unexpected, arrived in the Sheïkhlé Trappe.

[1] Letters of November 20, 1895; February 21, 1896; June 24, 1896.
[2] Letter of June 18, 1894.   [3] Letter of June 24, 1896.

"PARIS, *June* 15, 1896.—My dear child, I read and re-read your letter. I have made you wait long for my answer, when you were so thirsty! But I thought that you would not lose your time by studying theology and getting from it sure and broad ideas, and thus preparing, in that teaching, your mind and heart for a sure mysticism, free from illusions. . . .

"I had hoped, my dear child, that you would find in La Trappe what you were seeking, that you would find enough poverty, humility and obedience, to be able to follow our Lord in His life of Nazareth. I thought you might have said on entering it: *Hæc requies mea in sæculum sæculi!* I still regret that it is not so. There is a too deep-seated urge towards another ideal, and through the strength of this impulse you get out of your framework and find yourself dislocated. I don't think, indeed, that you can get rid of this impulse. Say so to your Superiors at La Trappe, at Staouëli. Tell them your thought simply. Tell them also of your profound esteem for the life you see around you, and of the invincible impulse which, in spite of all your endeavours, has so long urged you towards another ideal. . . . Not that I think you are called higher. . . . I do not see you higher up; no, indeed, I see that you feel yourself uplifted in another direction. I won't make you wait any longer. Show my letter, speak. Write to Staouëli.[1] I should have liked to keep you in a family where you are loved, to which you would have been able to give so much! I think, my child, that you have been well directed and formed in La Trappe; but inevitably, you see something else. Oh! how I pray for you! . . .

"I have been a priest twenty-nine years to-day! How I should have liked to have seen you, too, a priest!"

No sooner had Brother Marie-Albéric ascertained the contents of this happy letter than he submitted to his director the sketch of a rule for the future community of the Petits Frères de Jésus—a voluminous work, in which the extreme austerity of the convert and monk was given full scope. He hoped for approbation, but the reply was not in that sense. In an intimate note, Abbé Huvelin sets down clearly what he had in mind: "I have just received the letter. It is accompanied by a long rule of the community of the Petits Frères de Jésus, which you hope to found. The rule is impossible, and it contains everything but discretion. I am broken-hearted." And, as he is a very firm

[1] A Trappe near Algiers, no longer in existence.

adviser, able to check his penitent where required, with a sure hand now that he is carried away by ardour to the point of judging others by himself and their strength by his own, the Abbé replies in no less clear terms as follows :

"Fontainebleau, *Sunday, August 2,* 1896.—If your Superiors ask you to make another attempt, make it loyally! What would above all frighten me, my dear child, is not the life of which you are thinking for yourself, if you remain isolated . . . but it is to see you found, or think of founding something. . . . Your rule is absolutely impracticable. . . .

"The Pope hesitated to give his approbation to the Franciscan rule; he thought it too severe; but this rule! to tell you the truth it terrified me! Live at the door of a community, in what abjection you like, but draw up no rule, I beg you!"

Hence no foundation, no company. Henceforth Charles de Foucauld appears in the eyes of this priest, who is a connoisseur of souls, as a born solitary. A single permission was accorded to him; that of trying to live, outside the Trappe, a hidden life, in some corner of Syria or Palestine. Furthermore, before taking up so singular a part, he was to submit to the test of obedience and the study that his Superiors would doubtless require of him. But, on the main point of his vocation, of his attraction to complete solitude, Abbé Huvelin no longer hesitated, and he again said: "Yes, my child, I see the East with your eyes."

Therefore Brother Marie-Albéric wrote to the Father-General of the Trappists in Rome, praying him to obtain the necessary dispensations from the Pope. The reply arrived about the end of the month of August. The Superior-General of the Order, before deciding, imposed a trial on Brother Marie-Albéric; he ordered the latter first to go to La Trappe of Stauëli, where instructions would be sent.

The monk replied that he submitted with all his heart to what might be ordered, and set out by the next steamer.

"Algiers, *September* 25.—Reached Marseilles on Wednesday at 5 o'clock in the evening. I left there again an hour after, on the Algiers boat. Think of the time I spent in Algeria, and the life I led there, of my absolute impiety at that time, and beg for me to be forgiven."

He went at once to the Stauëli Trappe, and this is what he learnt:

"*October* 12, 1896.—I want to tell you immediately of some news which will give you much joy : . . . the test laid upon me is to go and study theology in Rome for about two years.

" I start in a fortnight, about the 25th. It was Père Louis de Gonzague who settled that in his great affection for me. It is a great blessing to make me thus drink at the purest fountain of religious teaching, and this favour is rarely accorded in our Order. . . . I shall be in Rome with seven other monks at the General's house, where we shall live under the supervision of the most reverend Father-General and council : from there we shall go and attend the lectures at the Roman College.

" You know that my desires are by no means changed, they are steadier than ever : but I obey with simplicity, with extreme gratitude, and with confidence that after this long trial the will of God will be manifested very clearly to all of us who have but one sole desire—to know the will of God in order to do it, whatever it may be, and to throw ourselves into it with our whole heart and strength."

His obedience and simplicity of heart shone forth in his acceptance of the trial imposed on him. This was all the Father-General was in quest of, as the event consequently proved. But Charles de Foucauld knew nothing of that. He had asked to leave the Order, and before according any dispensation, two years' waiting were imposed on his ardent nature. He obeyed, not only without murmuring, but with gratitude : he agreed to be kept under the Trappist Rule long after the fifth anniversary of his vows.

How long did he remain at Stauëli ? A few weeks. And at once he formed friendships : he was immediately venerated by his Brethren : they still recollect his passage as one of the more important events. After over twenty years one of these witnesses, questioned on the subject of Father de Foucauld, was moved at the thought of Brother Marie-Albéric, and replied :

" I was a novice then. How he edified the whole community ! In church, his eyes were always fixed on the Blessed Sacrament. He did not believe, he saw. He lived on nothing, being satisfied with the vegetables he found in the soup, not touching the soup itself or anything else ; and that only once a day at noon. He only slept two hours. He used to sit up till midnight, in a little infirmary chapel whence he could see the Blessed Sacrament. At midnight, he went and took a little rest, and at 2 o'clock he was in the choir with the community."[1]

Letter from Father Yves, February 16, 1917.

Some days passed: and he was in Rome. He lived in the Father-General's house, 95, Via San Giovanni in Laterano. There, he did everything that he was told to do; he became a student again amongst clergy younger than he; his strong will held him under obedience and, in truth, saved him.

"*November* 19, 1896.—Old and ignorant, and unfamiliar with Latin, I find it very hard to follow the lectures. . . . I shall be as great an ass in theology as in everything else."

"*December* 7, 1896.—Please God, I shall most probably spend three years here: this year, I am only taking philosophy. I take that as a trial which I am endeavouring to accomplish as well as possible, with obedience and gratitude . . . yet desiring another life with increasing ardour. . . .

"Pardon me if my replies are not long. *In conscience,* I am obliged to study hard,—and with my bad memory, my thirty-eight years of age, and but little time, it is tough work getting through, and I must try to benefit by the sacrifices which my Superiors are making for me through a very pure and disinterested kindness, since they are fully acquainted with my desires."

At Stauëli, Brother Marie-Albéric became intimately acquainted with Father Jérôme: the letters which he sent him from Rome are invaluable records. He seems to deliver his soul fully in them; they reveal it in his thoughts in his regular prayer, and they also disclose all the characteristics of a friendship which rarely flourishes except in the cloister or on the mountains near it.

"ROME, *November* 8, 1896.—After leaving Algiers, which was so sorrowful for all, but had the blessing of affording us the opportunity of offering a sacrifice to God— and that is still the greatest blessing, the only true one there is in life, the one which unites us most to our blessed Saviour —when one loves, what is sweeter than to give something to the beloved; above all, to give Him something to which we are attached, to suffer for love of Him, to give Him all our heart's blood? . . . I wanted to speak to you of our arrival in Rome, but here I am, still at the departure from Algiers. . . . It was so sorrowful for me! But blessed be God for it and blessed be all sorrow!

" We reached Rome on Friday at half-past 1 in the afternoon: we did not get out at San Paolo Station, which is

near St. Peter's; it was not very feasible, and we thanked
God for that; if we had got out there, we should have had
to take cab after cab, and it would have really grieved me
to enter, with so little poverty, the city into which St. Peter
and St. Paul both walked so poor and miserable, and
St. Peter in chains. . . . We therefore went on foot from
the station to the procurator, and stopped on our way at two
churches where we adored the Holy Sacrament on our first
steps in Rome, in order to ask Him that we might live there
according to His will. . . ."

He says that he frequently passed before the Colosseum,
"where so many martyrs gave their blood for our Lord
Jesus with such joy and love! How our Lord has been
loved within these walls! What flames of love rose up to
heaven! What are we in comparison with such souls?
However, we have hearts like theirs, our Lord loves us as
much as them, and we can and ought to love Him as much.
Oh, Father, how we ought to love! How you and I must
try to love this divine Spouse of our souls! If our hearts
are capable of loving passionately, and they are, let us
drown ourselves in this love! The Colosseum is quite
close to us: I can see it from my window; it is there that
St. Ignatius joyfully let himself be crushed for our Lord!
How these stones speak! What a strain of love still rises
thence to heaven!

"I did my best to commend you at the same time as
myself to St. Paul, to that Apostle who loved Jesus so
much, who worked so much for Him, who suffered so much
for Him. May he draw you and me after him, and teach
us to love!"

"*November* 29, 1896.—Dearest Father, how right you
are to speak to me at length of our Lord! If there are two
persons on earth who should speak only of God, are they
not we in whose friendship there is nothing terrestrial? Let
our conversation be, then, that of the angels, my dearest
Father. . . . But whilst the angels have tongues of gold
and hearts of fire, we stammer and are lukewarm; let us do
what we can . . . that will be a reason for helping each
other, for praying much for one another, for loving each
other all the more because we are weaker, for having to
sustain one another from afar, in order to follow, like our
Lord, the sorrowful way which He has shown us: "Take
up your cross and follow Me." I send you a little flower
that I gathered while praying for you in the catacomb of

St. Cecilia on the border of her tomb, on her feast; may this flower of martyrs recall to you, as to me, what the saints suffered, and what we ought to desire to suffer. . . . This is our advantage over the angels! . . . At least we have tears, sorrows, perhaps—would to God it were so—blood to offer to our Lord, in union with His tears and sorrows and blood!

"Manual labour is necessarily put into the second place at present because you, like myself, are in the period of infancy; we are not yet old enough to work with St. Joseph: we are still with Jesus the little child on the Virgin's knees, learning to read. But later on, humble, vile, despised manual labour will again take its great place, and then, with Holy Communion, the lives of the saints, prayer, the humble work of our hands, humiliation, suffering, and if it please God, at last, the death of St. Cecilia and so many others! With that we shall have the life of our Lord and well-beloved Master Jesus. . . . Permit one who has no right to give you the shadow of a counsel, one who is neither priest nor learned nor anything but a sinner, nevertheless to give you a hint. There is only one thing that authorizes me to do so—the fraternal love I have for you in our Lord; it is to consult your director in everything, about everything, even little things. I tell you this because I was always the better for doing so, and the worse for doing otherwise; I wish you to profit by my experience. This habit of asking what one should do, even in little things, has a thousand good effects: it gives peace; it accustoms you to conquer yourself; it makes you look upon the things of this earth as nothing: it gets one to make a host of acts of love: to obey is to love; it is the purest, the most perfect, the highest, the most disinterested, the most adoring act of love; it makes one, especially at first, perform not a few acts of mortification. . . ."

"ROME, *December* 21, 1896.—I do not want the feast of Christmas to pass without telling you that I shall do my best to be united with you at the feet of our Lord Jesus in these days of benediction. . . . Behold, then, our Lord on the way to Bethlehem; probably five days' journey, the last of two or three hours: from Nazareth to En-Gannin, from there to Sichar, from there to Bethel, from Bethel to Jerusalem, lastly from Jerusalem to Bethlehem. With what love, what meditation, the Virgin must have made this journey! With what burning desire for the salvation of men, for whom the Son of God had come down unto her womb! Every moment of this journey, our Lord saw not only His Mother and St. Joseph, and the angels adoring Him: He saw the present and the future, and every moment in the lives of all men; and His Sacred Heart already felt that immense sorrow which was His lot during all His mortal life at the sight of the sins, ingratitude, and damnation of so many souls. And He felt also along with the deep consolation afforded Him by His Mother's holiness a lesser but real consolation at the sight of many holy souls, of all the souls who had loved Him and would one day love Him, of all the hearts which unite with that of Mary to try and throb only for Him. . . . Shall we be of these, dear Father? Shall we be a consolation or a sorrow to our Blessed Saviour? If Christmas is the beginning of our joys, it is the beginning of the sorrows of Jesus. . . . Christmas is only eight days from the Circumcision. . . . Bethlehem is only 8 kilometres from Jerusalem. When one is in Palestine that strikes one painfully: after having spent the Christmas of 1888 at Bethlehem, having heard midnight Mass and received Holy Communion in the grotto; after two or three days, I returned to Jerusalem.

"The sweetness that I had experienced in praying in that grotto which had resounded with the voices of Jesus, Mary and Joseph, and where I was so near them, had been inexpressible. . . . But, alas! after an hour's walk, the dome of the Holy Sepulchre, Calvary, and the Mount of Olives rose up before me. I was obliged, whether I wished it or not, to change my thoughts and find myself once more at the foot of the Cross."

The study of theology, some walks in Rome, letters like those which we have just read or shall read later on, along with prayer, took up the end of 1896 and the two first months of 1897. Still, however firmly he might be anchored in obedience, he could not fail to perceive the dates coming closer on which a change would occur, an order be given determining his future. Brother Marie-Albéric thought of the 2nd of February. And, shortly before that anniversary, to a friend, this time not Father Jérôme, he set forth the suppositions and the probabilities on which he reckoned:

"The end of this month and the beginning of next are critical for me; on the 2nd of February five years ago I took my first vows. By the terms of the constitution, on that date I am to take my solemn vows or leave the Order. . . . To remain in the Order two years and a half more without taking my solemn vows, a dispensation of the Holy See, only granted for strong reasons, would be necessary. My novice master does not think that in this case there are sufficient motives to ask for a dispensation. It might happen that in a few days from now I may be obliged to come to a definite decision . . . that will depend upon the most reverend Father General, who will be here to-morrow or the day after. . . . The day on which my vocation is clearly known to my Father General and the novice master, and that it appears clear to them that God does not want me at La Trappe (at least as a Father), they will tell me, and ask me to retire, for they are too conscientious to wish to retain me a single day, when they see the will of God is otherwise.[1]

He consented to live thus for three years! His Superiors had no need of so long a trial to be sure that so humble a virtue could vanquish the dangers of a solitary life among men. By the perfection of his obedience, they recognized that the call he heard since the first days of his entrance to La Trappe was not that of a masked pride.

The General of the Order, who was travelling, reached Rome on January 16, 1897. Immediately, he made it his business to get a decision on the case of Brother Marie-Albéric by the members of his council. The latter suspected nothing. The General sent for him, and told him that the moment had come to inquire what were God's designs for his servant Charles de Foucauld; and that, if the Fathers, after prayer, study, and reflection, recognized that the latter had an exceptional vocation, outside the Rule of St. Benedict and St. Bernard, he must follow it without delay and with his whole heart.

"I laid before him in writing the state of my soul; then he gathered his council, and there, before God, having no longer but one thing in view, His will, the Father General and all the members of the council declared unanimously that the good God called me to a particular life of poverty and abjection, and that I should enter it without further delay. Consequently, I am to be given a dispensation, and all doors are open for me to follow God's call immediately. Our good Father General told me that yesterday. He at the same time said that he thought I ought to remain under obedience as to the matter of my vocation, but in that and in all, it was best for me to refer not to him, but to the Abbé. I wrote to him yesterday evening. As soon as I have his

[1] Letter to a friend, January 15, 1897.

answer, I shall set out. You know that I wish to be a servant in an Eastern convent, the Abbé will indicate which, and I shall go there."[1]

"My dear child," M. Huvelin replied, "I fear another Trappe for you, where I should prefer to see you nevertheless. The same thought will come to you there, the same comparison between the life you see and the life you follow after. I prefer Capharnaum or Nazareth, or some such Franciscan convent; not in the convent, but only under the shadow of the convent; asking only for spiritual assistance, living in poverty at the gate. Do not think of banding any souls around you, nor, above all, of giving them a rule. Live your life, then; if any souls come, live the same life together, without making any regulations. On this point I am quite clear.

"I admire the goodness and simplicity of the Father General; I admire the charity of the good Fathers, who love you and part with you. I am touched by their way of treating you."

The Trappists paid him the courtesy, the exquisite attention, of offering him a ticket on the boat, though he ceased to be Brother Marie-Albéric, and of conveying him thus to the door of the "Franciscan Convent."

"What a favour God bestows on me!" replied Charles de Foucauld. "How good He is to have made me come so far, to Rome, to give my vocation the very fullest and most entire confirmation that is possible in this world. I thought I came to Rome to study: I came here to be sent, without asking, by the very hand of our General, to follow the attraction which has been drawing me for so long."

The news that Brother Marie-Albéric had left La Trappe circulated quickly from the Convent of Rome to the other convents where he was known. It made more than one old monk weep. One of them, the former Prior of Notre-Dame at Akbes, who had become Prior of Stauëli, even wrote: "In leaving us, he has given me the greatest pain that I have ever felt in my life."[2]

Charles de Foucauld had spent seven years in La Trappe. All his life he preserved the greatest respect and gratitude for the venerable Order he left; later on he was to return

[1] Letter of January 24, 1897.
[2] Letter of Dom Louis de Gonzague to M. de Blic. The same monk had thus judged Brother Marie-Albéric in a letter dated the month of the preceding October: "For almost seven years I have seen him a Trappist, and faithful to all his religious duties, and I was wont to look upon him as a real saint; it is also the impression that he has left here amongst a community of eight hundred after a month's short stay.

and ask the Trappe of Notre-Dames-des-Neiges to receive him, for several months, as guest and friend.

One of his first cares, henceforward, was to advise Father Jérôme of the great event which had transformed Brother Marie-Albéric into a secular, and was to make him change habit, rule, and scene.

"ROME, *January 24*, 1897.—I believe it is my vocation to come down . . . all the doors are open to me, in order to cease being a choir-monk and go down to the rank of servant and menial. Yesterday I received this news from the very mouth of my good and excellent Father General, whose goodness to me touches me so deeply ! . . . But I needed obedience before he came to a decision; I had promised God to do all that my most Reverend Father told me, after undertaking the examination of my vocation, and also all my confessor told me. So that had I been told: 'You are going to take your solemn vows in ten days, and afterwards receive Holy Orders, I should have obeyed with joy, being certain that I was doing the will of God. . . . And even now I am in the hands of God and obedience. I asked where I must go on leaving here in a few days : it will be to the East; but in what house I don't know at all. God will tell me by the voice of my director. . . . You see I need my Brother's prayers. . . . I am bringing you down too, my dearest Brother, to be the Brother of a domestic, a servant, a menial; this is not glorious in the eyes of the world. . . . But you are dead to the world, and nothing can make you blush. . . .

"Thanks for having opened your heart to me about your desires for the priesthood : I thank God with all my soul for inspiring you with that desire : I do not for a moment doubt that it is your vocation, and, from the bottom of my heart, I thank God for it. . . . There is no vocation in the world as great as a priest's; and in truth, it is not of the world, it is, even here, of heaven. . . . The priest is something *transcendent*, exceeding all. . . . What a vocation, my dear Brother, and how much I praise God for having given it to you. . . . Once, I regretted not receiving it, regretted not to be clothed in that sacred character; it was at the height of the Armenian persecutions. . . . I should have wished to be a priest, to know the language of the poor persecuted Christians, and to be able to go from village to village to encourage them to die for their God. . . . I was not worthy of it. . . . But you, who knows what God reserves for you ? . . . The future is so unknown ! God leads us by such unexpected paths ! . . . If ever obedience brings you to these distant shores where so many souls are lost for want of priests, where the harvest abounds and perishes for want of workers, thank God, without measure. Wherever one can do most good to others, there one is best : entire forgetfulness of self, entire devotion to the children of our heavenly Father, that is our Lord's life, the life of all true Christians, that is above all the priest's life. . . . Also, if ever you are called to these countries where the people are seated in the shadow of death, thank God without measure, and give yourself up body and soul to make the light of Christ shine amongst these souls watered with His blood; you can do it in the Trappe with wonderful results; obedience will furnish you with the means. . . ."

Charles de Foucauld, in announcing his early departure for the East to his brother-in-law, asked him to keep it secret :

" The new life that I am going to begin will be much more *hidden,* much more solitary than that which I am leaving. I want you alone to know where I am; do not therefore say that I am in the Holy Land; say only that I am in the East, leading a very retired life, writing to nobody, and not wanting anyone to know where I am."

Charles de Foucauld left Rome in the beginning of February, to embark at Brindisi. He was going to lead the life he had longed for; it was to be an extraordinary one, a life adapted to him. Naturally, he was convinced that he was going into Asia for ever, where his bones would rest later on beside the dust of the Patriarchs. He was mistaken; other and wilder countries were awaiting him, and other labours. Nazareth and Jerusalem were to be for him only splendid experiments, two steps of the *Scala Santa* that he had commenced to climb.

CHAPTER VI
Nazareth and Jerusalem

"*BLESSED are the poor;* that is the beatitude I want. I have already been offered a corner where I believe my soul will be well. In any case, He who assigns each leaf its place can put me in mine," Charles de Foucauld wrote to his sister, when he was leaving Italy for the East. The boat was one of those calling at Alexandria, then at Jaffa, before going on to Constantinople. The pilgrim landed on the shore which is bordered by a semi-circle of square painted houses in filth at the bottom, but with very beautiful gardens of orange-trees extending at the back. He neither stayed in the houses nor in the shade of their gardens, and at once set out on foot, to reach by stages the town where he wanted to live: Nazareth. Having passed through Ramleh, Acre, Bethlehem, Jerusalem, and Sichar, on March 5, 1897, and quite unknown, like the poor who still stand at the town gates, he entered Nazareth the blessed. A week later the leaf had found its place. Charles de Foucauld wrote to his counsin, Colonel Louis de Foucauld, who had just been appointed military attaché at Berlin:

"I am settled in Nazareth henceforth; there you may henceforth write to the following address: Charles de Foucauld, Nazareth, Holy Land, *poste restante.* The good God has let me find here, to the fullest extent, what I wanted: poverty, solitude, abjection, very humble work, complete obscurity, as perfect an imitation as possible of the life of our Lord Jesus in this same Nazareth. Love imitates, love wants to conform with its beloved; it tends to unite everything, their souls in the same feelings, all the moments of existence in a kind of identity of life; that is why I am here. La Trappe made me ascend, made me a life of study, an honoured life. That is why I left it and embraced here the humble and hidden life of the divine workman of Nazareth.

"Keep my secrets; they are love-secrets that I entrust to you. I am very happy; my heart has what it yearned for so many years. Nothing remains now beyond going to Heaven."[1]

[1] Letter to Comte Louis de Foucauld, April 12, 1897.

What had happened, and what employment had he found?

Charles de Foucauld had at first presented himself to the Franciscan Fathers who gave hospitality to pilgrims to the Holy Land, and had asked them to accept him as a servant to the religious. They had no need of his services. He had therefore decided to live in the Franciscan house, Casa-Nova, for three days as an ordinary guest, but after making his confession to one of the religious, a chaplain of the Poor Clares of Nazareth, he looked so perplexed that his confessor said to him: " I shall speak of you at St. Clare's; they will perhaps find you a place." But already the traveller had been recognized by the Brother Guest-master of Casa-Nova, who remembered perfectly having seen him some years before in Nazareth, in quite another turn-out. The Abbess was therefore warned that a strange pilgrim would come to the monastery and offer himself as servant, and that this pilgrim, vowed to penance, was named the Vicomte de Foucauld. She was a woman to understand the greatness as well as the singularity of such a conjuncture, and then to contrive all for the soul's peace.

On the feast of St. Colette, at the exposition of the Blessed Sacrament, they saw a man still young come into the chapel of the Poor Clares, dressed in such a way that no one could tell to what nation he belonged, unless it were to that of the poor, which is immense and of all countries. He knelt down some way off before the altar, and remained there without stirring, for one, two, three hours, so that the attendant Sister, an Arabian, was quite anxious, and said to one of her companions: " I must watch that man, who does not leave the chapel. I fear he may steal something." The unknown one went out after doing nothing beyond praying a great deal. But three days later he came back and asked to speak to the Abbess of St. Clare's, the reverend Mother St. Michael.

To understand the sequel of this story, you must know that Charles de Foucauld, on disembarking in the Holy Land, had adopted a costume which might have some kinship with the clothes of certain Orientals—people of so many races are met with in the eastern crowds—but which caused astonishment even in that country. He wore a long hooded blouse with white and blue stripes, blue cotton trousers, and on his head a very thick white woollen cap, around which he had rolled a strip of fabric in the form of a turban. He had only sandals on his feet. A rosary of big beads hung from the leather girdle which tightened his tunic. In adopting this dress, no doubt the solitary meant to expiate the smartness of former days, and to excite to some extent the scorn of the passers-by and the mockery of the children in the street, and to take all this gladly. He knew the saying of St. Ignatius, used by so many saints of all ages: "I prefer to be regarded as a nobody and a madman for Christ, who was thus looked upon before me." He imagined that everybody would take him for what he was not—a poor beggar, without name, education or style. But the delicacy of his features, his accent and involuntary choice of words, his easy gestures and pose which just altered some fold or line—that is to say, nearly everything in the look of his dress—betrayed him. That is what happened when he was called to the parlour to interview the Abbess of Nazareth standing on the other side of the enclosure. She did not see him, but heard him.

The Abbess had no sooner questioned this visitor than she understood that she had not been misled. We can fancy her smiling whilst the pilgrim was asking for work, any job they liked to give him, provided they left him time to pray; a hut under the shadow of the monastery, and the guaranteed wage of just a slice of bread. As she was not only acute but advanced in spirituality, she very clearly felt that the man was sincere, and that he must be helped in the exceptional work he was undertaking.

"Very well," she said. "Nearly all the work within the enclosure is done by the Sisters: but we indeed want a sacristan, a man who will take our orders to the post and do other little jobs. You will be the man, and you will get the wages you ask for."

She had thought of giving him a gardener's quarters. He blankly refused, and looking round he saw a log-hut outside the yard about a hundred yards off. It was used as a lumber-room, and looked quite like a sentry-box covered with tiles. This cabin leant against a wall and was situated on the border of land belonging to the Poor Clares.

"That will do for me," he said, "I shall stay there."

They gave him two trestles, two boards, a straw mattress, a woollen wrapper stuffed with rags to use as a coverlet: this was all the hovel could hold. When the mattress and planks had to be lifted up, the pilgrim was too worn out by his journey to do it. His swollen and sore feet gave way under the weight; and he was obliged to drag his bed to the hut.

Here he is now a hermit, apparently lost in his often longed-for Nazareth.

To meet his wishes, some little jobs were given him in the days which followed; he was asked to pick lentils; then to repair the enclosure wall, which threatened falling in several places, with dry stone; then to dig a few beds in the garden. The attempts were generally not very successful. The Abbess soon saw that her guest was not accustomed to such work. She let him serve Mass, sweep the chapel, pray bowed and motionless in a corner as long as he wanted to do so; and then shut himself up in the hut, where he gave very few hours to sleep, and many to meditation, reading and writing. She learned by degrees that he was studying theology, and composing several works, especially meditations on the Gospels.

Being quite sure that she had received a holy man, she gave him more and more freedom to live as he was inspired to live, and ordered him to be given only the errands which the attendants could not do as well as he. Lastly, the Sisters were discreet enough to let him long remain ignorant of the fact that they knew his real name and something of his history.

He himself related his start in life in the East. To Colonel de Foucauld he revealed the place of his hermitage, to Monsieur and Madame de Blic he details " his use of his time."

" Coming here without knowing any trade, without a testimonial, with no other papers than my passport, on the sixth day I found out not only how to gain my living, but to gain it in such conditions that I have absolutely what I have longed to have for so many years, and one would say that this place was waiting for me; and, in fact, it was waiting for me, for nothing happens by chance and everything that takes place has been prepared by God: I am a domestic, servant, and menial of a poor religious community.

" You ask me for the details of my life.

" I live in a solitary little house, situated in a close belonging to the Sisters whose happy servant I am. I am there quite alone on the border of the little town : on one side is the Sisters' enclosure, on the other the country, fields, and hillocks; it is a delightful and perfectly solitary hermitage. . . . I get up when my good angel wakens me, and I pray till the *Angelus;* at the *Angelus* I go to the Franciscan convent; then I go down into the grotto which formed part of the house of the Holy Family; I remain there till about 6 o'clock in the morning, saying my Rosary and hearing the Masses which are said in that adorably holy place, where God became incarnate, where the voices of

Jesus, Mary and Joseph echoed for thirty years. It is sweet to feel one is looking at the walls of rock on which the eyes of Jesus rested and which His hands touched.

" At 6 o'clock I go to the Sisters, who are so good to me that they are really *my mothers*. In the sacristy and chapel I prepare what is necessary for Mass and pray. . . . At 7 o'clock I serve Mass. . . . After thanksgiving I put the sacristy and chapel in order. When sweeping is required (on Saturday only) I sweep. On Thursday and Sunday I go and fetch the letters (there is no postman, everybody goes and fetches his letters); I am the Sisters' postman. . . . By the way, put *poste restante* on the addresses no longer; put simply ' Nazareth.' Then I do what I am told, now one little job, now another; very often I draw little pictures (mere elementary drawings), the Sisters want them and get me to do them. . . .

" If there is a little errand, I do it, but it is very rare; in general I spend my whole day doing little jobs in my little room, near the sacristy; about 5 o'clock I prepare whatever is wanted for Benediction, when there is any, which is very often, thank God.

" From then I remain in the chapel till half-past 7 in the evening. Then I return to my hermitage, where I read till 9 o'clock. At 9 o'clock the bell announces evening prayers; I say them and go to bed. I read during my meals; I take them quite alone. I am the only servant, which is very pleasant for me; I see nobody in the world but my confessor every week for confession, and the Sisters when they have something to say to me; which is rare, for they are very silent.

" Besides I spend half an hour before 11 o'clock, and half an hour at 3 o'clock, in the chapel; they are the hours of Sext, None, and Vespers.

" The Sisters supply me with all the books I want; they are infinitely good to me.

" The more you give to God, the more He renders. I thought I gave up all in leaving the world and entering La Trappe, I received more than I had given. . . . Once more I thought I had given all in leaving La Trappe : I have been loaded and overloaded without measure. . . . I infinitely enjoy being poor, dressed as a workman, a servant, in that low condition which was that of Jesus our Lord; and by an overplus of exceptional grace, to be all that in Nazareth."[1]

[1] Letters to M. de Blic, April 24 and November 25, 1897.

He was no longer a religious, but he always lived like one. It must also be added that after being dispensed from his Trappist vows, at Rome he had taken the vow of perpetual chastity under his confessor—a Trappist of Rome; and also this—never to have in his possession or for his own use more than a poor workman has.

In landing, he had brought no luggage. In the hermitage only the smallest amount of furniture could have been listed: a few pictures, a much cherished crucifix inlaid with a piece of the true Cross, then a few books, given or borrowed. Perhaps the number of books exceeded that which would be found in a workman's library, but it might be replied that they were tools.

As to the table, it was neither abundant nor varied. The hermit adopted the diet of the Poor Clares. On Sundays and feast-days a few almonds and dried figs were added. But Charles de Foucauld did not eat any of them. One day one of the lay-sisters found, in one of the chapel stalls, a box in which he had put away the almonds and figs in view of distributing them to the children in the street or country when he went out. At first they readily used to mock the foreigner who walked with downcast eyes and a big rosary at his girdle. Soon they ran after him, begging the dainties which he had for them in his pocket, and with their naked uplifted arms and dancing eyes, they surrounded him with brightness. The other poor soon came to know his charity. They came to find him in his hut, knocking at the door behind which the hermit was studying or praying. One Sunday, towards evening, while the sun was still strong, but when the first fresh breath of night was passing over the stifled earth, three ragged travellers from goodness knows where, going right on begging for everything, stopped before the hermit and said to him:
"We have nothing left to clothe us. See, the night will be cold." He looked at them, was moved with pity, thought of St. Martin, and taking his knife, he cut in two the great woollen mantle which he wore. Then, seizing the spare tunic which was hanging on a nail, he beckoned to the third beggar, the one who had received nothing:
"Come along with me." They both went into the monastery yard, before the portress's lodge.

"Sister," Charles de Foucauld said to the lay-sister, I pray you fit my garment to this unfortunate man; a cut or two of the scissors and a few stitches will do."

"But, Brother Charles, it is Sunday to-day!"

"I will help you; I will cut and then you will sew; we

may work a little, because these poor people are in such need."

Every time he was asked by the rare passers-by, or by the chaplain or Sisters, he put himself out of the way and tried to oblige his neighbours. It was thus that one day he agreed to lie in wait. A jackal was robbing the Poor Clares' poultry-yard. It used to slip into the garden by a certain well-known path between two rocks, and carry off a still cackling hen; the next day it would be off with the best layer, and if there followed a little respite, it was because the fine fellow with the long pointed ears had paid a visit to a neighbour's hen-roost. The country must be rid of this offensive and thieving brute. And who would do it more easily than an ex-cavalry officer? A gun was borrowed from a consular agent; Charles de Foucauld lay hiding, at a good distance from the rock, and began to wait for the jackal. But no sooner was he seated with the loaded gun on his knees than he began reciting the rosary according to the custom which he loved, and to meditate upon the joyful, sorrowful, and glorious mysteries. Time passed delightfully for him. The eyes of the solitary wandered on to the terraces of the town which was going to sleep. He saw before him houses like one another and like our Saviour's former workman's home. He was happy and absent-minded. Mr. Jackal asked for nothing more. He came trotting along, stopped before showing himself, observed that the enemy's mind was elsewhere, entered the poultry-yard, killed a selected hen right off, and then galloped away with it. When the lay-sisters came to question Brother Charles, and ask him about the hunt:

"I have seen nothing," he replied.

This was his first and last lying in wait for game in the hills of Nazareth.

These stories and many others which are told of him, the singularity of his costume, his politeness, his charity, and his long daily prayers attracted the attention of all who lived in Nazareth or spent any time there. He came to be highly regarded: they tried to know why he had come to the country from so far; and as the idea of power, in the popular imagination, rarely goes without gold or precious stones, he was represented as a very rich man, and this gave him a place apart among the servants of the charitable establishments of the town. For instance, at the post-office he met a lay-brother of a Salesian house at Nazareth, and was accosted by him.

"Excuse me," said the brother; "they say lots of things

about you. I should like to know whether they are true?"

"What's the good?"

"It is said that you had a good position in France. ···"

"What position?"

"A Count's."

Brother Charles smiled, and replied carelessly:

"I am an old soldier."

His letters during this period of his life are particularly affectionate. He writes only to his relatives. How often lost in silence, the door of his hut open, gazing at the Eastern heavens, better jewelled with more numerous stars than ours, he thought of his sister and of his sister's children, of the peaceful hills of Barbirey, of his cousin Louis de Foucauld, of his cousins in Paris and Abbé Huvelin, of that little group of dear ones who knew his place of retreat, and wrote regularly to Brother Charles of Jesus, Nazareth. For he finally adopted that name, which hid his own, but disclosed his love. He was in infinite peace. Let me make a sort of psalm with the phrases of joy which are scattered through his letters:

"I am in infinite peace, flooded with peace overflowing.

"If you knew the joys of the religious life, and all the jubilation of my soul!

"How does God repay even here a hundredfold in inward grace what we give unto Him.

"The more I gave up all comforts, the more happiness I have found!

"I praise God daily for the life He has ordained for me, and I am overwhelmed with gratitude. Give thanks and praise with me!"

News comes from France, from the scattered family. He, the hermit, has none to give in return, but he sings the psalm that I have just spoken; and he replies promptly, letting speak each of his childhood's affections, which are now as lively as ever and always referred to God by some quotation betraying the practice of meditation.

He heard that one of his nieces was going to make her first communion: "How I shall be with you on that day!" he wrote. "Look for me quite close to you, in church; before and after and at home. I shall be with you everywhere."

His sister was going to leave Dijon to live in the country:

"My little Mimi, don't be frightened of going to Barbirey or of anything in the world. Fear not to find depression there: believe the experience of your old brother: God is the master of our hearts as well as our bodies: He gives us, as He wills, joy and sorrow, as well as health and sickness. Believe indeed that it is folly to say to yourself: 'This will make me happy, that unhappy'; for happiness or depression do not depend on this or that, but on God, who has a host of means of filling us with joy or sorrow."

His brother-in-law informed him of the birth of a child.

"My dear friend," Brother Charles replies, "how great and wonderful is a soul! Such a soul is your child's, and, after its time of trial it will live for ever in the glory, radiance, beatitude, and ineffable perfection of the elect at the feet of God! ... I am settled in Nazareth. ... I am as happy as one can be down here, in my life of a labouring son of Mary, endeavouring to follow, as far as my moral poverty permits, the vanishing and hidden life of our well-beloved Jesus, in whom I love you with my whole heart."

The envelope contained a second letter for Comte Louis de Foucauld. And Brother Charles added, as a postscript, this recommendation: "Be good enough, I beg you, to forward this letter to Louis de Foucauld. It worries me to make known to the persons who take my letters to the post, the names of those to whom I write: I am solitary, silent and unknown."

The little child of whom I have just spoken died a few months after its birth. Brother Charles consoled the father and mother, as his custom was, by setting heaven's gates ajar. He says how well he understands the parents' sorrow, and then tells them of their son's eternal happiness: "How great he is compared with you and with all of us! how high he is over us! ... None of your children love you as much as he does, because he drinks deeply of the torrent of divine love. ... I have already familiarly invoked my little nephew-saint. ... Pray to him constantly, dear Marie, and thank God well for making you the mother of a saint. A mother lives in her children: you are partly in heaven already! More than ever henceforth you will have 'your conversation in heaven.'"

All the correspondence of this period is in words thus "winged." I should like to quote at full length a very fine series of letters to a Trappist, on monastic obedience. I cannot interrupt my story too often. It ought to picture a life hastening on, and, above all, its example must be made plain.

I shall therefore only say that, during his hermit-life in the Holy Land, the requests for books and the thanks for books sent, are numerous. Brother Charles asked his sister to forward to the East the German translation of the Vulgate and also a history of the Catholic Church in German (he wished to lend them to some German Protestants who were then living in Nazareth); the last edition of two courses of Philosophy in Latin by Father de Mandato and Father Feretti, both Jesuits : the Roman *Ordo* for the breviary and the Mass—" I say the breviary," he added, and in my great love of Rome, as I am not bound to anything, I want to say it as Roman priests say it ";—four volumes by Abbé Darras; a "good" St. John Chrysostom; a little later on he took delight in a New Testament and a prayer-book in Arabic. Prayer, study, and solitude, these were to bring upon him the grace of God.

He was accustomed from the beginning of his conversion and while with the Trappists to go into retreats. He went on a twelve days' retreat at Nazareth, not to speak of one or two shorter ones. It took place at the beginning of November, 1897. The meditations were all written down; I have the text of them before me. They give some idea of his fervour and faith and power of self-analysis. I here give one of them, and reading it reminds one of certain chapters of the *Confessions of St. Augustine*: the same ardour of contrition, the same gratitude, the same frankness.

MYSELF AND MY PAST LIFE — GOD'S MERCY.
(*The Fourteenth Meditation of the Retreat.*)

"Lord Jesus, make Thou my thoughts and words. If I was weak in previous meditations, how much more so in this! . . . It is not material that is wanting . . . on the contrary, it overwhelms me! What mercies there are, God, mercies of yesterday, of to-day, of every moment of my life; before my birth and before time itself! I am submerged in them, flooded by them; they cover and enclose me on all sides. . . . Ah, my God, we have all to sing of Thy mercies, we who are all of us created for eternal glory and redeemed by the blood of Jesus, by Thy blood, dear Lord Jesus, who art close to me in this Tabernacle; but if all of us owe it Thee, how much do I, who have been from my infancy surrounded by so many graces, the son of a holy mother, learning from her to know Thee, to love Thee and to pray to Thee as soon as I could understand a word! Is not my first recollection that of the prayer she made me recite morning and evening : ' O God, bless papa, mamma, grandpapa, grandmamma, Grandmamma Foucauld, and my little sister'? And that pious bringing up! ... those visits to churches ... those flowers placed beneath the crosses, the Christmas cribs, the months of Mary; the little altar in my room, kept for me as long as I had a room to myself at home, and which outlived my faith! the catechisms, the first confessions seen to by a Christian grandfather ... the examples of piety given in my family—I see myself going to church with my father (how long ago that is), with my grandfather; I see my grandmother and my cousins going to Mass every day. ... And that first communion, after a long and careful preparation surrounded with the graces and encouragement of a whole Christian family, under the eyes of those I loved most in all the world, so that all was united together in one day to make me taste all the sweetness of it. ... And then the Catechism of Perseverance under the direction of a good, pious, intelligent, and zealous priest, my grandfather always encouraging me by word and example in the paths of piety; the most pious and most beautiful souls of my family loading me with encouragement and kindness, and Thou, my God, planting in my heart an attachment for them which the storms that followed could not uproot, and which Thou madest use of later on to save me when I was dead and drowned in evil. ... And then when I began to stray away from Thee, in spite of so many graces, with what gentleness didst Thou recall me to Thee by the voice of my grandfather, with what mercy didst Thou prevent me from falling into extreme excesses by keeping in my heart my affection for him! But in spite of all that, unfortunately I forsook Thee more and more, my Lord and my Life—and my own life, too, began to be a death, or rather it was a death in Thine eyes. ... And in that state of death Thou didst still preserve me. ... Thou didst preserve my memories of the past, my esteem of virtue, my friendship—sleeping like fire under ashes, but always existing—for certain beautiful and pious souls, my respect for the Catholic religion and priests: all faith had disappeared, but my respect and esteem remained intact. ... Thou gavest me other graces, O God—Thou didst preserve in me the liking for study, serious reading, beautiful things, the dislike of vice and ugliness. ... I did evil, but neither approved nor loved it. ... Thou madest me feel a sorrowful void, a depression that I experienced then only; ... it used to come upon me every evening, when I was alone in my rooms; ... it kept me dumb and oppressed during socalled fêtes: I organized them, but when the time came I spent them in dumbness, distaste, and infinite boredom. . . . Thou gavest me the vague uneasiness of a bad conscience, which was all asleep yet not quite dead. I never felt such depression, so ill at ease, such anxiety till then. O God, it must have been a gift from Thee; . . . how far I was from suspecting it! . . . How good Thou art. . . . And by this invention of Thy love, at the same time as Thou didst prevent my soul from drowning beyond recovery, Thou didst take care of my body: for had I then died, I should have been in hell. . . . Riding accidents, miraculously avoided and averted! The duels that Thou didst prevent! During expeditions, the perils that Thou didst turn aside! The many and great dangers of travelling, through which Thou hast brought me as if by a miracle. My health unaffected even in the most unwholesome places, and despite such great fatigue! . . . O God, how Thy hand was upon me, and how little I felt it! how good Thou art! How didst Thou watch over me! How didst Thou cover me with Thy wings when I did not even believe in Thine existence! And whilst Thou wert thus guarding me Thou didst deem it was now time for me to return to the fold. . . . Thou didst unloose in my despite all the evil ties that would have kept me far from Thee. . . . Thou didst even untie the good bonds which would have prevented me re-entering into the bosom of that family, in which Thou desiredst to make me find salvation, and which would have hindered me from being one day all Thine. . . . At the same time, Thou gavest me a life of serious studies, a hidden life, solitary and poor. . . . My heart and mind were far from Thee, but yet I lived in a less tainted atmosphere; not in the light nor in goodness, far from it; . . . but the mire was no longer so deep, nor the evil so odious; . . . the place was being cleared out little by little; . . . the water of the deluge still covered the earth, but it was subsiding more and more, and the rain was no longer falling. . . . Thou hadst broken the obstacles, softened the soul, prepared the ground by burning the thorns and bushes. . . . By stress of circumstances didst Thou force me to be chaste, and soon, at the end of the winter of '86, didst Thou bring me back to my family in Paris, and chastity became my delight and my heart's desire. It is Thou, O God, who didst that, Thou alone; unhappily, I had nothing to do in it. How good hast Thou been! From what sad and guilty relapses hast Thou mercifully saved me! In all this, Thy hand alone wrought the beginning, the middle, and the end. How good Thou art! It was necessary in order to prepare my soul for the truth; the devil's power is too great over an unchaste soul for the truth to enter in. . . . Thou, O God, couldst not enter a soul where the demon of uncleanness held the mastery. . . . Thou desiredst to enter mine, O Good Shepherd, and Thou thyself didst drive out Thine enemy, . . . and after having driven him out by force, in spite of me, seeing my infirmity and how incapable I was of myself to keep my soul pure, Thou didst set a good guardian to guard it, so strong and so gentle that not only did he not leave the least entrance for the demon of impurity, but made me feel the need and the charm of the delights of chastity. . . . O God, how shall I praise Thy mercies! . . . And after having emptied my soul of its filth and having entrusted it to Thine angels, Thou wouldst return to it anew, O God! For after receiving all these graces, it yet knew Thee not! Thou didst continually work in it and on it. Thou didst transform it with a sovereign power and astonishing rapidity, and it was completely ignorant of Thee. . . . Then didst Thou inspire it with a taste for virtue, for pagan virtue; Thou madest me seek it in the books of pagan philosophers, and I found there nothing but emptiness and dislike. . . . Then didst Thou let me see a few pages of a Christian book, and madest me feel their warmth and beauty. . . . Thou madest me suspect that perhaps I should there find, if not the truth (I did not think that men could know it), at least the teachings of virtue, and Thou inspiredst me to seek lessons of an altogether pagan virtue in Christian books. . . . Thus didst Thou familiarize me with the mysteries of religion. . . . At the same time, Thou didst knit more and more closely the bonds which united me to finer souls; Thou broughtest me back to the family, to which I was passionately attached in my young days, in childhood. . . . For these souls Thou madest me feel again my old admiration, and them Thou didst inspire to receive me as the prodigal son who was not even made to feel that he had ever abandoned the paternal roof. Thou madest them as kind to me as I might have expected had I never erred. . . . I drew nearer and nearer to this well-beloved family. There I lived in such an atmosphere of virtue that my life recovered visibly; it was spring restoring life to earth after the winter; . . . it is in that gentle sun that the desire for goodness grew, and the dislike of evil, the impossibility of backsliding into certain faults, the striving after goodness. . . . Thou hadst driven evil out of my heart; my good angel came back, and Thou gavest me a terrestrial angel as well. . . . At the beginning of October, '86, after six months of family life, I admired and desired goodness, but Thee I knew not. . . . What devices, O God of goodness, didst Thou use to reveal Thyself to me! What circuitous ways! What gentle and strong outward means? What a series of astonishing circumstances, where all united to urge me towards Thee; unexpected solitude, emotions, illnesses of beloved ones, ardent feelings of the heart, the return to Paris after an amazing event. . . . And what interior graces! the desire for solitude, meditation, pious reading, the desire to go into Thy churches, though I did not believe in Thee, the trouble of my soul, the anguish, the striving after truth, the prayer: ' O God, if Thou dost exist, make me know it.' All that was Thy work, O God, Thy work, Thine alone. . . . A fine soul was helping Thee, but by its silence, its gentleness, goodness, and perfection: it let itself be seen, it was good and exhaled its attractive perfume, but it did not act. Thou, O Jesus my Saviour, Thou didst all within me as well as without. Thou drewest me to virtue by the beauty of a soul in which virtue appeared so beautiful that it ravished my heart for ever. . . . Thou drewest me to the truth by the beauty of this soul. Thou then gavest me four graces: the first was to inspire me with this thought: Since this man is so intelligent, the religion which he believes so firmly could not be the folly I think it. The second was to inspire me with this thought: Since religion is not a folly, is the truth which on the earth is in no other nor in any philosophical system perhaps there? The third was to say to myself: ' Let us then examine this religion; let us take a professor of the Catholic religion, a learned priest, and let us see what it is, and whether we must believe what it says.' The fourth was the incomparable grace of applying to M. Huvelin for my religious lessons. In making me enter his confessional, between the 27th and 30th, I think that Thou, O God, gavest me every kind of good. If there is joy in heaven over one sinner being converted, there was joy when I entered that confessional! . . . What a blessed day, what a day of benediction! . . . And since that day, my whole life has been only a chain of benedictions! Thou didst put me under the wings of that saint, and I remained there. Thou didst open the door by his hand, and there has been only grace upon grace. I asked for religious lessons; he made me kneel down and make my confession, and on the spot sent me to communion. . . . I cannot help crying when I think of it, I don't want to check these tears, they are only too fitting, O God! What streams of tears ought to flow from my eyes at the thought of so many mercies! How good Thou hast been! How happy I am! What have I done for this? Since then, O God, there has been nothing but a chain of ever-increasing graces—a rising tide, always rising; direction, and such direction ! prayer, holy reading, daily attendance at Mass laid down from the first day of my new life; frequent communion, frequent confessions every few weeks; direction becoming more and more intimate and frequent, enveloping my whole life and making it a life of obedience in the smallest things, and obedience to such a master! Communion becoming almost daily, . . . the desire for the religious life growing, gaining strength, . . . exterior events independent of my will forcing me to detach myself from material things which had a great deal of charm for me, and which would have held back my soul, would have bound it to the earth. Thou didst violently shatter these bonds as well as many others. My God, how good Thou art to have shattered all around me, to have so reduced to nothing all that would have prevented me from being Thine alone! . . . The deepening feeling of the vanity, the falseness of the worldly life, and of the distance which exists between the perfect evangelical life and that which one leads in the world. . . . The tender and increasing love of Thee, Lord Jesus, the taste for prayer, the faith in Thy word, the deep sense of the duty of almsgiving, the desire to follow Thee, the words of M. Huvelin's sermon: ' Thou hast so taken the lowest place that no one can snatch it from Thee!' so inviolably graven on my soul; the thirst to offer Thee the greatest sacrifice I could possibly offer Thee by leaving for ever a family in which all my happiness was centred and by going far away from it to live and to die; . . . the striving after a life like Thine, in which I can completely partake of Thy abjection, poverty, humble labour, burial, Thy hiddenness, a striving so clearly shown in a last retreat at Clamart. . . . On January 15, 1890, the sacrifice accomplished, and that great grace being given me by Thy hand. . . . La Trappe, . . . daily communion, . . . what I learned during seven years of religious life, . . . the graces of Notre-Dames-des-Neiges, the graces of Notre-Dame-du-Sacré-Cœur, . . . the graces of Stauëli, . . . the graces of Rome, the town of St. Peter and the martyrs, the Holy Father, the Basilicas, the churches, the thousand marks of the Apostles and Martyrs, . . . theology, philosophy, readings, the exceptional vocation to

NAZARETH AND JERUSALEM

a life of abjection and obscurity. After three and a half years waiting the Very Reverend General told me, on January 23, 1897, that God's will is for me to follow the attraction which urges me to leave the Trappist Order for the life of abjection, humble toil and deep obscurity, of which I have had the vision for so long, . . . My departure for the Holy Land, . . . the pilgrimage, the arrival in Nazareth, . . . the first Wednesday that I spent there, O God, through the intercession of St. Joseph, Thou madest me a menial at the convent of St. Clare. . . . The peace, the happiness, consolations, graces, and marvellous felicity which I feel. . : . *Misericordias Domini in æternum cantabo.* . . . *Venite et videte, quoniam suavis est Dominus.* . . . O God, I can only tremble at such mercies; I can only beg the Holy Virgin and all the Saints and holy souls to give thanks for me, for I faint beneath the load of graces. . . . Oh! my Spouse, what hast Thou not done for me! What then wouldst Thou have of me that Thou hast thus overwhelmed me? What dost Thou expect of me to have thus overpowered me? O God, thank Thyself within me, within me do Thou Thyself create gratitude, thanks, fidelity, and love; I succumb, I swoon, O God; transform my thoughts and words and works, so that everything may thank and glorify Thee in me. Amen, amen, amen."

Thus the summer, autumn, and winter of 1897 were spent in Nazareth. About this period the renown of Brother Charles of Jesus reached as far as Jerusalem. The Abbess of the Poor Clares of Nazareth had written to the Abbess of Jerusalem about the benevolent servant, who dressed like a pauper, spoke and wrote like a scholar and prayed like a saint. Mother Elizabeth du Calvaire wished to see and question him. She had founded two monasteries and was, indeed, a sort of Superioress-General. They therefore hastened to obey her. She was a most prudent woman, and, in the circumstances, feared that the Nazareth community might be the victim of an adventurer. She would judge the case.

Brother Charles was therefore sent by Mother St. Michael, who commissioned him to carry an important letter to the Poor Clares of Jerusalem. He at once assented, and said that he was ready to start: he had no business to settle, no luggage to prepare. They suggested that he should take some provisions with him. He refused, saying that he knew the language of the country, and would beg his bread in the villages.

He left as he had come, alone on foot, and passed through

Galilee and Samaria, thinking of the Master who had made this long journey so many times for him and for us all. Christians gave him the bread and water he asked for; they put him up, nor did the Turks refuse him. Very tired, he came in sight of the walls on June 24, the feast of St. John the Baptist, but as night was falling he slept on the ground in a field near the convent.

Next day he was received by the Abbess, whose distrust did not last long after he had spoken for only five minutes. They could not think of letting the traveller, whose feet had been made sore by a bad pair of sandals, set out again for some time. There, too, he had an empty hut outside the enclosure, and built at some distance from another, in which lived a negro and his wife. As guardians of the Sisters' little ground, Brother Charles asked to be allowed to be the neighbour of these poor people, and to stop in the empty hut. He refused to lodge in the chaplain's rooms, which the Abbess placed at his disposal for a few days.

To explain this offer, we must say that Mother Elizabeth du Calvaire knew by the letter from Nazareth whom she was receiving, and that from her first meeting with Brother Charles, he saw that he was known, and had spoken of himself more fully than usual, telling what trials he had undergone and for what he had come to the East. He had related some incidents of his infancy, his conversion, his years in La Trappe, and let it just be seen that the hardest sacrifice for him had been, and still was, his separation from an excellent and beloved and united family. Then suddenly he ceased speaking. The man of silence reappeared. The servant had taken leave of the Abbess and begged permission to lodge outside the enclosure, not far from the negro guardian, in the country near the Holy Town.

In the evening Mother Elizabeth, speaking to her daughters, said to them: "Nazareth was not mistaken: he is truly a man of God; we have a saint in the house."

This venerable and highly spiritual woman was, as we shall see, to have a decisive influence in the determination to which Charles de Foucauld came less than two years later, to prepare for the priesthood.

He was at Jerusalem for some weeks at least; he led the same life there in the same conditions as at Nazareth, and he wrote to his relations in France: " I have just received your letter at Jerusalem, where I have definitely settled down in the Convent of the Poor Clares. The Mother Abbess of the Jerusalem Convent, who is the foundress of the two monasteries, asked me to come here. I do not know why she made me come, for I am not much good; I believe it is simply for her to be able to show charity towards me and to overwhelm me with kindness. She is a saint. . . . How beautiful God makes souls, and how good He is to let me see them! What treasures of moral beauty there are in the depths of these cloisters, and what fair flowers blossom there, for God alone! . . . I have a little house with its back against the great wall of the enclosure. . . . I live like a hermit, or an independent workman, getting all I ask for, and working as and when I wish at very easy work that they have been so considerate as to give me, so that I may say that I gain my bread. . . .

" My life here is exactly the same as at Nazareth with this difference, that I am still more solitary—that is to say, better. The convent is over a mile from Jerusalem on the Bethania road, in an admirable position, on the border of the Vale of Cedron, opposite the Mount of Olives. From my windows I see all Jerusalem, Gethsemane, all the Mount of Olives, Bethania, and, in the distance, the mountains of Moab and Edom, which rise up like a dark wall on the other side of the Jordan; it is extremely beautiful. . . . On the other side of the convent you can see the hills of Bethlehem to the South and those of St. John the Baptist (his birthplace and the deserts in which he lived) to the West. . . . The Cenacle, the road that Jesus took with His Apostles after the wedding-feast to go to the Garden of the Agony, the garden itself, the palace of the High Priest to which He was led after having been bound, Herod's Palace, Calvary, the cupola of the basilica of the Holy Sepulchre, the place of the Ascension, dear and beloved Bethania, the sole place in which our Lord was always well received, the whole road which leads from Jerusalem to Bethania which our Lord followed so often, Bethphage the temple in which Jesus so often taught, Siloë with the pool in which the man blind from birth bathed his eyes : all this is under our eyes and cries aloud, singing without ceasing of Jesus. . . .

" Why cannot you come here ? how you would enjoy it! how touched you would feel and happy to know that Jesus was speaking to your heart!

" I never go into the town, nobody comes to the convent; I have therefore a marvellous solitude which I profoundly enjoy. . . . God is good! . . . The farther I go, the more joy I find. I must humble myself for it : it shows I am not strong enough to endure crosses, but I must also be grateful to God, who, in His tender care, is so good as to save this poor shorn lamb from the least wind."[1]

Brother Charles rarely left his solitude except to go to the chapel. He used to say : " I have quite the life of a monk, except the habit."

He soon returned to Nazareth, but he really considered himself as a servant of both monasteries, and as Mother Elizabeth du Calvaire had expressed the desire that he would come back and live in Jerusalem, he returned there before the end of the year. What did it matter to him to be here or there, as the life was similar and the soul in safety ?

No one escapes entirely from his neighbour's eye. However hidden Charles de Foucauld might be, he was esteemed. He spoke very little; he avoided entering into conversation with the few people whom he met on his way; the Abbess, remaining in the enclosure, only spoke to him on rare occasions and if he wanted a permission of her; nevertheless, as at Nazareth, a murmured opinion at the outset, made up of astonishment, of hesitating admiration, of restrained but keen esteem, was being formed around this mysterious person. Like one of the poor he was seen going daily to fetch his meals from the monastery door and then returning without ceasing to read a book which he invariably carried; he was seen taking Holy Communion each morning, serving Masses, scrupulously doing the little jobs which were given him, spending an hour and a half after his midday dinner in the chapel, going back in the evening, if there was a service; they knew that he slept on two boards covered with a mat, with a stone for pillow, as at Nazareth; that he slept barely more than two hours a night; that he was extremely temperate and equally charitable. The Arabic or French speaking people who had conversed with him remembered his very kind eyes and his brotherly ways. They also wondered at the joy which they detected in this homeless man, without relations, riches, and without position.

Several in the country about Jerusalem and the town called him "the Poor Clares' holy hermit." Some inquired if they might consult him. The poor tried to get in his path when he went out.

At the French Consulate, where he sometimes went to transact business for the community, he was received with honour, and at once shown into the drawing-room in spite of his extraordinary and unprepossessing costume.

[1] Letters of October 15, and November 10, 1898.

The negro himself and his wife, neighbours of the hut, whom he always called "brother or sister," treated him with a great deal of consideration. One day, in order to try him, the Abbess said to the guardian: "Take this to the workman." "To the gentleman," quickly replied the negro.

A short time after he had settled in Jerusalem, and at the end of a retreat he had just made, Brother Charles declared that he would henceforth take to the Trappists' diet; at midday, milk-soup, figs, and some honey; in the evening, a piece of bread of the same weight as a Poor Clare's—180 grammes.[1] During Advent of 1898 and Lent of 1899, he contented himself with a piece of bread at midday and in the evening. Some nuns of the monasteries in the Holy Land remembered these things, and have written of them to me. One of them remarks by the way: "Trappist he remained in the full sense of the term; in all circumstances he used to remark, 'As the Trappist Rule says,' and this Rule he always carried about him."

Let it not be imagined, as certain people in the world might perhaps think, that piety and regular meditation had made of Charles de Foucauld a mawkish, insipid, and formal man. The man who lived the life of which I have just spoken proved that he had the gift of strength. Generally he exercised it in subduing himself; on some occasions, and when it was necessary, he showed hardness to others. One day a troop of Italian beggars succeeded in getting into the lay-sisters' yard; they made a great uproar because the Sisters rightly refused to give them dinner. The poor girls, insulted and threatened, did not know what to do, when Charles happened to arrive. Without reflecting, without saying a word, he threw himself on one of the worst fellows, seized him round the body and put him out; then it was the turn of a second and a third. With incredible and masterly skill, he succeeded in this little police operation in one minute. His eyes were blazing.

Next moment Brother Charles passed before the lay-sisters' lodge:

"Perhaps I have disedified you!" he said.

"Oh no; you have delivered us. Thank you!"

When she had seen him live thus for several months, and was sure of his great intelligence and singular virtue, Mother Elizabeth began to exhort him to take Holy Orders. She showed him that he would do much more good by becoming a missionary; but he changed the con-

[1] About six ounces.

versation, and went back to the hermitage. As she was a woman of very strong will and accustomed to guide souls that do not give in to every argument, but only to one, she returned to the subject, and observed to Brother Charles that, if he became a priest, there would daily be one more Mass in the world, and an infinite number of graces for men; that it was then in his power to pour down a fresh blessing on the earth, or to keep it in heaven. If he had received gifts, which he had increased by study and a long spiritual work, was it to make use of them for himself alone? Brother Charles, whom the thought of honouring still more the Blessed Sacrament had moved to the depths of his soul, reflected on the words which had been said to him, and then replied: "To be a priest is to put myself forward, and I am made for the hidden life."

The Abbess decided to procure one more holy priest for the Church, and set her daughters to pray, and, after some time, the solitary, having seen her again, said to her: "Write yourself to my director," and this was done.

Now, at this time an evil dispute had arisen with the Poor Clares of Nazareth, about a piece of land which belonged to them—the piece, I suppose, on which was situated the hut that Brother Charles had lived in. They wrote, begging the latter to retake possession of this disputed piece of their ground, to till it a little, and to undertake to arrange the difference, for no one could succeed in it as well as he.

He at once set out, accompanied by a priest who was going down to preach a retreat there. The travellers went from Jerusalem to Jaffa, where they embarked for Haifa, and, from there, reached Nazareth at the beginning of 1899.

Abbé Huvelin had been told of all these things by his penitent, who asked him for counsel. He had long thought that Charles de Foucauld was intended for the priesthood, and he had let him know it. In the little hut at Nazareth, Brother Charles had at last formed the resolution of preparing himself for Holy Orders. But he could not deny his particular vocation, studied, meditated, and proved for so many years; it was necessary to find a solution to the problem: to live as a priest, and also as a hermit. Where could he live thus? and how?

This man, tormented by an overflowing imagination which was at times chimerical, always grandiose in the choice of its dream, would have quickly made his decision; he would have bought the Mount of the Beatitudes; he would have set up a hermitage on the summit, and there quite alone—or perhaps with a few Little Brothers whose coming he always hoped for—he would have guarded that sacred spot; he would have adored the Blessed Sacrament, having brought it among fierce populations; he would have received the passing Bedouins and the pilgrims who ascended in the footsteps of Jesus Christ. A contemplative, unprotected, austere, and charitable priest, " he would have preached the Gospel in silence."

The book of intimate notes is here very touching. One finds in it the purity of intention, the generosity of this solitary who, in his log-hut, meditating on the near future, was only concerned with his own effacement and the glory of God. Here is what he writes:

" I believe it my duty to try and buy the probable site of the Mount of the Beatitudes. Clearly seeing that, either on account of obstacles placed by the Turkish Government, or on account of their actual burdens, the Franciscans cannot take upon themselves to set up immediately, nor in a given time, an altar with a tabernacle and a chaplain, . . . I cannot make any better suggestion to them than to take upon myself to maintain on the top of the mount an altar and a tabernacle in which the Blessed Sacrament will be reserved, and a chaplain entrusted to say Mass there every day, on condition that, whenever the Franciscans wish to take upon themselves the keeping up of the altar, tabernacle, and chaplain, the place shall immediately be handed over to them by me or my heirs.

"I had at first thought of setting up a hermit chaplain there, in a poor room, and to settle down near him, to serve him as servant and sacristan. But I find that I cannot on any account impose these charges on my family. Another means must therefore be found. I see only one: it is to be myself the poor chaplain of this poor sanctuary."

Brother Charles, continuing his meditation upon this subject, asks himself whether he will thus fill his vocation better, which is "to imitate, in the most possible and perfect way, our Lord Jesus in His hidden life." And he replies affirmatively, comparing what he does in Nazareth with what he would do on the Mount of the Beatitudes.

" Faith in the word of God and of His Church can be practised equally well everywhere, but there, on the Mount of the Beatitudes, in destitution, isolation, in the midst of very malevolent Arabs, I shall, so as not to lose courage, need a firm and constant faith in these words: *Seek ye the kingdom of God, and all things shall be added unto you.* . . .

Here, on the contrary, I lack nothing, and am safe. It is *there* then that my faith will be best exercised.

"There I shall be able to do infinitely more for my neighbour by the sole offering up of the holy sacrifice, . . . by setting up a tabernacle which will invisibly sanctify the environs by the simple presence of the Holy Sacrament, as our Saviour in His mother's womb sanctified the house of John, . . . or else by pilgrimages, . . . or by hospitality, alms, and the charity I shall strive to give to all.

"*Here,* my condition is lower in itself; *there,* it will be, in my eyes, of an infinite height, for nothing in the world seems to me greater than a priest. But where is there a closer imitation of our Lord? The priest more perfectly imitates our Lord, the Most High Priest, who offers Himself up daily. I must put humility where our Lord put it, . . . I must practise it in the priesthood as He did.

"*Here* I have more distractions through my surroundings. . . . *There* I can be much more before the Holy Sacrament, for I shall be able to keep at His feet part of the night. . . .

"Although *here* the abjection of my state be, at first sight, greater, *there* I shall be subject to ever so many more humiliations. *Here,* in my own eyes, I am above my rank; . . . *there,* an ignorant and incapable priest, I shall be far beneath my office in my own opinion. . . . Appearing in a strange habit, asking to live a special life, to set up a tabernacle in a holy place, the authenticity of which is disputable (though I have no doubt about it), from the first I shall be the butt of all sorts of mockeries, rebuffs, and contradictions. . . . Alone in a desert, with an indispensable native Christian, in the midst of a wild and hostile population, . . . courage will find much more field for its exercise."

He ends his "election" by giving a definition of himself. Who is it, he asks, who thus weighs the pros and cons? "A sinner, an unworthy, poor, ignorant fellow, yet a soul of good-will, desiring all that God desires, and that alone."

Such are the principal ends that Brother Charles proposed to himself, when he thought of buying the Mount of the Beatitudes. They are those of a great soul. In the sequel, if he pursued them otherwise and in other countries, one observes that they never ceased to be present in his mind. In other places he was what he contemplated being on the Mount where our Lord preached the eight Beatitudes of which the world knew not.

In June, 1900, Brother Charles, having come to a decision, set out and reached Jerusalem. He reached that town on the eve of the Feast of the Sacred Heart.

He wished to see Mgr. L. Piavi, for the authority to set up as a hermit priest on the top of the Mount of the Beatitudes could only be given by the Patriarch. No doubt in this interview he could also get the proposed Rule which he had drawn up for himself and the future " Little Brothers of the Sacred Heart " approved. Abbé Huvelin had only reluctantly accepted this idea. He knew he had the care of an extraordinary soul which " upset all estimates," and that is why he dare not go so far as a formal veto. But the terms which he used involved a forcible warning. He refused to decide : " My dear child, I have no light about that, and only see the objections; and I fear there is self-will beneath your self-sacrifice and piety."

The day after his arrival in Jerusalem, Brother Charles went up early to Calvary and heard a Mass; then he directed his steps to the patriarchate. In what a dress and in how pitiable a condition! He was not a traveller who had a change of dress in a bag, or possessed the wherewithal to buy a new one. On the way his sandals must have given out on the road; he had replaced them by mere bits of wood strapped together. Bands of thick paper tied up with string hid the holes in his breeches, broken at both knees. Besides, the poor traveller, walking all day long in the height of summer, without any precaution, had had a terrible sunstroke; his eyelids, forehead, and cheeks were swollen and freckled. When such a ragamuffin asked to be received by Mgr. Piavi, the staff of the patriarchate naturally offered some objections. It was only after waiting a long time, and on his renewed affirmation that he wished to speak to the Patriarch himself, that Brother Charles was admitted to his Beatitude.

Mgr. Piavi listened to him; then, imagining that he had to do with one of the visionaries who are often found in the East and elsewhere, and not suspecting that before him was a man of powerful mind and heroic virtue, he replied : " I will think about it, and now withdraw for a while."

He reflected indeed and made inquiries; he heard something of Brother Charles's exceptional life, and tried to get this queer petitioner to return to the patriarchate. But the dream was over. Brother Charles considered the rebuff a sign of the divine will. He therefore returned to Nazareth. At the same time, and whilst he yet thought himself actually in possession of the Mount of the Beatitudes, he discovered that he had been tricked by the seller, and that the latter—a born German—had sold the land on which the altar and cabin were to be raised without having any rights. The cash paid was lost.

Brother Charles tells us in his letters how he bore these deceptions and humiliations; and in doing so unsuspectingly sings his own praise.

"I saw the Patriarch, and I told him what I had to say to him. And, although he dismissed me quickly enough, I am very pleased. . . . I am in deep peace and great joy: I have but one thing to fear; being unfaithful to grace. . . ."[1]

"My desire for Holy Orders is stedfast, but all the rest is in doubt. . . . Be very certain of one thing, my dear; it is that the will of God will be done: either by men, or despite of them, He will do for us what is best. Don't be grieved because I shall not go to France this year. Perhaps, without knowing it, I am on the point of going there. . . ."[2]

"Do not let us attach importance to the events of this life, nor to material things; they are but as dreams after a night's carousal. . . . What is left us at the hour of death, save our merits and our sins?"[3]

Abbé Huvelin encouraged his penitent to prepare for the priesthood; he thought that the preparation would be short, on account of the philosophy and theology already learnt, and he hoped, as the idea had struck Brother Charles, it would take place at La Trappe of Notre-Dame-des-Neiges. Since the attempt made on Mgr. Piavi had not succeeded, yes, indubitably until the priesthood, it would be wise to ask the Vivarais Abbey, where the training was perfect, for a refuge. Besides, there was no hurry; he himself proposed in good time to take the necessary steps with the Father Abbot and the Bishop. The poor curate of Saint Augustine's was very poorly indeed, and, as he said, "enclosed in a network of pains." He wrote pretty frequent notes, in which abandoned plans and present ones were passed in review one after another. But the slowness of the mails, the impossibility of making themselves entirely understood at such distances, the violent instinctive need which urges us to seize upon the fringe of the morrow before us, overcame Charles de Foucauld's patience. He hastened things; he sent a note to tell Abbé Huvelin, and started for France.

[1] Letter to a friend, June 28, 1900.
[2] Letter to Madame de Blic, July 10, 1900.   [3] Ibid., July 21, 1900.

NAZARETH AND JERUSALEM

He left the Holy Land at the beginning of August, 1900, taking with him only a breviary and an old basket containing his food. He crossed the sea on deck, in the fourth class, and no doubt unknown. He went where he was called by a will which only unfolds its secrets little by little, but which clearly and with suavity orders what is essential for each day. He felt sure that he ought, henceforth, to accept the priesthood from which the thought of his unworthiness at first and for long had kept him away; he was sure that his vocation was to bear the Host into wild countries, among infidels, and to live ever adoring it in silence, but preaching only by the heroic charity which it instilled into his heart. But as he watched the houses of Jaffa and the land behind them fade away, he was in the deepest ignorance as to the country and people to whom he would soon be sent. The time for that revelation had not yet come.

In Palestine and Judea the renown of Brother Charles remained. Already legend had taken possession of the story of the hermit of Nazareth and Jerusalem and embellished it with its flowers, so often unprofitable and vain. It was rumoured in the villages that Brother Charles liked to be let down to the bottom of dried-up wells, and, being quite sure of being undisturbed there, prayed and meditated for hours. There was no truth in the story nor in several others like it, except the veneration which had inspired them.

The long years spent in the East were a time of preparation for Charles de Foucauld. They had accustomed him to a solitary life, to discipline without witnesses, to work without a set programme. He had served his apprenticeship, which would permit him to support much harder trials without weakness, with the joy of the one who obeys his vocation. But he did not know these things; he only went forward to meet them with confidence.

CHAPTER VII

Charles de Foucauld a Priest—The Desert Road

THE direction of a soul, two thousand five hundred miles away, is no easy thing.

What was Abbé Huvelin going to think of this sudden return to France? His advice had not been followed; the journey had been undertaken in spite of a telegram saying "Remain at Nazareth." He was at first displeased and troubled, but he had hardly seen his terrible penitent again, when he, like the others, submitted to the charm, and recognized his utter good faith and, what was much more and much better, the mysterious and certain call which Charles de Foucauld had obeyed.

At first, and when he had in hand Charles de Foucauld's letter telling of his coming, Abbé Huvelin, always quickly roused and smart at repartee, exclaimed: "The ball is shot; who will stop it?" Another letter came on August 16. Brother Charles had landed at Marseilles, and following the attraction of a former devotion, had run to Sainte-Baume, so as to pray to Mary Magdalen; he was now going to take one of the first trains for Paris, and, if he did not find M. Huvelin at Rue de Laborde, he would go to Fontainebleau, where, in fact, the Abbé was ill as usual and tormented with gout. M. Huvelin then decided to go back to Paris; he received the dear, strangely dressed hermit, who looked very tired—as anyone would be. He scolded him a little and then listened to him. Not having seen one another for so many years, they had a thousand things to say to each other. Twenty-four hours were not too many to tell, explain, and arrange everything. On seeing his penitent going away, Abbé Huvelin wrote these lines: "He dined, slept in the house, and had breakfast with me, and took the road to Notre-Dame-des-Neiges and Rome. . . . He is a very holy soul. He wants to be a priest. I showed him how. He had little, too little money: I gave him a little. He knew my mind very well. I had told him about it in a telegram; but something stronger drives him on, and one can only admire and love him."

I can imagine Brother Charles, in his third-class carriage, on this journey. He is sitting near a window.

Already reassured and quieted by the approbation he has received and the undiminished affection of his guide, he at times stops praying to look at the landscape. How this fresh scenery touches the traveller, how sweetly it speaks to him of former days! He is going down the valley of the Rhone; in his sensitive soul he finds an image of one of our great rivers which flow, reflecting the countryside, green even in summer; he beholds a picture of the mountains in the distance, the mist of which always softens the ridges and the line of the heights. I see him getting out of the express, and taking a slow train, accustomed to long delays, and about to enter into the valleys and slopes of the Ardèche. Those around him are astonished; they wonder who is this singular man, half monk, half layman, bareheaded and untonsured, dressed in a whitish cotton robe, with a rosary round his waist. He looks like a very poor man, hollow-featured; he goes along with downcast eyes, without bothering about the sun, or the laughter, or the raillery, or the pity, perhaps, that he excites in passing.

At what station did he stop to climb the last slopes which lead to Notre-Dame-des-Neiges? One can go as far as La Bastide-Saint-Laurent. But he who followed the counsels of poverty and mortification in the least things, must, I imagine, have got off the train long before Saint-Laurent, to make the long climb while thinking of Calvary, and of his approaching priesthood, of the years spent in La Trappe, and, now and then, of the splendour of the high plateaux of heather and rocks which, at this hour of sunset, displayed for a solitary traveller and God their treasures of colour, outline, and perfume. He was mistaken in thinking that he was alone in these great open spaces. Poor people like him, but who had always been so—wanderers more or less steady, more or less crippled, young or old, whose favourite trade is going from one shake-down to another with outstretched hand—were travelling by the same road or mountain paths. He, when he came in, altogether done up and brown with dust, found more than half a dozen of them at the abbey door, between the long low façade and the full-grown trees planted by the old monks. The brother-porter was not expecting him. He had not known Charles de Foucauld, a novice of Notre-Dame, ten years earlier. When he came out of his lodge, at the hour provided for by the regulations, to count the guests that the monastery would receive that evening for the charity of Christ, if he noticed in the darkness that one of the poor people was whiter than the others, it was to smile at his get-up. He had seen all sorts of them. So he only counted his boarders and said :

"Come in, my friends; you will get some soup, and then a nice corner to sleep in."

Brother Charles, glad of such an opportunity for following his Master, took good care not to give his name. Like the others, he ate his bowl of hot soup, slept with them in the barn, and only made himself known next morning when the convent bell rang for first Mass.

There, the incident is still fresh in all memories. To the old Brother who told me of it I remarked that the porter was really not very clear-sighted to be so mistaken.

"Ha!" he replied, laughing heartily, "Father de Foucauld looked so pitiful : he was dusty to the shoulders, and around his body, sir, a rosary long and big and heavy enough for tethering a calf!"

The laugh was very frank, but edification pervaded it.

Dom Martin welcomed ex-Brother Marie-Albéric, and at once zealously set to work to get the Bishop of Viviers to have him amongst the clergy of the diocese. He succeeded; for testimonials sought from several quarters represented Charles de Foucauld as a man of high virtue. Between the Abbot of La Trappe and de Foucauld, it was agreed that after a short stay in Rome he should return to Notre-Dame-des-Neiges, and there prepare for the priesthood. What was he going to do in Rome? At the moment of taking Holy Orders and of choosing his final abode, from which perhaps he would never return, he wanted to speak to some whom he had known there: and I hardly doubt that among the subjects about which he proposed to talk to them, the principal one was that dear foundation of the Little Brothers of the Sacred Heart, his dream now seven years old, the hope in which he took delight; that the hermitage amongst the Musulmans, the difficult and hard enterprise of poor Charles of Jesus, might not die with him.

Dom Martin let him go, after making him give up costumes more or less Eastern while travelling in Europe, and giving him one of the black habits which the La Trappe lay-brothers wear.

At the beginning of September, Brother Charles, having made a short stay in Milan, was in Rome.

"I am at Rome, in a little nook that God seems to have prepared on purpose; just opposite the Fathers of the Holy Sacrament, who have It exposed day and night at Saint-Claude-des-Bourguignons. These good Fathers whom I asked for hospitality and who could not give it me for want of room, found me a cabin in a very pious house, where I am as tranquil and solitary as possible, and can enjoy the Blessed Sacrament with as much facility as if I were in the convent itself.

"I think that I wrote you that it is no longer a question of my living on the Mount of the Beatitudes: according to the Abbé's advice, after being ordained priest, I shall return to Nazareth, where I shall continue to live as a priest, but in the shade."[1]

Even in Rome he led a hermit's life, hardly going out of the church close by, in which, day and night, the Blessed Sacrament was exposed. He studied theology there; he usually read on his knees the big books that he brought in; from time to time he raised his eyes towards Him of whom the books spoke to him; he prayed by way of relaxation, and from the morning Angelus to the evening Angelus, the hours passed as calmly as at Nazareth. He would have liked the desert: at any rate he found out and made himself a solitude everywhere. Two of the professors he wished to consult were in Rome. He saw them. A third religious, his friend, came back about September 20. Then, when it was time to leave the Holy City for shutting himself up in La Trappe, Charles de Foucauld impatiently awaited an answer from Abbé Huvelin: permission to stop on the way back, to go up to Barbirey. For ten years he had not seen his sister, nor his nephews and nieces whom he did not know, nor the nook in the hills of Burgundy, where he had only been in spirit.

"I do not yet know," he writes to Madame de Blic, "whether it is the will of God, or whether He prefers me to mortify myself by making this sacrifice. I shall do what I am told to be most perfect. . . . If I am told to go and see you, what joy it will be! How happy shall I be to embrace you, to find myself in your little nest, between you, Raymond, and your children!"

The reply came: M. Huvelin gave permission. Brother Charles left Rome and took the road to Burgundy. The whole family was overjoyed. Everyone knew that these days so long dreamt of, to be so long remembered, would perhaps pass more quickly than the rest, and that the sweetness of meeting again from the outset was already diminished by the nearness of the farewell.

He had to set out quickly for the Vivarais mountains, to

[1] Letter to a friend, September 3, 1900. He was lodging at Madame Marie Basetti's, 105, Via Pozetto, on the third floor.

cross the pine-woods, to knock at the Abbey door, and go into retreat.

The latter began on September 29, 1900. From that date and for nearly a year the eternal traveller remained in the enclosure of Notre-Dame-des-Neiges. It was in the monastery chapel that, on the feast of the Holy Rosary, October 7, he received the minor orders. The oldest Fathers, the oldest Brothers, still speak of the affection which they all had for Charles de Foucauld, and of the daily edification they received from him. The day after the feast Dom Martin wrote: "I cannot tell you how happy we were to possess our dear and holy hermit for some time. He is rather jaded just now, and we do not know how to set about taking care of him. . . . I had the happiness of conferring minor orders on him on the feast of the Holy Rosary; perhaps it is the greatest happiness of my life."

It had been decided to abridge, as much as possible, any delays in ordaining the candidate, for he had already studied so much, prayed so much, and so amply proved his vocation. On December 22 he was made subdeacon, at Viviers. Almost at once he went again into retreat for the sake of the diaconate. His life glided on in continual meditation. All day long he perused the Gospel, the Bible, and the writings of the Fathers. Accustomed to soar, his soul was carried away as if on wings by the sacred text, and far above the world blossomed forth fully in the divine light. We have books in which this assiduous annotator wrote certain of his thoughts and resolutions. Promptly enough, the question presented itself to him: "What shall I be?" and plans were outlined, and the way grew clear.

Recapitulating this period, he afterwards wrote: "My retreats for the diaconate and priesthood made me see that the life of Nazareth which appeared to be my vocation must be led not in my beloved Holy Land, but among souls most in need of the physician, sheep most in need of a shepherd. The heavenly feast of which I was about to be a minister must be offered not to kinsmen and rich neighbours, but to the halt, the blind, and the poor—that is to say, to souls lacking priests. In my youth I travelled over Algeria and Morocco. In Morocco, as large as France, with ten million inhabitants, there was not a single priest in the interior;[1] in the Sahara, seven or eight times as large as France and

[1] Letter to Abbé Caron, Vicar-General of Versailles, April 8, 1905. To-day the French Franciscans and nuns of the same Order have begun the establishment of missionary posts and charitable institutions in Morocco.

much more populous than was formerly thought, are a dozen missionaries! No people seemed to me more abandoned than those."

Above the walls, blackened by the burning of the former chapel, they took pleasure in showing me the window of the cell which Brother Charles had chosen when preparing for Holy Orders. It could only be reached by going up to the top of the arches. But the door opened out on a gallery from which you could see the altar, and the future priest used to spend many hours there.

In his cell under the roof Brother Charles used to do his cooking, which was very simple—a plate of haricot beans or a boiled cabbage. There, as at Nazareth and Jerusalem, he had his hermitage. His only walk was from the cell to the chapel. As the end of 1900 drew near, he resolved to pray very much for the world which was changing centuries. He spent the two last nights of the closing century and the two first of the new one before the Blessed Sacrament. How many others did as much?

It was just when the French Church was being severely and unjustly treated by public authorities. He was grieved by it, because weaker souls fall in times of persecution, and because it was an offence to Jesus, the raising of whose hand alone maintains France. He used to say: " But Jesus remains the Master; the more He seems to die, the more He rises again as God and Lord: *Stat crux dum volvitur orbis.*" He also said: " But how unfortunate are the fortunate!" Without allowing himself to be dejected, he endeavoured to employ well every minute given him, " little bits of the examination which mortal life is." He was ordained deacon on the eve of Passion Sunday.

In May, 1901, began the thirty days' retreat, which ended his preparation for the priesthood. His ordination took place at Viviers on June 9. Charles de Foucauld was ordained by Mgr. Montéty, in the presence of Mgr. Bonnet. The night before the Father Abbot Dom Martin said to him:

" I shall accompany you; make provision for us both." The two travellers set out a few minutes afterwards. When lunch-time came, Charles de Foucauld drew a little parcel out of his pocket, opened the envelope, and on the Abbot's robe put three figs for each of them, two walnuts, and a bottle of water.

Several of the clergy at Viviers were amused when told of this incident, and wondered : " What is he going to do at Monseigneur's, who has invited him to lunch after the ceremony ?" He did as everyone else, and was not singular in any way.

The same evening the new priest regained the Ardèche mountains, so as to say his first Mass, on June 10, at Notre-Dame-des-Neiges. His sister had preceded him. She lodged outside the monastery in a little house where this letter from her brother was handed to her on her arrival :

"BEST AND DEAREST,

"Thanks for coming, your arrival touches me to the bottom of my heart. I shall get there on the night between Sunday and Monday about midnight or 1 in the morning. Take care not to wait for me; rather go to bed very early, like the Trappists, at 8 o'clock. On my arrival, I shall go straight to church to worship the Blessed Sacrament, to whom I owe my first visit; and I shall remain in silence and adoration till the day after my first Mass. You cannot speak to me before my first Mass, but afterwards we shall make up for it, my dear; the community Mass is sung at half-past 6, before the most Blessed Sacrament exposed; I shall act as deacon. . . . As soon as High Mass is finished, I shall go to the sacristy and put on a chasuble, and shall reappear at the same altar as where High Mass was celebrated, to say my first Mass. I shall give you Holy Communion there, through one of the gratings of the little chapel where you will be. After the thanksgivings of my first Mass (three-quarters of an hour or an hour after) I shall go and spend a good long time with you. . . . Wait for me in your room then : take care to have a good breakfast after communion. Be assured that your arrival here is a *real joy for the whole community,* which is full of illusions about me and loves me a thousand times more than I deserve, and in particular good Father Abbot, who is going to Viviers on purpose to accompany me, though he is very busy. . . .

"Welcome, my dear, and thanks for coming. I embrace you as I love you : with all my heart in the heart of Jesus.

"✠ FR. ALBÉRIC."

From consideration, and during his stay at La Trappe, Charles de Foucauld had retaken his former Trappist name. After his ordination he continued to live in his cell at Notre-Dame-des-Neiges until the end of the negotiations, which were to prepare for the establishment in North Africa. They were of two kinds : they had to obtain the permission of the religious authorities, and those of the General Government and of the military chiefs.

The letters which I am going to quote are to my mind beau. 'iful for their honesty, clear-sightedness and affection, when they speak of Charles de Foucauld; and for their humility and ardour, when signed by him. It seems to me that any unbiassed mind must admire the priests of France, whether in him who offers himself for an unprecedented mission, or in those who commend him. By a mistake the first letters were addressed to Mgr. Bazin; it was quickly seen that Mgr. Guérin, the Prefect Apostolic of the Sahara, should have been written to, as well as Mgr. Livinhac, Superior-General of the White Fathers.

M. l'Abbé Huvelin to Mgr. Bazin.

"Martigny-les-Bains,
"*August* 25, 1901.
"Monseigneur,

"M. le Vicomte Charles de Foucauld, long a lieutenant in the African Army, then an intrepid and skilful traveller in Morocco, then a novice with the Trappist Fathers of Akbes, in Syria, afterwards devoted to the service of the Poor Clares of Nazareth, lastly returned to the Trappist monastery of Notre-Dame-des-Neiges, where he has just received Holy Orders and the priesthood, asks me to commend him to your Grace.

"When you see him, you will judge that my recommendation is quite unnecessary, for he is himself his own recommendation.

"You will find in him heroic self-sacrifice, unlimited endurance, a vocation to influence the Musulman world, humble and patient zeal, obedience in his zeal and enthusiasm, the spirit of penance without any thought of fault-finding and condemnation for anyone else.

"I have been his spiritual Father for fifteen years. I have always followed him, I have always found him, even in the midst of his enthusiasm and transports, prudent and knowing how to wait, taking refuge in prayer when action was forbidden him. I admire and I love him, as do the Trappist Fathers who testify to you for him. The Reverend Father Abbot of Stauëli had a most real affection for him, and saw in him a hope for his Order, even after he had left it.

"M. de Foucauld's difficulty was the question of Holy Orders. In his humility he long refused to take them; he required clear enlightenment to show him that his way lay in mission work sustained by prayer.

"It is a simple portrait I am sending you, not flattering, but true to life. I am unknown to your Grace, but I ' ope you will find an appearance of truth in my words, and will see in the priest who presents himself to you a help and benediction for work in Africa. . . ."

ABBÉ HUVELIN,
"Honorary Canon of Paris; Curate of Saint-Augustine's."

The Rev. Father Martin, Abbot of Notre-Dame-des-Neiges, to Mgr. Bazin.

"NOTRE-DAME-DES-NEIGES,
"*July* 15, 1901.

"I send you the enclosed letter of my dear and holy friend, for the Bishop of the Sahara.

"I have neither to judge nor to weigh pious plans: *Spiritus Sanctus posuit Episcopos regere Ecclesiam Dei,* and not Abbots. But what I can affirm is that I have intimately known M. Charles de Foucauld for eleven years, and that never in my life have I seen a man realizing so fully the ideal of holiness. Never, except in books, have I seen such prodigies of penance, humility, poverty, and of the love of God.

"I will add, what is less important, that this former pupil of Saint-Cyr, a cavalry officer, was an explorer of the highest rank in Morocco, Algeria and Tunis, that he belongs to a very noble family, and that he is connected with the best families in France."

Charles de Foucauld to Mgr. Bazin.

"LA TRAPPE DE NOTRE-DAME-DES-NEIGES.
"*August* 22, 1901.

"MONSEIGNEUR,
"I throw myself at your Grace's feet. . . . The remembrance of my companions who died without the Sacrament and without a priest, twenty years ago, in the expeditions in which I took part, against Bu-Amama, urges me strongly to set out for the Sahara, as soon as you have accorded me the necessary faculties, without a single day's delay, since a gain of one day may mean the salvation of the soul of one of our soldiers. I also look upon it as a duty of charity to write to you again, in order to be able to set out as soon as possible.

"I humbly ask your Grace for two things: (1) The

faculty of setting up between Ain Sefra and the Twat, in one of the French garrisons which has no priest, a little public oratory, with the Sacrament reserved for the needs of the sick, and to reside and administer the Sacraments there; (2) authorization to associate with me companions, priests or laymen, if Jesus sends them, and with them to practise adoration of the Blessed Sacrament exposed.

"If you deign to grant me this twofold request I shall reside there as chaplain of this humble oratory without the title of parish priest or curate or chaplain, and without any emolument, living as a monk, following the Rule of St. Augustine, either alone or with Brethren, in prayer, poverty, work and charity, without preaching, and not going out except to administer the Sacraments, *in silence and enclosed.*

"The object is to give spiritual help to our soldiers, to prevent their souls being lost for want of the Last Sacraments, and *above all* to sanctify the infidel populations by bringing into their midst Jesus present in the most Blessed Sacrament, as Mary sanctified the house of St. John the Baptist by bringing Jesus into it.

"I promise your Grace with all my heart to endeavour with God's help, despite my misery, never to be an occasion of scandal, and never to be a cause of expense nor material burden to your delegation; with my whole heart I promise you beforehand filial love and the most faithful obedience.

"I take the liberty of adding that the presence of your unworthy servant in the Sahara, although he be very poor, will probably save several souls who will otherwise die without the Sacraments, and that it will give your delegation one more tabernacle, and one more holy sacrifice daily.

"If your Grace wishes to speak to me, on a word from you, by post or telegram, I shall immediately go to Algiers.

"I am with the most profound respect, Monseigneur,
"CHARLES DE FOUCAULD,
"An unworthy priest."

M. l'Abbé Huvelin to Mgr. Livinhac.

"*Sunday, September 1.*
"MONSEIGNEUR,
"A week ago I sent to Mgr. Bazin, of the White Fathers, all the information about M. de Foucauld for which you ask me. He asked me to send it to Mgr. Bazin.

"What I can tell your Grace is good in every way: he has much enthusiasm, but wisdom—much zeal, but much obedience—love of a hard life with the minimum of alleviation, but under direction—his love of mortification is a need resulting from his love of God.

"His vocation always drew him to the Musulman world. His sojourn in Algeria, his journey in the interior of Morocco, his years spent in Palestine, have prepared and hardened him for this mission. I saw the coming of his vocation. I saw him grow wiser through it, more humble, more simple, and obedient. When I bade him to put it aside as chimerical, he put it aside, but it returned stronger and more imperious. In my soul and conscience, I believe it comes from God. Love of silence and hidden action you will find in him. . . . His difficulties in La Trappe all came from his repugnance to receive Holy Orders. He dare not!

"Nothing *queer* or extraordinary, but an irresistibly urging force, *a hard instrument for tough work*—that is what your Grace will find in M. de Foucauld.

"How often have all the objections which occur to you occurred to me! I gave in only after trial and many tests.

"Stedfastness, a desire to go to the end in love and in the gift of self—to bear all the consequences—never discouragement, never; a little harshness formerly—but now much mitigated!

"Let him come, and then see for yourself. I regret having destroyed the admirable letter in which he very humbly asked me to give you information about him. It is in all conscience that I am sending you this, which will complete what I gave Mgr. Bazin a week ago. Get him to come at his own risk and peril; see him at work and judge.

"Receive, Monseigneur, my respect, and my profound and religious devotion, and give me your blessing.

"I cannot tell you how touched and stirred I was by your letter, in which I felt the Spirit of God. You will quickly discern Who is leading my dear child.

"L'ABBÉ HUVELIN."

Dom Henri, Prior of Notre-Dame of Stauëli, to Mgr. Guérin, Prefect Apostolic of the Sahara.

"*September* 5, 1901.

"Father Duffourd spoke to me of a business you had to discuss verbally with a former officer of the province of Oran, who desired to go back to it. . . . I think it is a question of our former Father Albéric (Charles de Foucauld —or rather Charles of Jesus). I forward you the last letter

I had from him. If you have the good-fortune to have him as a collaborator I shall be very happy both for you and for him. He is the finest soul I know: with incredible generosity he advances with giant strides on the path of sacrifice, and he has an insatiable desire to devote himself to the work of redeeming the infidels. He can do everything, but perhaps he cannot follow direction if it is too narrow. The Reverend Dom Martin must have recommended him to Mgr. Livinhac: all that I can add is that, having lived intimately with him for ten months, I was profoundly edified by his heroic virtue. There is in him the material of many saints. His sole presence is a most eloquent sermon, and in spite of the apparent singularity of the mission to which he believes himself called, you may quite safely receive him into your apostolic prefecture. . . ."

The Bishop of Viviers to Mgr. Livinhac.

" NOTRE-DAME-DES-NEIGES,
" *September* 5, 1901.

" MONSEIGNEUR,

" I recommend to your benevolence the humble and holy priest who comes to bring you his co-operation, and I beg you be good enough to accept him.

" Abbé de Foucauld is an old and brilliant officer, who broke off his career to give himself more completely to God in the priesthood. I had him ordained priest; he is my subject, and I hold it a great favour for my diocese to have possessed for some time a priest of such merit and character. If a vocation of too long standing and too urgent did not call him to devote himself to the conversion of the Musulmans, I should be happy to give him employment in my ministry. . . . Here he has acquired the reputation of a saint, and our priests beg the happiness of having access to him for a few moments as a great favour.

" All this will tell you, Monseigneur, in what esteem I hold the priest who is going to you, and how obliged I should be to you to receive him with great kindness.

" ✠ J. M. FRÉDERIC,
" Bishop of Viviers."

At the beginning of September, Charles de Foucauld bade farewell to the Fathers of Notre-Dame-des-Neiges. The boxes in which the Brothers had put the provisions and all the furniture that the hermit would take with him were already nailed down and labelled. What did they contain?

What was wanted for the chapel, a small number of books, over 50 yards of rope with a small bucket to draw water from the desert wells, some strong cloth to make a tent, and some sacks cut up for carpets.

The poor luggage was put in a cart. The former Brother Marie-Albéric received a last blessing from the Abbot and went away, much affected. A few days afterwards he crossed the sea, and landed in Africa, *his* Africa. At Maison Carrée he was received by Mgr. Livinhac, " the Bishop of the Sahara "; he was given the necessary authorization to set up in the south of Oran, near Morocco. While he was waiting for the second authorization, that of the Governor of Algeria, to reach him—an old friend, Commandant Lacroix, one of the best known *Africains,* had taken the necessary steps[1]—he was invited to spend a few days at the Stauëli Trappe. There he again found the monks so long devoted to him. New and immediately intimate friendships sprang up between him and the missionaries of Maison Carrée. He was full of hopes and plans. " At Beni-Abbes, I shall *actually* be alone as priest," he writes, " two hundred and fifty miles from the nearest one.[2] My Prefect Apostolic, Mgr. Guérin, allows me to have companions ! " On his side, Mgr. Guérin said : " I have only known Charles de Foucauld since the beginning of September, but it did not take me long to esteem him as he merits and to recognize his wonderful goodness. I regard as a blessing from God the coming of this holy priest into the territory of the prefecture entrusted to me. A real saint, like Charles of Jesus, necessarily does good. He cannot help radiating round him some of the sweetness and goodness of Jesus, who is henceforth his whole life."

The favourable reply from the Governor-General and General in Command of the army corps came on October 14, and the start for Oran, and then the south, took place next day. The officers of the posts échelonned on the route from Oran to Beni-Abbes had learned that the celebrated explorer, their old comrade, now a monk, was on his way, he too following the call of the desert, but from other motives. They were waiting for him at the stations of the little strategic railway, at present laid down for two hundred

---

[1] Head of native affairs to the *gouvernement général* at Algiers ; one of the authors of that remarkable work, La *pénétration Saharienne,* by Augustin Bernard and Commandant Lacroix. M. Augustin Bernard, who was at that period professor at the *École Supérieure des Lettres* of Algiers, is at present professor at the Sorbonne.

[2] The nearest points at which a priest could be found were: Ain Sefra, El-Golea, Timbuctoo.

and fifty miles from Oran, and in 1901, ending at Ain Sefra; and they came to greet him, some bringing him provisions for the journey. At Ain Sefra, the little white town at the foot of the dunes, he might have found an inn. But General Cauchemez took him to the Arab Office, a white castle among European trees, and gave him a room, in which Charles de Foucauld lodged, we may be sure, but that the hermit-explorer had slept on the floor during the two or three days he stayed with his friend. He expressed much gratitude to the officers of all ranks who had welcomed him. And so as not to annoy them, after intending to go on foot to Beni-Abbes, he reluctantly agreed to start with Lieutenant Huot, who was returning from leave, and consequently to undertake on horseback—on a *maghzen* cavalry mount—and with an escort, the long route from Ain Sefra to Beni-Abbes.

They entered the desert regions.

About half-way are the oasis of Taghit and the redoubt, which commands a dangerous region frequently overrun by marauding bands. As the French travellers and their little escort approached Taghit, they saw a troop of horsemen coming. It was Captain de Susbielle, commander of the post, at the head of his *maghzen*. Hearing that the old lieutenant of the Chasseurs d'Afrique was coming soon, he was there to meet the man who had given himself up to the poor of the desert for ever. On his way he said to his men: " You are going to see a French marabout; he comes through love of you : receive him with honour." Foucauld, recognizing France, advanced at a gallop towards her, his white robe flying in the wind. He stopped his horse within three yards of the officer, and replied to M. de Susbielle's salute. At the same time, the fifteen troopers, faithful to native politeness, dismounted and surrounded the marabout, "who came for love of them," and several together bowed and kissed the hem of his *gandourah*.

This was the Sahara's welcome.

Brother Charles stopped for a few hours at Taghit. On October 24, before remounting, he celebrated Mass before the Frenchmen of the garrison. " It is the first Mass since the occupation," he said. " Probably no priest has ever been here. I am very much affected at bringing down Jesus into these places, where, in all probability, He has never been corporally."

Four days later, in the evening of a hot day, the travellers saw the first palm-trees of Beni-Abbes.

CHAPTER VIII
Beni-Abbes

BENI is an oasis of seven to eight thousand palm-trees. They grow on the left bank of the Saura in earth and sand in which are numerous fountains, and they form a long thick forest close up against a cliff which rises high above it. The Saura itself is no other than the Zusfana, coming from Figig, which, at twenty-five miles to the north of the oasis, mingles with a more abundant river, the Wady Guir, which comes down from the plateaux of the great Moroccan Atlas. After the manner of Saharan rivers, their mingled waters burrow so as not to be drunk up by the sun; they cross the deserts through tunnels; they only come to light at the entrance of the palm plantation, the border of which they follow—the right bank being almost without verdure—for over a mile, then disappear again, perhaps, a long way off, mysteriously to swell the course of the Upper Niger.[1]

Travellers coming from Colomb-Béchar and following the wide valley have a long ride across pebbles, between the dried-up bed of the Saura and the dunes which bound the desert to the left. When they have got beyond the Mazzer palm grove, with their feet deep in the sand they have to cross successive spurs of dunes, which edge the horizon in front of them. It is only from the top of the last dune that they suddenly see between the two cliffs, close to them, the bending river, the first small strips of water, the first waving tops of a large green palm plantation, a high plateau on the right, a high plateau on the left, and on the crest of the latter the white crenellated walls of the *borj* of the Native Office. You emerge from aridity and enter the region of shade, springs, cultivation, and life. The interval between the cliffs which hold the oasis in their arms is narrow at first, and then opens out like the bulge of a ewer; it is more than a wooded corridor—it is a little plain they embrace, divided by the river, without trees on the right bank, covered on the left bank with palms which shelter apricot, peach and fig trees and vines. There,

[1] It is probable that the Niger formerly had no connection with the sea. This immense river rose and was lost in the African Continent. Its waters filled the depression of the desert in which the Taudeni salt-mines are worked, and there formed a second Lake Chad.

towards the centre of the forest, is a fortified town into which one enters by a single gate, in which the streets are almost everywhere covered in; a village peopled by free men, who consider themselves as the aborigines of the place, the Abbabsa. Farther on towards the end is a second village with very high walls like those of a feudal castle, and it is inhabited by Arabs of the Rehamna tribe, who graze their camels and asses on the poor pasture-lands of the region. Negro gardeners, sowers, and barley-reapers lodge on the borders of the palm grove, along a ravine which gives access to the *borj* plateau. And the native population, divided thus into three groups, numbers from twelve to fifteen hundred souls.

Brother Charles had chosen this place for his apostolate because of the wretchedness to be found there, which no priest had been able to relieve; also on account of the nearness of his much loved Morocco, which he hoped some day to enter as missionary; he knew also that Beni-Abbes passed for one of the most beautiful of the South Algerian oases, the most beautiful part of the long avenue of palms which begins at Figig and ends at In-Salah. At the time of his arrival, there was not the great redoubt which commands the entry of the palm groves; a smaller one, now destroyed, was a little farther away on the crest of the cliff, and it sheltered the garrison.[1] He followed the track made by the feet of men and beasts. Hardly had he climbed the steep slope, bordered by huts, which leads to the top of the plateau, than he was struck with admiration. To the north and east Beni-Abbes was enveloped to some distance by the rose-coloured or golden sand-waves of the western Erg, the great mingled dunes sweeping away, several of which rose from 500 to more than 600 feet, whilst to the west, beyond the cleft of the ravine and palm groves, stretched the second plateau—a rocky, rigid tableland, without a tree, apparently without end. The traveller found himself at a junction point between the two Saharan deserts, between the sandy desert that covers the whole of the south of Oran, and the rocky Hamada, which goes to the frontier of Morocco. Splendour of light, poverty of soil, purity and silence of night, how often will Brother Charles make use of them in his meditations, and unfold the eternal meaning hidden in the most humble or most magnificent landscape!

He immediately sought a place in which to fix his abode,

[1] The first troops of occupation comprised three companies of African sharpshooters and a company of light infantry.

and, on the plateaux of the left bank, not on the edge but over 200 yards back, bought three little humps which he called mountains, and two untilled hollows which he called valleys, where several wild palms grew. Of course the price was excessive. Brother Charles paid 1,170 francs for these 22 or 24 acres of desert. The whole was shaped like a bent pumpkin. It was the " tillage land " of the future " Fraternity." Fortunately there was water, or at least some possibility of getting it. The property contained several springs and old wells. The wells were dug, the springs cleared. Brother Charles, with his lively imagination and his mind a day, month, or year ahead of the present moment, was delighted with this new residence, and was half a hermit already when he thought of living there, and he fancied that the fruit and vegetables of the garden would be abundant, that he would be able to give some away, and that famine would be thus avoided in years of great drought, and that he would be the foster-father, comforter and friend of many of the poor, particularly of French soldiers and slaves.

At first he lodged in the building of the Arab Office. In the morning he set out, with some willing sharpshooters placed at his disposal, to build the hermitage. This was never anything but a poor collection of earth huts, without any artistic feature, built in a ravine, and quite fragile: if they very nearly kept off the sun, they would have melted under two days' rain. Fortunately, it rains barely more than once a year in the Saura district, and sometimes it may not rain at all. Stones gleaned on the plateau, but chiefly bricks of dried clay, were used for building; a little earth mixed with water was the mortar; porous planks of palms did duty for beams; the veins of large leaves and reeds made the roofing.

Naturally the chapel held a place of favour, and was built first. Brother Charles describes it lovingly in a letter to a friend: "The roof is horizontal, of big palm beams in the rough, covered with mats of palm branches: it is very rustic, very poor, but harmonious and pretty. To carry the beams, there are four upright palm stems in the middle; in their rusticity they produce a very good effect and frame the altar very well; from the one which is near the Gospel corner is hung a petroleum lamp which lights me at night, and throws a great deal of light on the altar. . . . A tent-like canopy of heavy dark green canvas, absolutely waterproof, is hung from the ceiling to protect the altar and its steps from the rain."

An officer of the garrison drew four large figures of Saints for the chapel. Still, the principal decorator was the architect, Brother Charles. He painted on fabric—in the most modern manner, *i.e.*, just a few lines of the finest accuracy, which he so often exemplified in illustrating *La Reconnaissance au Maroc*—a picture representing Christ "stretching out His arms to embrace, to press closer and to call all men to Him, and to give Himself for all." On the Gospel side was a St. Joseph, from the Father's "factory." On the walls of the "nave" hung the fourteen pictures of the Stations of the Cross, drawn in black, blue, or red ink, not on canvas or paper, but on the boards of the boxes which Brother Charles had cut and planed a little. He never ceased adorning this Saharan chapel, of which he says : " It suits me perfectly; it is pious, poor and clean, and very contemplative." On the Epistle side, in a niche, he put an alarum—the Fraternity clock.

There he was to spend many an hour of the day and night in adoration or meditation : there at first he was to sleep, alone in this isolated hut. He lay down at length, and fully dressed, on the altar steps. He slept near the tabernacle, like a dog at his master's feet. Yet he thought himself unworthy of such a favour. As soon as the first buildings, which were to go along with the chapel, were begun, a non-commissioned officer of the sharpshooters, M. J., who was a friend of his, having got up very early to come to the hermitage, found the Father lying down under the shelter of an unfinished wall.

" What," he said to him, " have you given up sleeping in the chapel ?"

" Yes."

" You told me yesterday that you were all right there !"

" That is just why I have left it."

A little later, Father de Foucauld chose the chapel sacristy to sleep in. Now, the little room that he called the sacristy was not long enough for a man to lie down at full length on the sand in it. The same adjutant of sharpshooters observed this to the Father, who replied, " Jesus did not lie down at full length on the Cross."

The workmen went on working. Beyond the sacristy, they erected brick and dry mud huts, which were named the cells of St. Peter and St. Paul, and these little buildings, being perpendicular to the apse of the chapel, formed a right angle with the nave. At the back a courtyard soon extended, called the " Retreat Courtyard." Brother Charles built a few more huts, " the non-Christian guest-room," an infirmary to which the sick of Beni-Abbès and neighbouring tents came to be taken care of, a lumber-house, and the walls of a second courtyard, the "Almonry Yard," on the Epistle side. He hoped that some day, perhaps soon, an unknown priest, called by the same vocation which had urged the former cavalry lieutenant towards the souls of the poor people of the oasis, would come and join him at Beni-Abbès, and that the hermitage would number two companions while waiting for something better. The workmen and troopers were much younger than he, and worked deftly and willingly for one as poor as themselves. They felt he was better than they were, and his goodness secretly touched them. He never left them when his Rule bound him to manual labour; even at noon and when the heat was extreme, he was seen going with them over the waste ground around the hermitage, and stooping down, picking up and lifting stones which might do for the foundations, and generally the last to join the file and return to the workyard. Sometimes the stone he was carrying back on his shoulder was not very big, and he would make excuses. "My dear fellows, "he would say, laughing, " I know very well that I am the fly on the wheel, but I work up to my strength."

Thoughtful care of the least details was one of the notes of Brother Charles's mind. Must not those who entered the house be brought to God, and the walls tell something of Jesus Christ and His teaching? While he was finishing the building of the hermitage, Brother Charles adorned the completed rooms with "texts" appropriate to their use. He gave the thoughts which were his strength and joy to himself and others for meditation.

The texts in the sacristy were: "Follow Me!" "If any man will come after Me, let him deny himself and take up his cross, and follow Me!" "Live to-day as if you were to die a martyr to-night." "Be all to all, with the sole desire of giving Jesus to all."

Those in St. Paul's Cell: "I have come to cast fire on the earth." "I have come to save those who were lost." "Whatever ye do for one of these little ones ye do for Me." "Our Father, who is in heaven, willeth not that one of these little ones should perish." "Go ye into the whole world, and preach the Gospel to every creature."

Those in St. Peter's Cell: "Other sheep I have that are not of this fold; them also I must bring: there shall be one fold and one shepherd." "That they may be one, as we are one."

After the chapel and the rooms, an enclosure wall was made around the Almonry Yard; then Brother Charles thought he ought to bound and close the Fraternity grounds, for he had resolved to live in seclusion, and not to go out of bounds without very grave reason. In the beginning he was satisfied to mark the boundaries of his ground with lines of pebbles about the size of an egg. One of the soldiers who had most to do with him just then told me that he sometimes returned to the camp after sunset. Studious to win souls of good-will, and more polite and obliging to the humble and disregarded than to the great and powerful, Brother Charles used to accompany him. He chatted amicably; he would speak of God and the beauty of the night. Around them were absolute silence and the desert, above an immense sky which did not conceal a single star. The hot air rose from the sand, and the former officer and the soldier went along on a barely visible track, each thanking God for an unexpected friendship, of which He was the origin and end. And that would last some minutes. Then Brother Charles bent down and felt the ground with his hand to see whether he had reached the boundary. When he touched the row of pebbles, he used to say: " I cannot bring you any further, here is the enclosure; good-bye; we shall soon meet again."

Far, far away from their families and country, we can tell how touched the soldiers were by a friendship such as this! Their sensitive French hearts with an old-time politeness which survives many counter-influences, made them fear to take any advantage of it. Can one go and talk thus, almost as a friend, with a former officer, with a monk who after all has his business, and, as they clearly felt, with a highly educated man whom a sharpshooter's conversation could not always interest? They made excuses for not returning; they deprived themselves of a pleasant hour, in order not to take it from him. Then he wrote them letters like this:

" Dear Friend,
    " You told me that you are depressed at night and that your evenings are dull. . . . Will you—if you are allowed to leave the camp, which I do not know—come and spend the evenings regularly with me? We shall make them as long as you like, chatting fraternally of the future, of your children and your plans . . . of what you and those you love more than yourself want and hope for. . . . You will find a brother's heart, if nothing else.

"You would have liked a short account of St. Paul. . . . I should have liked to send you it, but I cannot, I have other urgent things to write at this moment. . . . I could tell you about it by mixing my poor words with passages from his letters. I have them and they are wonderful. . . .

"The poor man offers you what he has. What he offers you, above all, is his very tender and brotherly affection, his profound devotion in the Heart of Jesus.
"BROTHER CHARLES OF JESUS."

The natives, who were inquisitive, insinuating, tormented with hunger and thirst, and therefore ready pilferers, showed a kind of respect for Brother Charles's enclosure almost from the outset. Not that they stood upon ceremony as to entering the grounds and coming to visit the "marabout," but the reputation of holiness of the latter rendered sacred to them the things they found on the way and in the interior of the enclosure. The nomad unloaded his camel on the other side of the pebble boundary; the poor Arab woman, returning with her daily load of wood, threw her faggot down there; the butcher put down his bundle of blood-stained kid-skins; and, even if he had to be several hours or a whole night away, the caravaneer found his goods untouched, the woman her load of palm roots, the butcher his bale of fresh leather. Afterwards, the row of pebbles was replaced by a row of stakes, more or less twisted, on which were fixed two lines of barbed wire. Seven stout posts, with two sticks across on top of each, were set at intervals as props for the slight enclosure and as standards for the man of God.

The farming made very slow progress. It is no slight undertaking to hollow out a piece of desert which has perhaps never been dug; to secure water—that is to say, life—for the trees one plants and the seed one sows, when the temperature, as at Beni-Abbes, is always 86° from October to June, and afterwards rises to 122°! Brother Charles, as I said, began by deepening the abandoned wells of his property; he hollowed out irrigating canals to bring the water of the springs to the feet of the palm-trees which grew at hazard and were half covered with sand by the south wind. The work was of a kind that the poor gardener of Nazareth could not continue without help, for the most energetic will does not suffice—men learn it quickly —to be everything to all men and to all things. After a few trials, Father de Foucauld engaged two *harratins*[1] who were

[1] Arabs and negro half-breeds found in all the oases, whose social position is intermediate between that of the slave and the free man.

not lacking at Beni-Abbès, and he called them gardeners for the work he required them to do. Perhaps, after all, they knew better than the master of the property what care to give the palm-trees and the infinite precautions which must be taken in hot countries to keep the vegetable seed-plot from being at once burned up by the sun, after putting forth its first leaves. With but little supervision these blacks had to do with so good a master that they remained faithful to him a long time. He only found that they lost many hours daily in going from the hermitage to the oasis *ksar* and back. He would have liked to keep them and feed them at the hermitage. The blacks wanted nothing better. They were surely not used to dainty cooking, nor even to eat according to their hunger. But when they had shared in Father de Foucauld's fare several days following, they declared they might die but not live on that diet, for the marabout lunched on a piece of barley broad soaked in a decoction of a Saharan plant which bears the innocent name of " desert tea," and in the evening he dined on a bowl of the same tea to which he added a little condensed milk. The *harratins* went on as outside gardeners. By degrees their labour improved the land, and made a sensible distribution of the water. In the sand there were some young palm-trees, the promise of a few fig-trees, and even olive-trees and vines. Some years later, the name of " garden," at first given to these attempts at cultivation, began to be deserved. But just then the hermit quitted Beni-Abbès, and returned there on rare occasions only.

Sometimes Brother Charles accepted the invitations which the officers, his comrades, frequently sent him, and came out of the enclosure to go and dine with them at the *borj*. He seldom did so except to salute in passing a Saharan chief, like Laperrine or Lyautey, or a scholar sent on a mission into this desolate country, but which leads to all others, and where, as at an enormous cross-road, all the riches of Africa may one day meet. On those evenings he did not take a place of honour, but the lowest one, beside the youngest officer. They tried to get him to talk, and did not fail to question him about Morocco, which was quite near, and which he alone knew well. But the fear of pride made him dumb on that subject. To all other questions he replied, but without carrying on the conversation. His vocation was silence, self-effacement and retirement. He only agreed to appear in a circle of men of the world so as not to seem wanting in courtesy, or, somehow, in the discipline of his former profession. The story of military doings interested him in the highest degree. Brother Charles kept watch over himself less narrowly, if he was asked his opinion on a police operation which had just been executed, or that was contemplated. If the news came, for instance, of some movement of pillagers carrying off flocks and women, assassinating and mutilating men, at once reappeared the ardent chief, the lover of justice seen in the pursuit of Bu-Amama. "You must catch them up," he said, "and set about it vigorously." Next moment, he saw a mouse caught by a dog in the dining-room : " Poor little thing, what a pity !" he murmured. He withdrew early; he lit his lantern, and reached the hermitage, going through the dark by himself.

I should not be a faithful historian, did I not also say that, as soon as the chapel was built, Brother Charles dug his own grave in a corner of the garden, and blessed it for his own burial. He did the same afterwards in the various parts of the Sahara in which he stayed a little while.

Such were the frame and outward trappings of this unprecedented life, ordered by a powerful will. The rest was almost entirely hidden from men. Had they tried, they could hardly have found out the division of the hours between charitable duties, manual labour, reading, and the duties of prayer : the Rule to which Father de Foucauld had bound himself. They would miss the soul. Every soul is more or less of a secret to others. The mystery is greater when souls are great, when they turn aside from our pleasures and work, and from our ordinary thoughts which are hardly anything but ourselves; and when they give themselves to God for Him to set at the service of His poor. Then we see only what they bring us, their goodness, their fraternal works, the faint reflection of themselves on their faces and in their eyes. But with what efforts they keep themselves apart from the common life, in the constant presence of Him whose smile and peace are lost by a single little thought; what graces they have had, what combats, what delights, what dreams : all that, we know not.

His rule of life was unchanged from this period to the end. Brother Charles has himself set it forth in a letter addressed to the Prefect Apostolic of the Sahara.[1]

" . . . Get up at four (when I hear the alarum, which is

---

[1] This letter of September 30, 1902, reproduces the Rule almost as it may be read in a former letter to a friend (December 13, 1901). The sole difference to be noted is that the hour of getting up, originally fixed at three, is altered by an hour in 1902. I am inclined to believe that this was a concession asked for by Père Guérin.

not always !). *Angelus, Veni Creator,* Prime and Terce, Mass, Thanksgiving.

"At six, a few dates or figs and the discipline; immediately afterwards, an hour's adoration of the Most Blessed Sacrament. Then manual labour (or its equivalent: correspondence, copies of various things, extracts of authors to be kept, readings aloud, or explanation of the Catechism to anyone), until eleven. At eleven Sext and None, short mental prayer, particular examen until half-past eleven.

"At half-past eleven dinner.

"Midday, *Angelus,* and *Veni Creator* (this latter is sung. You will laugh when you hear me singing! Unintentionally, I have certainly invented a new air.)

"The afternoon is given entirely to God, to the Blessed Sacrament, except an hour devoted to necessary conversation, to various replies, to cooking, the sacristy, etc., necessary housework, and to alms; this hour is divided up throughout the whole day.

"From noon to half-past twelve, adoration; from half-past twelve to half-past one, Stations of the Cross, some vocal prayers, the reading of a chapter of the Old and New Testaments, a chapter of the *Imitation* and a few pages of a spiritual author (St. Teresa, St. John Chrysostom, St. John of the Cross, perpetually follow one another).

"From one to two, written meditation on the Holy Gospel.

"From two to half-past two, moral or dogmatic theology.

"From half-past two to half-past three, reserved for the catechumens.

"From half-past three to half-past five, adoration; after Mass and the night, this is the best moment of the day; work is over, I say to myself, I have only to look to Jesus . . . this is an hour full of sweetness.

"At half-past five, Vespers.

"At six, collation. . . .

"At seven, explanation of the Holy Gospel to some soldiers, prayer and benediction of the Blessed Sacrament with the holy ciborium, followed by the *Angelus, Veni Creator.* Then the soldiers leave after a short conversation in the open air. I say the rosary (and I say Compline, if I have not been able to say it before the short explanation of the Holy Gospel), and I go to sleep in my turn about half-past eight.

"At midnight I get up (when I hear the alarum), and sing the *Veni Creator,* recite Matins and Lauds: this is also a very sweet moment: alone with the Spouse, in the profound silence of the Sahara, under the vast sky, this hour of *tête-a-tête* is a supreme comfort. I go back to bed at one.

Thus he had six hours' sleep, divided by an hour's vigil, and prayer held the first place. The work of charity alone upset the Rule. This was a most acute trial for Brother Charles, whose contemplative soul thirsted for meditation. He accepted it, however. He was one who gave a fraternal welcome to the poorest and most unknown and undeserving of neighbours, who never let it be suspected that he was put out, and was willing to waste his time for talking with God upon unreliable nomads, corrupt slaves, beggars and bores. Every minute somebody would come and open the door, and Brother Charles appeared with his beautiful eyes full of serenity, his head bent forward a little, and his hand already held out. He wore a white *gandourah*, fastened with a girdle on which there was worked a heart surmounted by a cross in red cloth; he had sandals on his feet. As to the headgear, it was his own invention—it was made of a cap which he had stripped of its peak and covered with a white pugaree to shield the back of his neck. The picture of the Cross and the Sacred Heart told from a distance what this white man's Faith was. Nobody could fail to see it. That is why, on some desert post, many years after the time of Beni-Abbès, when General Laperrine read an article representing Charles de Foucauld as a priest who never spoke of his beliefs or did much preaching of the Faith, he seized his pen and angrily scribbled in his notebook : " What of his conversations ? and his dress ? " He wrote the truth : his habit was a sermon and, besides, Brother Charles's whole life proclaimed the Gospel. The natives were never mistaken about it.

We can now follow the events which marked his stay at Beni-Abbès, and, in order to do so, we shall only have to consult that most accurate and assiduous taker of notes, Father de Foucauld himself, who studiously entered in what he called his " diary " the little happenings of the day, his accounts, and even the names of his visitors.

" *October* 29, 1901.—Celebrated Mass for the first time at Beni-Abbès. *Ex voto* to Our Lady of Africa.

" *November* 5. — Erection of the first Stations of the Cross."

" *November* 30.—Formal opening of the Chapel of the Fraternity of the Sacred Heart."

"*December* 25.—First exposition of the Blessed Sacrament for over ten hours."

This man had given himself up to being forsaken so that in the far-off Sahara Jesus Christ at any rate might not be forsaken. The religious ceremonies of the first Christmas at Beni-Abbes therefore delighted him, and he wrote of them to his friends in France:

"We have had the Blessed Sacrament exposed from midnight to 7 o'clock in the evening. We shall have it on New Year's Day from 7 o'clock in the morning till 7 in the evening. I was far from hoping there would be enough adorers for it to be possible. Jesus provided them.

"The good-will, the unhoped-for piety of the poor soldiers round me enable me to give a reading and explanation of the Holy Gospel *every evening* (I cannot get over my surprise at their willingness to come and listen to me); Benediction is followed by a very short evening prayer. . . . This Benediction and Holy Mass are both a consolation and an infinite joy."

About twenty years ago a handful of Algerian sharpshooters who formerly had been taught the Catechism and had not forgotten it, assisted at the first Catholic offices celebrated in the earthen chapel of Beni-Abbes. They still speak of it readily. One of them who I met in Paris said to me:

"I was one of the faithful of Father de Foucauld. He used to say Mass when it suited us. If you asked him to say it at four o'clock in the morning or at noon he would always say yes. And what a Mass! If you were never at his Mass you don't know what Mass is. When he said the Domine non sum dignus it was in such a tone that you wanted to weep with him."

"*January* 9, 1902.—First slave ransomed; Joseph of the Sacred Heart. . . . This afternoon there was very little hope of freeing this child; his master refused to sell him at any price; but yesterday, Wednesday, the day of good St. Joseph, I had changed the name of the child to that of *Joseph of the Sacred Heart* and promised St. Joseph to erect an altar to him in the bay on the Gospel side, and one to the Blessed Virgin in the one on the Epistle side, if he obtained the liberation of the child for me. To this good Father everything is easy: at 5 in the evening, the master came to claim the child for the last time, and in two minutes accepted the price I offered him. I paid it on the spot, and you would have been delighted at the joy of poor 'Joseph of the Sacred Heart' reiterating that 'God was his only master.' . . . He is a Musulman, but more in name than in fact. I hope that, naturally and of himself (I shall avoid anything like pressure—he will be quite free) he will go to Jesus and to the Heart which willed him to be free."

This young man of twenty, very much touched by Father de Foucauld's charity and seeing his life, soon felt that religion was the principle of such great perfection, and asked of his own accord to be instructed in the Catholic Faith. He began at the hermitage; then, at the end of a month, finding an opportunity of getting out of the country and escaping from the influence of the society in which he lived, he went to Algiers, where the White Fathers looked after him. "He already looked upon himself as a Christian," the hermit wrote. It was a fine work of piety, mixed with some imprudence, for slaves were numerous around Brother Charles. Many must have begged him to set them free like Joseph. "It breaks my heart to have to leave them with their masters," he said. And he gave way more than once, as often as he had the means. After Joseph he redeemed a youth of fifteen whom he called Paul, and whom we shall meet with again later on.[1]

No doubt he must also have ransomed the little negro aged four, who is seen in several photographs seated on the Father's knees, or standing beside him and gambolling. Anyhow, we know that he freed other captives.

To buy back Saharan slaves, to feed the hungry, Father Charles would not have liked to ruin his friends; but he shrank less from troubling them a little. He collected small sums, but often. His family got used to it and lovingly let him do as he pleased; the White Fathers from time to time silently settled any arrears of heroic charity; the officers of the Beni-Abbès club, moved to pity for the slave, took their share of the purchase money; the safe of the Arab Office remained closed, decidedly distrustful. The liberator quite understood that wanting to ransom slaves ruined his credit; that political economy put him in the wrong, and that, perhaps, strict reason was on the same side. He then examined his conscience.

"I could get a small sum," he wrote, "by taking stipends for Masses. The good Father Abbot of Notre-

[1] Paul entered the Fraternity about October 15, 1902. Fourteen years later he was the chief witness of Father Foucauld's death.

Dame-des-Neiges has offered me some, and if I have no means of living and paying my debts, I shall make use of it; but as long as a glimmer of hope of my being able to do without it exists, I shall do so because I believe that *much more perfect:* I live on bread and water, which costs me seven francs a month. . . . As for clothes, Stauëli gave me a coat and two shirts with twelve napkins, a rug, and a cloak; these are a gift of good Father Henry, or rather a loan, because he has only lent me them, so that I may not give them away; a very nice officer here, Captain d'U—— offered me so graciously a rug and two small knitted vests that I could not refuse; you see I am well set up. . . . For myself I want nothing. To help me to get the slaves, travellers, and the poor together to tell them of Jesus and induce them to love Him, I want a small sum to buy barley; I asked C—— for thirty francs a month, for the slaves' barley, and M—— for twenty for that of the travellers. . . . I confess I must also pay for the ground I bought, and go to some expense in planting some dates which, in three years will provide food for me and the poor, please God. My only capital on leaving France was what it still is, the word of Jesus: ' Seek ye therefore first the kingdom of God and His justice, and all these things shall be added unto you.' I was quite at ease here up to the last few days; the purchase and freeing of Joseph of the Sacred Heart made me get to the bottom of my little purse, but our heavenly Father's is still full."

Again he wrote: "I wish to accustom all the inhabitants, Christians, Musulmans, Jews and idolaters, to look upon me as their brother, the universal brother. . . . They begin to call the house the Fraternity (the *Khaua,* in Arabic), and I am delighted."

This beautiful word suits our missionary and might describe him: he was truly the universal brother, not in words, but in deeds; he did not scatter political formulæ, or promises which only add to the weight of wretchedness, but he forgot himself for the sake of his nearest neighbours, he spent beyond his means to feed them and to ransom them if ransomed they could be. His way was the silent way. Before living four months in Beni-Abbés, he had already reckoned up all the material and moral wretchedness there which found no alleviation. In his long meditations before the altar, or while carrying his stone along with the hermitage masons, he forthwith planned out a better Beni-Abbes, but in his plan his own share of the work and self-sacrifice were to be the greatest.

Always building the ideal he asked himself : " What good can others, better than I, do for these people, and what above all can I do, who am but a wretched good-for-nothing ? " In a letter addressed to a friend in France, thus does he distribute the rôles. He confessed to this friend his great desire to obtain some Sisters of St. Vincent de Paul for the oasis of Beni-Abbes. " I am heartbroken when I see the children of the town idling at haphazard with nothing to do, without teachers or religious education. A place of sanctuary would do so much good ! It is just what we want for spreading the Gospel. . . . With God's help a few good sisters of Charity would soon give all this country to Jesus." Then, putting all his thoughts on this subject together, he draws up a regular memorandum and sends it to Père Guérin, Prefect Apostolic of the Sahara. In it we see his great heart, and the minutiæ which never leave him, even in his dreams. He goes beyond the present, beyond the good immediately possible, and the complaint of this Christian thrown among so many infidels gains a thrilling greatness from the slenderness of the means at his disposal and the breadth of the imagined conquest. From Beni-Abbes in the Sahara, he sends to his spiritual head his report for getting the world forward. I am obliged to condense these pages of boundless charity.

The first charity to undertake, according to the hermit, would be "slave relief work." They are miserable in every way, treated in the hardest possible manner by the Arabs and especially by the marabouts; they have every vice and neither hope nor friends. But they would soon consider the Christians who did them good as saviours, and perhaps they would be the first Saharans to become Christians, as the first Christians of Rome were largely made of slaves. The second charity would be meant to give a shelter and a meal to poor travellers, who sleep in the open when it is so cold at night. Also Christian teaching for the children must be thought of. There is no school in the whole oasis except a Musulman one. A crowd of children run about all day long, idle vagabonds and quickly perverted; it would at least be necessary to have a shelter where they could learn reading, writing, French, sacred history, and the Catechism, where they would be given a few dates in the morning and a little cooked barley at noon. This would cost at most " two sous a day." No doubt there would be few Arab children in this Christian school, but the little Berbers, children of a mild race and quite ready to take to the Latin they once knew, would all come to it. The Berbers are neither fanatics nor scornful. One may expect in the future that "when the Berbers are settled in the Faith, that will prepare and induce the Arabs to embrace it."

The memoir continued to enumerate the necessary charitable organizations: a civil hospital, a military hospital, visiting the sick in their homes, the distribution of remedies and alms at the Fraternity door, zeal for the souls of the soldiers, officers, Musulmans of all sorts, Jews, "of all the inhabitants of the country, of the prefecture, of the world and purgatory." There are fifteen paragraphs outlining fifteen projects.

Having thus described the work to be organized, Brother Charles sets forth for Mgr. Guérin the work he had done:

". . . I am alone for this immense task. . . .

"For *the slaves,* I have a little room in which I gather them and where they always find a lodging, a reception, daily bread and friendship; by degrees I teach them to pray to Jesus. Since January 15, the day on which their little room was finished, I have had some every night at the Fraternity. Sometimes I see twenty slaves a day.

"*The poor travellers* also find a humble shelter and a poor meal at the Fraternity, with a good reception and a few words to bring them to goodness and to Jesus; but the place is so small, the virtue of the monk and his skill are still less; more virtue, intelligence and means, would allow of much more good being done. . . . Sometimes I see thirty or forty travellers a day.

"*The infirm and aged* here find a shelter with a roof, food and attention when forsaken . . . but what inadequate care and what poor food! . . . And for want of separate places, I can only take in those who get on with the others, and women not at all; yet the women, even more than the men, need a home for old people.

"*For the Christian teaching of the children* I do absolutely nothing; it seems to me that I can do nothing. I sometimes see as many as sixty children in a single day at the Fraternity, and with a heart full of sorrow have to send them away without doing anything for them." And the list of replies continues; the military hospital, the civil hospital for the natives, visiting the sick at their homes, "are beyond my power and vocation; nuns are required." So it is with the visits to the homes of the poor. Doubtless he daily distributes remedies to ten or fifteen people, but he is very cautious, having little confidence in his talents. There is a doctor at the Arab Office, he is very good, but women and children cannot go to him—they come to the Fraternity, and the men themselves prefer applying to the marabout. What is to be done? Nuns would do all the good that he can only look on at, estimate and plan. At the hermitage gate, in a single day, taken at hazard, he has counted seventy-five poor people. He begins to know his people; but how much help was wanted! What need there was of intelligent almoners for such great poverty and so many outstretched hands!

" If I do not ask you to send any White Sisters out here, it is because I know that you will settle them wherever you can, and never have enough to put wherever they are required. . . .

" I am still alone : I am not faithful enough for Jesus to give me a companion, still less . . . I follow to the best of my abilities the little Rule you know. . . ."

This report, like all the correspondence of Father de Foucauld, shows the extreme humility of the man to whom were wanting neither pretexts nor opportunities for seeming proud. Race, fortune, superior intelligence, relations, the gift of sympathy were his, and he could have chosen a brittle branch on which to perch and sing his own praises. The very sacrifice he had made in leaving the world might have done for self-adoration, which can entrench itself among the ruins, provided they rise high enough. Instead of that, he showed a most respectful tone, promptness in obedience, a liking for checking inclination almost to the point of indifference, a great esteem for others, a great contempt of himself, and a great astonishment at being employed in a work that demands saints for workmen. Brother Charles never ceased blaming himself for the slow progress of his apostleship; if he were less unworthy, all the Musulmans, Jews, and bad Christians would have already been, or have again been, converted. At any rate he would have had help, instead of wearing himself out in solitude. He declared that his own conversion was evidently the condition of his converting others. But how far was he from it! He begged prayers from all to whom he wrote. The remembrance of the sins of his past life was rarely even alluded to, but it was always present. " I have all I need to do immense good," he exclaims, " except myself."

Charles de Foucauld was a humble man, and I firmly believe that his prime virtue, the principle of his influence over infidels and Christians, lay in that. This judgment may surprise. We readily imagine that humility breaks the ardour of nature, and that such an impulse as pride can do no more. But we do not observe that humility, if it destroys one energy, replaces it at once by another which is far higher. It consists in knowing the limits of one's powers, which is a reasonable thing to do, and to expect less of such weak powers than of God's. Hence no enterprise seemed to him impossible, no check held him back. Humility has nothing to do with timidity. Let us reckon up the audacity there was in the programme which Father de Foucauld had just laid down. A poor priest, lost in an oasis of the Sahara, proposed to found more institutions than a monastery quite full of heroes of charity could maintain; in his zeal he forgot no one; he allowed himself to be carried away far beyond the palm-trees of Beñi-Abbés; he wished for and aimed at the conversion of the whole of Africa, of the entire world. Was he, then, a madman? No: a very humble man, who knew the power of God.

The reply which Père Guérin sent to this long report is not textually known to us. It certainly counselled Brother Charles to ransom slaves only in rare cases, otherwise the poor hermit would get himself intolerably into debt.

"*May*, 1903.—Thirty years ago to-day I made my first communion and received my God for the first time. . . . This is the first time that I celebrate the Holy Mass on that day. . . . What graces I have received in these thirty years! How good God has been! How many times I have received Jesus with these unworthy lips! And lo, here I hold Him in my poor hands! He puts Himself into my hands! And now I officiate at an oratory; night and day, I have the holy tabernacle—I possess it, so to speak, as mine alone! Now, every morning I consecrate the Holy Eucharist, every evening I give Benediction with it! And here at last and above all I have the permission to make a foundation! What graces!"

The foundation to which he alludes is that of the "Little Brothers of the Sacred Heart of Jesus," the future religious family which he already contemplated in Palestine, an enclosed family, destined to adore the perpetually exposed Holy Eucharist day and night, and to live in a missionary country, in poverty and work.

This congregation of missionaries would not therefore directly preach the Gospel, but would make it known, admired, and loved by the life of prayer, charity, and poverty that the monks would lead among Musulmans. The Little Brothers of the Sacred Heart would be primarily adorers, bringing their Master into the midst of infidels. Brother Charles wished to establish them in groups wherever possible; he wished, not one oratory at Beni-Abbes, but a great number of them to be raised, whence the Blessed Eucharist and Sacred Heart should shine as the light of the world, upon many infidel regions, for ages.

A magnificent thought, which he never ceased to express all his life long! When he undertook some new journey, he rejoiced, as he did at Taghit, in consecrating the body of Christ in places where no priest had been for two thousand years. Thinking of Rome, he exclaimed: " I love Rome so much! That is where there are most tabernacles, where Jesus is most present corporally. One of my aspirations would have been to restore worship in the little chapel *Domine Quo vadis, via Appia.*"[1]

Here, at Beni-Abbes, if he asked for help, for companions to be sent him, it was because he wanted first of all to multiply the Real Presence among those who had no tabernacle or Host. He constantly thought of the immense peoples around him and among whom the Saviour did not dwell. He wanted to give Him to them. "For men die every day and souls fall into hell, souls redeemed at so great a price, dyed in the blood of Jesus, which St. Colette saw falling into hell, as thick as the snowflakes in a winter storm."

We shall soon see what came of these plans of foundations. I shall only note now that Father de Foucauld has entered into the life of recollection so long desired, and declares himself the happiest man in the world. When we compare his happiness with that which some of us pursue, we are confounded as to ourselves, and many of us have so little elevation of soul, that we can barely imagine the exultation of the hermit of Beni-Abbes. Did he eat and drink to sate hunger and thirst, since these satisfactions are called happiness? We know he did not. Did he keep any past habits of luxury or self-pleasing? Not the least. Did he try to find in the books he brought into the desert a diversion from the monotony of his days, with their servile tasks and boring conversations? With his artistic temperament he doubtless enjoyed certain pages of St. Chrysostom, and in more than one point he was too like St. Augustine not to be moved by the human beauty of the *City of God* or the *Confessions:* but his happiness was far above such pleasures as these. May it not be that

---

[1] Letter to a friend, December 20, 1903.

exceptional graces were granted him, and that in communion or meditation, or in the evening, when he could go on no longer through working so hard and giving consolation to so many, and grain and dates, and when suffering from the torrid heat, some sudden nameless immeasurable sweetness came down into his heart and filled it with delight? I hardly doubt it, although nowhere, to my knowledge, has this humble servant explicitly spoken of any heavenly favours bestowed upon him. But he spoke of his joy, and extolled it. Indeed it was the purest, the most detached from all that is human that anyone could experience. We can know no more.

At La Trappe, at Nazareth, he experienced periods of interior trials, and something like darkness. "I only managed to get through by entire obedience to the Abbé, even in little things: I clung to him like a child to its mother's dress. . . . At present I am in great peace. That will last as long as Jesus wills. I have the Blessed Sacrament, the love of Jesus; others have the earth, I have the good God. . . . When I am sad, this is my recipe: I recite the Glorious Mysteries of the Rosary, and I say to myself: what does it matter after all if I am miserable, and if I get none of the good I want? All that does not prevent my well-beloved Jesus—who wants it a thousand times more than I do—from being blessed, eternally and infinitely blessed.

"Our Well-Beloved is blessed: what do we lack? You know that to love is to forget yourself for another whom you love a thousand times more than yourself, that to love is to give up working and wishing to be happy, and to desire solely and with all the strength of your heart the happiness of the Beloved: well, we have what we desire. Our beloved Jesus is blessed, so we lack nothing! If we love Him, let us praise God without end, for our wishes are granted: He is happy!"[1]

Brother Charles was self-forgetful to a point which sometimes made his friends anxious. He had fever, rheumatism, and was utterly tired out. Some officers had to write to his family about it. One of Brother Charles's relations, thinking that the diet of bread and herb-tea was insufficient for a man still young, asked the missionary to accept a small sum monthly, on condition that this money should be used to buy some extra food. He replied: "I accept the ten francs, and so that you may know the menu, I tell

[1] Letter to Count Louis de Foucauld, September 3, 1902; letters to a friend, dated March 21, April 4, September 3, 1902.

you that I am adding some dates, which are very good and nourishing fruit, to my bread."

A short time after, his director, Abbé Huvelin, counselled moderation as follows:

"My dear friend, my dear child, bear with yourself! Be humble and patient with yourself, less anxious to overcome sleep than restlessness and that *anxious striving after the best* which torments you. Be at peace, in order to receive God's graces, and, if you have and keep your hatred of yourself, let it be a hatred as calm as deep water. . . . Possess your own soul; do not cut yourself down too much; eat a little; sleep as long as action requires."

Père Guérin wrote to him in the same strain, and I believe this was the finishing stroke for the " desert tea." In a letter of Brother Charles " cous-cous " is spoken of at the midday meal: perhaps it was on the great feasts.

Brother Charles's attack of fever had stirred the little military colony of Beni-Abbes. Immediately all flocked to the Fraternity: "the doctor with his advice and remedies, all the officers and non-commissioned officers, goats' milk, jam, coffee, tea, and I don't know what besides!"

And he was astonished that they did so much for him.

What is to be feared by such souls as this holding the highest within them above the world? Absolutely nothing. In the summer of 1902, one of his friends told him he feared that the Berbers might attack Beni-Abbes, and Brother Charles did not deny the danger, but rejoiced in it.

" I thank you for what you have told me about possible dangers; . . . I regard them with the peace of God's children. . . . If you knew how I desire to end my poor and miserable life, so badly begun and so empty, according to our Lord's saying on the night of the Last Supper : ' Greater love than this no man hath, that a man lay down his life for his friends !' I am unworthy of it, but how much I desire it ! Reports of war are reviving ; . . . it is very sweet to feel oneself always so near, on the threshold of eternity; it is extremely sweet and also good for one's soul."

"*July* 4.—There is nothing new in my life; oh yes, there is ! I have had the great joy of being able to buy and free a slave; he is staying with me provisionally as a guest, and working in the garden; . . . he appears to be twenty-five years of age. . . . Pray for his conversion ! Pray also for that of a good Musulman Turco who is most devoted to me . . . and pray for mine !"

The slave of whom Brother Charles here speaks was a Beraber, carried off in a raid by the Doni Meuia, who were not then very reliable friends, and a party of them were camping on the Beni-Abbes plateau. Moved by pity of this fine young captive, Brother Charles said to a French non-commissioned officer: "We must buy him from his master. But, if they hear that it is I who wish to free the slave, they will ask a price I cannot pay. Go, then, as if for yourself, to buy the captive and keep me informed of the negotiations." These lasted three days. We have still the notes he addressed to the adjutant. "Add another douro or two, my dear J——, but I can't give any more; indeed, I can't."

Next day, a fresh letter: "Well, yes, go up to 400 francs, and don't hesitate or haggle. . . . Our brother's freedom is priceless. . . . Jesus might have redeemed us by a word, but willed to do it with all His blood to show His love by the price He paid. Let us follow God's example."

At last the master gave way. The slave went to thank the great Christian marabout who had delivered him. They chatted for a moment, then Brother Charles said to the Beraber:

"Now you are free; what are you going to do?"

"Say good-bye to my captors."

"And then?"

"I shall go back to my first master, who treated me well. My wife is still there."

"*June* 28, 1902.—Saturday is the day for giving out the barley distribution. We must make our Sundays and feast-days known. It is a very inferior way, but just now the only practical method, I believe, of evangelizing."

"*July* 12, 1902.—First baptism at Beni-Abbès: Marie-Joseph Abdjesu Carita, a little negro of three and a half."[1]

"*July* 21.—Four soldiers of the garrison have died this month of extreme heat. Not one of them refused the Sacraments; two died very piously after a long illness. . . ."

"*August* 13.—I am still alone—the only religious—with Abdjesu, a negro of twenty-five redeemed and liberated some time ago; an artilleryman who serves my Mass; some

---

[1] "Abdjesu" means, in Arabic, "servant of Jesus"; as "Abd Ennebi," "servant of the prophet."

sharpshooters who are repairing the chapel, the roof of which is getting weak. The Fraternity, very silent at night and from 10 to 3 in the afternoon, is a beehive from 5 to 9 in the morning; and from 4 to 8 in the evening. I never stop talking and seeing people; slaves, poor people, invalids, soldiers, travellers, and inquirers; the latter—inquirers—I have but rarely, but the slaves, invalids, and poor increase. . . . I celebrate Mass, except on Sundays and great Festivals—I say it, on those days, when the military desire—to which nobody ever comes on weekdays, before daybreak, so as not to be too much disturbed by the noise, and to make my thanksgiving in some peace; but however early I may be, I am always called three or four times while making my thanksgiving."

"*September* 12.—What are wonderful here are the sunsets, the evenings, and the nights. . . . The evenings are so calm, the nights so serene; the great sky and the vast horizons half lit by the stars are so peaceful, and in silence thrill the soul by hymning the eternal, the infinite, and the beyond, so that one could spend entire nights in such contemplation; however, I curtail it and return after spending a few moments before the tabernacle, for there is more in the humble tabernacle: nothing is nothing, compared to the Well-Beloved."

14*th*.—Ransomed two slaves: a father of a family and a young man of fifteen, whom Brother Charles provisionally named Paul.

"*November* 5, 1902.—It has rained twice, so I hide the altar furniture under the altar; and the altar, as soon as the sky grows cloudy, under a waterproof covering—a little tarpaulin. At the Fraternity, as at the camp and in the village, it rains as much inside the rooms (and chapel) as outside. The roofs protect only from the sun. That, far from hindering, contributes to happiness: in making the inclemencies of the weather felt, God reminds us that Jesus had not a stone whereon to lay His head. All that makes us like the Well-Beloved unites us to Him and is perfect happiness. . . . The very sight of my nothingness, instead of afflicting me, helps me to forget myself and to think only of Him who is all."

The end of the year came. The buildings and repairs of the poor hermitage were finished—waiting for the Brothers to tell of their early coming and thus bring the workmen back to the workyard. Ordinary and regular life was, no doubt, beginning. It must be as strict as possible, and

Brother Charles, thinking of this obligation of his calling, thought it better to do without the daily help of a soldier who had been his "housekeeper." They told him he was overdone, but he maintained his decision; he gave this noble and witty reply: "Jesus had no orderly."

His only anxiety was for souls. Thanks to the two blacks he had redeemed, he could have exposition of the Blessed Sacrament in the not quite empty chapel when the soldiers were kept in camp. And then, on Christmas Day and the day after, he had an "immense joy"; some Moroccans came to pay him a visit. With what friendship he must have received them, and with what dreams beyond their understanding he must have followed them!

On these same days, he had surprises of another sort. For many centuries Christmas has been a season when friends have been accustomed to exchange gifts. Brother Charles saw a porter coming to the hermitage carrying a light parcel, carefully tied, that the ass-driver postmen had delivered at the Native Office.

"Where does it come from? The East? Do they still remember me?"

They remembered him so well that the nuns of a convent in the Holy Land where he had spent some time, wishing to give pleasure to the hermit whom they had known as gardener, porter, and messenger, sent him a Christmas present. But what can one give a hermit, when one is oneself poor? First of all relics for the chapel. There were several in the parcel: relics of the Saints, particles of the Holy Sepulchre or of the Nativity cave. The donors had added some flowers from Palestine, arranged as a bouquet and pasted on vellum; then, having sought such small things as a Father of the Thebaid might want for his household, they had put into one envelope a wooden spoon, a mousetrap, and a yard of white cloth. The man who brought the parcel, seeing this remnant and also Father de Foucauld's poor threadbare and tattered *gandourah* full of holes, surmised that pieces much needed by his friend's tunic might be cut out of this fine white cloth. No sooner was he back in camp than he went to the army tailor, and told him to go quickly to the hermitage. The tailor did not loiter much on the way. Perhaps he wanted to wait till the worst heat of the afternoon was over. Anyhow, a little before sunset he was back in camp, with discomfited expression.

"Nothing doing."

"What? won't he have his *gandourah* mended?"

"Not quite that; but he had no more of the cloth; he has given it away."

In fact, on the still burning plateau, they could see a little negro, running round with pride and showing himself to his comrades. He had just come from the hermitage clad in a sack as white as snow.

About the same time—perhaps a little sooner—an officer, who had to do with sending supplies to the oasis posts, remarked on the platform of Oran station a little cask addressed to the Révérend Père de Foucauld at Beni-Abbes. "Altar wine," he thought, " and it cannot fail to turn sour; the journey and the heat must already have damaged it. In what state will it reach the poor Father?" As soon as the discovery was made, they hastened to put the cask in the shade in a store. A man of good-will, who knew what to do for wine in danger, poured several buckets of water on the barrel, which was given into the charge of the guards of the train from Oran to Beni-Unif, and sprinkled two or three times *en route*. At Beni-Unif, when the time came to form the convoy for revictualling Beni-Abbes, the cask was put on the camel's back, and, as everyone was a great friend of Father de Foucauld, never was a parcel more closely looked after, better covered with wool while on the way, or unloaded with more care when the caravan in the evening halted for the night. At last the precious barrel was brought to the hermitage.

"Here is your altar wine, Father."

"But I have not ordered any."

"They have sent you some; look at the address."

Brother Charles decided to open the cask. It was then perceived that it was a bell, with a clapper well wrapped in rags, which had travelled under chestnut staves and had been refreshed with such touching care. It was hung from the top of a sort of small rectangular tower—I should say campanile, if the word here did not suggest immoderate ambition—at the side of the chapel. And it rang, a witness told me: "It used to ring oftener than we wanted sometimes, not only in the day, but at night, at 10, at midnight, at 4 in the morning. The sound, through the clear desert air, reached us in the redoubt, as if we had been under the clapper. It was Brother Charles summoning himself to say his Office."[1]

---

[1] At the same time (end of 1902), at the other end of the cliff of Beni-Abbes, the soldiers were building a monumental Arab Office, to which a redoubt was added. This is the vast mass of buildings surrounded by ramparts that you see to-day on your left as you enter the oasis.

"*January* 20, 1903.—Two *harratins* of Anfid, the fakir Barka ben Ziân, and the fakir Ombarek, known for their honesty, ask me to instruct them in our holy religion, and they seem sincere."

"*January* 21, 1903.—A child of thirteen, a native of Twat, a slave for six years, has been ransomed, and declares even before his ransom that he wishes to follow the religion of Jesus and stay with me. Ransomed to-day at noon, he immediately enters the catechumenate under the name of Peter."

In March came the visit of a former comrade, Henri Laperrine.[1] He reached Beni-Abbés on the 6th. He is chief in command of the Saharan oases—that is to say, of Gurara, Twat, and Tidikelt.

Henry Laperrine, who here reappears by the side of Charles de Foucauld, had been a sub-lieutenant in the Fourth Chasseurs d'Afrique. Of middle height, with a supple and muscular body, a pale and lean face, refined features, short fan-shaped light auburn beard, bright eyes —generally roguish, at moments hard—he was already regarded, at the time of his arrival, on his round as chief at Beni-Abbes, as an accomplished type of the colonial cavalryman. He was hardly ever seen wearing the linen helmet or dressed in Arab fashion or as a Tuareg. He allowed such fancies—and others—to his subordinates, in their stopping places. Under the blazing sun he wore his cloth cap cocked over his left ear, and the regulation uniform. He would ride for ten hours, with the thermometer at 102°, and reach the halting-place with his collar buttoned up and sitting bolt upright in the saddle. Few bushrangers were such men of the world as he in the desert. He made up for it by shunning towns and their ceremony, detested official visits, and used to declare that between submitting to an hour's wait in the antechamber of a minister and enduring a sandstorm, he would choose the storm. His good-humour was well known. He liked lively, even light

[1] Born at Castelnaudary on September 29, 1860, consequently two years younger than Charles de Foucauld. A pupil of the École spéciale Militaire, October 25, 1878; sub-lieutenant pupil at the École d'Application de Cavalerie, October 1, 1880; sub-lieutenant in the 4th Regiment of Chasseurs d'Afrique, September 10, 1881; lieutenant in the 1st Regiment of the Spahis, July 29, 1885; of the squadron of Senegal, March 22, 1889; captain in the 2nd Dragoons, November 1, 1891; in the 2nd squadron of Spahis Soudanais, September 13, 1893; in the squadron of the mounted *méhari* Saharan Spahis, November 6, 1897; squadron commander in the 7th Regiment of Chasseurs, October 7; Commander-in-Chief of the Saharan oasis, July 6, 1901.

stories, preferably those which introduced the people of the *bled*. But he was subject to sudden changes. This impressionable, spirited, absent-minded man had twenty and often thirty times a day reason for losing patience or being angry. The only thing he did not forgive was deceit. You won his confidence once, not twice. As for the rest, he easily forgot the wrongs of others and his own; he possessed in perfection the gift of sympathy, which in a man of feeling becomes an art. All good workers, all energetic servants of the cause—that is to say, of France in Africa— loved Laperrine. He could be amiable without being familiar. He had his rank in his look, gesture, and soul. In the desert he used to make his non-commissioned officers sit round the *burnous* spread out on the ground and used as a tablecloth for lunch. His officers on mission corresponded, in private letters, with their chief, even in service matters, each giving news of himself and telling stories, and commenting and complaining if there were reason to do so. He replied in the same way. His energy was prodigious, his exactness equally so. Hardly was he off his horse or *méhari*, after a ride of thirty or forty, and sometimes fifty miles, before having his work-table set up; he then drank a cup of tea, and set about writing. The messengers who joined him *en route* could set out again the same evening with his reply. During the siesta there was often only one man who was not asleep—Laperrine. There, in the desert, he was in his kingdom, the whole of which he knew, men and things. One of his disciples and friends said: "He was fully himself only from the moment he placed his bare foot on the supple neck of his *méhari*." His authority over so many of the tribes of Algeria, the Soudan and the Sahara, was obtained by the certainty, established by a hundred proofs in the hearts of the natives, that this great chief was not their enemy. Laperrine wished neither to humiliate nor impose on them; he wished to conciliate them, to get them to enter, as protegés, helpers, and friends, an extended France.

This constitutional liberalism, which was victorious and has brought France a much envied colonial empire, he expounded neither in a treatise of military art nor in an account of his campaigns. "It is in his correspondence as military commander that an historian, enamoured of the things of the Sahara, will go sooner or later to find the principles of civilizing the desert. If it be true that a man writes as he thinks, there is Laperrine in his entirety. The big books of instructions and orders are in his own firm and expressive handwriting; his matter sets aside the accessory to get to the essential. Even the jumbled spelling—Laperrine, like Madame de Sévigné, had a disdain for academic conventions—all reveals his inner fire. Everywhere one finds the impress left on Laperrine's mind by his youthful years. He adapted himself to his surroundings, became a nomad with the nomad, a counter-raider with the raiders, took from the native all the instinctive experience he could give, and surpassed him in moral ascendency, reasoning, and conscience."[1]

The vocations of Laperrine and de Foucauld were sisters, not similar nor of the same character, but both varieties of the same species, very French and very Christian. Their friendship, during forty years, is explained by their common understanding of the civilizing rôle of France. But I believe other elements formed and maintained it. Foucauld admired in Laperrine a loyal and ardent soul, capable of sacrificing to the ideal all his ease, repose, health, life itself and, what is more rare, promotion. Laperrine in Foucauld admired gifts similar to his own, placed at the service of a still grander ideal: his personal holiness and radiation of holiness among the natives.

Colonial military life, which is not that of a girls' boarding-school, the remoteness of Christian society, the preoccupation of a mind always on the strain or brought back to military duty, may have turned Laperrine away from religious practice. But this pupil of the *Dominicans* of Sorèze remained a believer at heart. His two dearest friends were priests, with whom he kept up a most constant correspondence—viz.: his brother Mgr. Laperrine of Hautpoul, and Father de Foucauld. And if any sally of his can be quoted to lead one to suppose that he had no faith, great care must be taken not to draw from so slight a cause, so grave and distressing a conclusion. We ought to accord quite another credit to some positive facts which shall, in their place, be related in this book, and to the affirmation of one of his intimates, who said to me: "On all serious occasions he used to speak of the things of religion with wonderful respect."

I should give a very incomplete sketch of this great Frenchman if I did not further say that he was generous. His purse was easily opened. On a journey he used to share his commander's provisions with the officers and non-commissioned officers whom he had invited; he was fond of

[1] " Notes sur le Général Laperrine" (*Bull. de l'Afrique française*, Mai, 1920).

distributing presents among the tribes, and one cannot think, without emotion, that many years after the one I am now speaking of, when setting out for that air journey to Hoggar which was to be his last, Laperrine brought as his luggage on board the aeroplane a little parcel of light silks for the Tuareg women and children.

Such was the visitor whose coming was a great joy to Brother Charles. They must have had a long talk, a little of the past, much of the future of *their* Africa. However, the diary makes no mention of it. Neither the arrival of this military detachment on the Beni-Abbes plateau, nor the reception given to this already legendary Commander, nor Laperrine's words, nor the conversation of the two friends, are related. How little of a romancer this Brother Charles was! Just a simple note, very short, a confidential intimation: " A few days ago he [Laperrine] had obtained authority for undertaking a triple operation next spring: 1st, to go from In-Salah to Timbuctoo, and definitively and militarily to join Tidikelt to the Soudan by force, if necessary; 2nd, to conquer the Hoggar and to push on as far as Agades; 3rd, to gain the Atlantic Ocean to the South of Dra, occupying Tabelbalet and Tinduf. But, after having thus given him authority, they have now almost immediately withdrawn it."

And Laperrine continued his round.

Days and months went by; but de Foucauld was always entirely alone, I mean in his apostolate. No other man offered to share the life of him who had gone out to be *vox clamantis in deserto*, like John the Baptist. The Baptist well knew he would have no companion: Brother Charles hoped to find one, and surely in the hardest days, when the body droops with weariness and the mind begins to ask *cui bono*, he took refuge in the hope of this help to come. How often is the flight of time, the lack of continuance which is one of the infirmities of our state, a consolation to us. But poor Brother Charles felt this trial keenly. Loving solitude, he did not suffer from it for himself, but for his fellow-men. Working by himself amidst total corruption, total ignorance, in which he never encountered even the glimmers, the veiled regrets, the power of resurrection felt to be latent in the souls of the baptized, he had tried in the course of years to induce a few Little Brothers or Sisters to prepare for the future community. His letters and cautiously distributed regulations did not seem to touch any heart. Can any generous idea fail to germinate in France? How could such a thing take place?

The answers may vary. Persons ever so little acquainted with ecclesiastical history will doubtless observe that religious Orders are not born in the abstract; that constitutions are not made *a priori,* but at first lived, tried, and proved by a band of men or women drawn together by the moral strength of their future chief. Others will point out that the regulations of Brother Charles overstep the mark, do too much violence to human weakness, presuppose a vigour of temperament and a power of will rarely associated. We shall see this opinion firmly, even hardly expressed by the Prior of a Trappe, who had not forgotten Brother Marie-Albéric, considering him an eminently holy man, but who believed he was not called to govern a community. We have arrived at that point of Father de Foucauld's "Life" where it will be necessary to explain why he so eagerly desired—as he does to the end—other priests, like himself, to become Little Brothers of the Sacred Heart, and to break into the Mohammedan countries. He had sought solitude; he had bought it dearly; he held to it. But the workman plunged into the harvest, and seeing the immensity of the task, was dejected at not belonging to a band. He did more, he accused himself unceasingly; in his correspondence and intimate notes he declares that his unworthiness is the cause of the isolation in which he lives.

"I am still alone at Beni-Abbes," he wrote to the Marchioness de Foucauld.[1] "More than ever I believe Beni-Abbes favourable for a community of poor solitaries, living to adore the Blessed Sacrament and for manual labour; it is so solitary and so central, between Algeria, Morocco, and the Sahara! Pray that my infidelities may not in any way hinder the designs of the Sacred Heart."

He was always lamenting such shortcomings. We find the same thought, the same fervour of contrition and supplication, in his diary, at Easter, 1903.

"Not a single postulant, novice, or Sister. . . . *Unless the grain of wheat die, it remains alone.* Lord Jesus, pardon my innumerable infidelities and slacknesses! Help me, Holy Virgin, St. Magdalen, Blessed Margaret Mary! Reign in me, Heart of Jesus, that I may at last die to myself, to the world, and to all that is not Thee and Thy will, and bear fruit for Thy glory.

"After great misdeeds the catechumen Paul has left me; the catechumen Peter has left me: he desired to return to his parents, and I have sent him to them; the catechumen Joseph of the Sacred Heart, sent to the White

[1] Letter of November 15, 1903.

Fathers at Algiers in February 1902, and brought back by them to the Soudan in October, has left me, and his was a bad leaving. . . . Two persons only remain with me at the Fraternity: the little Christian Abdjesu and the old blind catechumen Marie."

All at once it looked as if those men of mortification, prayer, example, and charity, whose coming Brother Charles implores, are going to be sent him. Two Fathers and two Brothers of La Trappe of Staouëli have spoken—no doubt vaguely enough—of imitating Father de Foucauld and putting themselves under his obedience. But look at him and see him as he is: he does not seek to attract them; he tests them from the beginning; he writes to one of them:

"DEAR AND VENERATED FATHER,
 "M. de la H—— tells me that you and another Father and two Trappist Brothers feel yourselves urged to share in my poor, abject, and solitary life of the hidden Jesus, the life which He put before us for thirty years at Nazareth. . . .

"My very dear Father, what all of you have to do is simple. Jesus never asks us to do things that are complicated, but He asks all of us to combine childlike simplicity with great prudence, which consists, as St. Paul says, in seeking carefully, by sure means, what is the will of God, so as to do it without mistake.

"It is enough for you and for each of the other three of you, the Father and Brothers, to know God's will, and then to do it, cost what it may.

"There is but one infallible way of knowing the divine will in such a question; it is by spiritual direction: open your soul fully to a *conscientious, learned, intelligent, meditative, unprejudiced director;* and take his reply as the divine will of the present moment, in virtue of the promise: 'He that heareth you, heareth Me'; that is the infallible means of doing the will of Jesus in this case and in all others; . . . If he says to you: 'Jesus calls you to leave La Trappe and join Brother Charles,' come, my arms and heart are open to you, I shall receive you as brought by the hand of Jesus. If he says to you: 'Wait,' obey and wait. If he says: 'Stay in La Trappe,' obey; in this last case, if, while obeying, you continue to feel yourself interiorly urged to come and follow Jesus in His poverty, abjection, solitude, and hidden life, again, tell him so from time to time, always keeping your soul open to him.

"But to know if you are called by God to share my

humble kind of life, you must know exactly what it is: it is fixed now by constitutions and a Rule which I submitted to my Prefect Apostolic: the latter permitting me to establish myself in his prefecture has also permitted me to gather round me a certain number of priests and laymen according to these constitutions and this Rule. When we are numerous enough, final authority will be sought for from Rome.

"Forewarn them well as to *dura et aspera*. Show them this letter, the constitutions and the passing of the preliminaries of the Rule. . . . Tell them frankly that besides what is generally demanded of postulants—namely, the good-will to practise the constitutions and the Rule to the best of their ability—I ask for three things as the first stones of this little building: 1st, readiness to have one's head cut off; 2nd, readiness to die of hunger; 3rd, to obey me in spite of my unworthiness, until there are a few of us and we can have an election (which, I hope, will replace me by one more worthy than I am, and put me, as I deserve, in the lowest place). . . .

"My thought is that, since we are accepted in the apostolic prefecture of the Sahara, where I have at the present time a little land, enough to feed from twenty to twenty-five monks, and the beginning of a monastery capable of being finished in a few weeks at very little cost, and where, what is more, an enormous amount of good can be done to the populations of the Sahara as well as to those of Morocco—sheep more lost than any—the best thing is for both Brothers and Sisters to concentrate and be trained here, *if it is possible*. . . ."

He was never to have, with one exception for a very short time, a missionary companion. Already the hope of the early establishment of some nuns at Beni-Abbes was abandoned. Brother Charles had corresponded, on this subject, with Père Guérin, and in one of his letters accepted the reply given him: "As for the Sisters, yes, it is very just and wise, not to send them to me here, as long as I am the only priest. You are a thousand times right."

The reason of the refusal must have been, I suppose, that the Sisters would be compelled to take the only priest there was within three hundred miles, as their spiritual director. Ecclesiastical law respects the liberty of souls, and prevents this sort of constraint as far as possible.

Therefore, no Sisters for the refuge, none for the little negroes or for the girls who lived in the oasis. He was with still more reason obliged to put off until later, till much later, the foundation of those Little Sisters of the Sacred Heart, for whom he had also thought out and written the sketch of a Rule.

As to the Little Brothers of the Sacred Heart, the reply was also in the negative, but Brother Charles did not know it. Some months previously Mgr. Guérin, desirous of helping him and sending him companions, had corresponded with the Father Abbot of Notre-Dame-des-Neiges. The latter replied:

" . . . You exhort me to give him a helper, a companion. For the moment I cannot, but could I do so, I should still hesitate. You know, Monseigneur, I have the deepest esteem for the heroic virtues of Father Albéric, and it is well rooted by twelve years of intimate companionship. The only thing at which I am astonished is that he does not perform miracles. I have never seen, outside of books, such holiness on the earth. But I must confess that I am a little doubtful of his prudence and discretion. The austerities he practises, and which he thinks of demanding of his companions, are such that I am inclined to believe that neophytes would soon succumb to them. Moreover, the intensity of mind that he imposes on himself and wishes to impose on his disciples, appears to me so superhuman as to make me dread lest such excessive tension of mind might drive his disciple mad before he had been killed with the excess of austerities.

" If you think that we may entrust anyone to him without danger for his head and for his life, I shall blindly agree with your decision, and shall set to work to find him a companion as soon as possible."

Staouëli said the same. One of the monks of that Abbey at the beginning of 1902—questioned, no doubt, by Commandant Lacroix—delivered himself with the same frankness about the desired companions.

"Our holy friend is at the height of his desires; thanks to your fraternal support, all the personnel of Beni-Abbes is devoted to him. . . . You can rely on him as on a perfect instrument of pacification and moralization. He will do yonder on a small scale what the great cardinal did in Tunis for French influence. My only regret is not to have anybody to send to second him. His life is so austere, that those among the Superiors of our Order who have the sincerest affection for him judge him more admirable than imitable, and fear to throw into discouragement any disciples they might be able to procure him. He will therefore be probably obliged to live alone, or by degrees recruit, on the spot, the elements of his future community."[1]

Brother Charles never read these letters. He continued to wait and be resigned. He had not to make his sacrifice just once; he made it yearly, perhaps every month, as long as he lived, seeing clearly that nobody came to relieve him. And how did he take this hard trial? Perfectly. It is proved by the lines which he chanced to write, not knowing what was thought of his plans:

"As for companions, I shall, my very dear Father, from the bottom of my heart, be perfectly content, whatever may happen. If one day I have some, I shall be satisfied to see in that the accomplishment of God's will and His name glorified. If I have none . . . I shall say to myself that He is glorified in so many other ways, and that His beatitude so little needs our poor praises and hearts! If I could—but I cannot—do otherwise than lose myself totally in union with His divine will, I should prefer for myself total failure and perpetual solitude and defeats all round: *elegi abjectus esse*. There we see the union with the abjection and the Cross of our divine Well-Beloved, which to me has always seemed most desirable of all. I do all I can to have companions; the means of getting them is, in my eyes, to sanctify myself in silence. If I had some, I should rejoice in many annoyances and crosses : having none, I am perfectly joyful."

Indeed, nature cannot be more completely overcome, and this soul is great among the great. Men suspected it : even during his life they called Brother Charles a paladin, and they spoke truly. But several added, a paladin who mistook his century. A quip which marks an era. The war proved it; never were so many paladins seen as in the twentieth century, and in each province of France, and in the most humble families. And these were thoroughly men of their time! So was Charles de Foucauld. In other circumstances calling for devotion and self-sacrifice, he was one of them, born before them. And, if he had no disciples, who could say that they will not come to him, now that death is over, and the experiment has been made? For heroes are not lacking : it is the causes which have need of them that they want to know.

[1] Letter of January 5, 1902. It will be remembered that Abbé Huvelin, at the time of the hermitages in the Holy Land, had expressed himself in the same manner as the Abbot of Notre-Dame-des Neiges and the Trappist of Stauèli.

"*May* 5, 1903.—The old catechumen Marie is very ill. The doctor is away. Fearing that she might die, I baptized her, on her very clearly expressed desire, after having made her recite, in Arabic, the *Pater*, the *Credo*, the acts of faith, hope, charity and contrition, and having got her, once more, formally to ask for baptism."

This baptism of the poor Musulman negress was a missionary's joy. Brother Charles communicates the news to a priest whom he knows to be very devoted to the Saharan work; it gives him an opportunity of humiliating himself.[1]

"I ask your prayers for the poor old negress whose soul is so white, who would this evening be in Paradise were she to die now. I had much better ask them for the old sinner now writing to you.

"Indeed, Monsieur l'Abbé, it is a sinner who thanks you. One thing alone equals and surpasses the sins of my youth —the infidelities, the cowardice, the lukewarmness of my riper years, my daily wretchedness: it is the graces and the mercies with which God overwhelms and confounds me. Pray, I beg you, that I may at last be faithful. Pray that I may love and serve. Pray that my life may be all *alleluias* and obedience. . . . Pray that this little atom that I am may accomplish, in the midst of these millions of souls which have never heard Jesus spoken of, the work for which He sent me. Pray for Morocco and for the Sahara, which are unhappily a sealed tomb. Pray that, like the Angels, we may work with all our strength for the salvation of men, rejoicing with our whole soul in the happiness of God."

The hermit was going to receive another visit. Père Guérin, who had set out from Ghardaia, and was making a "round of inspection" of the White Fathers' stations, was expected at Beni-Abbes from the first weeks of the year 1903. Brother Charles was delighted; Captain Regnault, his friend, chief of the Arab Office, planned to go as far as Ksabi to meet the traveller—a desert politeness which recalls the time of the stage-coaches, when our fathers used to go as far as the next posting-station to meet a friend. But the journey was lengthened; after Tidikelt, the Prefect Apostolic of the Soudan visited Twat, Gurara; there he stopped, and Brother Charles's letters followed him as best they could. I will quote some fragments of this correspondence, because they show even better than others the ardent soul of the solitary, all affection, prayer, hope, and repentance.

[1] Letter of May 25, 1903, to Abbé Laurain.

He wrote on February 27 :

"My very dear and Reverend Father,
"With my whole heart I follow you, with thought and prayer on your journey. . . . Oh, yes, with my whole soul I consent, in spite of my ardent desire to see you, to your arrival being delayed beyond anticipation, if a journey farther to the South is to cause this delay : *Adveniat regnum tuum.* . . . My beloved Father, I am poor to the last degree, yet, seek as I will, I find no other desire within me than this : *Adveniat regnum tuum! Sanctificetur nomen tuum!* Do not think that in my kind of life the hope of enjoying sooner the vision of the Well-Beloved stands for anything : no, I wish for one thing only : it is to do what pleases Him most. If I love fasting and watching, it is because Jesus loved them so much : I envy His nights of prayer on the mountain-tops : I would like to keep Him company : night is the time for the *tête-à-tête.* . . . Alas ! I am so cold that I dare not say I love : but, I want to love ! That is why I love watching. Unhappily, less and less am I able to watch. . . . As to the fasting, in obedience to your letter, I shall mitigate it with all my might. I shall eat better and drink some milk : besides, in conformity with Abbé Huvelin's order, I have for several months been taking great care of myself, using condensed milk, and I eat according to my hunger. . . . Be certain that your letter and recommendations will have an immediate and serious effect on my sleep and food. . . .

"Thanks for what you tell me of my big negro Paul : you will judge. . . . I do not think there is any reason to bring him here ; he is not trustworthy. . . . I am not surprised at Joseph's flight [another young ransomed slave] : the most encouraging example, which I call to mind at every moment in order to guide me, is that of our Lord's behaviour towards Judas Iscariot. We are surrounded with nothing but negroes, Arabs, and revellers. I think also of the Epistles to the Corinthians, which show the Christians of St. Paul in a very sorry light. It was for our hope that those lines were written : for, seeing what surrounds us, we are terrified. What is impossible for us is possible for God : let us pray to Him to send His angel to roll the stone away from the tomb. . . ."

This sets us thinking : is it not a pity for a man of such worth to condemn himself to live among such people ? But Brother Charles is right : it is just these beautiful souls so closely akin to Jesus Christ that are required to draw together and reconcile the most unfortunate.

While Father Guérin continued his journey, raids increased round Beni-Abbes. That home of gossip, the desert, talked about the exploits of the Berbers, who were attacking convoys and sometimes carrying them off. The Zusfana tracks were not very safe. More than one sign suggested agitation amongst the tribes; the Governor-General of Algeria, M. Revoil, had just sent in his resignation; the news from France was depressing; religious persecutions were spreading; both men's Orders and women's were upset; irreproachable Frenchmen were being unjustly stripped of their property, deprived of the free choice of a vocation, and driven to leave their dear fatherland; it was to be feared that similar measures would be taken against the Algerian missionaries and Sisters. Charles de Foucauld went on writing the journal of the poor Christians of Beni-Abbes for Father Guérin.

The Father's arrival was at last announced for the end of May. Brother Charles rejoiced, and asked God to bless the journey. "May He let you long enjoy His little tabernacle at Beni-Abbes, and long enjoy your adoration therein! I dream of many days and nights for you here before the Most Blessed Sacrament exposed. It must be long since you enjoyed hours of silence at the feet of the Sacred Host."

On May 17 another letter gave the arrangements made and final advice. "Do not let yourself be monopolized by the others! They will want to receive you! There are even three officers, at this moment, messing together at Beni-Abbes. The first two days they will quarrel about your visit. . . . It goes without saying that you and your suite—*mehara* included—will lodge at the Fraternity. There you are *at home*. Captain Regnault strongly insisted on putting you up at the *borj* of the Arab Office, where you might be more comfortable, but I told him your place was under the roof of the Blessed Sacrament, and he understood. But your cook will not take a holiday. You would have only me, if your cook did not lend a hand, and I do not wish to kill you with my cooking.

"I shall receive you as a poor man receives his dearly beloved father—that is to say, very poorly; but you will do whatever you like, you will be the master: if you wish, I will be your guest. I shall not press you in any way, you will have complete liberty, you will be at home.

"Abdjesu and Marie—who did not die, I believe you

will find her alive—are impatiently awaiting you. Ten times a day, Abdjesu asks me where is the Pope now, Charles? Do what I will, he will not give up calling you the Pope.

". . . It goes without saying, that on your arrival I shall first of all get you to go into the chapel to the feet of the Master, of the All."

Father Guérin and his companion, Father Villard, remained five days at Beni-Abbes, from May 27 to the evening of June 1. We can imagine what must have been the first meeting, the prayers in common, then the conversations of these monks brought together for a moment in the course of the long journeys which were their vocation. They can hardly have spoken of what other travellers willingly relate—their impressions of the route, of the misery or discomfort of the resting-places, of the beauty of the landscape: they were taken up with the subject that was, is, and shall be, the greatest; with souls, with the ignorant and hostile multitude which they met in dry mud houses and under tents, and with the share of eternal life which is nevertheless promised to every one of these poor people.

We know that on May 31, Whit-Sunday, Father Guérin celebrated the principal Mass, and the diary bears this note: "The first time for many centuries, absolutely the first time, perhaps, three priests are at Beni-Abbes." Presently we shall see a few of the observations that Father Guérin made in reference to the missionary methods of Father de Foucauld. I will first quote the letter which the latter wrote to his Superior, two days after Père Guérin had quitted the hermitage plateau and descended the bank of the Zusfana in the evenhing, taking the track which leads in the direction of Taghit. He had just heard that a lady named Tavernier, a kinswoman of Père Guérin—he did not know how close—had just died, and to console him he sent him such condolences as only one near to God can give or receive. What a distance between our formulæ, our efforts to console our neighbour, our poor inventions, even those into which we have put our whole heart, and this sort of hymn of probation and alleluia of suffering, written hastily on a small sheet of paper by Father de Foucauld from his renewed solitude:

"WELL-BELOVED AND MUCH VENERATED FATHER,

"Sorrows follow closely upon joys. . . . It is in sorrow that I write to you to-day, for I know that your sojourn in Taghit will not be spent without sadness. . . . It is by the Cross that Jesus wished to save men, and by it he continues to save them; His apostles, who carry on His life here below, do good in proportion to their holiness, but only on condition of suffering and according to their sufferings. . . . In order to be an *alter Jesus,* if *we* are no longer to *live, but Jesus live in us;* we must above all things be holy, before all burn with love like His Heart; we must also carry the cross and be crowned with the crown of thorns.

"The trial which you feel is a divine dew for the Sahara mission: all your sorrows, all your tears are souls. . . . It is by the crosses which Jesus sends us, much more than by mortifications of our own choice, that we drink of the chalice of the Spouse and shall be baptized with His baptism, for He knows much better than we how to crucify us. . . .

"Well-beloved Father, I do not say to you: Be resigned; I say: Bless and thank God, lose yourself in thanksgiving; Jesus is giving you souls; your suffering is their salvation. . . . If you could only suffer much in order to save many! . . . If you could only die of grief to save the greatest number possible! . . . How good Jesus is to share His chalice with us; how good He is to mark the month of His Heart by piercing yours; how good He is to hear your prayer and make you suffer in order to make you a saviour!

"I don't know if you feel as I do: separated so long from souls so dear, when I hear of the departure of one of them for the fatherland, it seems to me that it is not a separation, but the beginning of reunion; I can speak to them and they hear me; pray to them, and I hope they help me; it is the beginning of eternal union.

"I felt myself *alone* for the first time for many years, on Monday evening, when you gradually disappeared in the dusk. I then understood and felt that I was a hermit. . . . Then I remembered that I had Jesus, and I said: 'Jesus, I love You.' . . . Well-beloved Father, how much I thank you for your visit, for the good you have done me. . . . I shall do my best to conform to all you said in order to mend, improve, and correct myself according to your wishes and desires.

"P.S.—Tell Abdjesu that I embrace and bless him, *complexans eos, et imponens manus super illos.* . . . If he ever asks my name, tell him that I am called Abdjesu. Pray that I may be so!

"Yesterday, a long visit from two men of Tafilelt, two

marabouts. They heard you spoken of, and asked me whether you had gone to Tafilelt. ' No, he will go another time !'—' Marhaba ! Does he travel on foot ?'—' No, on a camel.'—This question asked by marabouts, made me reflect. . . . They went on foot, leading their asses. . . . We are disciples of Jesus, we want Jesus to live in us, *Christianus alter Christus,* and we are always talking of poverty . . . they are disciples of Mahomet. I turn to the example of our brethren the Apostles. . . . We are in such infidel countries as St. Peter and St. Paul were in. . . . If we wish to do their work, let us follow their example. . . .

" Every time I pray to Jesus, the same answer seems to come back : ' Do miracles for Me, and I will do them for thee.' . . ."

Now that the Vicar-Apostolic of the Sahara has left Beni-Abbes, let us again open the diary, and we shall know what were the conversations of Fathers Guérin and de Foucauld.

"*June* 1, 1903.—Mgr. Guérin left for Taghit. Here are some of his remarks :

" 1st. Talk a good deal to the natives, and not of things commonplace, but always bring the talk back to God; if we cannot preach Jesus to them because they would certainly not accept such teaching, prepare them little by little to receive it, by unceasingly preaching natural religion in our talks. . . . Speak much and always so as to improve and uplift and bring souls nearer to God, and prepare the ground for the Gospel.

" 2nd. Arrange benches and shelters in the yards, make visitors sit down, and don't leave them standing. . . . When people are sitting conversation more easily takes a serious and intimate turn.

" 3rd. Make temporal alms help the soul by speaking of God, and give the spiritual alms of good instruction to those to whom you are giving material alms.

" 4th. The work of evangelists in Musulman countries is not only to take children and try and inculcate Christian principles in them, but also to convert grown men as far as possible. . . . Children will not be able to make the evangelical seed cast into their souls germinate, if they do not find the society in which they live somewhat prepared beforehand and well disposed. Besides, all men are made for the light, for Jesus; all are His heritage, and not one, *if he has good-will,* is incapable of knowing and loving

Him. . . . Musulmans are then by no means unfitted for conversion. . . . Let us try hard to evangelize men of riper years, first by conversations turning only to God and natural religion; then, according to circumstances, giving to each such truth as we hope to get him to accept.

" 5th. While evangelizing the poor, do not neglect the rich. Our Lord did not neglect them; neither did St. Paul, His imitator. On account of their influence their reformation is a blessing to the poor. Their sincerity is less doubtful, there is less reason to fear that they are 'soupers' listening to Christian truths only for material interests.

" 6th. I build too much: stop, don't go on building. . . .

" 7th. The Musulmans of the Sahara receive their false religion solely through *confidence* in their ancestors, in their marabouts, in those who surround them, solely through the authority which these have over them, and without a shadow of reasoning or verification. . . . We ought, then, to try more to gain their *confidence*, and to acquire more *authority* than those who surround them and indoctrinate them. For that, three things are necessary: 1st, to be very holy; 2nd, to *show ourselves* to the natives a great deal; and 3rd, to speak a good deal to them. *Holiness*, which is the main thing, will sooner or later give us the authority and inspire confidence. *Constantly seeing us* will bring them round to our cause, and, if we are holy, that will be preaching without words, and strengthening our authority.

" 8th. To bring Musulmans to God, must we try to make them esteem us by excelling in things which they esteem; for instance, by being audacious, a good horseman, a good shot, and slightly ostentatious in liberality, etc., or by practising the Gospel in its abjection and poverty, going about on foot and without luggage, working with our hands as Jesus in Nazareth, living poorly, like a petty workman? It is not from the Chambāa that we ought to learn to live, but from Jesus. . . . We ought not to take lessons from them, but to give them some. Jesus said to us: 'Follow Me.' St. Paul said to us: 'Be ye imitators of me as I also am of Christ.' . . . Jesus knew the best way of bringing souls to Himself, and St. Paul was His incomparable disciple. Do we hope to do better than they? Musulmans do not make a mistake. Of a priest who is a good horseman, a good shot, etc., they say: 'He is an excellent rider, none shoot better than he'; and maybe they will add, ' He would be worthy of being a Chambi!' They do not say: ' He is a saint.' Let a missionary lead the life of St. Anthony in the desert, they will all say : ' He is a saint.' For natural reasons they will often give their friendship to the first, to the Chambi; if they give their confidence in matters of the soul, they will only give it to the second."

The question thus treated between Fathers Guérin and de Foucauld is of great importance : it is, besides, for France and other nations, the first of colonial questions. I must therefore stop a little and say, in the first place, that it is but little known, and that, generally, it is answered off-hand.

In drawing rooms and at meetings, if there is talk of the better administration of our African possessions, one is certain to hear this opinion expressed : " Musulmans are incapable of conversion "; or, as they used to say at the beginning of the nineteenth century : " You can't associate or mingle with them." It became a maxim. Undoubtedly, it grieves, it galls several of those who hear it, but it finds few contradictors among them. Unhappily, the immense world which it condemns and despairs of is far from our eyes. We do not see clearly enough the injustice we help to commit by thus keeping silence. Those whose purely worldly interests nearly always direct such efforts do not measure the danger that the very development of our colonial power makes us run, if we do not know how to conciliate men's minds and hearts. Or even, in spite of many warnings, they imagine—and it is an infirmity of the intelligence called " practical " — that mechanical and economic civilization has the power of changing men fundamentally, and of transforming into faithful friends nations whose religion stirs them up to despise and curse us, and who learn, in the tent or earth-walled house, to repeat the proverb : " Kiss the hand you cannot cut off."

Yet note how inhuman and uncharitable is this widespread opinion ! Several hundred millions of men must therefore find it impossible to know the truth and rise to true civilization. The Musulman must be perpetually an inferior being. There must be on earth two sorts of men, pagan, Jewish, and Buddhists, who can perceive the transcendent beauty of the Christian religion, be converted and fraternize with Christ's people, and then the Musulmans, incapable of understanding or incapable of the act of will which enters into all conversions? Can we grant this? Can so great an insult be offered to men?

Is it not in the first place offered to God? Does it not

deny His power, His grace, His express word, since He ordered the Gospel to be preached to all nations? Reason, and revelation, which exceeds and satisfies it, forbid us to condemn any human race, any followers of a false religion, so cruelly.

Such is the objection on principle. I shall presently return to that which they claim to draw from experience. What is beyond doubt is that successive French governments in the last century and in this, have acted as if it were certain, *a priori,* that Musulmans cannot become Christians.

Ninety-one years ago France began to conquer Algeria. Since then an immense territory has been added to the first coasts on which French troops landed in 1830. Since then, also, many efforts have been made to assimilate the natives. The African empire has been provided with roads, railways, tramways, post and telegraph offices; the French have spread new crops or new agricultural methods, established hospitals and dispensaries, built schools where everything is taught except the Christian religion. Are the natives nearer to them in mind than at the beginning of the conquest? Readily making use of several of the advantages which their civilization has brought them, have they accepted it, and can it be said that they consider themselves as the faithful subjects of France and for ever?

It is enough to know slightly the history of the last thirty or forty years, not to speak of the regions recently annexed, but only of the three old departments—Algiers, Oran, and Constantine—to reply: No. Even less is enough; just walk for an hour in the midst of Musulman crowds, and read their looks. Doubtless, during the Great War, thousands of Arabs or Berbers, French subjects, came and fought alongside of our metropolitan troops, and many died for our salvation.

In that there is a proof of loyalty which will never be forgotten. But many tribes and nations, since the world has been a world, have made war to uphold causes which were not those of their heart, but rather of their courage, interest, or pride. It would be false, and therefore dangerous, to believe that, since 1914, the Musulman populations of North Africa have become assimilated to us or simply come near to us, and that between them and us there are the only durable bonds of understanding, esteem, and friendship.

The fault of this belongs to the men of very different origin and talents but similar in their illusions or prejudices, who have guided our African policy during the last hundred years. They have never understood that our civilization is essentially Christian. Some of them have never been able to cast aside all religion for themselves; they cannot prevent all our national history being Catholic; our feeling, habits, manners, and charity from showing the stamp of our Faith. In our present state, if they fail to recognize this truth, it appears evident to the Musulmans, the inhabitants of our colonies, who call all Frenchmen Christians. In this the Musulmans are in the right against the very short-sighted politicians. They think that this historic power, against which theirs has in the past clashed more than once, has remained fundamentally the same. We are for them the *Roumis*. Our State neutrality, our acts of persecution and speeches, even the favours imprudently accorded to Islamism, do not prevent them from seeing that the vocation of France has not changed. And besides, if ever— of which there is no appearance—the French were to abjure the Catholic Faith, they would gain nothing from the African Musulmans, and more surely and irretrievably earn the contempt of such religious races.

This ignoring or negation of souls is an error with such inevitable consequences that, in seeking to conciliate the natives, we have often worked against our own interests.

I will give two proofs only:

In the first place, we made mistakes in organizing the schools. The evidence abounds: I quote only one of the most recent. In its number of *December* 11, 1920, a French Review, *La Renaissance,* published an article on " La Politique musulmane," by an African. The author denounces this sort of "educational fury" which everywhere for the children of the primitive races in Algeria has set up schools, the main business of which is to exalt "liberty, the rights of citizens, the electorate, and the whole considered as the supreme good"; an ideology baneful in France, and still more so between the sea and desert. What results could we expect from a teaching so inappropriate? Exactly such as have followed. "In a general way experience has shown, that the more the natives had acquired French culture, the more they had a tendency, in secret or openly, to hate us: this manifestly disappointing statement represents the unanimous opinion of those who have impartially watched the results."

Publicists, witnesses acquainted with the errors committed, and foreseeing the dangers ahead, have proposed this remedy: that the education given to the natives should be henceforth quite elementary. That is not worthy of a nation such as ours. Besides, we do not see how the little Arabs, remaining ignorant or nearly so, would love us so much better because they had learned less. The evil complained of would not be cured. It lies in the very principle of the education given. Exalting the rights of the individual, and offering him as a first truth the proud and fallacious notion of equality, no wonder it promotes still further the Arabs' spirit of insubordination. It spreads amongst their sons scorn of their environment and ordinary calling, and urges them to leave home surroundings for what is called "a good place." It thus makes a great number of nondescripts, who will be the disillusioned of tomorrow and next day, the irreconcilable enemies of the French authorities.[1] Lastly, as it furnishes the little Arabs with no morality beyond an ensemble of precepts without obligation or sanction, it cannot seriously correct any fault. It leaves him provided with a collection of proverbs, hygienic recommendations, fragments of election speeches, in presence of all the passions, all the cupidities, all the temptations of revolt that he has in his blood, through his age, race, and religion; and if he succumbs, as almost necessarily he will, we have provided him with the means of being socially more dangerous than his fathers, since he will be better educated.

The other error consists in favouring and spreading Mohammedanism. That we have deliberately done it, no examples are needed to show; they abound, and the *Mufti* of Algiers could reasonably say to a friend of his: "Our religion is the only one recognized by the French State." Now, the history of fourteen centuries and the daily experience of those who live among Musulman populations tell us that animosity against the Christian is, in fact, developed and taught in the law of the Koran. One of the men who is an authority on these questions, the Dutchman Snouck Hurgronje, said not long ago (1911) in one of his celebrated lectures at the Academy of the administrators of the Dutch Indies: "According to the letter and spirit of the sacred laws [of the Musulmans], it is in violent measures that the very best means of propagating the faith are to be sought. This faith considers all unbelievers as enemies of Allah. A small party of Mohammedans actually appear, it is true, as partisans of the adaptation of Islam to

[1] M. Jules Cambon, then Governor-General of Algeria, said in the Senate, January 8, 1894: "I have asked myself if, in developing [primary instruction] beyond measure in a people which is not yet fitted to receive it, we are not going to make a lot of wasters."

modern conceptions, but they represent as little the religion of which they are adepts by birth, as Modernists do that of the Catholic Church. On this question no divergencies are found between learned legists of the different schools in successive periods." We may conclude from this that any act of public authority which tends to develop the teaching of the Koran is directed against ourselves. It is enough not to infringe the religious liberty of Musulmans, to leave them their worship and customs, to be perfectly just and good to them :[1] if we go any farther, we are weak, and even rather more than weak.

When these truths of common sense have been recognized by those who direct the Musulman policy of France, what ought to be done? Neither our heart nor interest counsel us to restrict our ambition to some inferior and precarious economic alliance with the Musulman peoples who live in the French possessions. As the Dutchman quoted a moment ago said finely, "Material annexation must be followed by spiritual annexation." Now that is an aspiration one may make without being a Catholic. From the day on which the Musulman understands the beauty of Catholicism, he will have understood France; and in proportion as he admires Christian charity, he will love us.

Does this mean that we should just try what can be done to convert the Musulmans and make them Christians? The prescription would be ambiguous: it would not specify how slowly, gently, and fraternally such a conversion, if God permits it, is to be accomplished. It is better to say this: France, being responsible for a numerous colonial family, must at last take cognizance of her whole maternal mission; and that Musulman, as well as pagan, subjects of a great nation—Catholic by its history, its genius, by its whole soul, and even by its trials—must be able to know Catholicism and come to it, if they wish.

At any rate, they will know it, and that, in the first place, by its charity. Charity will be its ambassador. So let charity go to them; let it not be shackled and suspected, but

[1] The Palestinian law of the Crusaders shows the dispositions inspired in our fathers by this spirit of justice, and by the respect of religious men for the word of religious men. Thus the oath of the Saracen, taken on the Koran in the commercial court, was as good as the oath of the Christian on the Gospels or of the Jew or Samaritan on the Pentateuch. In case of a dispute between a Saracen and a Frank, the Saracen got his discharge by swearing on the Koran (*Assises de Jerusalem*, t. xi., chap. 241 and 60). This example is all the more significant as in ordinary Musulman law the testimony of a Christian or a Jew is not received against a Musulman.

amicably supported. In our own possessions, we are in the presence of an immense population, compacted of errors, agelong furies and hatreds, some of which are justified. The first work to be done is " to break in the Musulmans," according to the expression of Father de Foucauld and his friend General Laperrine, who so often led " training tours " in the desert. In doing that our officials and officers can play a magnificent rôle. Through them may the justice of France—that is to say, Christian justice, the kindness of France—that is to say, Christian kindness, become manifest to those who thirst for something more than water from the wells. But let charity, both adroit and mighty, for two thousand years familiar with all human suffering, be also free to console, care, heal, and endure, as evil and suffering endure, by self-renewal. Let it found its asylums and schools, its dispensaries and hospitals, its orphanages for young boys and girls, its homes for the old who have been left in the lurch by all men. It will take in the unfortunate without testimonials of character and conduct, without asking for police records, nor concern itself with the beliefs of its clients. It will preach its God silently, if it is so splendid that they cannot help seeing that its radiancy is divine. That will take years, perhaps many years. It has all the years before it, and so has France: they can wait.

Surely, combining its efforts with those I have already spoken of, it will win this grand triumph: that the Musulman peoples, without yet accepting Christian doctrine, will at least have the knowledge, the esteem, and here and there the secret desire of it. And if, later, Musulmans, thus persuaded that there is nothing in Islam which is as good as charitable and religious France, came to say: " If the disciple is thus, what must the Master be? Teach us the law which makes you so great of heart." What a gain it would be to the State, what a victory for France in Northern Africa! It would mean a regenerated world, a greater France, our authority recognized, our future assured, the highest glory that a civilized nation can desire and obtain: creation in its own likeness!

Here we come into collision with the commonplace objection: Musulmans, in fact, do not get converted; there is, so to speak, no example of it. This is a less grave error than to pretend that they cannot be converted; but it is one.

All the apostolic life of Father de Foucauld was founded on the conviction that it is possible, by prayer and example, and by preaching which takes into account the inveterateness of their errors and the weakness of poor human wills wrestling with the centuries and with a whole population, to lead Musulmans gradually into the full grace of Christ.

He shared the hope which had sustained Cardinal Lavigerie; the hope of the Church shown in that letter of Pope Leo IX, conferring on the Bishop of Carthage, at the moment of the worst Arab persecutions, the title of "first Archbishop after the Roman Pontiff, and Major Metropolitan of all Africa," and proclaiming that this privilege would last till the end of time, "whether ruined Carthage remain a desert or one day revive in glory."[1]

The difficulty is not so much in persuading a Musulman of the truth of the Christian religion, as of ensuring the perseverance of the convert. Arabs who become Christians can no longer live where they used to live. They are outlawed. Everything is put in motion to make them abandon the Faith; even their life is threatened, and the fear of seeing them apostatize—that is to say, loaded with a monstrous crime—is the reason which often prevents the request of catechumens from being granted, and their being baptized. The time of collective preparation for receiving the Faith cannot be short. The public mind must be changed before achieving individual conversions. Dwelling in centres of Musulman population, self-sacrifice, charity, the school, and conversation on high points open to reason, ought to prepare the preaching of revealed doctrine. Those who have most loved Africa have not ceased recommending this method. They did not pretend that the Musulman was unconvertible.

After having made a summary of Father Guérin's counsels, Father de Foucauld quoted in his diary passages from the life of St. Peter Claver, who, in Cartagena of the Indies, devoted himself to the conversion of the Moors. The book relates that the Saint by his charity vanquished many of these fierce and hostile souls. "As soon as Father Claver heard of the arrival of any fleet loaded with Moors, he at once went to find them, either on the vessels, or in houses in the town; he tried by degrees to make

[1] The text is inscribed in gilt capitals on the walls of the new basilica of Carthage, as Louis Bertrand reminds us in his fine book, *Les Villes d'Or*, in which he is one of the first to urge with such force, that "in re-entering Africa we are only recovering a lost province of Latinity." (Paris, 1921).

friends with them, interested himself in their affairs, asked them if they needed anything. At the same time, he gave them to understand that they could make use of him, and that he was ready to help them in anything that depended upon him. In a word, he did so well, by his perseverance and services, that he won them insensibly to Jesus Christ."

The history of the Franciscan missions, of the Trinitarians and of St. Vincent de Paul, a captive of Barbary pirates, would no doubt afford similar examples. We could easily name Musulmans converted by a sort of miracle of grace, or through meditation on Christian dogmas, or by the study of mysticism, or through admiration for the superior morals of Christians. There were conversions of entire Musulman families (the families of Emirs Chéhab and Bellama in Syria at the end of the eighteenth century). There were mass conversions of Musulman colonies—often Berbers—in various Spanish provinces, the conversion of the *Maragatos* around Leon and Astorga in the tenth and eleventh centuries; of the husbandmen of Majorca in the thirteenth; of those of Jaen in the fourteenth, thanks to the preaching and example of St. Peter Paschasius; and the same in Italy and Crete. In our time, an Orthodox Russian Society devoted itself to the conversion of the Kazan Musulmans, and succeeded by a method which approaches that of Father de Foucauld. But have we not, quite near us, the spectacle of groups of Kabyle Christians round the stations of the White Fathers? Beginnings, no doubt, small Christian societies disseminated amidst eleven often distant points of this mountainous country, each composed of thirty, forty, or fifty families, but the living proof that it is possible to bring Musulmans to Catholicism. I visited in Upper Kabylia one of these missionary posts, that of Beni-Mengallet. I heard High Mass amidst a congregation of eighty people. The men and little boys occupied the upper, the women and young girls the lower part of the chapel. I looked at these young Berber husbandmen, white-faced, with moustaches, solid, grave, attentive, and I found them, except their costume, very like our French peasants. After Mass, I chatted with them, for they know French. In the eyes of most, I read that welcome, that confidence prepared from afar, in which one is not deceived. The mission began about thirty years ago. There, as elsewhere, it has been favoured but little by the authorities which stand for France in Algeria; it has often been thwarted by the general policy of our country; for various reasons the governors did not understand, or did not appear to understand that African peace will be the certain sequel and reward of the conversion of Africa, and that all other means, force and weakness, repression and flattery, the abundance of riches and inventions, will not bring closer to us a nation which looks upon us only as pagans, and so calls us. It must perceive the greatest, the most essential, the highest of all things—religion. It is to hearts won by holiness that it will one day be possible to explain our teaching.

We have seen that St. Peter Claver acted thus. The founder of the White Fathers, Cardinal Lavigerie, explained his views in known documents, dated September 24, 1871, April 3 and July 6, 1873, and December 15, 1880. He had no illusions about the duration of this first period, all of sacrifice, in which the best workmen would perish and be replaced by others who would die in their turn, without either of them having the joy, which comes yearly to tillers of the land, of seeing the corn turn yellow. In a retreat lecture he said to his missionaries: "Before beginning the preaching of the Gospel among them (the Musulmans) it is necessary to prepare for conversion *en masse*. This preparation will perhaps last a century. I am a bishop; I have a crosier and mitre: well, it is no use to put my mitre on top of my crosier, and lift my arm as high as possible; I shall disappear with you in the foundations of the new African Church."

Let us go back to the Gospel: our Saviour did not employ any other method. He also addressed an obstinate race which was far from recognizing the Messias in the Man who was going to be and was already the Man of sorrows. He did not begin by teaching dogmas. He disclosed His divinity only by degrees; having such a splendid message to transmit, He delays doing it. He fears to scare and repel his friends the Jews. But he begins with preaching what can best touch, uplift, open, and attract souls: charity, humility, fraternity, the forgiving of injuries, and disdain of riches. The Sermon on the Mount gathers up all these features of Christ's first preaching. And it is the Sermon on the Mount that Father de Foucauld repeated all his life to the Musulmans.[1]

If we do not change our present methods of colonization, this very French and reliable witness does not hesitate to

[1] See *Le Dieu Vivant*, by Jules Lebreton, professor of the history of Christian origins at the Institut Catholique de Paris, pp. 76 *ff*. (Paris: Beauchesne, 1919.)

foretell that within fifty years we shall be driven out of North Africa.[1]

"*June* 21, 1903.—A few days ago I received from Commander Laperrine d'Hautpoul, chief in command of the Saharan oases, a letter containing the following passages: 'At the time of the massacre of the Flatters mission, a Tuareg woman of a "noble" family took up a splendid position, opposing the killing of the wounded, receiving and looking after them in her own house, shutting her door against Attisi, who, returning wounded from the battle of Amguid against Dianoux, wished to finish them off himself, and when they were healed she had them sent back to Tripoli. She is now from forty to forty-three years of age, regarded as having a great deal of influence, and is renowned for her charity.'

"Is not this soul," continues Father de Foucauld, "ready for the Gospel? Would there not be grounds for writing to tell her that the charity she practises so often, and with which, twenty years ago, she received, took care of, defended and sent back to their country the wounded of the French mission, is known to us, and we are filled with joy and gratitude to God? . . . 'God says: "The first commandment is to love thy God with thy whole heart. The second is to love thy neighbour as thyself." Wondering and returning thanks to God on seeing you practise charity so well towards men, we write this letter to tell you that among Christians there are hundreds of thousands of souls, men and women, renouncing marriage and terrestrial riches, consecrating their lives to prayer, meditating the Word of God and habitually doing good, and all these monks and nuns on hearing of you will bless and praise God for your virtues, and will pray to Him to overwhelm you with graces in this world and glory in heaven. . . . We write to you also to ask you very earnestly to pray for us, certain that God, who has put in your heart the will to love Him, will listen to the prayers you address to Him. We beg of you to pray for us and all men so that we may all love Him and obey Him with all our soul. To Him be glory, benediction, honour and praise, now and for ever. Amen.'

"I have just sent a copy of this draft of a letter to Mgr. Guérin, asking him whether he wishes to write himself, or if he desires me to write, offering—if intercourse

[1] See Father de Foucauld's letter to me on July 16, 1916, given in the last chapter of this book.

is opened up and if I remain alone—to go on foot and pay this lady a visit."

The man of the world and the Christian, courtesy and charity, have together dictated this letter to a "lady" of the Tuareg Red Cross.
Brother Charles even had had the idea of asking the Pope to write himself to this charitable nomad. And why not? It was too great a liberty to venture on.
Here we see revealed for the first time the still secret resolution which the hermit formed of pentrating as far as the regions inhabited by the Tuaregs, and of winning to Christian civilization, then to the Christian religion, this nation of Berber race said to be proud, intelligent, and much less fanatic than the Arabs. Charles de Foucauld had certainly heard about the Tuaregs through *Duveyrier* in Paris when drawing up the notes of his *Reconnaissance au Maroc*. He lived among African officers, the people of the oasis, the caravaneers, hawkers of the stories and legends of the tribes: lastly he had recently conversed with Commander Laperrine, who was haunted by the military and poetic dream of a great Frankish Kingdom, of an Africa renewed by French genius, and they had spoken of Hoggar as much as of Tidikelt and Timbuctoo. Wherever the officer had wished the civilization of France, in a durable peace, to be established—how fine these conversations of which nothing remains must have been—Brother Charles had promised himself to bring the prayer and charity of the missionary nation. Laperrine had persuaded him, as the diary thus testifies.

"*Feast of St. Mary Magdalen.*—Seeing that, in consequence of religious persecutions, the Prefect Apostolic could send no priest to the Tuaregs, nor to Tidikelt, Twat, Gurara, nor into the Saura and Zusfana, I wrote on June 24 to Mgr. Guérin, to ask his permission to go—until he is able to send priests—and settle among the Tuaregs, and as much as possible in the heart of the country; I shall pray there, study the language, and translate the Holy Gospel: I shall get into intercourse with the Tuaregs; I shall live among them without enclosure. Every year I shall go up North to confession.[1] On the way I shall administer the Sacraments at all the stations, and talk to the natives of God. I shall wait for M. Huvelin's authorization. . . ."

[1] " Next October will be two years since my last confession" (letter to a friend, March 16, 1903).

"*June* 29.—I am writing to Commandant Laperrine, communicating this project to him, and asking his authorization to execute it."

"*July* 13.—Received letter of authorization from M. Huvelin."

"*July* 22.—Letter of authorization from Commandant Laperrine."

"*August* 1.—Letter from Mgr. Guérin, asking for time to reflect."

Brother Charles, hermit and missionary, depending on Providence, waits for permission to set to work. In the reply of his Superiors, he will see God's command. He is deeply imbued with Father de Caussade's doctrine : "The present moment is always like an ambassador, declaring God's command. All our learning consists in recognizing His command in the present moment." Assuredly the ardent imagination of a Charles de Foucauld dreams, demands, and prepares great plans; but hearkening to every complaint, and also to every bit of news coming from the world in which he lives, he is always ready to respond and to consider himself as under orders. The summer of 1903 suddenly offered him the opportunity of bringing the help of religion to Frenchmen in danger of death. He was the only priest in these vast regions; our stations had no chaplains; although the highest virtue of obedience and sacrifice was expected of them, their souls had been neglected. He did not hesitate a minute : he was off, and fulfilled one of the great offices for which he went deep into the Sahara. Here are the facts :

The attacks on convoys or posts were increasing; the agitation might at any moment turn to revolt. The subdued tribes had just risen; a serious defeat would have meant their defection. Were not the French military forces scattered in small parties over so vast a space, and likely to be surprised, surrounded and forced to surrender in detail; was this not the expected opportunity, the signal for all the horse and foot of the Sahara to rise and bundle us out?

On July 16, at 3 in the morning, a *rezzu* of 200 Berabers, mounted on *meharis*, attacked a detachment of fifty Algerian riflemen of the Adrar company, which lost twenty-two men, and under a non-commissioned officer beat a retreat, fighting all the way. The counter-thrust was prompt. Nine days after, Captain Regnault, chief of the Arab Office of Beni-Abbes, set out as soon as the news was received with forty-five men of his *makhzen* and forty *meharistes* of the Timimun Company; took up the fresh traces of the *rezzu* in the Tabelbala dunes, to the south-west of Beni-Abbes; surprised the Berabers near the Bu-Kheila wells, killed thirty of their combatants, and put the others to flight.

Soon much greater enterprises were going to be attempted against us and the allied tribes. This was known. Information flowed in from all parts. What was not known was which of our posts of the Zusfana or Saura would be first attacked. Would it be Beni-Unif? Taghit? Beni-Abbes? Brother Charles was told of these rumours which were flying about the desert. Priest and ex-officer, he was thoroughly roused and demanded to serve. He conjectured and calculated that the Taghit post was more threatened than the others; a company of riflemen, a company of the African battalion and three score horsemen of the *makhzen* made up a very feeble garrison; besides, the post was dominated on several sides. There would be killed and wounded; there would be danger. Certainly, there his duty lay. Brother Charles wrote on August 12 to Captain de Susbielle, commander of the Arab Office of Taghit, asking him: "Could you send for me? They will not let me set out alone, because the roads are not safe." He was ready and expecting every moment to leave Beni-Abbes, and by way of precaution, took the Blessed Sacrament out of the tabernacle of his little church. All at once news broke down. For six days no courier reached Beni-Abbes.

The great storm-cloud was on its way. A *harka*, an expeditionary column composed of 9,000 men, women, and children from all the divisions of the Berabers, from all the districts upon the Moorish district of Tafilelt, were going to fall upon the Zusfana. It was commanded by one of our most determined enemies, Muley Mostapha, Sherif of Matrara. It numbered nearly 6,000 combatants, of whom 500 were on *meharis;* most of them were armed with breech-loading guns; there were 600 pack-camels loaded with stores.

Captain de Susbielle had the village of Taghit, where some subdued tribes of our protégés had taken refuge, put into a state of defence. They could only muster 470 men and two small mountain-guns against a whole army of enemies. On the morning of the 17th the column was signalled, and Lieutenant de Ganay went out first at the head of a cavalry detachment of *makhzen,* to reconnoitre the enormous gathering, which he forced to deploy. The shells threw the Moroccan masses into disorder, and they retired to the shelter of the dunes and into the palm grove, two miles from Taghit. But next day, the battle began again. On the 18th, 19th, and 20th of August furious assaults were delivered. Taghit defended itself victoriously; its small garrison performed prodigies, and—a marvel which might give courage to the least brave—it was relieved. Once more the young Saharan officers had displayed a decision which saved both honour and life at stake. On the 8th at dawn Lieutenant Pointurier arrived from El-Morra with his mounted company of the foreign legion which had covered forty miles in the night; on the 20th came Lieutenant de Lachaux, hastening up to the gun, riding in at a gallop under fire with his forty troopers from Beni-Abbes who had set out from Igli on the evening of the previous day.

The *harka* was decimated, and raised camp on the 21st. It had 1,200 men *hors de combat.* It went back to the north-west, carrying away the arms and clothes of its dead, instead of the expected plunder. The success of our arms was splendid. " It is the finest feat of arms in Algeria for forty years!" says Brother Charles, in a letter to the Marchioness de Foucauld.

He rejoiced at the victory, but regret tormented him at not having been there. Among the defenders, nine were killed, twenty-one wounded. And he, the chaplain of the Sahara, could not console, absolve, and bless! A less delicate and humble conscience would not have been disturbed. Had he not asked to set out, spoken to officers on the spot, written to those out yonder? No doubt, but he was not at ease. He ought to have done without an escort. " I must draw lessons from the difficulties I have had in doing my duty," he jotted in his journal. And at once he made resolutions. Henceforth he will " accustom himself by hard work to walking," so as not to need a mount; he meant to be the poorest of travellers; he would go on foot, without a servant, and, since he must have a guide, he would make sure of finding someone, even in hours of danger, by showing redoubled kindness to everybody.

The danger was, in fact, only averted; it was not over. The marabouts continued to preach the holy war, and the revolted tribes were roving over the sandy and stony desert. On September 2, twenty miles to the north of Taghit, and at the hour of the long halt—that is to say, about 9 in the morning—a half-company of the mounted squadron of the 2nd Foreign Legion, escorting a convoy, were suddenly attacked on a level with El-Mungar by a band of several hundred robbers. These, Ulad Jerir, old supporters of Bu-Amama, after becoming detached from the *harka* victoriously repulsed from Taghit on August 20, had hidden in the dunes, waiting for an opportunity of taking their revenge. They attacked the convoy on the plateau between the Wady Zusfana and the great sands. The first discharge from the bandits brought down, killed or wounded, the two officers of the mounted company, all the non-commissioned officers and a great number of soldiers. The survivors banded together on a projection of the ground and, under the overpowering heat which was increasing from minute to minute, decided to fight to death. Two spahis, from a quarter of a company which completed the escort were able to cut a passage through the enemy and, at a gallop, went to give the alarm to the Taghit garrison. Half an hour after being informed, Captain de Susbielle left the post, bringing all his *makhzen* and spahis, and, at top speed, in the height of the afternoon, went to relieve our encircled soldiers.

He arrived on the scene of battle at 5 o'clock. As soon as they perceived the dust made by the troopers launched against them, the robbers disbanded and took refuge in the dunes. It was time to relieve the besieged, who were reduced to a handful of men exhausted with thirst. They were about thirty, commanded by a wounded soldier, Quartermaster-Sergeant Tisserant, who had been hit by two bullets. They continued to fire on the Moors scattered around them, hidden behind the smallest undulations of the ground, and thus protected, besides their own lives, forty-nine wounded lying around them. A detachment was sent to a distance to bring water. Tisserant, with his head covered with blood, stood upright to fulfil his duty as quartermaster. He went from one to the other of the wounded, made out a list, picked up cartridges and arms which had fallen on the ground, and before leaving the place of battle, in a loud voice called the roll of the killed. During the night the forty-nine wounded were transported to Taghit.

Three days after, at 7 in the morning, the news of the battle reached Beni-Abbés. Brother Charles ran to the

Native Office. He renewed his demand. This time it was granted. The chaplain of the Sahara might go to the wounded. He was given a burnous and spurs; one of the *Mokhazenis* lent him a horse. At the last moment, someone there tried to stop what he thought was a mad adventure.

"How can we allow the Father to go without an escort? He will be killed on the way!"

"I shall get through," said the Father quite simply.

"Yes, he will get through; let him go," replied the Captain of the Arab Office, who just then came on the scene. "He can't tell you so, but he can go right through the whole of the rebel country unarmed; nobody will lift a hand against him; he is sacred."

At 10 o'clock Brother Charles was in the saddle and started with the courier. On the way he met two horsemen bringing him a letter from Captain de Susbielle, asking him to come immediately to the wounded. They travelled all day and night; they covered as fast as possible the seventy-five miles between Beni-Abbes and Taghit, where they arrived about 9 in the morning.

No sooner had he dismounted than without the slightest thought of the fatigue of such a ride Father de Foucauld first said Mass. Then he asked to be taken to the wounded, who were assembled in two rooms of the redoubt, and began his mission of friend and priest. Witnesses of this apostolate of Father de Foucauld with the Taghit wounded exist, and those witnesses have spoken to me. During the twenty-five days that he spent in the redoubt, Father de Foucauld, to whom one of the officers' rooms had been given, did not for a single night sleep in the bed that was kept for him. All his time, except the few hours given to sleep—and those not every night—and the time for his Mass and rapid meals, the Father devoted to the wounded. He chatted with each of them, spoke to them of their country and families, and wrote their letters. When he entered one of the ambulance rooms, all the wounded called out to him with one voice: "Good-morning, Father," and each wished to be the first to receive the visit of the friend of all. They recognized one who loved the soldier and understood him. Certainly, most of these legionaries were not accustomed to speak to a priest; piety was not their dominant characteristic; but the sweetness, the affable and sprightly manner, the self-sacrifice of this priest who devoted every instant of his time to them, rapidly conquered them one after the other. The presence of this monk became indispensable to them. An officer of the post, whom I questioned, said to me: " It is beyond doubt that his influence on their morale had a great deal to do with this singular fact: of these forty-nine wounded, of whom several were seriously injured and with many wounds, only one succumbed. I remember a certain legionary, of German origin, whom we considered a not very commendable subject. At El-Mungar he had had a bullet through his chest. Father de Foucauld took him in hand as the most seriously wounded and the least sympathetic, indeed, quite the reverse. Received at first more than coolly, with his patience and sweetness he ended in conciliating this poor man to such a point that the latter called for him at every moment, and related to him the intimate history—not always edifying—of an old African soldier. I believe I may affirm that all the forty-nine wounded, each in turn, received communion from the hands of Father de Foucauld."

Only once did Father de Foucauld leave them. It was on September 18. That day, accompanied by some officers and non-commissioned officers and a company of the *makhzen,* he went to the battlefield of El-Mungar, and blessed the tombs of the two officers, and the grave in which the other victims had been buried.

He took the road to Beni-Abbés once more on September 30.

In the two following months he again returned to pay his Taghit convalescents a visit. Then, towards the end of the year, he went into retreat. The retreats of Father de Foucauld, as we have already seen, were for him occasions for the most minute examination of conscience, and of the most genuine resolutions. This time he wrote to his director, Abbé Huvelin: ". The three principal things for which I have to ask pardon of Jesus, for the year 1903, are: sensuality, lack of charity toward my neighbour, lukewarmness to God." Now he never ate according to his hunger, he prayed night and day, and refused none of those who importuned him. But to advance, the perfect need—humility.

A very grave question occupied his mind, and without doubt, in that retreat at the end of 1903, he had studied it in its inmost recesses, putting, according to St. Ignatius' method, the reasons for and against in juxtaposition.

It will be remembered that Brother Charles had requested

M. Huvelin, Commander Laperrine and Mgr. Guérin, each having a particular right to be asked, for permission to go on reconnaissance into Twat and Tidikelt, and to settle eventually amongst the Tuaregs or elsewhere, without altogether abandoning Beni-Abbes, to which he would return and make visits. The hermit would have several hostelries in the desert. The last authorization had reached him on August 29. A few days earlier he had received a letter from Commander Laperrine, urging him to start, and adding : " I believe there is a great deal of good to be done, for if we may not hope for immediate conversions and to get *doctrine* accepted, we can, by example and daily contact, put in evidence the Christian *morale* and spread it."

The battles of Taghit and El-Mungar did not allow Brother Charles to carry out the plan. He was obliged to launch out on a trail which was not that of the Hoggar country. But at the end of the year, when he came out of retreat, the rebellion appeared to be quelled, and he asked himself anew : " Where is my duty ?" Contrary to what we should have expected, the idea of plunging deeper into the desert did not please him ; the conquest of souls, above all the high ambition of bringing Jesus to new nations, tempted the imagination and the great heart of the apostle, but regret at leaving Beni-Abbes pulled him back. What would the natives and soldiers who loved him say ? And what would become of the work begun ? He wrote to Abbé Huvelin :

" I am in great uncertainty about the journey that I had planned to the south, to the oases of Twat and Tidikelt which are absolutely without a priest, where our soldiers never hear Mass, the Musulmans never see a minister of Jesus. . . . You remember that after receiving the three authorizations from you, Mgr. Guérin and the military authorities, I was going to set out in September when I was called to Taghit for the wounded. . . . Now that peace seems re-established, ought I to carry out my plan ? This is a big note of interrogation for me. I know beforehand that Mgr. Guérin leaves me free ; it is from you, therefore, that I ask for advice.

" If Mgr. Guérin could and would send another priest there, I would certainly not go : my very clear duty would be to remain at Beni-Abbes. But I believe he will send nobody there, I even believe he cannot send anybody.

" In those conditions, ought I not to set out, found a

pied-à-terre, so to say, in the far South, which would enable me to go every year and spend two, three, or four months there, and use the journey to administer or at least offer the Sacraments in the garrisons, and show the Cross and the Sacred Heart to the Musulmans, speaking a little about our holy religion to them? . . .

"Nothing is, just now, easier for me than that. I am invited and expected. Nature is excessively opposed to it. I shudder—I am ashamed to say—at the thought of leaving Beni-Abbes, the quiet at the foot of the altar, and at flinging myself into journeys, of which I have now an excessive horror. If I did not believe, with all my strength, that such words as *sweet, painful, joy, sacrifice,* should be crossed out of my dictionary, I should say that I am rather sorry to absent myself from Beni-Abbes.

"Reason, too, shows many drawbacks: leaving the tabernacle at Beni-Abbes empty, going away from here, where perhaps, if not very probably, there will be fights; getting dissipated by journeys which are not good for the soul. Should I not glorify God more by adoring Him as a solitary?

"Although reason and nature oppose it, I feel myself extremely, and more and more interiorly, urged to this journey.

"A convoy starts for the South on January 10; ought I to take it? Ought I to wait for another? There will perhaps be none for several months, and I have reasons for fearing that I shall then not find the same facilities as now.

"Ought I not to start at all?

"I feel quite clearly that I ought to set out on January 10.

"I beg you to write me a line on this subject. I shall obey you.

"If I get nothing from you before January 10, I shall probably set out."

January 10 passed. M. Huvelin's reply had not come. On the 13th a convoy was to set out for the Twat and Tidikelt. Brother Charles, considering that he had a chance of visiting these regions, and that "perhaps no other priest would have one for several years," decided to undertake the journey which cost him so much. He writes, on January 13, 1904: "This morning I take the reserved Sacrament from the tabernacle, and at eight I start from Adrar, the capital of Twat." He thus began a new phase of his career. He was going towards the unknown, the Tuaregs of the Hoggar who were to have the greater portion of his friendship and apostolate, and with whom his sacrifice would one day be consummated. As he wrote to his Superior, Father Guérin: "You ask me whether I am ready to go anywhere else than Beni-Abbes for the propagation of the Gospel? For that I am ready to go to the end of the world and to live till the last judgment." He often used to say: "*Dread is the sign of duty.*"

CHAPTER IX
Training Tours[1]

THEY set out on the morning of January 13, 1904. Brother Charles joined a big caravan escorted by fifty soldiers, commanded by Lieutenant Yvart of the Second Chasseurs d'Afrique. They started, as one of his letters neatly phrased it, with the catechumen Paul, "an ass carrying the chapel and provisions, her foal carrying nothing, some new sandals, and two pairs of esparto shoes."

His friend, Captain Regnault, fearing the fatigue of such a journey for him—above all, that of the first stage—had ordered two *mokhazenis* to accompany the convoy for a little while, and had provided them with a led horse, on which Brother Charles could mount in case of need. But they soon came back, saying that the marabout had persevered in his idea, and stood the tramp like a young man, behind the ass and her foal.

We have the precise information of the diary as to the route of the column. The first considerable cluster of humans towards which they directed their steps was Adrar, the capital of Touat. But, on the way, Brother Charles notes in his pocket-book all the points at which they halted for the night, the little *ksours* he visited, the encampments, wells, and even the palms he met with and the distance traversed. Wherever he could he entered into relations with the natives, distributed remedies and alms, and regretted not having any vegetable seeds to give these poor people. He chatted with them. He was well received. The soldiers gave him their confidence. Mass was celebrated every morning in a tent. He rejoiced at the good he was able to do in various ways to his wandering parishioners, to Christians and others.

After eighteen days on the road the convoy, on February 1, entered Adrar. "I find," writes Father de Foucauld, "Commandant Laperrine there; in his own house he gives me a room which I have transformed into a chapel. The Commandant informs me that, of the six large divisions which make up the Tuareg people—Azjers, near Rât; Kel-Ui (Ahir); Hoggar (Jebel Ahaggar); Taïtok

---

[1] *Les Tournées d'apprivoisement*—i.e., "*civilizing rounds*" for *breaking in* the wild tribes.

(Ahnet); Iforas (East Adrar); Illemeden (on the banks of the Niger)—three have this year given their submission into his hands; that is to say, in the last twelve months, the Iforas, Taïtok, and Hoggar. The chief of the latter, the most important, the most warlike of the six divisions, the one that massacred Colonel Flatters and has, up to the present, shown itself the greatest enemy of the Christians, is at this very moment at In-Salah, where he has just arrived with eighty Hoggar notables to make his submission and present that of his tribe. This news is very important, for it shows the whole Tuareg country, hitherto so closed against Christians, is open from to-day. Commandant Laperrine is disposed to facilitate with all his influence my entry, journeys, and establishment. He voluntarily offers me to go with him on the very important tour he intends to take among his new subjects of Ahmet, Adrar, and Hoggar. I believe he will not accord these facilities to any other priest but me. I therefore accept, thanking God for the good He has given me to do, and begging Him to render me faithful. Perhaps in his next tour, which will begin in five or six weeks, Commander Laperrine will push on to Timbuctoo. If he does so, I shall accompany him, for the more I travel, the more natives I shall see, the more also I shall be known to them, and I hope to obtain their friendship and confidence. . . . The best place to study Tuareg (Tamahak) is Akabli, where all the inhabitants speak it, and where there are constant Tuareg caravans.[1] It is therefore decided that I am to go there and study Tuareg as hard as I can, until Commandant Laperrine comes and takes me with him on his tour."

Brother Charles then set out for In-Salah, whence he went to Akabli, the place for study. He went with another officer, Lieutenant Besset, and the diary again takes up the enumeration of the stages, 20, 21, 25, 28, 38 miles long, and of the stopping-points which in this region are described five times out of the six days' journey as "desert." He only stopped thirty-six hours at In-Salah, and went on to Tit, where he makes a note of the visits he paid to the caïd, the marabout Sidi-Ali, and settles down at Akabli on February 20. His first care was to see Sergeant Brun, commanding the detachment of the Aulef Saharans, the sergeant commanding the well-sinkers, the cäid, his calif, and others; and next day he began to take Tamachek

[1] Tamahak, or Tamachek, is the spoken language; Tifinar, the written language.

lessons from a Settaf man who had travelled for a long time among the Tuaregs.

The sojourn at Akabli lasted a little more than three weeks. Brother Charles was worried at having to give so many alms in the journeys that he was about to undertake in quite new and, just lately, hostile countries, and at having to buy both an express and a pack camel in order to accompany Laperrine. Where was the money to be found? The best thing to do was to write to the family and beg for it; in fact, who would be the chosen almoner? He reflected, made up his mind, and jotted down the arguments which had determined his choice, and, perfectly certain that, in six months at most, the amount demanded would have reached his treasury, the chief of the Arab Office of Beni-Abbes, he committed to his travelling diary the extraordinary permissions Father Guérin had given him for the celebration of Mass on long journeys. Permission to celebrate Mass an hour after midnight; to employ any lights, if beeswax is lacking; to celebrate even without lights in the very remote regions which do not produce olives and where no supplies for lamps are to be found. These Latin prescriptions, taken from canon law, give a curious touch of civilization to the pages of a diary full of barbarous names.

The weeks in Akabli were weeks of work and meditation. Brother Charles was all his life an extraordinary worker. He never lost an hour. His notes contain nothing of the picturesque; he writes: "The populations of this region, like those of Morocco, speak less Arabic than Berber, the old language of Africa and Palestine, which the Carthaginians spoke and so did St. Monica, whose Berber and not Greek name signifies 'queen.' I learnt it formerly, and then forgot it; I am tackling it again, so as to be able to talk with everybody." But this great worker was before all a priest. His notebooks as well as his letters were always marked with the sign of the cross. The thought of Christ made science of greater value, and poverty dearer in his eyes. "Among other comforts, there is one that I have been asking of Jesus for a long time; it is, for the love of Him, to be in similar conditions, as to well-being, to those in which I was in Morocco for my pleasure. Here my establishment is just the same."

On March 14, Commandant Laperrine, faithful to the rendezvous, left Akabli with his companion and friend, who, this time, rode on a *mehari*. He intended to push on as far as Timbuctoo. He would pass through In-Sis,

Ahmet, Adrar, Timissao, In-Uzal, Mabruk; stop a few days in Timbuctoo and return by Adrar and Hoggar. " If public opinion is ripe for it," wrote Father de Foucauld, "our idea is that, on the return journey, I shall be left with the Hoggars and settle down there." Under his orders Laperrine had Lieutenants Bricogne, Nieger, and Besset.

On the first day they only travelled seven miles and a half and stopped in the desert. On the evening of the 15th they camped in the bed of the Wady Keraan in the desert, after a thirty-mile ride; on the 16th in the desert, near the Tin-Tenai wells; on the 17th in the desert; the 18th in the desert, where they bivouac for a day; on the 20th still in the desert; on the 23rd at the Tinagart wells the Commander received the visit of Aziouel, the nominated successor of the *amenokal* of Taïtok. Near other wells, they were visited by Taïtok or Kel Ahnet warriors; during the great heat they stayed near a nomad encampment. "A pacific paternal tour for training and encouragement, for winning confidence and friendship, a true episcopal round." This is French policy, the only one worthy of a nation which dominates a country solely to pacify it, a strange race solely to elevate it, and which has no sooner ceased fighting, punishing, subjecting, than it lays aside all, and even legitimate, anger, and employs its genius only to make itself beloved. Brother Charles had not given up his hope that one day the Little Brothers of the Sacred Heart— no matter whether he were dead or alive—would undertake to give these poor people of the desert the most beautiful present that France can bring them, Jesus Christ. On Good Friday evening, April 1, stopping at the Wady In-Sis, two and a half miles from the wells, he thus meditates and dreams : " The In-Sis well is in the rock; and at the bottom of it there is always a spring of excellent and abundant water. Every caravan can always get water there. We met two caravans there, going from Gogo to Akabli : one from Iforas, the other of Akabli people : each composed of five or six men, a few camels and some sheep. When it rains, the Wady In-Sis is covered with abundant vegetation. Four years ago, after the rains, 500 tents— Hoggar, Ahnet, and Iforas—spent several weeks there drinking from the well. It is a place in which a fraternity might be founded, for it is : 1st, very desert; 2nd, a place of passage for travellers; 3rd, always sufficiently supplied with water for them to drink; 4th, sufficiently provided with earth for a few small gardens."

He had the same desire a few days later, on April 6, when the column stopped at the Timissao well, the finest they had come across, a well at which any caravan could draw water "not only without drying it up but without the water becoming less limpid. It would be a still better place to establish a fraternity—yes, preferable to In-Sis, for everything is ready, water, ground easy to cultivate near the well, and almost a place for lodging, since at a little distance, in the perpendicular side of a rock, there is a very large natural grotto covered with inscriptions, and surrounded by several lesser ones . . . which would make an excellent lodging for the Brothers, as long as they were not very numerous. . . . Settle in the grotto with dates and flour, begin a small garden, cover the well with a dome; always have halters at the disposal of travellers, and some dates or a little flour for the poor."

In proportion as the mission went deeper into this region, it received more numerous visits from native Tuaregs, friendly tribes, Iforas, Taïtok, or Hoggar. One evening, one of our most implacable enemies, the marabout Abidin, who had long fought against us, sent a rather insolent peace message to the Commander; he would not come himself; but he sent his messenger to salute the great chief. Laperrine understood the desert, and sent back word to the marabout that he would grant him peace, *aman* (safety), and pardon. The other then promised a visit, which he would pay soon with the prince, the *amenokal* Musa ag Amastane.

I picture the Commander bringing his *mehari* to the right of Brother Charles's and speaking to his friend about the Hoggar country, into which the mission was to enter in a few weeks. For the notes dispersed through the diary, and summarized hereafter, were jotted down in the notebook in the evening after the conversations on the ride. They give us the living words. And who could be a better master or as reliable an informant as Laperrine?

"Hoggar is a country of mountains and high plateaux. The temperature is therefore cooler than that which we sometimes expect to kill us here. In the greater number of deep hollows, valleys and ravines, there are trees, above all gum, and *ethel* trees; some of them were splendid. Hoggar extends in width from Jebel-Udan to the village of Tamanrasset; in length, from Wady Igharghar to Abalessa. It has what might be called four gates: In-Amadgel is the northern gate, Abalessa the western, Tazeruk to the east, Tamanrasset to the south. The vil-

lage of Tit is the centre; a village famous for Lieutenant
Cottenest's fight with the Hoggars, which led to the submission of the whole country. Among these shepherds
you will find some features which recall our Middle Ages;
a few poor nobles; the *Dag*-Rali, vassal tribes much reduced by the losses Cottenest inflicted on them; a relatively
large and wealthy division which is neither noble nor
vassal, a kind of nomad bourgeoisie, and the *harratins*,
negroes of Twat or Tidikelt, freed slaves or the descendants
of the freed, and these are the only ones who do a little tillage
of the ground. However, they cannot be compared with
our former serfs attached to the soil : they are free to leave
the country; they may be considered as foreign workmen.
They have no share in public affairs. These are all more
or less subject to the *amenokal*, a king without pomp, without personal retinue, who, as sign of his authority, has
only a big drum placed before his tent, an authority as
variable as that of the first Capetians, depending on the
valour of the man and the number of his vassals. I shall
introduce Musa, the present *amenokal*, to you and tell
you his story."

Thus the mission goes very peacefully until April 16.
That day, at the Timiauin well in the desert, Commandant
Laperrine's troop, arriving towards evening, met a French
column composed of twenty-five Soudan sharpshooters,
ten Kenata auxiliaries, and commanded by two officers.
This troop had set out from Timbuctoo when informed of
the Commander's march; it had passed through Aslar, Suk,
Attalia, and Tessalit; it came to make him abandon the
plan of crossing the Sahara to Timbuctoo. Strange as
such an enterprise may appear, yet the French from the
Niger colony lay claim to prevent the French of the
Algerian colony from travelling in the southern territories,
in the region which they consider as a dependency of the
Timbuctoo post. The limits had not been fixed by the
higher authority of Algiers or Paris. Therefore, the
South had resolved to defend its morsel of the Sahara.
They had got excited. In these extreme climates, jealousies
become ferocious, dissensions degenerate into obsessions,
the worst of fancies may fasten upon an honest man and,
if he does not react, dominate him entirely. After the first
salute, Commandant Laperrine saw that he must show a
more plentiful discretion. Fully master of himself, he
parleyed with his comrades from the Niger. He observed
that the latter had not even forgiven the Iforas for having
submitted to France through the intermediary of Algeria.

According to them, that tribe should have asked for peace from the Nigerian authorities. The difference was so serious that calm discussion was impossible. And night was coming on. Laperrine broke off the discussion and made arrangements to prevent any fighting between the two opposing troops, and then reflected. He would have no violence or outburst at any price. He would give way however hard the sacrifice might be. At daybreak the two troops had already parted, and the Commandant, renouncing the coveted glory of crossing the desert in peace from one side to the other, retraced his steps. But he had got the Commandant of the Nigerian force on his side to retire immediately, without molesting or disturbing the Iforas who had submitted. The question of the zones of influence would, later on, be settled by the minister. And this was done.[1]

Father de Foucauld, on this occasion, restrained himself with difficulty. It was not the traveller suddenly stopped and obliged to retrace his steps who showed his vexation: it was the ex-officer, the colonizer, the friend of the Saharan nomads, the priest, who judged this wayside incident with a severity of which his pen shows no other example.

However, he succeeded in concealing his condemnation. He wished to keep silent, and he did. The officers from the South misused their strength—that was his principal grievance—in going through the camp of the Iforas. He privately made a note of it that evening in his diary, and ended thus: "After fraternally shaking hands with them on their arrival, to-morrow I shall set off without bidding them adieu. . . . I shall not utter a single word of reproach to them: 1st, because it would do them no good; 2nd, because it might estrange them from religion; 3rd, because that might make a row between them and Commandant Laperrine's officers."

The latter gave up his hope, changed his course, and arranged to march first to the East, as far as Tin-Zauaten, by 19° 57' North Latitude, where he met several Tuareg chiefs and conferred with them. They had crossed the Ahnet; they returned by the Adrar and the Hoggar. It was a year of drought, and after the column had resumed its road northwards, Brother Charles noted that it took sixty hours to water 150 camels and fill 150 goat-skin bottles at the Tinghaor wells. Everywhere, for several weeks, the word "desert" recurs in the diary. One day

[1] The line of demarcation adopted gives the South Saharan territories to the Nigerian colony, and the rest to Algeria.

Brother Charles wrote that he could not say Mass on account of a storm of wind. Another day, after a halt, he celebrated it at noon! On May 17, the feast of St. Pascal Baylon, he prayed thus: "I put under your protection, O Protector of all Eucharistic associations and families, the sanctuary and the Fraternity of the Sacred Heart of Jesus, which I should like to found in the heart of the Tuareg country. With my whole soul I recommend the conversion of the Tuaregs to you. I offer you my life for them." Then Brother Charles set forth the various points of his meditation: "If I can stay in the Tuareg country, how am I to act? Who am I? What ought I to set myself to do? Where shall I settle? What helpers shall I find?" and then Brother Charles enumerates: "Jesus, the Blessed Virgin, St. Joseph, St. Margaret, St. Pascal Baylon, St. Augustine, all the Saints, all the Angels, all the souls in Purgatory whom I now supplicate, all good souls living in this world who help me with their prayers, counsels, commands, and with all sorts of good." "Why should I settle in this country? How?" And he replied: "Silently, secretly, like Jesus at Nazareth; obscurely like Him; gently, disarmed and mute before injustice like Him; allowing myself to be shorn and immolated like Him, without resisting or speaking."

At every moment, in this journey of discovery, an abundant well, as at Silet; a fairly good crop of wheat, as at Abalessa; a group of palm trees, here or there suggesting a former palm grove; the crossing of frequented tracks, awakened in Brother Charles the idea of founding a Fraternity or mission, of rebuilding a village, or even of erecting a convent.

Small sketches are jotted down on the margin of the diary, minute signs of the sites of habitations, of the best methods of civilizing, of the most profitable kind of example to give. Here a dispensary would be of assistance; there an agricultural or, still better, a horticultural centre. Here two Brothers could do the work; there ten at least and ten Sisters would be wanted. All along the route Father de Foucauld placed subjects of an Order then non-existent. Inspired with charity, he imagined and then built. Like the great monastic pioneers, he already saw a new civilization growing up amidst these wild countries; he was alone and did not despair: the boldness of his purposes would justly be called madness, if it belonged to those whose trust is only human.

They stopped for five days in Abalessa. On Whit-Sunday, May 22, "with great emotion" he celebrated Mass there in the presence of Laperrine and several officers. There the Commandant was visited by two notables of the Kel-Rela, coming by forced marches and bringing a letter from Musa ag Amastane. One of these notables, a very near relation of the *amenokal* and his designated successor Soua, was the brother of the young girl whom Musa loved and could not marry.—This romance of the desert was known yonder.—In this letter, the Hoggar chief showed himself very well disposed and declared that he was a friend of France, so much so that Brother Charles asked himself whether it was not time for the hermit to stop and found a hermitage in the village of Tit, which was reached on May 26, and was the most central of the Hoggar. Laperrine considered it safer not to grant permission then. They therefore continued the enormous round riding on camels. Each day the diary mentions the presence of some native in a big tent. On June 7 it was a woman's, a Taïtoq, Tarichat Ult Ibdakan, the very woman who had been so courageous at the time of the massacre of the Flatter column, taking in and protecting our wounded. Brother Charles had formerly wished to pay her a visit; he met and thanked her. The diary, which does not tell a story, and was not written for curiosity, recorded only this: "She is from forty to fifty years of age, *distinguée,* talking little, of simple and modest attitude, very nice in every way and speaks Arabic fairly well." However, a few pages farther on, so as not to be too incomplete, and without doubt to remember better the fulfilling of the commission he accepted, Brother Charles, at the moment of quitting the encampment where Tarichat's tents were, added these words: "She commissioned me to write in her name to rifleman Amer, whom she had saved and sent back to his own country. He promised her her weight in silver, and never sent her anything. She has debts: and 50 or 100 douros would give her great pleasure."

His mind was always busy with what might help his Tuareg brothers, and he took advantage of this halt in the desert to write a very long note, in which he summarized the experience which he had just had in this five months' travel, visits, conversations with the natives and Saharan officers, and he entitled this note: *Observations on missionary journeys in the Sahara.* It may be said that everything is found in it and in proper order. What ought the missionary to do to keep his soul right? What provisions should he take with him, and how choose his *mehari* and pack-camel? What place should the missionary take in the military or civilian convoy? Ought he to eat with the officers? etc. I commence by giving the replies to these last questions: " Let the missionaries be alone whenever possible," says Father de Foucauld. " Let them eat alone, to lose less time, and to have more for spiritual exercises and good works, in order not to be obliged to listen often to bad talk, not to lose popular respect by showing their defects, and to be more accessible to the poor. But when the good of souls requires, the Brothers will eat with the officers."

Other questions are treated in this practical and unbiassed spirit which directs everything invariably to one end—the good of souls. Father de Foucauld appears to be writing the constitutions which were to be followed by his missionary successors, the civilizers whom his experience and thought will bring forth from that inexhaustible treasury of mission work—France.

Of these observations, one may also say that they are a kind of portrait of Father de Foucauld painted by himself. I shall therefore reproduce some of them.

In the first place take these lines on the use of camels by the missionary:

" As on a journey, one may have to go very long stages, and cross long distances without water, the missionaries and their servants must be mounted. That will not prevent both doing the greater part of the stages on foot, in order to imitate our Lord, by penitence, abjection, poverty, and to save their animals as well as the money belonging to Jesus and the poor."

And now, " what ought the missionary to do for the souls of others"—of Christians, native soldiers and civilians; of the inhabitants, particularly those of the Saoura? The counsels are marvellously graduated, and I regret giving only fragments of them.

"*Christians.*—Talk a good deal with them; be the friend of all, good and bad. . . . Render them every service compatible with your state, with perfection. . . .

"*Native Soldiers.*—Always speak seriously and gravely to them of heavenly things, never of temporal; be easy of access and very civil to them, but not familiar, not talking aimlessly, and accept no presents; give them helpful advice in family matters, if they ask for it. Never give them any advice as to temporal business.

"*Other Natives.*—You must first gain their esteem by an exemplary and holy life, then obtain their friendship by kindness, patience, and all sorts of little services that you can render to all, small alms, remedies, and hospitality. . . . Try to have as much intercourse as possible with them; . . . but be discreet, reserved, without excessive eagerness, so as to draw them to you, rather than go to them; . . . don't enter their villages, tents, or houses unnecessarily, unless you are called there. . . . Live as much as possible as they do; try to be friendly with all, rich and poor; but go, above all and first of all, to the poor according to the Gospel tradition. In speaking to them, take great care not to go too quickly into such matters as are rather new to them. Try to make them ask questions, and lead them to be the first to speak of what you want to talk about. . . . Avoid theological discussions at present; more curiosity than good-will would enter into it; reply briefly, without admitting discussion; keep to natural theology and, except for special reasons, don't set forth Christian dogmas. In most cases, now is the time to say: *Cast not your pearls before swine.*

Slaves.—Father de Foucauld ascertained that in general the slaves were better treated by the Tuaregs than in the Saoura. "Nevertheless, their condition is worthy of pity and their dignity as human beings totally unacknowledged. There is neither family nor chastity, nor probity, nor truth, nor goodness, among the greater part of the slaves. The young negro servant-girls are all put to immoral uses by the Tuaregs: it is the same, more or less, in all the other parts of the Sahara. The Tuaregs generally have only one wife, but when their fortune allows it they also have several young negresses as concubines. We must therefore work with all our might to suppress slavery very quietly, progressively, and really, so as to improve not only the material condition, but the minds of the slaves. The best way seems to be to spread the method of Commandant Métois in Tidikelt. He permits all slaves to redeem themselves by paying the master back the amount they cost or what they are considered to be worth; and in order that they may be able to procure this sum, he gets those who ask for it enough work to do to wipe out in wages the ransom required. . . . Freedom is obtained by degrees, and the slaves trained to work. . . . With the slaves thus liberated Commandant Métois then makes new villages, beside freshly worked springs. All this is excellent and worthy of imitation."

What means, then, are best for starting the moral education of this poor Musulman people, and what part will the Gospel have in our first intercourse with them? Father de Foucauld's experience is too full, his authority too considerable, not to put on record his observations intended for those who may continue or imitate his work.

"*The Saura and Tuareg.*—It is somewhat difficult to have religious talks with the people of the Saharan oases, or of the Saura; they tend to become embittered, and to set a gulf between us instead of strengthening the bonds of charity. The best is to keep to short but reiterated advice on natural religion and Christian morals. . . . Read them from the Holy Gospels some of the clearest passages about natural religion, but do not put the whole book into their hands; . . . when they esteem us, we can have long religious talks, without fear of estrangement, with those whom we know to be serious and men of good-will. In certain cases that may be done soon; when they reach this point we must be ready to put the Holy Gospels before them. It seems, therefore, that it would be a very good thing to prepare a translation immediately in Algerian Arabic, to read to them or make them read, and this even the least educated will understand.

"The same order is to be followed with the Tuaregs. . . . Prepare at once a Tamahak translation for them. Above all, this translation should be read to them. . . . There is no reason in trying to teach the Tuaregs Arabic, which brings them nearer the Koran; it is, on the contrary, necessary that they should be diverted from it. They must be taught Tamahak, an excellent and very easy language, and by degrees we must provide it with words indispensable for the expression of religious ideas and Christian virtues, and improve, without changing, its system of writing. . . . Read them passages about natural religion or morals, such as the parables of the prodigal son, of the good Samaritan, of the last judgment; comparing it with a shepherd separating the sheep from the goats, etc. It goes without saying that, as soon as conversions begin to take place, we must have a Tamahak catechism."

Commander Laperrine's column was at Aseksen on June 12, when it was rejoined by a detachment of the Tidikelt company, commanded by Lieutenant Roussel. While the Commander returned to In-Salah, Lieutenant Roussel with Quartermaster Duillier, two corporals, and seventy-five native *méharistes* were ordered to continue the "training tour." They were to spend three months amongst the Hoggar Tuaregs, to go slowly and stop from time to time. Brother Charles was much perplexed, and wrote in his notebook: "Sacred Heart of Jesus, I have something to ask You: ought I to go with him (Roussel), if I am allowed? Or ought I to visit Twat, Gurara, and go and spend some time at Ghardaïa with Father Guérin, and return to the Saura, continuing to study Tamahak and translate the Holy Gospels which I began to do a few days ago? What does Your Heart wish?" according to his custom, Brother Charles made a parallel of the pros and cons, and, after choosing what he thought best—that is to say, the most divinely useful—noted in his diary on June 14: "This morning I asked Laperrine to permit me to stay with Roussel, as long as Roussel is out of In-Salah. He gladly gave me permission, and himself told M. Roussel, if he sees Musa, to try to arrange with him for my actual and immediate settlement in Hoggar. He is leaving me, after having loaded me for five months with all sorts of kindnesses for which I can never be grateful enough, and telling me that it is in Hoggar he hopes to see me again."

Thus started a second pacific mission, and Father de Foucauld along with it. On June 22, they cleared twenty-five miles, and the troop stopped for the night between Aseksen and Tin Tunin. For most of these travellers the route was new; they met unknown faces; the programme was the same; they opened up intercourse, lessened prejudice, and even won, if they could, some friendship for far-off France. A magnificent work, which presupposed in our Saharan officers, even in the youngest, qualities of tact, diplomatic patience and kindness, and also an education which would not be so easily found in all armies. This mission of Lieutenant Roussel was to succeed in every way. Father de Foucauld, writing to a friend on July 3, thus defined the character and conduct of this journey:

"We go from spring to spring, to the pasturages most frequented by nomads, settling amidst them and spending several days there. With Holy Mass, prayers, the needs of one's body of death, the frequent tramping, and the time given to one's neighbour, my days are taken up with the study of the language of this country—a very pure Berber tongue—and with translating the Gospels into that language.

"The natives receive us well; not sincerely: they yield to necessity. How long will it be before their feelings are what they pretend to be? Perhaps they will never be.

If some day they are so, it will be when they have become Christians. Will they know how to distinguish soldiers from priests, to see in us God's servants, ministers of peace and charity, universal brothers? I do not know. If I do my duty, Jesus will pour down abundant graces, and they will understand."

However distrustful, however malevolent these "suspicious brothers" of the Hoggar often appeared to him, he judged them "much less separated from us than the Arabs," and the idea of settling down in this *milieu* continued to haunt his mind. However, he recognized that the hour had not yet come. He was to return with the mission to the Saharan towns of the North.

At this point I shall only give short passages from the diary or letters, which may complete the knowledge we already have of this great apostolic soul, and I shall leave to others, as occasion requires, the care of noting the thousand details of river-geography, essays on tillage, temperature, habits and the names of tribes and divisions of tribes, which frequently recalled the celebrated work, *Reconnaissance au Maroc*. The traveller of 1904 was still the careful scientist who would record only the most certain observations, the ardent geographer, the psychologist who, in the eyes, gestures and words, quickly discovered the secret thoughts of those who came to him; but a singular nobility was superadded to all that; a heart athirst for justice, full of charity, ready to sacrifice itself for each of his unknown and hostile brothers, animated these humble jottings, and interspersed learned notes with prayers, desires, and aspirations.

"AMRA, *July* 2.—Feast of the Visitation. Patronal feast of all the fraternities of the Little Brothers and Little Sisters of the Heart of Jesus. Dearest Mother, . . . do to all, by visiting with heavenly grace and by the visits of holy monks and nuns and holy souls, what you did in visiting St. John the Baptist! Continue your Visitation; visit the Tuaregs, Morocco, the Sahara, the infidels, and all souls, . . . unworthy me; visit me, beloved mother; convert me, I ask you on my knees. . . ."

"*July* 8.—As our stay is prolonged, I have the happiness of putting the reserved Host in the tabernacle for the first time in the Tuareg country. We have built a chapel of branches, surmounted by a wooden cross: a tent pitched underneath forms a daïs over the altar and protects it from the dust. . . . Sacred Heart of Jesus, thanks for this first tabernacle in the Tuareg country ! May it be the prelude to many others and foretell the salvation of many souls ! Shine from within this tabernacle on the people who surround You without knowing You ! Send saints and numerous Gospel workers wherever they are wanted here !"

"WADY AGELIL, IN THE DESERT, *July* 22.—Feast of St. Magdalen. St. Magdalen, I lay at your feet the intentions of my soul; inspire me. Are there any resolutions that please the Heart of Jesus which I ought to make? In what must I correct myself? What must I do?"

On August 3 they were in the village of Tazeruk, at an altitude of over 6,000 feet. There was then some talk of returning. "These are the probabilities," writes Brother Charles to a friend. "I shall be back in In-Salah about September 20; I shall not stop there, but shall go through Tidikelt, Twat, and Gurara quietly, stopping at each village—there are 300 of them—leaving at each a few remedies, some words : from there I shall go to Ghardaïa, then to Beni-Abbes."

The extreme fatigue of so long a journey, and in the hardest season, impaired Brother Charles's health. A photograph taken at that period shows us that he was evidently exhausted, his eyes sunk in their sockets, his face thin and ploughed with deep wrinkles. He would not acknowledge it. To a friend of his in France who inquired for news of him he replied : " Yes, I need rest, but not in the sense you think; it is not spiritual solitude that weighs upon me, it is the lack of material solitude : a few days' silence at the foot of the tabernacle, that is what I feel the need of !"

The better to assert his will to accomplish the second part of the journey " as a workman of the Holy Gospel," he recorded in his diary how much to give to the poor villagers. "I intend to give an alms of seven francs in each small or average *ksar*, fourteen in every larger village, and twenty-one in every very large one."

His forecasts were right. On September 20 Father de Foucauld was at In-Salah, where the troops took up their country quarters again : he did not stay there. Henceforth without convoy or armed force, with a single native soldier as his guide, he continued his journey through Inghar, Aulet, Adrar. According to promise, wherever there was a tent, a group of huts (*gurbis*) or mud houses, he stopped to let the wild people of Africa see what the heart of a Christian Frenchman is like. At Timimun, "populous, rich, accustomed to Europeans, and a prospectively flourishing mission centre," he remained three days. Then, with his guide, he resumed his solitary journey, sleeping in the open air, during the whole week encountering only one inhabited place, Fort MacMahon, where there were some Christian soldiers, and some Musulmans, "and a native chief who gave me a good welcome." He hardly stopped at all at El-Golea, where three White Fathers welcomed him: he was in a hurry to reach the Ghardaïa mission station again, and his great friend, the Prefect Apostolic of the Sahara. The latter was impatiently awaiting the traveller, and went to meet him. They met at Metlili, a day's walk from the residence, and conversed on the way. When at last the two companions hove in sight, it was hard to believe that this poor lame ragged pedestrian, who was also leading his camel by the head, was their old officer of the Chasseurs. He looked like some dervish beggar. But his eyes were full of joy, and his smile betrayed him.

Ghardaïa was his resting-place. Brother Charles lived for six weeks, from November 12 to the day after Christmas, 1904, in this small town, the capital of Mzab. "I am resting in silence and solitude, in the pleasant friendship of Pére Guérin and his missionaries." There were many questions to settle with his Superior and friend. He gave him the whole of the finished translation of the four gospels in the Tuareg language, at which he did not cease to work while on the march, or even at night in his tent. He laid before the missionaries his principal observations on the new countries through which he had just passed, and gave them advice on the future evangelization of the people who lived there or passed through. And, after leaving "a report of many little things" in this connexion in order to complete and recall his conversations, he made his annual retreat.

Among the resolutions he took in those days of self-examination, there were two which reveal his deep interior life. He thought of his constant stream of visitors at Beni-Abbès, of the many journeys or doings which interrupted meditation, and he notes: "Take care: 1st, to make a spiritual communion every time I go into chapel, or talk to anyone, or write to anyone; 2nd, in all goings and comings, and travels, when I am not making any other spiritual exercise, recite some *Aves* for the universal reign of the Heart of Jesus: also during manual work; when I wake at night; lastly, whenever my mind is not engaged in some other duty."

During his stay at Ghardaïa he avoided appearing as much as possible among those houses and hovels, those narrow streets and half-covered little squares—*sol y sombra*—in which the curiosity of inhabitants and nomads is always on the watch, and always murmuring. But a man of his holiness and renown could not pass unnoticed. Although the people of the Mzab were of a close disposition and distrustful of Europeans, notables came to solicit the favour of a reception by "him who had sold this world for the other": the little people, who dared not do any more, tried to see "the great marabout," at work or in prayer, at least through the window. One of those who paid a visit to Father de Foucauld, one of the most important bourgeois in the town, said: "When I went in, he said to me, *The Lord be with thee!* and that moved my heart." There were always children on the watch near his house, and they used to get up on each others' shoulders so as to be able to boast of having seen him.

On December 26, very much touched by the reception of his friends and the people of the Mzab, he left Ghardaïa. Two White Fathers went with him from Ghardaïa to El-Golea. He knew the road and, always walking by his *méhari* so as not to be distracted in his meditations and prayers, he went on in front like the caravan guides who always go on fifty yards ahead. Not having a watch, he had asked one of the Fathers, while the light lasted, to tell him when a new hour began. And every time the hand arrived at the top of the dial, the timekeeper, mounted on his camel, struck a few blows on a pot or tin can. The noise was carried along by the hot air, which was otherwise soundless. Then, far ahead, the perpetual walker never stopped but turned round and made a bow of thanks.

They reached El-Golea on January 1, 1905. Brother Charles there found his friend Laperrine appointed Lieutenant-Colonel, and wished him a happy New Year. Two days later he set out with him for Adrar, "where there was a chance of going to Beni-Abbes." I see by the diary that between them *en route* there was often talk of Saharan missions. At last, on January 24, Father de Foucauld again took possession of his dear hermitage. He did not find Captain Regnault, who had been appointed to another post and was replaced by Captain Martin. But many other friends welcomed and made much of him! They thought he was lost: he came back. He at once resumed his former

Rule: he did not mislead anybody when he told officers, soldiers, native alms-collectors, invalids or visitors, that he wished never more to leave the enclosure nor the cabin of sun-roasted earth, which he had made his grounds and enclosure. " I return," he said, " without meaning to go away again; above all, with the great desire that the White Fathers in the future may do what I have done this year, with the great desire of staying in this dear Fraternity, which only lacks one thing: Brothers amidst whom I can disappear. . . . Being alone, every moment I am obliged to run to the door, reply and talk. Terrestrial troubles are sent in order to make us feel our exile, to make us sigh after the Fatherland. . . . Jesus chooses for each the kind of suffering which He sees best suited to sanctify him, and often the cross He imposes is the one that we would have refused had we dared, while accepting all the rest. The one He gives is the one that we least understand. . . . He directs us into bitter pastures which He knows to be good for us. Poor sheep, we are so blind!"

No sooner had he arrived than he received a telegram telling of the death of the mother of the Prefect Apostolic of the Sahara: He wrote at once to Mgr. Guérin:

"Beni-Abbes,
"*January* 28, 1905.
"Very dear and venerable Father,
"My Mass was for that soul so very dear to you, much dearer to the Heart of Jesus. We love with the poor hearts of sinners, He loves with His divine Heart. She is in good hands in a good place, the place where you so much desire to be, where one day you will be with her and with Him whom she taught you to love. She is at rest. Yet she has no need of rest. She has entered into the abundance of peace, where there is no longer either wind or winter, because these things have passed away. When shall we be there? . . . For myself I hardly dare think of that resting-place of which I am so unworthy. Should we dare have hope if God did not make it our duty? Hope is faith in His Heart. Our conversation will be more and more in heaven. There you will find not only the only adored One, but also your dear mother. Henceforth for her no more distance, no more absence: night and day she will hear you, watch over you, reply to your questions, your demands, by her prayers: for her the barrier is passed, the wall broken down, the night over. . . . How happy she is! . . . For the few years which perhaps

remain to you of life, the separation is a cross—a cross you accepted with all the rest, when you told Jesus that you loved Him. An apparent cross, for joy at the happiness of that much loved soul, daily more intimate and continual conversation with her, increasing aspiration for total union with Jesus, and growing weariness of the life of earth, will soon leave you only the joy of feeling her near Jesus and the desire of rejoining her there. . . . Let us kiss the cross that Jesus sends. One can, in this life, only embrace Jesus by embracing His Cross. And let us praise Him for the happiness of her beloved soul.

"I meant to write you a long letter. . . . General Lyautey's visit to Beni-Abbes prevented me doing so. He got here to-day and is going off again to-morrow to Ain-Sefra."

This beautiful letter was therefore cut short because there was a guest of mark at Beni-Abbes, and that day courtesy had to make devotions and silence give way, and many things that one would have liked to finish had to be let go.

Marshal Lyautey remembers this meeting at Beni-Abbes very well indeed. He spoke of it like this: "We dined together with the officers, on Saturday, in the redoubt. After dinner a phonograph gave us some songs of Montmartre. I looked at Foucauld, saying to myself, 'He will go out.' He did not; he even laughed. The next day, Sunday, at 7 o'clock, the officers and I heard Mass in the hermitage. A hovel, this hermitage! his chapel, a miserable corridor with rush-covered columns. For its altar, a plank! For decoration it had a calico panel with a picture of Christ, and tin candlesticks! Our feet were in the sand. Well! I have never heard a Mass said as Father de Foucauld said his. I believed myself in the Thebaid. It is one of the greatest impressions of my life."

Father de Foucauld had again taken up the sedentary life he led a year before. The bell again began to be heard at midnight on the desert plateau. The natives were more numerous than ever in begging the marabout's sous, dates, and barley, and in endlessly telling him of their complicated affairs.

However, he was no longer as robust as before the great journey which he had just finished, and he confesses it.

"I'm not ill," he says. "I celebrate Holy Mass; I am up, but I have great headaches and some fever, and a lot of ailments. I don't think they are serious."

His strength returned, but he had no help. It was again

suggested that he should go back to the Hoggar, and he was authorized to settle as the first priest among the Tuaregs, whose language he was almost the only one to speak and write well. He left his first chosen residence with its poor and beloved chapel and the silence of hours set apart to plunge still deeper into the desert and recommence elsewhere the now promising work begun at Beni-Abbes.

For a vocation is a terrible thing to one who obeys it resolutely with a virile will. While waiting he rejoiced to be in the hermitage once more. He wrote to Commandant Lacroix: "You are at the top of the heights, I am at the bottom of the well; my place is the easier and pleasanter. I would far rather be at the Hoggar, or in the dunes, than at Algiers. Oh! how good is solitude!"

CHAPTER X
The Settlement in Hoggar

THE invitation to return to Hoggar also came from Commandant Laperrine. By two letters, of April 1 and 8, 1905, he proposed to Father de Foucauld to go and spend the summer at Hoggar with Captain Dinaux, chief of annexation of In-Salah, commanding the Saharan company of Tidikelt. The latter was to start at the beginning of May, and go over Ahnet, and Adrar of the Iforas and Aïr.

Brother Charles at first replied that he could not leave the Saoura before autumn. At that moment he would decide either to live finally enclosed at Beni-Abbes, or to divide his life as a travelling priest between the Saura, Gurara, Twat, Tidikelt, and the Tuaregs.

At heart he was extremely troubled. He wrote to Abbé Huvelin, and one gathers from his letter that the hope of at last attracting some Little Brother of the Sacred Heart to the Fraternity of Beni-Abbes, to transform his personal and precarious work into a durable foundation, went for a great deal in the uncertain reply given to Laperrine. Though so quick to conceive and so ardent and firm in execution, he was slow to make up his mind, through love of perfection. He also hinted that such great journeys were not free from fatigue. Nevertheless he would do what his director and Father Guérin advised.

On April 22 he received from Father Guérin, then in France, a telegram which expressed the opinion of the Prefect Apostolic and Abbé Huvelin: " We should be inclined to accept invitation."

Brother Charles at once made inquiries. He learnt that Captain Dinaux would not leave Akabli before May 15. There was time to get there. On May 3 he set out for Adrar with Paul. At the two first stops, twenty-two miles from Beni-Abbes, at the village of Tametert where he slept, then forty-four miles off at Geurzim where he breakfasted and spent the hours of the great heat, he was welcomed. His many sacrifices were not made without some return, and the distant stranger sometimes gave thanks for neighbourly charity.

The words " very well received " occur again and again in the diary, coupled to the names of the *ksurs* at which the traveller asked hospitality for a night. On June 5 in one of these villages Brother Charles met Aziuel, the future successor of the *amenokal* of the Taïtok, " quite changed since last year, full of confidence, quite civilized."

Three days later, near a well in the Twat region he at last found Captain Dinaux, who had four French " civilians " as companions, three at least of whom were very well known : M. E. Gautier, an explorer and geographer; M. Chudeau, a geologist; a writer, M. Pierre Mille; and a post and telegraph inspector on mission, M. Étiennot. The conversations between these men, so different in temperament, studies, and in their spirit of inquiry, must have been more than once worthy of being recorded. Their words are still in the desert. The order of the march joined Brother Charles to M. Étiennot, whom fifteen men mounted on *meharis* escorted; but he was often found elsewhere apart, according to the precept he had himself drawn up, going along on foot, with his head down, keeping silence, the better to hold his soul in peace. " Poor dear Father de Foucauld," Pierre Mille said to me, " I believe we all recognized his worth : he was an admirable man and a saint, tinged, perhaps, with Orientalism : we loved him. We used sometimes to smile at his extraordinary love of the desert. With the freedom of youth we used to call him between ourselves " The man who can't stand tramways."

War chief, scientists, artists, and religious, each one went seeking his own good, and all desired, too, the good of France. They usually set out under the stars, so as to cover more road before the extreme heat stopped the doleful steps of man and beast. Father de Foucauld frequently said his Mass at 2 o'clock in the morning; then he would fold his tent, to prevent delay and to inconvenience nobody. Whenever possible, tents were pitched as soon as evening drew near. On June 23, while the mounted men were driving the tent-pegs near the In-Uzel well under the eyes of two young Tuaregs of about ten years of age and two slaves who were grazing a flock of camels, a man was signalled as coming, the only one in sight. He was quickening his *mehari*. He was soon recognized. He was a courier sent by Captain Dinaux in search of the new *amenokal* of Hoggar. He found the latter at Tin-Zauaten. He was bringing a letter from Musa ag Amastane announcing the approaching arrival of the chief of the Hoggar Tuaregs. In fact, two days after Musa entered the camp and saluted the French Commander. Brother Charles thought well of him. " He is a good fellow," he says, " very intelligent, very open, a very pious Musulman, willing the good as a liberal Musulman, but at the same time ambitious and loving money, pleasure and honour, like Mahomet, in his eyes the most perfect of men. He is entirely devoted to the Bey of Attalia, from whom he says he has received everything.[1] ... Upon the whole, Musa is a good and pious Musulman, having the ideas and life, the qualities and vices of a logical Musulman, and at the same time as broad-minded as possible. He very much wants to go to Algiers and France. ... As agreed with him, my setting up in Hoggar is decided."

For a fortnight the young chief—he was about thirty-five —accompanied the Dinaux mission. There was mutual instruction from which all learnt something. Then the column grew thinner. Musa went off as a nomad, I know not where, M. E. Gautier and Pierre Mille, escorted and guided by three chiefs of the Tuareg Ifors, undertook to cross the south of the Sahara, reached Gao and Timbuctoo, and got back to France after visiting Senegal. Captain Dinaux continued his expedition towards the lofty Hoggar plateaux, and twenty-eight days later entered the valley of Tamanrasset.

This name of Tamanrasset, underlined three times on the margin of the diary, is followed by these lines in which Father de Foucauld's emotion is plain : " By the grace of the divine Well-Beloved Jesus, it is possible for me to settle down in Tamanrasset or any other place in Hoggar, to have a house and garden, and to get established there for ever. ... I choose Tamanrasset, a village of twenty homes, right in the mountain in the heart of Hoggar and of the *Dag*-Rali, the principal tribe, far from all important centres. I don't think that there is ever likely to be a garrison, telegraph station, or a European here : it will be long before there is any mission : I choose this abandoned place, and here I stick."

Thus speaks charity. Then the colonist comes out. He would like to attract and settle in Hoggar (the list is curious, and an economist would not perhaps have drawn it up so well): " a nurseryman; a well-sinker; a doctor; a few women weavers of wool, cotton, and camel-hair; then one or two traders in cotton goods, hardware, sugar, and salt; but honest folks who would get us blessed and not cursed."

The only fault the hermit finds with Tamanrasset is the absence of any priest in the neighbourhood, or even within a reasonable distance. " At an ordinary pace, it takes sixty

[1] A marabout of the family of the Kunta, residing in Attalia.

days to get to Beni-Unif, the only point at which I can conveniently find a priest. I do not think the precept [of confession] is binding in such conditions. In spite of my misery, I am tranquil and in great peace."

As at Beni-Abbes, so at Tamanrasset, Brother Charles began building a "house," or rather a sort of corridor, twenty feet long by six feet wide, to be the chapel and sacristy. For himself he first had a rush hut some way off to work and sleep in; then he lengthened the corridor, and separated the chapel from the library and room with a curtain. He celebrated his first Mass in Hoggar on September 7, 1905. He reckoned to stay there until the autumn of 1906, then to set out for Beni-Abbes, where he would spend the autumn and winter, then go back to Tamanrasset at the beginning of the summer of 1907. He would thus divide himself between the two hermitages. He would be a wandering monk with two huts, the friend of two neglected peoples. At least such was the plan, God willing.

What country, what people could he see from his cabin door? The high plateau of Tamanrasset is at an altitude of about five thousand feet. The dry bed of a fairly wide river crosses it, and it is only there, in a depression of the ground, that there were some very primitive and poor attempts at cultivation when Charles de Foucauld built his oratory and hut near the left bank. All around was undulating stony ground, in which grew tufts of hard grass at every ten yards; *guettaf*, whitish saltworts, a yard high; *um rokba*, of a yellowish-green, not quite so tall; *diss*, a kind of rush somewhat similar to alfa: in a word, rather poor camel pasture. The faded tint of its growth does not rest the eyes and does not give them any pleasure. The beauty of the valley, its grandeur, is given by its frame of mountains, for on the north, within from two to three miles of the hermitage, the solid mass of the Kudiat rises up dominated by the Ilaman peak, ten thousand feet high, bare, heaped-up and rocky mountains, coloured by the sun, above all towards evening, with rose or fawn, with gloomy or dark purple tints, undimmed by mist or dust: to the east, and closer, is the little Hageran chain: to the west the undulations through which the In-Salah track penetrates and winds: on the south the split rock of Mt. Hadrian, famous in Tuareg legend.[1] At these great heights the air is of such perfect transparency as our

[1] The legend relates that long ago the giant Elias split the mountain with a blow of his sword.

eyes have never seen. Autumn is the fine season; the days are mildly warm, the nights sparkling with stars : one has not to go a long way up to see the Southern Cross. What a magic name! The very mention of this heavenly jewel gives plenty of food for imagination, and allows us to reckon how far infinite charity has led Father de Foucauld from Europe.

He is there on the threshold of his cabin, dressed in his white robe, which bears a red heart and cross on the breast. If he looks again into the plain, he will see but a single tree there, an *ethel,* a sort of enormous round tamarisk, which grew in the bed of the wady. In the shade of this only spot of verdure he suspended his barometers and thermometers, except the large mercury barometer over six feet high, brought with so much difficulty on camel-back, and now hung up in the hermitage. At that period a single tree and no house, only a few *zeribas,* rush huts similar to his own, half hidden in the bed of the Wady Tamanrasset, in which lived some *harratins,* who grew a little barley, carrots, and red Guinea pepper. They were his ordinary companions. There were others who passed by. In the expanse, except in the great droughts, Tuareg shepherds, dwellers in great tents, guarding troops of camels, asses, sheep and goats, were nearly always wandering about. One morning, without any noise having revealed the march of a caravan, appears the ungainly outline in shadow of a few extra camels, whose feet and bellies make windows, and not far away are three or four hillocks which were not visible the evening before, brown molehills made of animals' skins under which the nomads sleep. These " masters of the desert," as the Tuaregs are often called, lead the most nomadic life possible. They fill the desert with their name, but they are not very numerous. Tamanrasset ordinarily only numbered about sixty inhabitants. Father de Foucauld estimated the various Kel-Ahaggar tribes at from eight to nine hundred families, whilst other groups of tribes of the same people—the Iforas, for instance— amounted to at least two thousand families. Summer drives them away and compels them to convey their cattle to immense distances, as far as the Sudan, where they pay very high for pasturage. They also travel for commerce. Caravans set forth to sell sheep and goats in the markets of Tidikelt, and bring back cotton goods, dates, and millet. Other Tuaregs carry on traffic with Rhat and Rhadames : others lead their camels loaded with salt from the celebrated mines of Taudeni as far as Timbuctoo.

A wretched people, on the whole, often tormented with hunger and thirst. It does not know whence it comes, nor through what event it was obliged to retire into so rude a region. For a long time the legend of the European origin of the Tuaregs was upheld, on account of the whiteness of their skin, and the cross which they carry as an ornament on the pommels of their saddles and on their clothes. It is now thought that they are Berbers thrust back by Arab invasions into the depths of the desert, "simply Libyans, the last survivors," says M. E. Gautier. And Father de Foucauld, who studied them more closely than anyone, was of the same opinion. "They are," he wrote, "certainly Hamites; their language shows it clearly. When of pure type they have the physiognomy of the ancient Egyptians: very white, slender, long-faced, regular features, large eyes, slightly receding forehead, arms and legs rather long and thin—the Egyptians of the old sculptures. Their customs are very different from those of the Arabs. They are Musulmans with a great deal of faith but no practice or education."[1] The Middle Ages seem to have known them: annals of the time of the Crusaders speak of veiled men, the *Multimin*. They have, in fact, their faces veiled up to the eyes by a blue bandage, the *litham*. Their pride is immense, their coquetry greater than that of women. When these tall thin devils, leaning on their lance, approach a stranger they hold their heads straighter, they affect a more solemn walk than if they were princes of former times.

Up to the beginning of our century war and expeditions of vengeance and plunder were the most lucrative industry of the Tuareg tribes: the free man does not work. Emile Gautier describes the warrior thus: "The accoutrements of the Tuareg warriors are well known: the long fine lance, all of iron, inlaid with brass, with fierce barbs; the great long straight sword, with round point and cross-hilt, ... the antelope-skin shield, painted with barbarous figures. They are dreadfully 'poor,' far beyond our usual conception of the word: the cost of a Winchester rifle and its annual supply of cartridges, doubled or tripled by the carriage across a thousand miles of desert, is about as

---

[1] Letter to Comte de Foucauld, April 3, 1906. The Tuaregs believe in God, but do not observe the Ramadan fast, nor say the five daily prayers. E. Gautier said: "Nowhere in the rest of the Berber world does the primitive man appear under so superficial and scaly a varnish of Islam." No doubt that was one of the reasons which decided Father de Foucauld to settle in Hoggar.

disproportioned to the resources of an average Tuareg as, for instance, the upkeep of a 60-h.p. motor-car to the income of a rural postman."

The fighting men, when they go on an expedition and it is time for the night halt, bring several shields together and sleep thus under shelter. The family tent is not quite so primitive. "A big skin made of an infinite number of sheepskins sewn together, fixed by cords to twelve stakes, a long central pole which raises the skin, and there your Tuareg family lodges," says a traveller who recently visited Hoggar.[1] "The Dag Rali that I visited were rich, and had tents of fine skins and carved stakes. To complete their dwellings, through which the wind passes without meeting any obstacle, the tent is surrounded by a sort of screen formed of fibre mats which the Tuaregs make themselves. At night the tent is closed by the mat; in the day the mat is rolled up. . . . The furniture is reduced to nothing: a few coverlets, kitchen utensils, the *rahla* to mount the camel, the woman's violin (*imzad*), and arms—that is all. Of course, they have no beds: all sleep on the ground. . . . Around the tents negro and negress slaves attend to the household duties. The men, at least at this season, do nothing, spend their time in palaver or sword-fencing with great skin shields. The women are busy with the children and cooking, which is really too inadequate; they play the *imzad* and make visits in the evening."

The nomad women not only pay visits to one another. Frequently at the end of the afternoon, before the hour for milking the animals, they go to a gallant party which brings together the young girls, the young widows or those cast off, the young or comparatively young and unmarried men. There is great liberty of speech. Sometimes the *ahâl* is held in the shade of a tree, if there is one, or a rock; at other times, under the tent of a woman living alone, or a tent put up on purpose. They sit beside one another. They meet old friends, they chat, invent witticisms, a woman plays the *imzad*, a violin with one string, the men accompanying in an undertone: the men often recite poetry of their own composition or poems that have been handed down in the family or tribe from generation to generation. Young Tuareg warriors sometimes go from 60 to 120 miles to be at an *ahâl* of a woman reputed for her beauty or wit. A traditional etiquette regulates everything in this corner

[1] Doctor Vermale, *Au Sahara pendant la guèrre européene*, 1913-1917 (written notes). Doctor Vermale was killed by the Tuaregs in the battle of Ain-el-Hajaj, February 13, 1917. He was twenty-nine years of age.

of the desert *en fête*. "Clothes, behaviour, and conversation are all governed by a graded worldly code, discreet, absurd, and inflexible. Flirting is naturally the great occupation."[1]

The Hoggar confederation, like the other Tuareg confederations, is commanded by an elected chief, the *amenokal* chosen among the nobles :[2] each tribe obeys an *amrar*. We already know that when Father de Foucauld began to build his hermitage at Tamanrasset, the Hoggar *amenokal* was Musa ag Amastane. He succeeded two declared enemies of the French : Ahitarel, who governed the confederation at the time of the massacre of the Flatter mission; then Attisi, who had himself taken part in the massacre. More clever and also more intelligent than his predecessors, Musa entered into negotiation with the military chiefs of the oases even before his election as chief of his nation. At the beginning of 1904 he concluded a treaty of friendship with the French at In-Salah, had himself recognized chief of the Hoggar Tuaregs, and—cleverest of all in the chief of a band—obtained from France pardon for the former *amenokal* Attisi, who had become unpopular and retired towards the south-east, to the Azjer Tuaregs.

Such was the country in which Father de Foucauld proposed to live, such were the Tuaregs whom he was going to have as companions and witnesses. He could still change his mind and go back north. That was proposed to him. Captain Dinaux, who had followed his journey and run over the Aïr region, again at the end of five weeks passed through Tamanrasset on October 15, 1905. He inquired about the hermit's plans : they had not changed. Then he bade him adieu, put in his report this memorable fact that a civilized man had asked as a great favour to be left in Hoggar, and added : " He will remain thus alone in the midst of the Tuaregs, 425 miles from In-Salah, and will be united to us only by the monthly courier which we are going to try to inaugurate."

What faith and what moral energy to support such a trial victoriously ! No one of his race and education. No help for body or soul ! No hope for years and years of altogether winning a people to his Faith across such a distance and so many obstacles ! He knew for a certainty that he would die before getting the reward—that is to say, before securing the full conversion of a single soul to the

---
[1] Emile Gautier, *La Conquête du Sahara*.
[2] The Hoggar noble tribes are the Kel Rela and the Taïtok : both have vassal tribes.

law of salvation and Christian civilization. And yet, not to doubt, not to hesitate, to offer himself resolutely for a task which no human attraction recommended, to break with all that he loved on earth and in the mind of Europe, to obtain the difficult, the uncertain distrustful sympathy of nomad shepherds, of warriors accustomed to robbery, and of miserable negroes—that is the life which Father de Foucauld chose. Most men, even of the stoutest type, would have succumbed to one or other of these temptations : discouragement or corruption. He remained pure : he made progress in the art of sacrifice, the longest of all to learn and the one the mastery of which is never assured; he rendered France the incomparable service of allowing a glimpse of her to be caught, for she was present and recognizable in him; he rendered other services to science; he prepared a whole people for missionaries to come; he was the great solitary sower whose steps nobody has been able to count. He never counted them himself. I believe the words of one of his near relations are quite right : " Hoggar. This is the period of his life in which Charles showed all he could do."

His self-surrender was apparently complete : yet it was to be much greater.

Faithful to his unchangeable resolution to prepare for the conversion of the infidels, Father de Foucauld, as soon as he had taken possession of his hermitage, made his retreat, and noted in his diary the means he would use for such a blessing.

" Do my utmost for the salvation of the infidel peoples of these countries by the total forgetfulness of self.

" Every year make a round of the *arrhem*[1] of Hoggar; accept invitations to journeys in the Sahara, if they are useful; if possible, spend a few days every year in the tents of the Hoggars."

With the help of Abd en Nebi, a Tamanrasset *harratin*, whom he paid twenty centimes a lesson—a price which was then and there sufficient—he at once undertook the translation into Tuareg of extracts from the Holy Scriptures.

Total forgetfulness of self, a life of prayer, charity, and study : how could a man faithful to such an ideal be unsuccessful in gaining the sympathy of these camel-drivers and savage traders, even of giving them a glimpse of the moral superiority of Christians? How doubt that France, of whom he was a model son, would benefit by such an exile? Captain Dinaux, the refined and cultivated officer who had

[1] Little colonies of agriculturists are thus described.

brought him to Hoggar and then left him there, said in his report to the Governor-General of Algeria: "The Father's reputation for holiness, the results he has clearly obtained in curing the sick, will do more for the extension of our influence and the rallying to our ideas, than a permanent occupation of the country. . . . The manner in which he was received and installed is a characteristic proof of Musa's good dispositions." He added these lines, which do him honour, and which should be remembered: "On the same grounds, we should encourage the establishment of the half-nomadic White Sisters as much as possible: the position of the Tuareg woman would further the improvement of their race by contact with European women. . . . Their devotion, their kindness, and spirit of sacrifice would have the happiest influence on the Tuaregs."

Father de Foucauld's Rule was still the same as that of the Little Brothers of the Sacred Heart, but he was obliged to make two modifications in them: he devoted a great deal of time to the study of Tamachek, and at first he had to leave the enclosure, in order "to be in contact" with his changing neighbours. "He had to take the first steps:" the Tuaregs would not come of themselves when there was no material profit to be hoped for. Brother Charles would therefore go into the gardens where the *harratins* were working: he would go and chat with the shepherds and their slaves around the tents scattered in the plain. He gave out remedies and little presents of coloured pictures, and above all needles that women riding on donkeys came from very far to beg for, since the greater part of the time they had to sew with thorns, to the end of which they fastened a piece of thread. Later on he learnt to knit, so as to give them knitting lessons: he thought of the great material and moral gain of establishing little workrooms managed by French Sisters in this country, "where they work so little and talk so much," and where the women "die of idleness." If only they could be taught to weave wool! When the sheep falls, unfortunately its wool along with the camel's hair are carried off by the wind. "Nobody makes anything of them: a little goat's hair is used to make cords, the rest is unused." The thought of "his people" never left this colonizing monk.

He also saw Musa ag Amastane, and spoke of him in his letters, and the opening sketch of the *amenokal's* face helps us to a much clearer idea of him.

"I again saw a lot of Tuaregs whom I saw last year: we are on very good terms. As to the natives, I see no other duty than that of praying for them, and making them like me, and, should an opportunity offer, giving them good advice very discreetly. . . . I endeavour to prepare the way for others, praying to Jesus to send them. It seems to me that at present the most necessary things in Hoggar are education and the reconstitution of the family; their ignorance is so profound as to render them incapable of distinguishing the true from the false, and the looseness of family life, the sequel to that of morals and numerous divorces, leaves the children to grow up as chance may decide and without education. . . .

"The setting up of French authority among the Hoggar and the Taïtok has made great progress since last year.

"As long as France has not a European war, we seem to be safe. If there is a European war, there would probably be risings in the whole South and here as elsewhere. . . .

"Actually both are entirely subject and pay France tribute: the *amrar* of the Taïtok and the *amenokal* of the Hoggar were solemnly invested with their authority in the name of France by the chief of the dependency of In-Salah, to whom they are subordinate. The Taïtok has an *amrar* Gidi ag Geraji, an intelligent old man but without great authority, and not a very responsible character. The Hoggar have Musa ag Amastane as *amenokal;* he is a very intelligent man, animated with good intentions, seeking solely the welfare of the Musulmans and Tuaregs; large-minded, he devotes his life to make peace reign among the Tuaregs, to protect the weak against the violence of the strong, and by that acquires, as well as by his liberality, piety, amiability, and courage, a universal veneration from In-Salah to Timbuctoo; the good he does, his efforts for peace and justice, are not restricted to Hoggar, but extend to the neighbouring tribes—Azjers, Kel-Ui, Taïtok, Aulimmiden: his moderation, his spirit of peace, and his constancy in upholding the poor and oppressed against injustice, are remarkable; he is open-minded, wise, and moderate; if God gives him life, his influence will go on increasing and will last for a long time. It is very interesting to see this mixture of great natural gifts and profound ignorance in this man who, from certain points of view, is a savage, and, from others, has a right to esteem and consideration; for his justice, his courage, and the elevation of his character have made for him a peerless position from Twat and Rhât as far as the Niger. My relations with him are excellent. I had not seen him last year; this year I have not left him for four months; he is here even now; he has no residence, and is a nomad like all his compatriots. Do his fine qualities exclude ambition, sensuality, and disdain and hatred in his heart for non-Musulmans? I do not think so, but he seems to have enough real piety, so that striving for the general good influences his conduct more than private interest, and he is intelligent enough to change to good whatever is false and bad in his mind and heart."[1]

This detailed analysis of Musa ag Amastane's character shows frequent intercourse between him and Father de Foucauld. The above letter alludes to it, but does not give any detailed account. What subjects were approached in these conversations between the European Christian and the African Musulman? The happy influence of Father de Foucauld, even his moral authority over the Hoggar chief, is undeniable. It will be clearly seen later, when I have to speak of the last moments and last words of the *amenokal*. But what sort of talks went on with the hermit of Tamanrasset when he paid or received visits from the chief? In spite of his personal fervour, did he confine himself to vague counsels with distant or discreetly veiled references to the law of Christ? This has been maintained, because many require positive proofs in order to believe in goodness, especially in a certain courage in which they are wanting; and so far these proofs could not be given. But now we have them.

After Father de Foucauld's death in his hermitage at Tamanrasset, among many other papers dispersed and thrown in the dust was found a pocket-book of intimate notes, a sort of memento, which I have under my eyes in writing these lines. Several pages are headed: *Things to say and letters written to Musa*. These things were not said or written at the beginning of his stay at Tamanrasset, but they are clearness itself; they reply to a question still more general than the one which has been put. About what did Father de Foucauld speak to the Tuaregs and, in a more general way, to Musulmans; and up to what point did he use that right of counsel which he bought so dearly and which his strict duty forbade him to drop? Here it is. I shall reproduce the greater part of the two documents, of which the first is dated Easter, 1912, the second 1914, but which both explain the whole of his dwelling at Tamanrasset, and reveal the secret of an action, always French, but also essentially and always religious.

[1] Letter to Mgr. Livinhac, October 26, 1905.

" *Tell Musa:*

" 1. Surround yourself with worthy people, keep no good-for-nothings about you.

" 2. Keep away all strange Arabs who only come to settle here in order to eat up the country and to eat up you, Musa.

" 3. Encourage settlers.

" 4. Reduce expenses. Be humble. God alone is great. He who thinks himself great, or who seeks to be great, does not know God.

" 5. First of all, love God with your whole heart and above all things; next, love all men as yourself. From the love of your neighbour as yourself follows the triple law of *fraternity, equality (imrad), liberty* (slaves). ' When Adam delved and Eve span, where was then the gentleman?' Where was the *imrad,* where the slave?

" 6. If he wants to know how the prophets think, speak, and act, he must come to see me. I shall read the Gospels to him.

" 7. Don't ask for, and don't accept presents. By asking for presents from his friends, he burdens them heavily; by accepting presents from anyone, he becomes the slave of the riff-raff.

" 8. Pay all debts and don't incur new ones: don't borrow of friends, because that is unworthy of you and will weigh heavily upon them. Don't borrow of unknown people, for that will make you their slave. In the holy books, God often tells chiefs not to take gifts. If the man from whom they have taken a gift asks them for an unjust thing, they find it hard to refuse; if he does wrong, they find it hard to punish him; it is to be feared that they will prefer him to others, who have given nothing, as good or better than them.

" 9. Don't give presents or hospitality without necessity, otherwise you will always be: (1) in money difficulties and debts; (2) surrounded by riff-raff, for it is they and not worthy people whom hospitality attracts; (3) to provide for it you will have to get considerable presents given you by those of the *imrad* who are most devoted to you, and they will end by hating you on account of your requests for money, for your waste and his bad company.

" 10. Have fewer slaves; a band of wasteful good-for-nothings who make you ridiculous are no good to you.

" 11. When you are near an officer, go frequently to see him quite alone; many things are better treated in a *tête-à-tête;* and speak to him without an interpreter, quite frankly as to a real friend; *never tell the shade of an untruth.* Treat all grave affairs always in a *tête-à-tête* with the officer without interpreter.

"12. *Never lie to anybody;* all untruth is hateful to God, for God is truth.

"13. Always furnish thoroughly good men as guides, because often all the other Tuaregs get judged by them.

"14. Never praise a person to his face; when one loves and esteems anyone, that is shown by confidence and acts; there is no use in talking about it; to flatter is a low thing good enough for the Arabian *thalebs*.

"15. Don't be slow and lazy, manage to husband your time.

"16. Try hard to get your people to learn French, to become naturalized French, not to become our subjects but our equals, to be everywhere on the same footing as we, so as to be everywhere free from annoyance. That will come sooner or later; those who see what is coming prepare for it; thanks to that, and probably in a short time, all the military and employés of Ahaggar will be natives.

"17. Never make a real present to any Frenchman; that rather annoys than pleases those to whom you give them; for it is an expense to you (which they wish to spare you), and also to the receiver (who will always make a present in return); when a Frenchman takes a gift, it is only through politeness and with regret. Never ask the captain for sugar, tea, or anything; bring what is necessary, and if you lack anything, put up with it. If you ask, you get what you want, but at the same time you obtain what you don't wish for—contempt."

"*Letters to Musa:*

"Love God above all things, with your whole heart, your whole strength, and your whole mind.

"Love all men as yourself, for the love of God.

"Do unto all men what you wish they would do unto you.

"Do to none what you would not wish them to do unto you.

"Abase yourself inwardly: God alone is great; all men are little: the man who is puffed up is mad, for he knows not whether he is going to heaven or hell.

"God sees all your thoughts, words, and deeds; remember and do them all as in His sight.

"Do each act as you would have it done at the hour of death.

"The hour of death is unknown : let your soul be as you would have it at the hour of death.

"Each evening reflect on the thoughts, words, and deeds of the day; ask pardon of God for those that are bad and for all the sins of your life, as if you were going to die in the night, and say to God from the bottom of your heart :

"'O God, I love Thee with my whole heart, above all things.

"'O God, Thy will in all things is mine.

"'My God, all that Thou willest me to do, I will do.'"

Is not that the summary of all evangelical morality, and is it necessary to remark that such teaching, commented on by frequent conversations, either with Musa, or with the Tuaregs and *harratins* of Hoggar, was excellently calculated to prepare the chief and his people to receive and understand Catholic dogma? Is not the poor Saharan who undertakes to examine his conscience and say the above prayer in the best dispositions for deserving and desiring to know the whole truth? And how near us he would be! And how much better would treaties hold with men thus taught!

Brother Charles, living in the midst of them, and having intercourse only with them, quickly judges the Tuaregs. He compares them to the Arabs; in both cases there are the same ignorance and violence. But the ignorance of the Tuaregs can be more easily combated and overcome, because they are of a more amiable nature, and more inquisitive. Their greatest fault is pride. These nomads of a Saharan tribe, "the proudest of men," look upon us as savages. They esteem themselves as the most perfect of mankind, "the best on earth." They even take us for know-nothings, and no doubt this would be a sign of madness if they had not some slight excuse—pride is contented with little and sometimes even with nothing—in their manner of life, and in their extreme remoteness, and in the obstacles of all sorts which make their country so inaccessible. One of the best-known officers of our African Army, an expert in all Saharan questions, whom I questioned in Algiers about the incredible contempt for us which the natives feel or affect, replied: "They feel that we are at their mercy whenever we ask them to act as guides in the desert, or advise us about a police operation. The natives think we are their inferiors in their own surroundings, and that is enough. Our machinery makes little impression upon them. A picture or a legend seems an explanation to them, and satisfies their very superficial desire for knowledge. Thus, to them an aeroplane is only a ' tent that flies '; the wireless, the utilization of the wind which we send from one post to another; the motor, an iron box in which we have imprisoned the genii of fire. It is the genii that make the wheels turn. And the proof is the drubbing (the turning of the crank-handle) we give them at starting, to force them to work. When once a native has heard these poor explanations, he considers himself well-informed, and as he feels no need to change his customs, the camel caravans seem to him the best means of transporting dates, millet, and salt, just as do runners for sending news; he agrees to use our inventions but does not esteem us on account of them, having been able to live at less expense, freely and as he pleased, before they were known."

That is not the whole explanation of the natives' pride. They were told, and thought there were many signs that Europeans, and particularly the French, were unbelievers. It is another error, another want of knowledge, more serious than the first, but which is explained by our fault, and they say: "You have the earth, but we have heaven."

Father de Foucauld, who was familiar with the subject, might then quite rightly conclude thus:

"Our civilized nations—which have among them many savages, many who are ignorant of primary truths and as violent as the Tuaregs—are very guilty for not spreading the light and propagating the right, education and laws of peace, in these backward countries. How easy that would be! But instead of that, they waste their substance in follies, or wars, or mad contradictions."[1]

Such were the companions among whom it may be said Father de Foucauld lived in solitude. He had his refuge in the adoration of the Blessed Sacrament and the celebration of Mass. But the consecration of the Body of Christ demanded some one to serve Mass along with the priest. Now, a letter to Father Guérin, on April 2, 1906, let it be seen that the negro, the former slave brought from Beni-Abbes to Ahaggar, would have to go: " Paul goes from bad to worse—morally—the impossibility of saying Mass without him alone makes me keep him. If I were obliged to part with him, or if he, of his own accord, leaves me, might I say Holy Mass, every fortnight, alone, in order to renew the holy species? Might I myself communicate daily as priests in prison do? . . . Thanks be to God!

[1] Letter to the Comte de Foucauld, April 3, 1906.

I am the happiest of men; solitude with Jesus is a delicious *tête-à-tête*, but I should like good to be done, to spread and be propagated; nevertheless, *non mea voluntas, sed tua fiat!* . . . My soul is in great peace. I am full of miseries, but without any serious thing tormenting me. I am happy and peaceable at the feet of the Well-Beloved!"

The will of God was that trial should come and the courage of His priest appear with more splendour. On May 17 the diary tells us that Paul left the Fraternity of Tamanrasset. Brother Charles gives no explanation; he has only a cry for pity: "O God, make me go on celebrating the holy Sacrifice! Let me not lose my soul! Save it."

In his letters he spoke of a coming visit to Hoggar: " I am expecting the visit of my old and good friend, Motylinski, a former army interpreter, one of the most learned men in Algeria, who has asked to spend the summer with me, in order to study Tamachek. . . . I am preparing a grammar, a Tamachek-French and a French-Tamachek lexicon, and a translation of extracts from the Bible, making both an abridged Bible-history and a collection of the most useful passages for this place, from poetic, sapiential, and prophetic books. All that is fairly forward, and may be finished two or three months from now."

On Whit-Sunday, June 3, 1906, Motylinski arrived. "A very good-hearted man," wrote Father de Foucauld, "and he will contribute to making the Tuaregs our friends." And Motylinski agreed to serve Mass. "The good God has sent him here just in the nick of time to allow me to continue to say it."

M. de Motylinski's stay in Hoggar lasted three months, during which the linguistic work made great progress. At the beginning of September the two friends set out for the "north," as the extreme south Oranais is here called. Father de Foucauld wished to see Beni-Abbes again. There he received a welcome which, in his modesty, he did not expect. "I was very satisfied with what I found at Beni-Abbes: the French, beyond all expression, and the natives of the Saura beyond all hope, were just perfect to me." It was a very rapid journey: Father de Foucauld, whom Motylinski had left at El-Golea—on the way to Ghardaïa and Biskra—went farther north, spent a few days at Maison Carrée with Father Guérin and his friends the White Fathers, and then hastily returned to Hoggar. "Hoggar is still so new," he said, "so little accustomed to our presence, that I think it very desirable to be absent the shortest time possible." And he set out from Algiers on December 10, with the intention of spending a few weeks at Beni-Abbes, then of going full speed to the South and regaining Tamanrasset.

For a wonder, the hermit had a companion, not an exploring amateur or scientist, but a companion who said he meant to follow him into the desert. This was a young Breton, a fisherman's son, who had spent three years with the White Fathers, then three years in a Zouaves' regiment in Africa. He was seeking his final career, and believed he had found it when he heard all about Father de Foucauld's mission. They therefore set out together. After having spent the whole evening and night with the natives in one of the compartments of the little train which starts from Oran and nears the Moroccan frontier and touches it at Beni-Unif, the Father and Brother Michael, dressed in Arab fashion, got off at Ain-Sefra Station, the chief town of the military sub-division. It is a large village built on the left of the railway, beyond a wide space where the sand flies; bright houses, the Information Office and club built in Moorish style; the little shops of a southern station; among the roofs, tufts of trees; and quite in the background are seen the projecting spurs of the great dunes, and a mountain. About fifteen officers had come to the station to wait for their former comrade, among them General Lyautey, who offered him hospitality. "I found him," the Marshal told me, "poor and neglected, though he used to be so refined. And that was intentional. Nothing was left of the former Foucauld. Yes, something: his eyes, which were beautiful, illuminated. The officers adored him. He rode with them barefooted. I had given him a room. Next day when he left us, I just received a telegram announcing that friends were coming. I said to the orderly:

"Hurry up and get the room ready!"

"It will be ready very quickly, sir."

"Why?"

"The bed has not been touched; not a thing has been moved; he slept on the floor."

It had become a habit.

From Aïn-Sefra, the two travellers gained Colomb-Béchar by train. They stopped, however, twenty-four hours at Beni-Unif, and, at the invitation of Commander Pariel, who was already popular and quite safe in the Moroccan oasis, visited Figig, where the Governor-General of Algeria had been welcomed with rifle-shots three or four years earlier. It was but a little thing, a walk under the palms and in the *ksurs*, a few minutes' conversation with the natives, looking white in the blue shadow of the winding-streets, a salute, a friendly word, an alms. However, certain people have a mysterious power: they pass, and he who has only seen, touched, or heard them for a moment, cannot forget them. After over thirteen years, in the spring of 1920 I found the recollection of Father de Foucauld's visit very enduring at Figig. One of the soldiers of the *maghzen*, a magnificent trooper in his high-coloured costume, a man with a serious and mild face, when I questioned him, replied:

" You are speaking of the Christian marabout? Yes, I remember him."

" What did you think of him?"

" What everybody thought: he was a good man."

After Colomb-Béchar, there was no railway or road to Beni-Abbes, and the companion began his real apprenticeship in Saharan travel. He wrote his impressions; he formed his opinion of his " Superior," and the pages he wrote are one of the most informing records of Father de Foucauld's life on the tramp through the desert or at Beni-Abbes.

Brother Michael's Story.

" We reached Colomb-Béchar, the railway terminus. At the station the French officers of the garrison again came to seek my venerated Superior, who received hospitality at the house of one of them, whilst I went and lodged, as agreed, in a modest hotel. On our arrival, the first care of the Father was to hire a servant who could be trusted to lead and take care of the two camels that carried our luggage and provisions across the Sahara. He was a big boy of thirty, a negro, a former slave in Timbuctoo, called Ubargua, a drinker and stubborn, vain, a liar, lazy and greedy, repulsively dirty and without any religion. Thinking the Father was very rich, he had joyfully agreed to serve him in the hope of having abundant and delicate food, and also very little work. At the end of a few days his disappointment was great, when he saw that instead of good cheer he had only just enough. He had also made up his mind to leave his place with us as soon as he found another in which he would be better fed.

" The next day we entered the desert, escorted by five or six African privates under a sergeant. The soldiers were always a few paces ahead of us, searching carefully every bush, every bit of cover in the land, to see they did not conceal any caravan robbers. After three days' march without any disagreeable encounter, we at last reached Beni-Abbes, where the Father had established what he called his first hermitage, and where we were to rest for a few days. It was a very modest convent, built with earth and wood, like all the cabins in the country. The cells, to the number of seven or eight, intended for the future monks, were so low that a man of ordinary stature touched the roof on raising his hand a little over his head, so narrow that in stretching out one's arms in the form of a cross one could touch the wall on the right and left. No bed, seat, table, or a prie-dieu to kneel on; one had to sleep, fully dressed, on a palm mat spread out on the floor. The sacristy was large enough and did for the Father's library and store, bedroom and study. The chapel was built like all the rest with wood and earth and surmounted by a dome; inside there was no other furniture than a very simple altar and two prie-dieu; therefore, during the long offices and the daily and nightly exercises of piety, one had to stand, or kneel, or sit on the mats. Near the sacristy there was a fine room, completely empty, which the Father intended to keep for passing strangers, for the Prefect Apostolic, for officers and other distinguished people who might come to visit him. . . . We spent every Christmas in this hermitage. At midnight Mass there were a hundred present, all officers, non-commissioned officers or soldiers, who filled not only the church but also the sacristy. I remarked a single woman in this numerous assembly. She was an old mulatto, very poor, quite blind, a beautiful soul enshrined in an ugly body, whom the Father had baptized three or four months ago, and whom he kept alive by his alms. She spent all her days in prayer and did not fail to go to communion every time that the holy Sacrifice of the Mass was offered at Beni-Abbes. At the departure of her benefactor, she wept bitter tears and uttered cries of grief.

"Here is the Rule we followed during the ten days we spent at the hermitage. As we had no lamps to light us, and were obliged to economize the wax and candles for the long and frequent liturgical ceremonies; our rising and going to bed were regulated by the sun. The Father loved punctuality, and himself fulfilled the difficult office of timekeeper, assigned in most communities to the youngest and least worthy. In the morning he came and wakened me

THE SETTLEMENT IN HOGGAR

at daybreak. As we slept fully dressed, our toilet was quickly finished, and a few minutes after getting up I said the *Angelus* in my cell. At the sound of the bell I went to church. My Superior then recited a long prayer, half in Latin, half in French, which I answered; he exposed the Blessed Sacrament, singing the *Tantum ergo*, then celebrated holy Mass, which I served, and during which I communicated. We remained in silence and adoration for more than two hours. The thanksgiving and meditation over, the Father said his breviary in a low voice, while I said some *Paters* and *Aves*. Before leaving the chapel the Father gave Benediction with the Blessed Sacrament and shut the holy ciborium up in the tabernacle. About 9 o'clock we went each to our work: my Superior shut himself up in the sacristy, where his books and manuscripts are, and wrote letters, or worked at his dictionary of the Tuareg language, always writing, for want of a table, on a simple box. As for me, I retired to my cell, the only one that had a chimney, and which served at once as workshop, kitchen, and refectory. There I read a pious book; then I set to work, either grinding wheat between two stones, as the people of the country do, crushing dates with a pestle and mortar, baking thick flat cakes in the ashes, or cooking. At 11 o'clock we had our meal, preceded by the reading of a chapter of the New Testament and particular examen. After saying grace, the Father stood up and read aloud two or three passages from a chapter of the *Imitation;* then we all sat on our mats around the saucepan placed on the ground, just off the fire, the Father, our negro servant and myself, and we ate in the greatest silence, fishing food out of the dish with a spoon, and drinking water out of the same vessel. The menu varied very little; it was composed now of a dish of rice cooked in water and, very exceptionally, with condensed milk, sometimes mixed with carrots and turnips which grow in the desert sand, sometimes with a sort of marmalade of a fairly pleasant flavour made with wheat-flour, crushed dates, and water. There were no napkins, table-cloth, plates, or knives or forks with which to eat this slight collation. We stood up at the end of a quarter of an hour or twenty minutes, and after thanksgiving and grace, both went to the chapel chanting the *Miserere*, to pay a visit to the Blessed Sacrament, and for spiritual reading in common. About 2 o'clock we returned, each on our own side, to our usual occupations, the Father to his studies, and I to manual work. At 6 in the evening we had supper with only one course, like the other meal. It was taken in the same way and despatched with the same rapidity. About half-past 6 we went to church for mental prayer before the Blessed Sacrament exposed, then a long evening prayer followed by Benediction with the Blessed Sacrament. We finished the day with the hymn *Veni Creator*. Bedtime was regularly fixed by twilight, but it was always dark when we went to rest.

" We remained more than a week in the oasis of Beni-Abbés, faithful observers of the austere Rule which I have just described. On December 27, 1906, we continued our journey, accompanied by several officers, among others the captain who commanded the garrison, and two native soldiers. The officers accompanied us for a whole day. In the afternoon a herd of gazelles passed before our caravan, at a fair distance, and stopped to look at us. One of our men on *meharis* at once aimed at one and brought it down. It was cut up and roasted. The supper was a real feast, in which all took part, even my venerated Superior.

" Next morning the officers left us, after an exchange of good wishes and hearty handshaking, giving us two native soldiers to protect us. The Father at the moment of parting gave the keys of his Beni-Abbes hermitage to the captain, saying to him : ' Watch well over the house of God;' I entrust it to you.'

" During the whole crossing of the desert, which took place in winter, the day temperature was from 59° to 68°, that of night from four or five degrees below freezing-point. In the morning we sometimes found frozen water in the cruet, and the ground covered with a thin coat of ice. From time to time a violent wind blew and made thick clouds of dust, driving sand into our eyes and small pebbles into our faces. When we arrived in a village at night, we were always offered hospitality, and we passed the night in a house. More often we slept under the canopy of heaven without any fire, in a hole large enough to lodge a man's body, which we ourselves hollowed out with our hands in the sand, and which served us as a bed. Benumbed with cold, rolled up in our camp blankets, we turned and turned again and again on our mats all night, to warm ourselves and induce sleep, but without succeeding. Towards noon we used to halt for a good hour, which enabled us to light a fire for cooking our dinner ; a little before sunset at the place where we were to camp, we had supper. The menu of these two meals was that of the hermitage, to which a cup of coffee was added. One day the Father invited some officers to his table as a joke. They accepted the challenge; but during the whole meal they appeared very ill at ease, ate with extreme repugnance, and were soon satisfied: they had no wish, I presume, to accept a second invitation to such a feast.

"In the depths of silent nature, in this dead land, where never had human being fixed his abode, it was easy for us to lead the life of solitude and contemplation. The Father did not once miss celebrating the holy Mysteries on a portable altar at sunrise, generally in the open air, only three or four times in the tent we had pitched the evening before, so as not to suffer from the gusty squalls.

"Like Moses, I was only to see the promised land from a distance. Already anything but well at our departure from Algiers, I felt seriously ill a little more than two months after our departure from Beni-Abbes, and I felt incapable of continuing so toilsome a journey on foot in the sands. I was obliged to stop at In-Salah, and, to my great regret, renounce the Tuareg mission. The good Father at first tried to keep me, but having been examined by the garrison doctor, . . . seeing very clearly, too, that my strength was exhausted and that I should be rather a hindrance than a help, he gave me a good sum of money and abundant provisions, and confided me to two trustworthy men. . . .

"I remained with the Reverend Father Charles de Jesus from December 2 or 3, 1906, to March 10, 1907. I therefore lived with him in the greatest intimacy for three months. I can affirm under oath that he always edified me greatly by his tender devotion to the Sacred Heart, to the Most Blessed Sacrament and to the Blessed Virgin Mary; by his ardent zeal for souls and his charity towards his fellow-men; by his spirit of faith, his firm hope, and his complete detachment from worldly goods; by his profound humility, his imperturbable patience under trials; and above all, by his terrible mortification. To tell the whole truth, I ought, however, to point out one imperfection, common enough in men who have for a long time exercised authority, that I perceived in my worthy Superior. From time to time, when things did not go as he wished, he betrayed a sign of impatience, but it was promptly checked. Apart from this slight fault, which he must have corrected, I esteem that Father Charles practised to an heroic degree the three theological and the four cardinal virtues, as well as the moral virtues which belong to them.

"*Charity towards God.*—He passionately loved Jesus Christ, his God, Brother, and Friend, and his great happiness was to converse with the Prisoner of love, really present in the tabernacle. Prayer was his delight, it was truly his life and the breath of his soul. He spent the greater part of his days and nights kneeling before the Blessed Sacrament, adoring, supplicating, giving thanks, and making reparation. As, on Christmas night, he did not quit our church for a single instant, I was bold enough to ask him next day how he could remain awake so long in the darkness: 'One has no need of seeing clearly,' he replied, 'to speak to Him who is the Sun of justice and the Light of the world.'

"*Desire of Martyrdom.*—He would have wished to give to Jesus Christ the greatest proof of affection that a friend can give to a friend, by dying for Him as He died for us. He desired and earnestly begged martyrdom from God as the greatest of all favours. The prospect of immolation, the beauty and greatness of which exalted his generous faith, transformed his always bold and ardent speech into true hymns of joy. 'To be killed by pagans,' he used to exclaim, 'what a beautiful death! My very dear brother, how honoured and happy should I be if God hearkened to me!'

"*Humility.*—This old pupil of Saint-Cyr was the most humble of men. I never heard him speak to his own advantage. One had to question him to learn anything of his family, his past, and his successes. One day I asked him how many pagans he had converted. 'A single one,' he replied modestly: 'the old mulatto woman you saw at Beni-Abbes hermitage.'

"'Have you not made other conquests?'

"'Yes, it is true I also baptized a little child in danger of death, who had the happiness of almost immediately leaving this world to fly to heaven. Indeed, I administered baptism to a boy of thirteen, but it was not I who converted him. He was presented to me by a French sergeant, who had taught him the Catechism and had prepared him to receive the Sacraments. You see, my dear brother, that I am truly an unprofitable servant.'

"He loves, he seeks affronts, derision and insults by an outward get-up that he strives to make extravagant. He always walks in rough sandals, his feet bare and chapped by the cold. He wears an unbleached linen robe, always too short and often stained and torn. He cuts his own beard and hair without using a glass. How does it matter what people say and think about him? Provided he pleases God, he is not going to put himself out for what men think of him.

"*Mortification.*—Like all the Saints, Father Charles of Jesus never stopped crucifying his flesh. On the railway he always chooses a third-class carriage; in the sandy plains of the Sahara, he always goes on foot, although he is an excellent horseman. When the soldiers who escorted us dismounted to stretch themselves, they offered us their mounts: once the Father was extremely fatigued, and consented, on my urging him to ride. When we halted, jaded and covered with perspiration, he would give me his burnous to cover me, while he, wearing nothing but his light linen robe, trembled with cold. I never saw him drink wine or liquors, and he never allowed me to accept any when the officers offered me some. On this point of his Rule he was inexorable, and declared that he would never give me a dispensation. He only once ate meat in my presence, with all who belonged to the caravan. During our stay at Beni-Abbes I never saw him breakfast in the morning; he was satisfied with dinner at eleven o'clock and supper at six in the evening, of which I have given the menu. He made me, on the contrary, break off mental prayer and go out of the chapel for ten minutes every day about seven in the morning, to take a cup of coffee and a piece of thin cake.

"*Poverty.*—He never went to any expense without absolute necessity. As he travelled about six months in the year, I advised him to buy a third camel, which he could use as a mount instead of going on foot. 'No,' he said energetically; 'I live at my family's expense; besides, I must help the poor. I have no right to go to that expense. I have two camels, necessary to carry our travelling provisions and baggage; a third would be superfluous.'[1]

[1] "He made use of everything: packing-cases took the place of bookcases for the books, and of cupboards to put away our two poor ornaments for Mass and other things needed for divine worship. When one of his robes was so used that it was past mending, he used to cut it into several pieces, and these rags we used as handkerchiefs and towels. Instead of throwing the envelopes, letters, and prospectuses that he received into the waste paper-basket, he collected them carefully and used them as scribbling-paper and for making notes."

"I shall remember till the end of my life Father Charles's Mass, which I so often had the happiness of serving. He said it without slowness as without precipitation, devoutly, with dignity and humility, with faith and an air of compunction which greatly impressed me.

"*Generosity.*—This nobleman ... was generous to prodigality, and gave without reckoning. When we entered a village, which happened nearly every day, and even from time to time twice in the same day, the inhabitants in great numbers, the caïd at their head, attracted by the reputation of holiness of the great monk, came to meet him, and pressed round him to see and hear him. They saluted the Father with veneration, kissed his hand, and gave him the title of Sidi Marabout. Sometimes a European with a photographic apparatus slipped into the crowd, and tried to take a portrait of this extraordinary man. Above all, a multitude of beggars ran up and besieged him whom they called their benefactor, to get alms. The Father then distributed, in small coins, a sum of fifteen to twenty francs, to those who seemed to him the least poverty-stricken; to those who were ragged and almost naked he gave pieces of material, recommending them to make it into a garment.

"*Work.*—Father Charles meant to earn his bread by the sweat of his brow; there was no unemployed moment in his day. In the desert, at the hours of halt, instead of taking the siesta or resting, even when he was weakened by a long tramp in the sun, he used to work at his dictionary which 'he had at heart to finish before his death to facilitate the work of future missionaries.' I can declare that he never smoked, even when he was in the company of members of his family or of his former regimental comrades. . . .

"During our stay at the hermitage, when he was not praying in the chapel, I was sure to find him in the sacristy, with a pen or a book in his hand. I never saw him take a walk outside the enclosure, or in our garden. He never took any recreation. To rest after prayer and study, he used to make little wooden crosses which formed the sole decoration of the poor cells: he painted pictures of the Sacred Heart or the Blessed Virgin, and drew all sorts of religious emblems with which he adorned our modest chapel and sacristy: he wrote on placards in a fine round hand or in Gothic characters the most edifying sentences from the ancient Fathers of the Thebaid, the maxims of holy doctors or holy martyrs the most likely to inspire the spirit of sacrifice, and placed them on all the walls.

"It has been most agreeable for me to speak of the reverend Father Charles of Jesus, who gave me so often such beautiful examples of all the virtues during the too short time I had the happiness of living in his intimacy. I was his first and last disciple. God grant me to imitate him according to my strength."

The slight hope of having a mission companion, perhaps a successor, went north with Brother Michael.[1]

At the same time Colonel Laperrine, passing through In-Salah, informed Father de Foucauld of the death of M. de Motylinski, which took place on March 2, 1907. This sorrow and the disappointment which preceded it did not discourage the energetic Brother Charles, but he thought of the precariousness of his work. He soon wrote to Father Voillard (May 6, 1907): "I am getting old. I should like to see someone better than I replace me at Tamanrasset, another better than I installed at Beni-Abbès, so that Jesus may continue to reside in those places, and that souls may get more and more there."

While waiting for the joy of a working successor who was always farther off, Brother Charles "sets up"—which is rather a big word for an owner with no furniture—a little house at In-Salah. It cost him 160 francs. He chose it in the middle of the native quarter, in the Ksar-el-Arab, quite close to the dunes. "One must foresee and prepare one's halting-places, because," he said, "if I am not a parish priest, this corner of the earth, which is as it were my parish, is 1,250 miles from north to south and 625 miles from east to west, with 100,000 souls scattered over it." During his stay at In-Salah, he continued his studies of the Tuareg language with Ben Messis, whom his pupil's extraordinary energy for work astonished and fatigued a little. M'ahmed Ben Messis was one of the most intelligent and sympathetic persons in the Sahara. The son of a Chambi father and a Tuareg mother of a noble tribe of the Azjers, he was considered by the Tuaregs as one of them, in spite of the lively enmity that he met among them, the cause of which was Ben Messis' devotion to France. It was Ben Messis who denounced the greater part of the assassins of the Marquis de Morès; he, again, who served as guide to the 150 African troops of Lieutenant Cottenest,

[1] The latter is at present a monk in a foreign Carthusian monastery.

when the latter, on May 7, 1902, defeated 300 Tuaregs at Tit, and brought about the submission of several tribes. No native of those regions spoke Tamachek better, none knew the traditions of the country better. He was a very devoted friend to Father de Foucauld.[1]

So, when a detachment of eighty men, commanded by Captain Dinaux, left In-Salah on March 8, going by short daily stages through Adrar and Hoggar, Father de Foucauld, who highly esteemed the captain, and was also sure of travelling with the Tuareg Ben Messis, willingly agreed to make the tour. He therefore set out as both a missionary and a philologist. We know how he was accustomed to work during his marches and halts, and even at night by candlelight, if the wind did not blow: he did not alter his habits. As the journey was for training the natives, stays were made near shepherds' encampments, and they were fine weeks for a scholar who wished to collect traditions, and also poetry which nobody had written, and which men have only kept in memory. " Precious records for grammar and lexicon; one gets examples for the grammar, when in doubt; one gets many words not often used in conversation for the lexicon. On arriving here— it was at Durit, 100 kilometres to the south of Timiauin— I promised a small payment for the verses which might be brought me; this promise, at a time when the country is poor, sufficed to fill my tent for a month. I was also told, by neighbouring *douars,* that they wished for a visit from me, so that the women, too, could give me some poetry. I have therefore been several times in the *douars,* spending hours under a tree or in a tent, in the midst of all the children and women, writing verses and giving little presents. I am very happy about my training work, which is getting on; it is only a first step, very small and humble, but, in fine, it had to be taken to break down a great deal of prejudice, antagonism, and suspicion. I shall do all in my power to finish the Tuareg-French lexicon this year. I begged Laperrine to get published by anyone he likes, as if they were his and belonged to the military commander of the oases, the Tuareg grammar and the French-Tuareg lexicon, which are finished, as well as the Tuareg-French lexicon at which I am working, and the pieces of poetry which I collected on the sole condition that my name does not appear, and that I remain entirely unknown and ignored. Next year, I should like to have nothing to do

---

[1] M'ahmed Ben Messis, decorated with the military medal and the Legion of Honour, died at In-Salah in 1919.

but correct the holy Gospels and Bible extracts previously translated, and after that no other work except giving the example of a life of prayer and manual labour, an example of which the Tuaregs are so much in need."[1]

A little later he reiterated his express injunction : " I wish to remain unknown." His extreme humility revolted at the idea that the work he composed might bring him some reputation. " These are not the means God gave us to continue the work of the world's salvation. The means which He employed in the manger, at Nazareth, and on the Cross are : poverty, abjection, humiliation, abandonment, persecution, suffering, the Cross. Behold our aims! We shall not find anything better than He, and He is not outworn."[2]

Brother Charles promised one sou a verse, and all the war and love-songs of the Tuaregs, those of distant and uncertain date, and those of to-day, those of famous and of unknown poets, fell once more from the lips of the reciter, and were set down in writing by a scholar. Their fate was changed, they escaped oblivion, and were born to book-life, which would carry them elsewhere. A learned work, no doubt, but a missionary work in intention. Father de Foucauld's correspondence shows proofs in abundance of his considered purpose, which he retained to the end, not to regard the gaining and vulgarizing of the Tuareg language as his goal. He always had in view the far-away people who were the parish of his desire : for them to be better known, more loved, and one day more easily evangelized, he translated their poetry ; to enable them to understand revealed truth better, he undertook the translation of the Holy Scriptures ; for them, and for those who followed him as teachers and preachers, he compiled his grammar and lexicon. In the letters of this period, it appears clearly that he worked in the hope that the White Fathers would soon begin to evangelize those whom he had brought nearer to them. The little house in In-Salah would provide them with quarters on the way, as well as a home for himself.

On the whole, the Adrar and Hoggar tour was very fortunate. "I spent a few days more in the pastureland with the detachment, in order to make use of Ben Messis and push on my Tuareg studies with him : in four or five days he sets out for In-Salah with Captain Dinaux, who is always very good to me, like all the French in the detachment. I shall at once take the road to Tamanrasset.

[1] Letter to Père Guérin, May 31, 1907.
[2] *Ibid.*, Christmas, 1907.

"Thanks to the French in the detachment, never since my departure from In-Salah have I lacked someone to serve Mass. How shall I manage in Tamanrasset? It is for the divine Master to arrange things. . . ."[1]

The rest of this letter to Père Guérin is a reply, and we shall see how far charity carries a missionary—*i.e.*, as to the point of giving up Mass from which as a priest he drew strength to meet his daily trials.

"The question which you put: Is it better to live in Hoggar without being able to celebrate Holy Mass, or to celebrate it and not go there? I have often put to myself. Being the only priest able to go to Hoggar, while many can celebrate the Holy Sacrifice, I believe it is, after all, better to go to Hoggar, leaving to God the care of giving me the means of celebrating, if He wishes (which up to the present He has always done in the most various ways). Formerly I was inclined to see, on one hand, the *Infinite*, the Holy Sacrifice; on the other, the *finite*, all that was not It, and always to sacrifice everything to the celebration of Holy Mass. But this reasoning must be faulty somewhere, since, from the time of the Apostles, in certain circumstances, the greatest Saints have sacrificed the possibility of celebrating to works of spiritual charity, such as travelling, etc. If experience proved that I must make very long stops at Tamanrasset without celebrating, I think there might be means of shortening them, and of not binding myself to keep company with detachments, *which is not at all the same thing as residing alone*. Residing alone in the country is good; one has some influence even without doing much, because one 'belongs to the country'; one is so accessible there and so 'very small'! . . . Then, at Tamanrasset, even without daily Mass, there is the Blessed Sacrament, regular prayer, much time for adoration, and I get great silence and recollection, and grace for the whole country upon which the Sacred Host shines.

"I considered the establishment at In-Salah as a great blessing, rather thinking of the future and of you than of myself. No doubt in going to and fro I shall spend more time there than in the past, and shall try to have some intercourse with the poor and accustom them to have confidence in the marabout, but I am *a monk and not a missionary*, made for silence, not for preaching; and in order to have influence in In-Salah, there must be intercourse and going about and visiting, which is not my vocation: I only

[1] Letter to Père Guérin, July 2, 1907.

try to prepare the way a little for what will be your work."[1]

Brother Charles again found a plain and mountain horizon at Tamanrasset. They came at once to beg alms, for Hoggar was suffering from a great famine. The hermit had a provision of wheat : he quickly raided it and gave it out to the poor women who held out their empty porringers; he arranged little dinners for the children, and each day brought the little ones together to satisfy their hunger. He waited on them and forgot to keep a part for himself.

One thing made him uneasy, and justly so: Musa's efforts to islamize Hoggar. " Taking advantage of our organization of Hoggar being so far rather nebulous and uncertain, rather that of a little self-governing kingdom than of a country directly governed by us, he hastened to organize it as a Musulman country.

" Two years ago there was complete anarchy: no rule, no submission to rule, robbery everywhere, religion nowhere. To-day Musa is obeyed; he assesses the taxes, names the subordinate chiefs, makes himself obeyed, raises armed forces, prohibits, under very severe penalties, robbery, theft, and murder; he has set up a cadi to judge all according to Musulman law. He is going to build a mosque and *zaouia* at Tamanrasset, which he makes his capital. Must I flee to a more deserted place, or see the hand of Jesus extending my influence more easily? The religious tithe is to be raised throughout Hoggar for the upkeep of this *zaouia*, in which the cadi will probably preside, and the *tholbas* of Tidikelt or Twat teach the Koran, religion, and Arabic to the young Tuaregs. It means the islamizing of Hoggar, and also of the Taïtok. It is most serious. Up to the present the Tuaregs, not very fervent Musulmans, easily made acquaintance with us, becoming very familiar and frank. If once this very bad, narrow, close spirit of the people of Twat and Tidikelt, which is so full of antipathy

[1] This letter of July 2, 1907, contains this passage, relating to the publication of works that were ready : " For twenty-five or thirty years Motylinski was attached to M. Basset, director of the École des Lettres at Algiers, a scholar of great merit in all Arabian and Berber matters. Believing that he was going to publish the records gathered by my dear friend, I wrote to him as soon as I learned the sad news, putting myself at his disposal to send him, as I did to Motylinski, all information needed to complete the work. I have just received his reply : it is he indeed who is to publish everything in Motylinski's works ; he will publish a little grammar, lexicons, dialogues and texts. You know what I feel and think, and how I rejoice in it. I have demanded that my name shall not be mentioned anywhere, and that I shall be treated as if I did not exist."

towards us, takes hold of them, the *tholbas* teaching the children, it will be very different, and it is to be feared that in a few years the population of Hoggar may be much more hostile than to-day. To-day it is distrustful, fearful, and wild; in a few years, if the Musulman influence of Twat gains the upper hand, it will mean a deep and lasting hostility.

"As I said to you, Tamanrasset tends to become the Musulman centre of Hoggar, Musa's capital. Musa is carrying on big tillage works: he now has his fields and gardens there; he usually pitches his camp close by; . . . he is going to set up a regular market there with shops."[1]

Brother Charles, watching these efforts at organization and Islamitic teaching, and suffering, therefore, through his love of Catholic truth and dear colonizing France; Brother Charles spending months without any news from Europe, for the posts are still very irregular; Brother Charles without Mass, because there are no servers, writes to his brother-in-law on *December 9, 1907* : " I am happy, happy in resorting to the presence of the Blessed Sacrament at any time, happy in the great solitude of the place, happy to be and do—excepting my sins and miseries—whatever Jesus wishes; happy, above all, in the infinite happiness of God. If there were not this inexhaustible source of happiness and peace, the eternal, immutable, and infinite happiness and peace of the Well-Beloved, the evil that one sees around one on all sides, and also the miseries one sees in oneself, would quickly lead one to depression. If, in Christian countries, there is so much good and so much evil, think what these countries can be, in which there is, so to speak, nothing but evil, where good is almost totally absent : here all is lies, duplicity, cunning, all kinds of covetousness and violence, and how much ignorance and barbarism ! The grace of God can do all things, but in face of so many moral miseries . . . one sees clearly that human means are powerless, and that God alone can effect so great a transformation. Prayer and penance! The farther I go, the more I see that these are the principal means of acting upon these poor souls. What am I doing in the midst of them ? The great good that I do is that my presence procures that of the Blessed Sacrament. . . . Yes, there is at least one soul between Timbuctoo and El-Golea who adores Jesus. Lastly, my presence in the midst of the natives familiarizes them with Christians and particularly with priests. . . . Those who will follow me will

[1] Letter to Father Guérin, July 22, 1907.

find men's minds less distrustful and better disposed. It is very little; it is all that can be done at present; to wish to do more would compromise everything in the future."

His will to stay there did not change; despite the ordeal he never tried to go to places in the Sahara where there were Christians, servers, and talk according to his mind. Obstinate in doing his duty, he refused proposals of travel : " May the will of the Well-Beloved be blessed in everything ! As for me, I see clearly that it is His will that I remain here until the lexicon is finished, because it is a work of the first necessity for those who come after me. . . . Besides, it produces an unexpected good : shut up from sunrise to sunset with a very intelligent and talkative Tuareg (the Khoja of Musa), I learn many things, and have the opportunity of teaching him many, and of rectifying not only his own ideas on many points, but those of others, for words run. May the Well-Beloved bless you from His manger ! May His will be done in Africa, as it is in heaven, after so long a night !"[1]

Nevertheless, though his inward peace set him above discouragement, he was not therefore insensible. He would not be human if he never uttered a groan. I open his diary or the letters at the end of 1907, and read there, like a refrain, the complaint of the priest who no longer enjoys the lofty privilege of consecrating the Body of Christ. On great Feasts above all, Brother Charles, while committing himself herein to God's grace, says : " Dost Thou not forget me ? "

"*August* 15.—Well-Beloved Mother, have pity on this people for whom your Son died; give it your help; your poor priest invokes you for this people."

"*September* 8.—Two years ago to-day Thou didst deign to inhabit this poor chapel l O Thou, who hast never been invoked in vain, convert, visit, and sanctify this people that is Thine. No Mass, for I am alone."

"*November* 21.—Dwelling in Hoggar would be of an extreme sweetness, thanks to solitude, especially since I now have books; if it were not for want of Mass.

" I have always the Blessed Sacrament, to be sure; I renew the sacred species, when a Christian passes by, and I can say Mass. I never thought I had a right to give myself communion outside of Mass. If I am mistaken in

[1] Letter to Mgr. Guérin, Christmas, 1907.

that, be quick to tell me so; that would make an infinite change in my position, for this is a question of the Infinite."

"*December* 25.—Christmas; no Mass, because I am alone."

"*January* 1, 1908.—Unite me to all the sacrifices offered up to-day. No Mass, because I am alone."

While he was thus imploring, someone in Rome was asking the Pope for the extraordinary permission so much wished for. A petition had been prepared on choice vellum. The Prefect Apostolic of the Sahara, after summarizing Father de Foucauld's life in a few lines, told the Pope : " For six years this very holy priest has not ceased leading the most heroic and most admirable life in the apostolic prefecture of Ghardaïa. Actually he is absolutely alone in the midst of the savage Tuareg tribes, which he has succeeded in civilizing, and to which he does the greatest good by the example of his life of extreme poverty, of charity as unfailing, and of continual prayer. For long, no doubt, he will be the only priest to go into the midst of the Tuaregs. The Prefect Apostolic of Ghardaïa therefore most humbly supplicates your Holiness to consider both the eminent virtues of this servant of God and the very great good he is doing, and therefore to deign to accord him the very signal favour. . . ."

The petition was not presented. In a private audience which he had obtained for other reasons, Father Burtin, Procureur of the White Fathers, asked for the privilege of celebrating Mass without a server, which was immediately accorded.

It was by a letter from Colonel Laperrine, his great friend, that Father de Foucauld heard the news, on January 31, 1908. "*Deo Gratias! Deo Gratias! Deo Gratias!* O God, how good Thou art !" sings the hermit : " To-morrow I shall be able to say Mass ! Christmas ! Christmas ! Thanks, my God !"[1]

This joy came to him at the moment when illness obliged the relentless worker to cease all work, and one who never complained to speak of himself. Writing to Father Guérin, he confided to him, as a secret to be rigorously kept, that there was " a big hitch in his health " : general fatigue, complete loss of appetite, "then something in my chest, or rather heart, which made me pant so much at the slightest

[1] From the *Diary*.

movement, that one might think the end was near." He had to keep quite motionless. To feed him, his friends the Tuaregs milked all the goats that had a little milk and brought it to the Christian marabout's cabin.

To a friend in France, whom he told of everything, he wrote:

"At my age there is always something wrong; it is the Father's warning from above. . . . I have no more teeth or hair; my eyes are good for some way off, but weaker and weaker for anything close." But he wrote at the same time to others: "Don't be uneasy. I do not believe there is any reason for being so. But absolute rest and a month's entire cessation of work are ordered, and afterwards I shall have to set to work again much more moderately than in the past. . . . I am getting the most varied sorts of food sent from In-Salah in order to recover my strength: condensed milk, wine (1), dried vegetables, some jams; I am doing all that is necessary."

In the same letter—and it suggests some doubt as to these fine resolutions to work less in future—Brother Charles asks the White Fathers to send him the *Summa Theologica* of St. Thomas, the *Summa Contra Gentiles*—that is to say, ten Latin octavo volumes—and three other volumes of philosophy. "The farther I go," he says in explanation of the request, "the more opportunities I have for carrying on serious conversations with the best natives." Then returning to his illness, and fearing they may be uneasy at Ghardaïa and Algiers, he says: "Jesus is giving me a month of recollection and a very sweet retreat by this enforced rest; I enjoy it at His feet."

When he recovered from this rude shock he felt himself incapable of the least continued manual labour; he could not therefore manage to work at leather-dressing or saddlery, as he intended, " and I regret it. For one thing, this humble and low work formed so intimate a part of Jesus of Nazareth's life, the model of monastic life; and then nothing could do more good than such an example amidst these races eaten up with pride and laziness!" The gravity of this illness, in spite of the precautions taken by Father de Foucauld, was soon suspected by the hermit's friends, and first of all by Colonel Laperrine, whom he had to tell that he could not go to In-Salah at the beginning of spring. One after the other, on February 3 and 13, Laperrine wrote to Father Guérin letters which he need not have signed, so far do the traits of the Saharan life and their lively and pleasant tone proclaim their author.

"*February* 3.

"Reverend Father,

"I was going to reply to your letter of January 13, when I received a long one from de Foucauld; he does not think he will be here before March 15, and yet he does not give that date as certain. He feels worn out. . . . This letter worries me very much, because if he admits he is worn out and asks me for condensed milk, he must be really ill. I do not yet know what to do. I am waiting for authorizations. But the actual situation inclines me preferably towards the east, to come back by Ahaggar. I am going to read de Foucauld's letter again deliberately, and should such be the case, I shall make a loop to take in Ahaggar, or send the doctor there, if his condition gets worse. He must have wanted to push penance and fasting too far, but our strength has its limits. I am going to abuse him, and get your authority to tell him that penance up to the point of progressive suicide is not permitted. . . . The 15th of March following the 15th of February, which followed the 15th of November—these dates don't inspire me with confidence. If I send a detachment down, perhaps he had better stay there and have a few meals with the officer, so as to get into condition for the journey. Pardon this scribble, reverend Father. My respects to the Fathers at El-Golea.

"Yours, etc.,
"H. Laperrine."

"*February* 11.

"Reverend Father,

"A few lines at a gallop, to give you news of de Foucauld. He puts off his journey till October. He has been more ill than he admits; he had fainting fits, and the Tuaregs who took great care of him are very anxious. He is better. I sent him a lecture, for I am strongly of opinion that his exaggerated penances have a great deal to do with his weakness, and the overworking at his dictionary did the rest.

"As the lecture was not all that was wanted, we added three camels with provisions, condensed milk, sugar, tea, and various preserves. Besides, he felt he would have to cut boiled barley out of his régime, since he asks for milk. . . . In any case, I think it indispensable that on his approaching return to the north, you put your grappling-irons on him and keep him a month or two at

Ghardaïa or Maison Carrée, so that he may fill his hump again—excuse the Saharan expression."[1]

Colonel Laperrine's and Captain Nieger's stay[2] at Tamanrasset was a great joy to Father de Foucauld, who for five months had received no news from Europe.

His health improved by degrees. Letters from the invalid became more frequent. One of them, written during this period of convalescence, in reply to questions put by Father Guérin, illustrates his energy of will and ardent courage, qualities which a person so self-effacing only expresses in moments of surprise and provocation. It also acknowledges that he is the author of the works on the Tuareg language. The letter is divided into paragraphs as the interrogatory was.

" I do not hesitate to prolong our talks and to let them last very long, when I see they are useful to souls; I sometimes spend days in explaining and showing books of pious pictures, or in reading passages from the holy Gospel to the Tuaregs. It is with this idea that I intend, next year, entirely to revise, or rather renew—because they are no good—my translations of the Gospel and of part of the Bible in Tuareg. That will be of use to me now, and afterwards help others.

" As to the question of signing the linguistic works with my name, in spite of the authority of Father Voillard, in whom I have so much respectful confidence, and in spite of yours, I have not changed my mind. What you and he say would probably be true of a White Father, but not of me, vowed as I am to a hidden life. . . . What determined me to write those works, to put the finishing touches to them, and to have them printed, is precisely because the great good of their publication can be effected without my appearing or being named at all. . . .

" The Well-Beloved has turned Musa's efforts to organize Hoggar into a regular and fervent Musulman kingdom to the good of souls. His efforts have totally and piteously failed; not only failed, but produced an inverted effect. He nominated a cadi to whom he entrusted important sums to build a mosque and *zaouia*, and gathered tithes for religion all over Hoggar. In three months his cadi had made himself hated of all, had dissipated all the

---

[1] To ascertain a camel's state of health and vigour, one first sees whether its hump is full or flabby.

[2] Colonel Laperrine, then chief in command at In-Salah, had as a companion, Captain Nieger, commanding the Saharan company of In-Salah, and another very dear friend of Father de Foucauld.

sums entrusted to him, and built nothing; the collection of tithe made everybody discontented; so that now . . . only the recollection of a disagreeable adventure and the horror of cadis and tithes remain. Let us pray and do penance.

"Had I been called up for the Moroccan expeditions, I should have started the same day, and I should have done seventy-five miles a day to arrive in time; but nobody gave me a sign of life. If they want me, they know I am ready to go. I told General Lyautey that in *whatever place* there was an important expedition, he had only to telegraph for me, and I would come directly."

He, too, and from the beginning of his mission, had put to himself the very objection which they did not fail to make afterwards, when Father de Foucauld's work got to be known: "Is the Sahara worth so many sacrifices, so much time and work? Is it not too costly, to take so much trouble for a few wandering tribes, who do not ask to be converted?" Father de Foucauld replies on this point:[1]

"No doubt the Sahara is not one of the most inhabited countries, but after all the oases, including the Tuaregs, contain 100,000 people, who are born, live and die without any knowledge of Jesus who died for them nineteen hundred years ago. He gave His blood for each of them, and what are we doing? It seems to me that two things are necessary: (1) a sort of third Order, having for one of its objects the conversion of infidel peoples—a conversion which is, at the present time, a strict duty for Christian nations, whose position in the last seventy years has totally changed with regard to the infidels. On the one hand, the infidels are nearly all subjects of Christians; on the other hand, the rapidity of communications, and the exploration of the entire world, now give comparatively easy access to all. From these two facts follows quite a strict duty—above all, for nations having colonies: the duty of christianizing.

"(2) Not everywhere, but in countries where there are special difficulties, like yours, we ought to have missionaries, *à la Sainte-Priscille*[2] of both sexes. They might be gleaned either here and there, or grouped in order to give them a common preparation before sending them. The thought of a kind of third Order, having for one of its aims the conversion of infidels, came to me last September, at the time of my retreat. It has recurred to me very often since, with the consideration that it is a duty and not solely a work of zeal and counsel for Christian nations to work

---

[1] Letter to Père Guérin, June 1, 1908.   [2] *I.e.*, Catechists.

energetically for the conversion of infidels and, above all, of those of their colonies. There would, I think, be occasions for showing this duty to those who appear to have no suspicion of it, and for urging them to accomplish it. During Holy Week and Easter Week I put down what the association might be. I am revising this and re-copying it. . . . I shall show it you in November. If you think it contains anything good, you will make use of it. But certainly there is something to be done. . . . For twenty years France has had an immense colonial empire, which imposes evangelizing duties on French Christians. . . . It is not with ten, fifteen, twenty, or thirty priests, even if you were given them, that you will convert the vast Sahara; you must therefore find other auxiliaries.

" Pardon me, my well-beloved Father, getting mixed up in what is none of my business, and an old sinner and quite insignificant priest of very recent ordination, and still a poor sinner, who has never been able to attain anything, or even to get a companion, who has had nothing but desires without effect, and whose plan of life, constitutions and Rule are always but useless papers, daring to expose my thoughts and continuing to form plans. My excuse is the souls around me who are being lost and will perpetually remain in that state, if we do not try to find the means of acting efficaciously on them."

In the summer of 1908 the military administration decided that a detachment of troops should be sent to and maintained in Hoggar; from time to time it was to go on rounds there, and a fort was to be built. Laperrine wished to name it "Fort de Foucauld," but the hermit refused. It therefore became Fort Motylinski, over thirty miles from Tamanrasset. Brother Charles also heard that next year Musa ag Amastane would certainly be taken to France by an officer. He asked himself and Father Guérin whether it would not be a good thing if other Tuaregs were to travel in our country, to obtain some idea of a society so different from theirs, and live for a week in some French family, so as to bring back with them the conviction that we are not *pagans* and *savages* at any rate: these were the names used in Hoggar to describe the French, and Europeans in general.

Further news: the *amenokal* of Hoggar is getting an important house built in Tamanrasset—in sun-baked bricks and dry mud, of course; several of his near relations were imitating him. Laperrine was in the country; he saw Musa and rejoiced at his colonizing efforts; he was specially glad to find his friend, Father de Foucauld, whom he looked upon as lost, in fine health. On July 22nd, 1908, he sent this good news to Father Guérin :

"Reverend Father,
"I send you a few lines from Tamanrasset, where I have been with de Foucauld since July 16. He came to meet me at twenty miles from Tarhauhaut on June 29, and we spent June 30 and July 1, 2, and 3 together. He is very well, and glowing with health and gaiety. . . . On June 29 he came galloping into my camp like a sub-lieutenant at the head of a group of Tuareg riders. He is more popular than ever among them, and appreciates them more and more. On the other hand, he has very little esteem for the negroes settled here, who are all lazy, and of the lowest type.

"I am leaving him this evening to return to In-Salah by the longest way. . . . De Foucauld intends to go and see you in November; I leave him here putting the finishing touches to the enormous Tamachek work which he undertook; this work will be thoroughly complete.
"Yours, etc.,
"H. Laperrine."

Several months ago Brother Charles had formed the plan to go and spend a few days at Ghardaïa. Would he not go farther? As far as Algiers? Why not to Burgundy? It was one of the subjects of epistolary conversation between him and Madame de Blic. The latter did not lack good arguments to prove to him that a visit to France was not only expected, but more than advantageous: it was quite necessary. Had he not been seven years absent? Was it not cruel that a brother and sister should live thus separated one from the other by thousands of miles? He was also an uncle; was not the family of nephews and nieces whom he hardly knew, growing up? The hermit tried to find an answer which might be accepted. "I am a monk," he said, "and monks ought not to travel for their pleasure. We shall together offer this sacrifice to the well-beloved Jesus. He offered up so much of all sorts! How often did He leave His Mother alone during His life! In what solitude did He leave her by dying!

"Perhaps we shall see each other again here below. God may, as He has already done, so dispose circumstances that it will be more perfect to go and see you than to stint myself. Because if you say you would be happy to see me again, you so surrounded, how happy should I be, who am alone in the midst of savages? Here no new love has come to take the place of the old ones. . . . You are deceiving yourself very much in believing that I should do good, my dear: I gain a great deal by not being seen, and from a distance I am thought better than I am. . . ."

Shaken by the earnest entreaties of "dear Marie," he finished by writing: "If you wish me to come, ask God and M. l'Abbé Huvelin, my interpreter of His will." He wrote these things and many others on old envelopes, "because," he said, "I am a hundred miles from a paper dealer."

When consulted, M. Huvelin replied: "My heart very much desires this little journey to France that you will take to see your family. . . . I do not see any objection to your journey with or without a Tuareg." Mgr. Guérin was of the same opinion.

In consequence, Brother Charles left Tamanrasset at noon on Christmas Day, alone, without any Tuareg, none being sufficiently prepared. On January 22, 1909, he arrived at El-Goléa, where Fathers Richerd and Périer of the White Fathers were: a few days later he saw Mgr. Guérin, who had come from Ghardaïa to meet him: on February 13 he was at Maison Carrée, among his friends the White Fathers, who were under Mgr. Livinhac. He again saw the convent gardens, the Mediterranean, which he was about to cross, and beyond which was France. Maison Carrée, as we know, is a small town to the east of Algiers, near the coast; and the residence of the White Fathers, a little more to the east in the open country, has no hill or forest before it, which prevents it looking towards France. The garden, of orange and lemon trees, descends towards the market-gardeners' fields, which continue the dunes covered with locust-trees and rushes, asphodels and African marigold. The violet mountains of Kabyle bound the horizon on the east side; on the west, Algiers, similar to a bright quarry of rose-and-white marble, raises the headland of its Arab quarter above the sea. In this religious house, young men, under the direction of missionaries back from Central Africa, are preparing to conquer for Christ, for civilization here, for eternity afterwards, the blacks who surround Lakes Chad and Victoria Nyanza; and other peoples, where the number of Christians is rapidly increasing: they are waiting for the Master of the world to be free to make known His incarnation, His passion, and His law to Musulmans. It is a place of prayer, work, and peace. Brother Charles loved it, and wished the house were always full of "workers" and of special workers for Musulman lands.

I was told that during this stay at Maison Carrée he was with Father de Ch——, a friend of his, and was talking to him, when the bell rang.

"Excuse my leaving you alone," said Father de Ch——.

Without reflecting, Brother Charles replied:

"Oh! I am never alone!"

Then, having said too much, he hung his head.

Although he loved this great and brotherly house, he did not tarry there, and, in the same way, he only passed through France. The least Saharan tour took him ten times longer than he would give to his human joy. He had to resume divine work without the least delay. On January 17 he embarked at Marseilles, of course as deck passenger. His route in France comprised Paris, Nancy, Notre-Dame-des-Neiges, Toulon, and Grasse, where Father de Foucauld's sister was. Lastly, twenty days after leaving Africa, Brother Charles was back again, having given just enough time to his visit to escape being convicted of "cruelty."

For three weeks, then, he changed customs, costume, landscape, and the idioms of habitual conversation. I shall let him travel, and take advantage of his absence to quote some of the Tuareg proverbs he had collected, and some of those pieces of poetry he got recited to him at the doors of the nomads' tents.

CHAPTER XI
Poetry and Proverbs

NOTHING is more sober than pride; it feeds upon nothing and slakes its thirst on the wind which blows. Do not let us be surprised that the inhabitants of the Sahara consider themselves the first of men; the most beautiful, of course; the most intelligent; the only ones worthy to lead the world and to be its models. I am persuaded that they consider their poets, not knowing any others, as the greatest of all. They will one day know they are mistaken. But we must acknowledge that these nomads without education are not without intelligence. They write verses, which sing of love, anxiety, defiance, the pride of youth and pluck, or of beauty and courtship; poems on incidents which do not lack features, but in which the work of composition is to seek. It is a wild sourish grape, which does not produce any wine, but the fruit of which may be eaten, and more than one author whom our little reviews praise has not yet found as many happy expressions as a shepherd warrior of Hoggar puts into his verse, when rhyming his song for the next *ahâl*.

Father de Foucauld said that among the Tuaregs "everybody writes verses: always rhymed and of various rhythms." Would free verse, therefore, be condemned in the Sahara? So his words seem to say, but the question of prosody in a tongue which is unknown to us, is one of those which prudence bids us avoid. Let us leave it to scholars. When the pieces collected, translated, and annotated by the Father are published,[1] we shall be able to judge; I think he has said everything. I will only tell here of one of the observations he made.

"The usual subjects of the verse by the Kel-Ahaggar and the Kel-Azjer and Taïtok are the same: love, war, camels, travel, and epigrams. Often the warlike poetry and epigrams give rise to answers; an enemy poet or the person attacked replied in verse. A poetic duel was sometimes engaged: the pieces of verse, the attacks and

[1] This collection as well as the other works of Père de Foucauld and M. de Motylinski, will be published by the celebrated Berber scholar at the head of the Algerian Faculty of Letters, M. René Basset.

replies, followed one another in great numbers. In wars, poetic hostilities always accompanied armed hostilities.

"There is no difference of language between verses by the Kel-Ahaggar, the Kel-Azjer and Taïtok. As to groundwork and form, there is.

"The poetry of the Ahaggar is at times somewhat sentimental and philosophic; that of the Kel-Azjer is full of ardent, warlike images; that of the Taïtok, elegant in form, has little substance in thought; echoes of Islam are more frequently found in it than elsewhere.[1]

I have gone over a great number of sheets which were found dispersed in the room Father de Foucauld worked in at Tamanrasset. They were rough copies of the works he had finished. I shall cite some of the pieces which appeared to me charming, or curious, and, mixed with those, others which M. Henri Basset, deputy-lecturer to the Algiers Faculty of Letters, was good enough to communicate to me.

Successful Raid of Musa ag Amastane

(*Date:* 1894.)

Musa, son of Amastane, rides amidst the sandhills.
We follow him as, with his foot, he urges on his enlisted
  mehari,
Which has a (high) hump and is girthed with white
  muslin.
On its flank rests his rifle.
  Musa has given him a great number of horses as companions.

You have no honour left, O bad Imrad!
  You have rejected Musa and let him go alone into
    Ahnet, the country of violins, to recruit his companions.
  In none of your men has awakened the sense of honour.
  Look! all follow Musa, even the lame and the one-
    armed, but not you.

---

[1] There is no really reliable census of the Tuareg populations. Around the so-called Tuaregs, we find tribes more or less tainted with black blood, and speaking Tamachek. Here is the statement of one of the officers best instructed in all things of the Sahara. *Tuareg populations speaking Tamachek :* (1) Azjer Tuaregs, Algerians and the people of Tripoli, about 5,000; (2) Hoggar Tuaregs, about 4,500; (3) Tuaregs of Air, about 17,000; (4) Tuaregs of Feuve (the Sudan Sahara), about 38,000; (5) Tuaregs of the Niger loop, about 40,000—or an approximate total of 105,000, speaking Tamachek.

The lame Akamadu with his white-footed camel rides close
    by the side of Musa's,
Kaima the one-armed with his bundle tramps side by side
    with Musa and his men.
At the well of I-n-Eelren, there we left our women,
Whose temples and cheeks are rimmed with indigo.
Bekki, from whom shall I hide my love of thee?
For it is not in my hand, from which a blow might dash
    it to the ground;
It is firmly fixed in the centre of my heart.
Hekhu's skin is as sweet as the bread
Of sugar that all young men love;
She is like an antelope fawn following along the River
    Tigi, going from gum-tree to gum-tree, browsing on
    their leaves through the summer nights.

The Battle with the Iullemeden

(Date: 1895.)

I send a decree to all women who go to gallant parties,
To those of this country and even to Arab women:
Whenever you find the men who hid from the fray near
    you,
Shower down your curses on the cowards.
We saw them that day, in the morning.
When the Iullemeden came straight on to the attack:
Then took place a festival of powder and bullets,
And the javelins flung in such hosts as to make a tent
    over the heads of the fighters.
When the enemy fled, I took my sword in my hand,
I struck at their legs, which flew off like jerjer stalks[1]
I defy them to use them hereafter on march.

The Battle of Tit

*(One of Lieutenant Cottenest's disciplinary rounds
in Ahaggar. Date: 1902.)*

I tell you so, women of sense,
And all you who put blue between your mouth and
    nostrils:
Amessara,[2] there we fought on both sides to a finish
With javelins, pagan rifles
And the sword unsheathed.

[1] A plant the stalks of which are carried away by the wind of the desert.
[2] The valley of Amessara touches the Tit field of battle.

I flew at the enemy; I smote, and was smitten,
Even until blood covered me all over like a wrapping
Inundating me from the shoulder down to the arms.
The young women who gather round the violin will not hear it said of me that I hid in the rocks.
Is it not true that after falling three times they had to lift me up,
And that they bound me unconscious on a camel with cords?
On that account,
Defeat is not dishonour:
Even against the prophet himself, pagans have won the victory in days of yore.

Starting for the "Ahâl"

My parents had stopped me from starting for the *ahâl;* they had, it seems, no ulterior design.
I remained, I shed tears, I went back to the tent;
I wrapped myself up and hid my face and lay down:
Even that seemed to increase my sorrow.
I could not rest: I put on my crossed sash; I ran through the place where the camels were crouching
I seized a well-trained one;
I put the saddle on the top of his hump where the hair ends;
I was evenly balanced on him, and made him go down into the valley of Isten.
When I stopped short, on getting near the *ahâl,* they said to me: "What has happened?"
I replied: "Nothing has happened
But depression and a gloomy face."
And now, There is but one God! it is written:
I shall see the maiden with the white teeth.

Declaration

One thing is no wise doubtful but certain.
It is that if the torment of love could kill,
By God! I should not live till this evening;
The sun would no longer rise for me to see it.
Geggé, thy love is hard for my heart:
It has dissolved the marrow in my bones;
It has drunk my blood and my flesh: I do not know what has become of them.

I have only my bones which hold together
And my breathing which heaves slowly and silently beneath them.
You have never yet seen a soul in which exists a whole town full
Of torments, and yet alive
Going to gallant parties, playing and laughing.[1]

To Amenokal Amud

Kenua ult Amâstân, a woman of the noble tribe of Taïtok, is, of all the persons actually living with the Kel-Ahaggar and the Taïtok, and all those who have lived there for half a century, the one who has the greatest reputation for poetic talent.

Amud el Mektar, an important person, travelling among the Taïtok, one day stopped to take his siesta near a tree, in the vicinity of Kenua's encampment. While he was resting with his companion under the shade of a burnous fastened to the branches, Kenua came and invited them to follow her to her tents; she offered them hospitality, and put them up for two days. The day after their arrival, she composed this piece of poetry in honour of Amud:

> This year have I seen
> Dates such as the hand gives not to the tongue;
> This year have I seen
> A green date-tree loaded with ripening dates;
> This year have I seen
> Gold and silver intertwined;
> This year have I seen
> Heaven; I reached it, but did not sleep there;
> This year have I seen
> Mecca; I prayed, but did not spend the noon there;
> This year have I seen
> Medina; I was there and did not take a meal there;
> This year have I seen
> The waters of Zemzem, but I did not drink thereof;
> This year have I seen
> Tender young antelopes like children who speak in gentle tones;
> They were making a sunshade of wool under which they were having their midday nap:

[1] Communicated by M. Henri Basset.

Made for play, capable of playing,
They were in a bed of silk and silver.
This year have I seen
A colt whose love has wounded me.
He is in a wheat-field, standing, grazing there.
If only he were for sale, I should give for him
A thousand young men! . . .

A Poem of Eberkau

(A woman celebrated for her beauty and wit.)

Shall I compare him to a white *mehari*, to a shield of Tarmai?
To a herd of Kita antelopes?
To the fringe of Jerba's red scarf?
To grapes which have just ripened
In a valley where alongside of them ripens the date?
Amûmen is the thread on which have been strung the pearls of my necklace.
He is the cord on which are hung the talismans on my breast;
He is my life.[1]

Thanks

A poor woman of a tribe belonging to the *imrad*, having received alms from the French officer, thanked him thus:

>I leave the tents after morning prayer,
>I take a walk full of anxious reflections;
>I left Tekadeit and Lilli yonder,
>Hungry, exhausted, crying:
>Grasshoppers are the death of the poor.
>I went to the captain, who had pity on me:
>He is a young man who tries to do all good.
>He is valorous in war, he is benevolent;
>He makes women shout with joy and wins merits in the eyes of God;
>His challenge none takes up.
>He excels above all the pagans.

When one has read many improvisations by Tuareg poets, one remarks that they repeat themselves, and that in the Sahara more than elsewhere, certain metaphors, which at first amused or touched one, are tricks of style

---

[1] Communicated by M. Henri Basset.

and hackneyed. It matters little here. I wished simply to add a few features to the picture of the people among whom Father de Foucauld lived the last years of his life, to whom he was so devoted, whose traditions, customs, vocabulary, language, and poetry he had spent so many hours in studying. And with this same intention, I shall choose some Tuareg proverbs from those which he collected. In these we shall see still better the quick mind of these Ahaggar people, and their good sense, in which all the human hope of Charles de Foucauld must have been bound up.

Tuareg Proverbs

Part your tents, bring your hearts together.

When you see a halo round the moon, a king is travelling by its light.

Fear the noble if thou make little of him: fear the base man if thou honour him.

He who drinks out of a jug (the sedentary) is no guide.

However long a winter night may be, the sun follows it.

The viper takes the colour of the country it lives in.

Laugh at baked clay (terra cotta).

Kiss the hand you cannot cut off.

Whoever loves thee, even a dog, thou wilt also love.

It is better to spend the night in anger than in repentance.

Reasonings are the shackles of the coward.

A single hand without a fellow will not untie a double knot, whatever it may do.

When a noble spreads the rich material of his dress for thy carpet, sit not right in the middle.

Hell itself holds dishonour in horror.

Living people often meet.

If a man puts a cord round his neck, God will provide someone to pull it.

In your native land, birth; in a foreign land, dress.

The palm of your hand does not eclipse the sun.

The beetle, in its mother's eyes, is a gazelle.

The beaten path, even if it winds: the king, even if he is aged.

CHAPTER XII
Tamanrasset

ON Passion Sunday, March 27, 1909, Father de Foucauld, travelling in great haste, again took possession of his first hermitage, so as to have Mass at Beni-Abbes on that day. He spent Eastertide there. To the last he wanted to be at the disposal of the Christian officers and soldiers who wished to make their Easter duties, and was visited by French, Berbers and Arabs, and, in the hours of solitude, put the finishing touches to the rules of the association for the development of the missionary spirit, according to the suggestions of Mgr. Bonnet who was interested in the project. It was, indeed, a fine idea of the great African monk to band the French and Algerian Christians together, especially the Saharans who belong to both countries, but also those who live at home and never cross the sea, and to get them to pray daily for the conversion of "our Musulman brothers" who are subjects of France. The idea is simple, too, and a practical one, which will deeply affect Christian France, accustomed, from time immemorial, to understand these sorts of fraternal and extended developments of the communion of saints. Already, although the work has remained humble and without means of propaganda, travellers, officers, sailors, parents and relations of missionaries, and communities of men and women have promised to intercede for the neglected peoples who belong to us. At the end of the book I shall tell what has been done, and what that very simple rule of this union of prayer is, Father de Foucauld's legacy to many who know nothing of it.

After about a month's stay in the hermitage of Beni-Abbes, then the hermit became a pilgrim once more. He made or bought the two pairs of sandals required; he would put on the second when the stones had worn out the soles of the first pair, or the heat hardened and shrivelled up the leather; and now he was off on his journey. The reception given him everywhere was his reward. No doubt there were many beggars among those who came to the marabout. But to many he was the friend of whom they sought counsel. When walking by his camel, when going through a *ksar*, or lying down for a midday siesta in the shade of a tree or rock, someone would slip close up to him and entrust him with some anxiety or trouble; there were so many of them! Here is an example of this sort of apostolate. About this time a soldier came to the Father. He was living with a negress, a slave that her Arab masters had been obliged to liberate, because they ill-treated her. This woman was looking forward in terror to the soldier's approaching return to France. The latter loved and esteemed her; although he was living irregularly, he had at heart the faith of the old country, and perhaps a little through remorse, and because we are naturally missionaries, he had taught this woman the principles of the Christian religion. He even declared that she might already be regarded as being of our religion, her soul was so much disposed to receive it. But what would she do when he left her? Knowing that she regarded the Arabs with horror and could not stay on where she had suffered so much at their hands, he was most perturbed. He laid the matter before the ambulant monk, the universal brother. The answer given him is to be found in a letter to Father Guérin: "I urged him to ask you to take this woman into your Ghardaïa workroom. He was to take her and she was to remain there, living entirely with the Sisters, where her work would pay for her board. She looks very well, and the corporal esteems and loves her very much; besides, it would be a soul's salvation. . . . She has always led a regular life; when she was freed, the Frenchman received her; according to her own ideas, her position has never ceased to be regular." What became of the poor "quiet and hard-working" negress of thirty? It is one of the countless stories of which we shall never know the end.

Back in Tamanrasset, Father de Foucauld found his hermitage somewhat enlarged by the care of his friends, Motylinski and the village *harratins*. A young officer gave him the additional surprise of discovering amidst the lumber of the corridor he called his house, a bed, a camp-bed brought on camel-back. . . . He did not grumble, but acepted the gift with thanks, and for the first time in twenty-seven years, being thoroughly tired out, slept on canvas. As soon as he had got into the hermitage again he started with his old ardour on his works in the Tuareg language, and hastened to finish them, in order "to work more directly for the one end: to see more people, and to give more time to prayer and spiritual reading."

This idea of progressive evangelization, which he never gave up, inspired all his acts and prompted him to draw up a few forms of prayer for his poor Saharans, and, in the same letter, he submitted to Father Guérin the sketch of a simplified rosary for the use of infidels. At the beginning they would make an act of charity, and then, in any language, say on the little beads: " My God, I love Thee "; and on the big beads: " My God, I love Thee with my whole heart!" " Would you think it right," he concludes, " to ask for indulgences for this very simple rosary, which is also good for the use of Christians?" And this letter ends with this noble outburst, revealing the memories that helped this great soul in his poor life with its want of response in all around it:

" To-day is the feast of SS Peter and Paul. It is delightful to write to you on this day. Let no difficulties daunt us; they conquered many far greater ones, and they are always with us. Peter is always at the helm of the barque. If Jesus' disciples could have been discouraged, what a reason for discouragement Roman Christians had on the evening of the martyrdom of both? I have often thought of that evening; how sad it must have been, and how all must have appeared to have gone under, had it not been for the faith in their hearts! There will always be struggles, and always real triumphs of the Cross in apparent defeat. So be it."

He expected Colonel Laperrine from day to day; he remarks, as a happy event, the nomination, as Musa's secretary, of a young man brought up at Tlemcen, speaking French well, having a good French and an excellent Arab education, very French in his ideas, and by no means fanatical. It is to be hoped that this new arrival will destroy the bad influence of the so-called *thalebs*, ignorant fanatics from Rhât. " When shall we rejoice at the arrival, not of Musulmans, but of Catholic priests?" he asked. " With what ardour I desire a priest as companion to instruct by example and daily talks, so as to lead souls by degrees to another teaching!"

Laperrine, "after a very successful and fruitful round, pushed on as far as Gogo," spent a week at Tamanrasset, and took his friend Father de Foucauld with him; they made the tour of Ahaggar in such a way as to see the principal inhabited cantons. This time he had resolved to take a fresh census of the Hoggar warriors, and to review the troops available against the Azjers, and had distributed rifles of the 1874 pattern. This was both a proof and an earnest of trust: Musa and the Colonel deliberated together as to where to order the assembly, and decided on the high valley of the Wady Tmereri, which is "provided with water and pasturage," and covered with very fine *ethels*.

On the day and hour agreed, Laperrine was on the summit of a hillock in the middle of the valley, and the valley was still deserted. Around him were Lieutenant Saint-Léger, Lieutenant Sigonney, Doctor Hérisson, Father de Foucauld, and four orderlies. Near the French commander was the war-drum, the *tebbel*, which signals the call to arms.

In a neighbouring valley, where he had convoked his warriors, Musa ag Amastane began to make his troops pass into the Tmereri plain. Between the trees was seen the glitter of arms and moving shields, and outlines of the foremost warriors riding high, and *meharis'* heads. Then the Colonel had the tocsin beaten: the dust rose between the *ethels*, and 252 *meharis* of Musa dashed towards the great French chief, who was immobile but secretly delighted.

After the *fantasia* there was a long chat. Laperrine spoke of the customs to be kept, of others to be given up—for instance, the raids. The rumour went round that he wished to forbid *ahâls*—that is to say, gallant and "fashionable" parties. Laperrine, who knew Tamachek imperfectly, turned his head, looking for a good interpreter to contradict the report. "There was one," he says in his *Annales de Géographie*—" there was Father de Foucauld, but I hardly dared ask him to do it. . . . He began to laugh, and after having told me that I was getting him to make very uncanonical interpretations, he translated my phrase to the great joy of all the young people, and in particular of Alkhammuk, who saw in it a splendid opportunity for teasing the Father on their long rides."

On returning from this expedition towards the end of October, the Father was visited by Captain Nieger at Tamanrasset. Fort Motylinski was built. For a traveller like Brother Charles thirty miles was a walk, and when a French soldier fell seriously ill, the hermit was told of it. He at once left the hermitage, and heard the dying man's confession. "There is nothing new," he writes to Father Guérin, "in the country, which the presence of the officers is getting more and more in hand; the farther we go, the more it is prepared for the arrival of your Fathers. At present, the officers' work is the best one can desire; it opens up the ways, establishes contact, makes safety prevail, and gives a good opinion of us, for the Colonel, Captain Nieger,

M. de Saint-Léger and the others, are wonderfully good to the natives."

So many efforts are not and cannot be vain. All the evidence agrees in proving that civilization had made a beginning in Hoggar. "Our training is making great strides." Father de Foucauld gives all the honour of it to the officers, but we know that, in this beginning of civilization, he had a very considerable share. "Wherever an officer has been, the population, once wild and suspicious, has become friendly. . . . A biennial fair has been started at Fort Motylinski (Tarhauhaut), in March and October; people are invited from all sides, from Agades, Zinder, Aïr, as from In-Salah, Wargla, etc. The constant presence of a detachment of a hundred soldiers in Ahaggar has brought to light the resources of the country. This detachment finds all its supply of wheat, meat, vegetables, as well as barley for its horses, on the spot. Wheat costs 40 francs a hundredweight, barley 30; a goat 7·50 francs, a sheep 10 francs, butter 1·50 francs a pound. All French vegetables are grown in the gardens; their quality is excellent. Water and land are abundant; much more could be grown, only hands are lacking."

To know the daily life of the hermit in detail, and just what he does not tell us, we took a few pages from Brother Michel, a passing guest of Beni-Abbes. To depict his life at Tamanrasset, we shall give the notes which Surgeon Hérisson was good enough to put into my hands, referring to the years 1909 and 1910.

Doctor Hérisson resided for many months in Hoggar as assistant Senior Surgeon of the Motylinski station, in charge of the medical mission among the Tuareg tribes. He, too, and in the sphere of science, was one of the invaluable agents of the "training" system invented by Laperrine.

He was in the Tripolitan oasis of Janet, when he received from the Colonel a service letter which rather surprised him. The Colonel wrote to him to go to Hoggar, and there to put himself at the disposal of Father de Foucauld, to receive instruction as to how to act with regard to the Tuaregs, and especially to ask him in what tribes, in agreement with Musa ag Amastane, it was advisable to vaccinate and provide medical care. Father de Foucauld had hardly spoken to the young doctor, when he invited him, according to his custom, to come to Mass next day. M. Robert Hérisson replied that he was a Protestant, and regretted he could not accept the invitation.

"I addressed Father de Foucauld with curiosity and some reserve, knowing that he was going to be 'my instructor.'

"I saw a man of sorry appearance at first sight, about fifty, simple, and modest. In spite of his habit, recalling that of the White Fathers, which I had seen in Wargla, there was nothing monastic in his gestures or attitude. Neither was there anything military. Beneath very great affability, simplicity and humility of heart, were the courtesy, the *finesse* and refinement of a man of the world. Although he appeared badly dressed, without any care for elegance, and though he was very accessible to all, French workmen or native corporals, the vivacity and penetration of his look, the height of his forehead, and his expression of intelligence made of him a 'somebody.' He was below middle height; at first sight he looked of no account, but I had quickly the impression that Father de Foucauld was a highly intellectual man, both sensitive and tactful.... He was very winning.... I felt myself attracted to him.

"I saw he was adored by all the French who already knew him, and there was, even amongst the non-commissioned officers and artisans, a certain pride in talking with Father de Foucauld and in writing letters to him as familiarly as to one of their old comrades.

"The Father was really singular.

"'What do you advise me to do about the Tuaregs, Father?' I said to him. 'I am ordered to follow your instructions.'

"He spoke at length.

"'You must be simple, affable and good to the Tuaregs; love them and make them feel they are loved, so as to be loved by them.

"'Don't be the assistant-surgeon, not even the doctor with them; don't take offence at their familiarities or their easy manners: be human, charitable, *and always gay*. You must always laugh even in saying the simplest things. I, as you see, am always laughing, showing very ugly teeth. Laughing puts the person who is talking to you in a good humour; it draws men closer together, allows them to understand each other better; it sometimes brightens up a gloomy character, it is a charity. When you are among the Tuaregs, you must always laugh.

"'Give them your medical assistance patiently, cure them; they will get a high idea of our science, power, and kindness. If they ask you to attend a goat, don't be annoyed.

"'In my opinion, you should reside long near a Tuareg

encampment, not mixing with them, but on the edge, not to be in the way, but ready to receive them should they wish to come. Remain here, without stirring from the spot, for three weeks; you will have time to cure them, and also to know them and to get known.

"'They do not know us. Absurd legends about the French have been put in circulation. It is said we eat children, that at night we turn into animals, etc.

"'Use an interpreter, to tell those who want to come and talk with you about our intimate family lives, our manners and customs, the birth and sponsorship, the religious education of our children, marriage, marriage laws, and duties between husband and wife and their children; about deaths, ceremonies, legacies, wills, what deeds we honour, those we despise. . . .'

"He advised me to show the Tuaregs verascopic photographs, representing agricultural work in France, our flocks, country life, the rivers, farms, oxen, horses. . . . 'Make them understand that a Frenchman's life is made up of peaceable honesty, work and production. Show them that the foundation of our peasants' lives is the same as theirs, that we resemble them, that we live in our country as they do, but in a more beautiful country.

"'You will doubtless have leisure, for the country is very healthy, there are few patients and the population is very thinly scattered. What do you intend doing?'

"'The Colonel,' I said, 'commissioned me to collect samples of plants and send them to Algiers to M. Trabut, the botanical professor, who will ascertain the species. I am also going to try and make a kitchen-garden at Tarhaouhaout.'

"'It would be interesting,' Father de Foucauld said to me, 'to know if any other race than the Tuaregs has inhabited the desert. There are very old tombs here—pagan tombs, anterior to Islam. They are very probably the Tuaregs' ancestors, but they will not acknowledge that. You would be able to make excavations. They will see no harm in your exhuming these bones. You can then ascertain the relationship of race existing between those pagans and the Tuaregs of the present day.'

"Father de Foucauld was the soul of Hoggar. Colonel Laperrine did nothing without taking his advice, and Musa ag Amastane did the same.

"The natives held him in such esteem that they made him their judge. One morning I saw this very remarkable scene. He was before his door, slightly bent towards the ground, dressed in white: before him in the foreground were two immense Tuaregs dressed in black, their faces veiled with the *litham,* in full dress, with swords at their sides, with daggers on the left forearm, and lances in the right hand; behind were four or five other Tuaregs, squatting, as witnesses or hearers. It was a story of camel robbery, and blows given to the negro, the owner's slave and guardian of the drove.

"The one accused, the other denied. Both assumed the emphatic theatrical attitude of the Hoggars, the imperious gesture, the marked accentuation, though deadened by the *litham,* which acted as a slight gag.

"Finally a Koran was brought; the accused protested his innocence by swearing on the Koran before Father de Foucauld.

"'About 10 o'clock every morning the Father used to call his negro; he gave him a wooden bowl full of wheat, and a handful of dates. The day on which he invited me to lunch he warned me the menu would be detestable. I accepted through politeness and curiosity, but never again.

"The negro went and ground the grain in a stone handmill, as the Berbers in the Atlas and the natives of the Moroccan countries do. This mill broke the grain but did not make flour of it. With the broken wheat, without any yeast, he made a flat round cake, which he put to bake under the ashes. In a little wrought-iron saucepan he had boiled some coarse dates, full of sand and camel-hair—and lunch was ready.

"Father de Foucauld then took away the books and sheets of paper which were on the table, and laid two hollow plates and two wrought-iron spoons on it, and said to me:

"'Have you ever eaten any *khefis?*'

"No."

"'It is my usual food. I do not know whether you will find it good, but I can offer you nothing else. I had still a few little tins of "bully" (*singe*) that Saint-Léger's sergeant wanted to leave behind on his last visit; I gave them to Corporal X——, who wanted to invite me when he was here. *Khefis* seems to me a perfect food, which is easily prepared and suits my poor teeth.'

"Here is the recipe for *khefis.* You take the wheaten cake, break it up into small pieces, quite hot, and put it into the wrought-iron plate. Stone the dates, pour the stewed dates on the pieces of cake. Then take some old melted Arab butter and spread it over the cake and dates. Now take all this by the handful, triturate and crush it, and make a sort of putty of it. The taste is insipid, sugary, but not bad.

"A glass of water and a cup of coffee complete the meal.

"To-night we shall have a couscousou without meat—'my usual dinner, that will please you more.'

"It was not good for much.

"Before sunset the Father took an hour's recreation. He used to walk to and fro before his hermitage. Then he talked amiably of everything. We walked side by side. He put his hand on my shoulder, laughed, spoke about the Tuaregs and his memories. At first he used to ask me every time how I had spent the day. He got me to make a sort of examination of conscience, and blamed me if I had not attended some Tuaregs, learned Arabic or Tamachek. . . .

"The day on which I saw Father de Foucauld really annoyed was when I confessed to him, a few months before my final departure from Hoggar, that I had not made any anthropological researches for seven to eight months.

"I saw, I told him, that I was not going to get any result. I should be quite as ignorant as before as to what race those pagans belonged to. Were they the ancestors of the Hoggars, or were they another people? My work was condemned beforehand to mediocrity.

"Father de Foucauld reproached me for being wanting in perseverance. 'The little that you would have done, and which you would have left to your successors, would have been work already done; others, taking up the even negative results of your researches and going on with them, would have carried the matter further. By abstaining from following up your researches, you hinder the work. To be held up by the idea that your work would only be mediocre, is nothing else than pride. Your abandoning the pursuit of these researches may discourage at the outset those who come after you.'"

"One had to work. One day while I was there, a negro came and asked him for alms. He was dying of hunger, he said. He was well set up, but appeared thin. He was about twenty-five years of age. Father de Foucauld asked him why he did not work in the Tit, Abalessa, and other centres of civilization. He replied that there was nothing to do there. Then Father de Foucauld, showing him a little wooden box which was used to mould bricks, said to him: 'Make me twenty bricks, and I give you a measure of wheat.' There was hardly an hour's work: he had only to make twenty little pies such as children make at the seaside; the negro refused. The Father held out, and gave him nothing, except advice to work for his living."

On other occasions, there was a lesson for the Tuareg nobles. Surgeon Robert Hérisson tells us, for instance, that one evening, at sunset—that is to say, at one of the hours of Musulman prayer—five or six Kel-Ahaggar and Kel-Rela were talking with Father de Foucauld and the *amenokal*. The latter, his cousin Akhammuk and Aflan, Dassine's husband, rose up, adjusted their blue *lithams* on their faces, and prepared to say the prayer. The other Tuaregs, indifferent, continued talking. But the Father stopped them sharply:

"Well, don't you pray?" he said.

He thus excited them to honour God in the only manner known and recognized by them. They understood, and at once got up to imitate Musa.

Dr. Hérisson saw Laperrine and Father de Foucauld live side by side in Tamanrasset. Between these two men there was fraternal affection and a great mutual esteem, with that little shade of deference that Laperrine knew how to show towards his great senior of Saint-Cyr, a cavalryman like himself. When he was passing through Hoggar, they always took their meals in common.

"For lunch or dinner, a big rug is spread on the ground in the shade of some tree if there is one, or in the Colonel's tent, which is quite large. Each gives his table-gear, can, and cup to the cook, who places them anyhow. There is no precedence.

"When all is ready, they sit down to table, squatting like tailors on the edge of the rug. The cook brings the dish. Each man has his little wheaten cake cooked under the ashes. The Colonel calls upon anyone he likes to help himself the first. Then they talk away and there is no constraint. The Colonel always invites all the French in the neighbourhood to his table—quartermasters, corporals, gunsmiths and joiners. They will pay nothing to the mess. Sometimes he has them served first. They take any place whatever at table, just by chance. Father de Foucauld always comes at noon, with a bottle of white muscat, his sacramental wine. We drink a claret-glass of it at the end of the meal. We protest, and call out on seeing the bottle: 'Father, you will run out of stock; it is too much, you will exhaust your supply: we won't drink it!' But he laughs and insists: 'You may drink it.

I only bring you what I can.' And, of course, we drink it with delight.

"At table, we do not talk about serious things; we tell stories, jokes, and chaff the Colonel's cook. Father de Foucauld laughs. The Colonel has a very varied and amusing stock of stories, which he says are true. He is a very charming raconteur. Father de Foucauld smiles when everybody else laughs. But if the story goes a little beyond the limits of propriety, he hears nothing, he is deaf, and seems to be thinking of other things. Then someone remarks that the conversation has taken 'a silly turn,' and that the Father must be scandalized; but if excuses are made, he protests that he was not listening and did not hear; no one was embarrassed.

"During the 'rounds' he used to come with a negro servant and a hired camel, without tent or camp-bed. He slept on the ground in his blankets. The greater part of the time he took a pack-camel without a saddle (without a *rahla*). Not to lose time, he wanted us to go on, and to come and join us at the place agreed upon, doubling his stages, and doing fifty miles a day at three miles an hour, and, as far as possible, using a route still unexplored by the French.

"He then arrived with little bits of paper full of notes and sketches, quite small, but very clear, like those of his Morocco exploration, and put them all into the Colonel's hands.

"At meetings and palavers, he used to refuse to sit on a camp-stool alongside of the Colonel; he wished to squat on the ground beside him. The Colonel made use of him as an interpreter. These Tuaregs, indeed, did not know the Arab language, or did not know it well. The Father not only understood them and expressed himself perfectly in set speech, but, by his knowledge of their characters and habits, he knew what had to be made clear to them, the doubts or apprehensions that might arise, etc. Lastly, his moral valour was held in such consideration and so highly esteemed that everything said by him carried greater weight.

"The Tuaregs used to say: 'He knows our language better than ourselves.'

"During evening recreation, when walking to and fro before his hermitage, at sunset, with his arm on my shoulder, he told me that personal distinction is not due to birth or education, but is innate, and that he had found amongst the simple at La Trappe a remarkable loftiness of feeling. ' We lived beside each other without knowing one another's origin or name, doing our work according to our aptitudes. There was a peasant without any education, who had inspirations, perfectly beautiful thoughts which came from his heart. He was unconscious of their worth. I was delighted to hear him. He was eloquent, and that without art, quite naturally and simply.'

"Father de Foucauld, unlike what is said of celebrated men, became immeasurably greater when one saw him every day and close by."

Do not these lines with which Doctor Hérisson's manuscript ends, recall the judgments passed on the hermit when he lived at Beni-Abbès? Did not these re-echo the many praises of Akbès, Nazareth, Jerusalem, and Notre-Dame-des-Neiges?

In 1910, two great friendships, two supports, were taken from Father de Foucauld. On May 14 the mail coming from In-Salah brought news of Father Guérin's death, at thirty-five, worn out by the fatigue of the Saharan life. The long voluminous correspondence between him and Father de Foucauld showed the respect that these two men had for one another. When two men, thanks to the faith which fills them, are almost free from self-love; when they become, as much as nature permits, entirely noble influences, ever waiting to obey the slightest sign from God, the understanding between them is immediately perfect, whether silent or expressed, and the confidence which they have in each other surpasses all other friendship in sweetness. In their numerous letters there is not a trace of disagreement. On either side is the same certainty that the friend addressed—one asking counsel, the other replying—was only thinking of the reign of the Sovereign Beauty over the world. Father de Foucauld submitted all his plans of journeys, and distant future foundations to his director-friend, and, if he did not render him an account, as he did to M. Huvelin, of his spiritual state, he nevertheless did not mark off the limit between these two domains—the one outward, the other inward—and very often spiritual confidences, resolutions, hesitations, and passing depression found expression in the letters of the hermit of Beni-Abbès or Tamanrasset to the Prefect Apostolic of Ghardaïa.

" God has just inflicted a trial upon us both," he wrote to Father Voillard, two days after the news came. " You have lost a very good son, and I a very good Father; lost in appearance, for he is nearer to us than ever. . . . I had never thought that he might not survive me, and I leant upon his friendship as if it would never fail me. You know the void that his departure has left me. Jesus remains: blessed be He in all things! Blessed be He in having called our very dear Father Guérin to his reward! Blessed be He also for having lent him to us for a few years!

"This unforeseen departure makes me wish all the more for the company of a priest who may continue the very small work begun here. He might live along with me, living the same life or not. I don't want to be his Superior, but his friend, ready to leave him alone as soon as he knows the routine. . . .

"From 1905, Captain Dinaux, then Chief of the Arab Office at In-Salah, asked for some White Sisters for Ahaggar: now that there is a permanent garrison, a French officer, a doctor, several French non-commissioned officers and corporals, and a hundred native soldiers permanently in the country, with the mail twice a month, great security and the conveniences of life, we might reasonably think about it. Sisters are not sent apart from White Fathers; but there might be grounds for considering the possibility of a foundation for the White Fathers. . . . The Tuaregs of Ahaggar are Musulmans only in name; they detest the Arabs. Their submission to France introduces into the country Arab Musulmans, Musulman *Khojas* in the service of France, as soldiers or interpreters. Arabs from Tidikelt and other countries are allowed to circulate freely, to carry on commerce without fear of being robbed; whence will probably follow an islamic propaganda and a renewal of islamic fervour: it would be useful to be beforehand . . .

"I am preparing for a greater spiritual activity by getting a little hermitage for two built about forty miles away in the heart of the highest mountains in Ahaggar, and where tents are quartered in larger numbers. There I shall be much more at the centre of the inhabitants than here. Next year I mean to divide myself between it and Tamanrasset. . . .

"I ask you to pray for my director, M. l'Abbé Huvelin; he has been my Father for twenty-four years; nothing could explain what he is to me and what I owe him. The news about his health is lamentable. At each mail I fear to learn that he, too, has fulfilled his time of exile."

Less than two months later, in fact on July 10, Abbé Huvelin died. The one whom he had led back to God wept and then, like the best, raised his eyes to heaven, and there found immutable joy to comfort him. To one of the White Fathers expressing sympathy with him in the circumstances, he replied:

"Yes, Jesus is enough: where He is, nothing lacks. However dear be those in whom His likeness shines, it is He who is all. He is all in time and in eternity."

As if all supports were to be taken away from the finished building, a third friend of Father de Foucauld was to leave Africa that same year. Colonel Laperrine, who had been in command of the oases for nine years, asked for the command of a regiment in France; he left those territories organized by him in peace, and enlarged by the whole Tuareg country.[1]

Why did this great Saharan quit the Sahara? For the best of reasons. Brother Charles, his confidant, said in fact: "He is right; we must not seem to cling to office." Only the highest type of man thinks thus. The life and death of Laperrine justify us in thinking that Brother Charles was not mistaken.

Laperrine never returned to Hoggar, until the middle of the Great War. He never again saw his friend alive. As almost always, it was an unconscious adieu. Foucauld not only had a tested love for the man who had been the comrade of his youth, he admired the commander who had done so much for the greatness of France in Africa—that is to say, for the civilization of the nations who are confided to us. A few months before his departure, he paid this tribute to him in a letter: "Laperrine spends himself beyond measure; he has impressed all who are under his orders with a wonderful energy and activity. The last six years, the amount of work the officers under his orders have done, and what has been effected from the military, administrative, geographical, and commercial points of view, are unheard of."

On Laperrine's departure he summed up his colonial career thus: "Since the age of twenty-one he has not spent three years in France; one summer as lieutenant, fifteen months as captain, and six months as commander; all the rest in Algeria, Tunis, and above all Senegal, the Sudan and the Sahara. It is he who gave the Sahara to France, *in spite of her*, and at the risk of his career, and he it is who united our Algerian possessions with our colony in the Sudan."

[1] He was appointed Colonel of the 18th Regiment of Chasseurs, on November 8, 1910.

Before leaving Africa, the Colonel had decided on taking Musa ag Amastane to France. Some noble Tuaregs accompanied the *amenokal;* they were made to assist at gunnery experiments at Creusot; they visited the breeding studs, factories and towns, especially Paris and its "curiosities," among which was certainly one of the least Parisian and most cosmopolitan—the Moulin Rouge. It was a lightning visit of rapid skipping without respite, meant to astound rather than to appeal to the heart, a visit such as governors who have no paternal feeling of responsibility can order. Brother Charles received some news of this promenade, which was too official for his taste; but he rejoiced at the thought of the good the Tuareg chief would nevertheless derive from this very partial experience of a superior civilization. "On his return," he wrote, "I shall try to make him understand that three things are necessary if he wishes to work for the eternal salvation of his people: (1) To get education for the children and youths, who are as neglected as animals. (2) To get a certain amount of instruction imparted to them. (3) To work to make his people settle down and give up the nomad life, while keeping their pastoral character.

"This third thing is the *sine qua non* of the two firsts, for education and instruction seem incompatible with the nomad life.

"For the Kel-Ahaggar, or at least for most of them, the transition from the nomad to the settled life would be easy; the strongest tribes are almost stationary; the camels, under the care of a few shepherds, go and graze a long way off; but the tents with the families and the flocks of goats are almost settled—they only move within a circle of about twenty-five miles. . . . Moreover, the peace of these three years of French occupation has already had the effect of stabilizing the inhabitants. On my arrival there was only one house in Tamanrasset, the other dwellings were huts; now there are fifteen or twenty houses; they are constantly being built; the huts will soon have disappeared; it is the same, they say, in the other villages. . . . Tillage is increasing. Every Tuareg in slightly easy circumstances has fields. Unfortunately, they do not cultivate them themselves; they get them cultivated by the *harratins* of Tidikelt or negroes. The Tuaregs superintend the work, and harvesting, but they despise putting their hand to the hoe. The settlement in this country of monks cultivating with their own hands would be a great blessing. . . ."

No sooner was the Hoggar chief back on African soil, than he wrote to his friend, Father de Foucauld; and here is the letter he addressed him, on a sheet of the *Hotel de l'Oasis* paper:

" Praise be to the one God, and may God bless Mahomet.

"From Algiers, for Hoggar,
"*September* 20, 1910."

" To his honoured excellency, our dear friend above all, Monsieur le Marabout Abed Aissa,[1] the Sultan Musa ben Mastane salutes thee, and wishes thee the grace of the very high God and His benediction. How art thou? If thou wishest news of us, as we ask for thine, we are well, thank God, and we have only good news to give thee. Here we are arrived from Paris, after a good voyage. The Paris authorities were pleased with us. I saw thy sister and remained two days at her house; I also saw thy brother-in-law. I visited their gardens and houses. And thou, thou art in Tamanrasset like the poor man![2] On my arrival, I shall give thee all the news in detail.

" Wani ben Lemniz and Sughi ben Chitach salute thee.

" Greeting !"

The hermit remained at Tamanrasset until the end of the year, and at the beginning of 1911 undertook a second journey to France, a little longer than the first. The latter lasted three weeks. In 1911 Father de Foucauld took a month to get over the following complicated itinerary: Marseilles, Viviers, Nîmes, Notre-Dame-des-Neiges, Paris, Nancy, Lunéville, Saverne, Paris, Bergerac, Angoulême, Paris, Barbirey, Lyons, Marseilles.

On May 3 he was back in Tamanrasset, after having made a stop at Beni-Abbes, where he spent only three days. The calm of Hoggar appeared, after those four months travelling, very agreeable to him, and his reception by the Tuaregs touched him. He wrote, on May 14, to Father Voillard, who had become his spiritual director since Abbé Huvelin's death : " At this moment, there are a great many people here on account of the harvest; I shall remain here about three weeks more, to take advantage of their assembly, to see various people, to talk with Musa, and to give the poor of the neighbourhood

---

[1] Abed Aissa—servant of Jesus.
[2] *El meskine* is the poor man, an object of pity by his destitution.

their share of alms; then I shall go to Askrem, the mountain hermitage, for a year at least. I shall work there with all my might at my Tuareg books, so as to finish them in a year and a half from now. . . . I was very well received by the whole population; it is making progress in confidence and civilization, it is also making material progress . . . an intellectual movement will certainly follow."

Summer came. Suddenly letters became less and less frequent. Father de Foucauld's correspondents must have thought that he was ill or lost in the Sahara. Lost would perhaps be nearly true. The man who had settled in one of the most unknown places in the world was tempted by the inaccessible. On July 5 he had set out for Askrem, where he dwelt in a hovel nearly ten thousand feet up, assuredly the highest point on earth where a hermit had ever lived. Must we think that he was led there by a whim, by some fanciful eccentricity of an adventurous nature? That would be to form a wrong opinion of him, and we already know it. His villeggiatura in Askrem is only fresh evidence of his charity and fearlessness. He went yonder to seek, through cold and storm, the souls whose wandering pastor he had made himself. The dryness drove the Tuaregs from the Ahaggar plateaux; they went and camped in the Kudiat valleys, where there was a little green grass for the flocks. And Brother Charles went up to them. They came not only from Tamanrasset and neighbourhood, but from several deserts around the Hoggar heights, and nomads of divers tribes were there for a short time, shivering, but no longer famishing.

The road was long and rough. The last part could hardly be done except on foot: the camels stumbled on the fallen and broken stones. It took at least three days to reach Askrem, the citadel of the country—a plateau enveloped in a fantastic landscape of peaks and points and tabular heights, and grottos carved on the tops of the lower mountains. To the north and south nothing stops the view. Here and there are statues of men or animals upright in the limpid air, changing in colour, shading and expression, according to the height and secret power of the sun. In our European mountains there is rain; here is wind, always blowing the drifting sand; it has worn away the friable rocks, and leaves standing the harder pillars with resisting angles, and fine or enormous spires, like the Ilaman peak which dominates the rest. The Askrem plateau has not only this strange beauty: it reminds the scientist of the first ages of the world; it is the watershed. The great Saharan rivers, to-day dried up, flowed from its flanks. On all sides one can follow the beds which they have hollowed out, and which go, some towards the Taudeni basin, others towards the Atlantic, others, like the Wady Tamanrasset, towards the Niger.

Father de Foucauld loved with all the ardour of his poetic and contemplative soul this extraordinary solitude. "It is," he said, "a beautiful place to adore the Creator. May His reign be established here. I have the advantage of having many souls around me, and of being very solitary on my summit. . . .

"Since I was twenty I have always relished the sweetness of solitude, whenever I got it. Even in my non-Christian days, I loved the solitude of beautiful nature along with books, but now all the more when the sweetness of the invisible world prevents one's solitude from ever being lonely. The soul is not made for noise, but for meditation, and life ought to be a preparation for heaven—not only by meritorious works, but by peace and recollection in God. But man has launched out into endless discussions: the little happiness he finds in loud debates is enough to show how far they lead him away from his vocation."

At Askrem as at Tamanrasset, he had chosen a commanding position. His house was but a corridor, built in stone and earth, and so narrow that two men could not pass abreast. But in this poor refuge he had a chapel, and, beyond, a number of things in wonderful order, a great number of books, provisions, and packing-cases, opened and unopened. He slept on one of the latter. In the daytime he used it as a table. Around him the wind blew, with the noise of the sea when the tide is rising. Abbé Huvelin had sent his friend two hundred francs, to help him build this shelter; he had also given him the little altar for the chapel, and Brother Charles, enraptured and grateful, had exclaimed: "I hope Holy Mass will be said on this altar long after my death."

There, more than once a week, he received the visits of Tuareg families; men, women, and children all came up together from the innumerable valleys hidden in the Kudiat. They were both pilgrimages and pleasure parties. They came a long way, at least one or two days' march. They had to rest up yonder, sup, and spend the night. Brother Charles joyfully spent his precious time in welcoming his guests; he made them little presents; he shared his meals with them. "One or two meals taken together, a day or half a day spent together, put us on far better terms with one another than a great number of visits of half an hour or an hour, as at Tamanrasset. Some of these families are comparatively good, as good as they can be without Christianity. These souls are directed by natural lights; although Musulmans by faith, they are very ignorant of Islam, and have not been spoiled by it. In this direction, the work I am now doing is very good. Lastly, my presence is an opportunity for the officers to come into the very heart of the country."[1]

All the rest of the time—and there is plenty of time when one gets up long before the sun—Brother Charles prayed or worked. He brought with him a native whom he called his "Tuareg teacher"; he gave him five sous an hour to pay for his trouble, but as the sittings of questions and answers lasted on an average nine hours a day, the pupil found the professor's fees a heavy expense, and the latter that so much diligence wearied a nomad's head.

This weariness, so new to an Ahaggar, the distance from the wells from which he used to go and fetch water every day, perhaps the austere solitude, perhaps the cold at night, with winter coming on, made the "coadjutor" ask to be sent back to his country. Brother Charles, who had taken his provisions of books and preserves "like someone who plans a sixteen months' voyage without having to call at any harbour," was forced to give way and go down. At the beginning of December, he again entered the Tamanrasset hermitage.

There he resumed his usual charitable and hidden life, answering the appeals of poverty, which is always great among the tribes. Brother Charles gave himself up entirely to almsgiving, and distributed his provisions. He just came to hear of news which was stale for the rest of the world: the war between the Italians and the Tripolitan Arabs. His friends were anxious about the reaction this war might have on the Sahara. "Don't be alarmed," he wrote to one of them, "about the preaching of a holy war. The Sahara is large, the Turks are certainly doing all they can to get the holy war preached among the Arab tribes of Tripoli, but that does not touch us. The Tuaregs, very lukewarm Musulmans, are equally indifferent about the holy war and about the Turks and Italians. It is all the same to them; what solely interests them is their flocks, the grazing and the harvest. Before

[1] Letter to Father Voillard, December 6, 1911.

their submission to France, they joined to these callings the profession of highwaymen; now that is forbidden them, they devote themselves with all the more ardour to the others.

"I found Tamanrasset and the neighbouring inhabitants in a terrible state of misery, and I thought I ought to give much more in alms than I foresaw. The reason of this misery is twofold: (1) drought has prevailed for twenty months: hence it follows that milk, butter, and butcher's meat, which are the principal riches of the country, have been lacking for twenty months; (2) in 1911, the two harvests (there is a wheat harvest in spring and a millet harvest in autumn) were failures, owing to greenfly eating away the inside of the ears just before they ripened. Results: (1) there is nothing to eat in the country: I could not buy a *litre* of any grain whatever here (wheat, barley or millet); (2) nobody has any clothes, because they can only get them by selling butter, animals, etc. I have something to eat, because I have stores, but there are few people here who have two meals a day, and many who live entirely on wild roots. . . . I cannot feed the people, but I have given much more clothes than I usually do; it is the cold season.

"Since my return, I have so far done little beyond praying to God and receiving visits from my neighbours one after another. . . . I have not yet taken the work of the lexicon and grammar up again: I shall set about it after New Year's Day: in the first place, I would like to be able to stay at the foot of the Crib during this holy Christmastide, then I must see all my poor neighbours who begin to be old friends, for I am in my seventh year at Tamanrasset."

He brought back little presents which he distributed to his visitors of both sexes, and which were highly treasured in Hoggar. The most ordinary gifts were needles; further, there were safety pins, then boxes of matches; scissors were kept for the great ladies, and knives for the more influential Tuaregs.

As time went by and experience increased, Father Charles was strengthened in his conviction that his missionary methods were not mistaken. Dwelling among the native camps in the high mountain provided him with fresh proofs of it. "I help as far as I can; I try to show that I love. When the opportunity seems favourable, I speak of natural religion, of God's commandments, of His love, of union with His will and love of one's neighbour. . . . The Tuaregs have the character of our good rustics in France, of the best of our peasants: like them, they are industrious, prudent, economical, opposed to novelties, and full of suspicion as to unknown persons and things. Ignorant as they are, they can receive the Gospel only by authority, and the authority necessary to make them adopt it and reject all they know, love and venerate, can only be acquired after long and intimate contact, by great virtue and God's blessing.[1]

"Some—very few—seriously question me on religious matters; in my counsels I keep to natural religion, insisting on avoiding sin, on night prayers with an examination of conscience, and acts of contrition and charity."

These good countryfolk of the Sahara are not wanting in vices, which Brother Charles enumerates without dwelling on them, for fear of letting it be thought that he was in an evil neighbourhood. They were extremely violent, proud to the point of madness; laxity of morals was general; the Tuareg rules of honour allowed women, and even advised them, to do away with children born outside marriage, and there were so many infanticides that " perhaps a third of the children perish at birth."

"Send some White Sisters," he wrote to Mgr. Livinhac; "they will start a round for the newly-born, and that will be the remedy until conversion takes place."

At each page in the voluminous correspondence of the Tamanrasset hermit, we find him thinking out the best human means of raising this people to whom he was the first missionary. He came with a complete civilization in his heart. For him civilization "consists of two things: education and gentleness." Nothing was indifferent to him if it helped to protect children, to free slaves, to teach the ignorant, to settle nomads and draw them closer to France.

He preferred solitude, and we have heard his praises of it; but for the good of the 100,000 souls in the Sahara, whose chaplain he was, that solitude had to be enlivened, that silence disturbed. Post and telegraph, railways, biennial fairs—he called for such "progress" with a county councillor's passion, though caring but little about it for himself. He rejoiced at the speedy coming of a mission of engineers, officers, and geologists charged with inquiring into the eventual line of a trans-Saharan railway to follow the great curve of Oran, Beni-Unif, Beni-Abbes, Twat, Aulef, Silet (forty-six miles west of

[1] Letter to Father Voillard, July 12, 1912.

Tamanrasset), In-Gezzam, Agades, Chad. "I am very happy about it, for the railway in these regions is a powerful means of civilization, and civilization a powerful help to christianization; savages cannot be Christians.[1] Above all, let them hasten to build the railway!" And immediately after that wish follows this sentence which shows the officer, the great and true Frenchman: "It is a necessity for the preservation of our African empire, but also for bringing all our forces, in case of need, to the Rhine."

Fresh good news came in. Near Fort Motylinski had just arrived an officer, "who was charming and distinguished, Lieutenant Depommier." There was also an "extremely nice" doctor. These were causes of joy to which was added a last one of another order, wished for, called for, and long expected: Morocco had come under the protection of France. Letters told Brother Charles of it. He at once replied in these lines, which are well worth reflecting on: "Here is our colonial empire greatly enlarged. If we are what we ought to be, if we civilize, instead of exploiting Algeria, Tunis and Morocco will, in fifty years, be an extension of France. If we do not fulfil our duty, if we exploit instead of civilizing, we shall lose everything, and our uniting these people will turn against ourselves."

In the constant desire of civilizing which filled his mind with aspirations and plans, he contemplated making another journey to France in a few months, and taking with him a young Tuareg of an important bourgeois family, "if one may speak thus." He began to prepare Madame de Blic and his cousins in France to receive the tourist, dressed in a waistcloth, with plaited hair and cheeks covered with a blue veil. He introduced him by making a favourable portrait of him. According to Brother Charles, no one in Ahaggar was equal to his candidate, who was "not only affectionate, intelligent, and gentle, but exceptionally steady. The son of one of the principal men of his tribe, first cousin to the chief, he has been half adopted by the latter, who had no children; he entirely manages the material affairs of his adopted father, whose stepdaughter he is going to marry. He is nice in every way and of the best plebeian family. We are here in a country of castes; there are plebeians and patricians, the

---

[1] Letter to a friend, February 1, 1912. The mission comprised four engineers of bridges and roads, a geologist (M. René Chudeau), and two captains, old Saharans; it was commanded by Captain Nieger.

first incomparably superior to the others in moral value, and making all the strength and hope of the country." But, before undertaking this journey, Brother Charles had many pages to write, and the fiancé had to set out in a caravan, with the healthy men of the country, to fetch millet from Damergu.

Spring, like winter and all the seasons, found Brother Charles shut up in his hermitage, bending over the packing-case which he used as a table, surrounded by his manuscripts and books, in difficult passages consulting his "teacher," who had a headache. He finished the dictionary, and promised himself to send the work soon to M. René Basset, who would publish it "under the name of our common friend M. de Motylinski." The trans-Saharan mission traversed Ahaggar. It stopped at Tamanrasset. "Very well managed and well composed, it has accomplished an extraordinary amount of work. I saw the members of the mission; several have long been my friends. They hope that in about a year the work will begin. What fields are opened for the holy Gospel: Morocco, the Sudan, and the Sahara!" There were frequent comings and goings between the camp and hermitage. Brother Charles mentions Captain Nieger, M. René Chudeau, Captain Cortier of the colonial infantry, M. Mousserand (a mining engineer). He notes also that he receives numerous visits from Tuaregs, who have formed the habit of coming to see him at sunset on Sundays, a day during which they observed that the marabout received them still more willingly and chatted at greater length than on other days.

The mission went away; great heat fell upon the Tamanrasset plateau. Suddenly a serious accident interrupted work. Charles de Foucauld was bitten by a horned viper. The bite is nearly always fatal. The shepherds and blacks in the vicinity of the hermitage heard of the occurrence. They ran up and found their friend lifeless. No European doctor was there. They therefore nursed the marabout according to their custom, burning the wound brutally with hot irons, bandaging the arm to prevent the venom from spreading to the whole body, then, as the syncope persisted, they applied the red iron to the soles of his feet; a terrible blister, administered through compassion. The hermit at last came to himself. He was extremely weak; they searched everywhere in the valley for milk to feed him. But the heat was great, the goats no longer had any grass. Musa became anxious, and ordered two cows to be brought from very far away to Hoggar to save the marabout. Brother Charles was long unable to study or walk. He ended, however, by recovering from the viper's bite, and from the treatment which had saved him.

He never dreamt of complaining. In that he was like my old professor of chemistry. When he caught a fever, and the doctor told him that the illness would be very serious, he joyfully exclaimed: "What luck; I shall be able to have a rest!" Charles de Foucauld rested a moment before his door, and long in his chapel—only one step away—in meditation and prayer. And we know that, in that autumn of 1912—autumn is the favourite season of Europeans who have lived in Ahaggar—two principal thoughts made his soul rejoice and his life of solitude light. The first was: "The farther I go, the more I enjoy the beauty of nature. How beautiful are the works of God! *Benedicite, omnia opera Domini, Domino!*" And the second: "The time of Advent is always sweet, but particularly so here. Tamanrasset, with its forty hearths of poor husbandmen, is very much what Nazareth and Bethlehem may have been in the time of our Lord."

I ascribe to this period a story which I have not been able to date exactly. It was and is still being told all wrong. In the reviews or newspapers, one may read of "Musa ag Amastane's mother" falling very seriously ill, when Father de Foucauld was called in to her. To encourage her in the hour of death he found nothing better than to recite some suras from the Koran: "He came and fulfilled his office of comfort and laid the old woman to sleep in Allah, with appropriate verses from the Koran." When these lines fell under my eyes—many months ago— I at once felt that the truth must be otherwise. I thought that a Catholic priest might, indeed, have suggested to the dying woman to recite suras expressing timely truths— exhorting, for instance, to repentance or to hope in God. This would have simply meant translating an act of contrition or Christian charity into the language most intelligible to the woman. But I could not believe that Father de Foucauld had done it, knowing how he dreaded the extension of Islam, and therefore that he would avoid quoting the Koran, even if appropriate, as much as possible. I wished to know whether I was right, and wrote to the *aménokal* of Hoggar. I asked him to call to mind the very words of his friend Father de Foucauld. He well understood the sense of the question I had put to him. Though uncivilized, he was intelligent.

He answered me a few months later in the following letter:

" Praise to the one God! There is none but He!

" Tamanrasset,
" 5 Chabân, 1338,
" *April* 25, 1920.

" To the most honoured of French scholars, Réne Bazin, of the Academy.

" To thee, thousands of greetings, a thousand divine favours! From the servant of France, the Emir Musa, son of Amastane, *amenokal* in Hoggar.

" Thy letter reached me, in which thou askest me to give thee details about the great friend of the Hoggar-Tuaregs. So be it! Know that the marabout Charles held me in great esteem. God bless him, and make him dwell in Paradise, if it be His will.

" Now, here are the details thou askest me for: about his life, in the first place. The people among the Hoggar-Tuaregs loved him deeply during his life, and now still they love his tomb as if he were alive. Thus the women, children, poor, and whoever passes near his tomb, salute it, saying: ' May God raise the marabout higher in Paradise, for he did good to us during his life!' All the people of Hoggar also honour his tomb as if he were alive—yes, indeed, quite as much.

" Then, thou askest me what took place when he was present at the illness of my mother—that is to say, my aunt (Tîhit), my father's sister, at the time of the illness of which she died. The marabout Charles said to her in Tamachek: ' Oksâd massinîn ' [fear God], and afterwards he left her. She died the next day. We carried the body to the tomb, and he was with us; whilst we were praying for her, he was standing, the colour [of his face] impaired on account of her death. He did not pray with us for her. When we placed her in her tomb, he kept standing on the edge, buried her with us, and said to us: ' God increase your consolation on the subject of Tîhit! May God give her Paradise in her tomb!'

" One of my days, a year before her death, she came to see him in his cell, and found him praying: she stood motionless behind him, waiting till he had finished his prayer, then she said to him: ' I also pray to God, at the hour at which thou prayest.'

" As to the fame of the marabout, it is always enduring

in Hoggar, and the persons to whom, as to us, he did good —that is to say, all the people of Hoggar—honour his tomb as if he were living.

"Such is the information that thou hast asked me for, given without fault. I hand this letter for thee to Captain Depommier, the commander-in-chief with us.

"May God bless thee in thy life! Mayest thou live in good health! Greeting.

"(*Seal of*) Musa ag Amastane."

The answer is clear; I was right. The incident helped Father de Foucauld's memory more than I expected. It led, indeed, Musa's *thaleb*, Ba-Hammu, who worked for ten years with Father de Foucauld, to make some most interesting statements, sent on to me by a witness along with the letter. Here they are:

"We know well that the marabout could not tell us to say the *shahada* [the Musulman form of prayer]; we are in no doubt about this. That was inconsistent with his office as a Catholic priest; we all know it. A fact well known to everyone here proves it. Father de Foucauld was continually visited by the poor, the aged, the sick, women, children, and numerous Tuaregs who came to ask for his help and counsel. At the beginning of his installation, it happened that some of his visitors, coming out of his house at the Musulman hours of prayer, stopped near the hermitage to pray. Father de Foucauld amiably invited them to move away from the hermitage, telling them that they must understand that he did not want them to pray near his house, as they could not themselves want him to pray near a mosque. . . . He said these things in such an amiable and kindly way, that we all soon got to know them, and would not think of violating his wishes."[1]

The very well-informed witness who told to me these memories of the *thaleb*, added this personal reflection: "If we strip Father de Foucauld's intercourse with the Tuaregs of all purely formal considerations, it is absurd and untrue to say that he ever did or said anything which did not aim at their evangelization, which was, after all, his object."

The journey to France with a young Tuareg was one of the thousand means devised by his charity to diminish the

[1] In order to understand Father de Foucauld's words better, we must realize that the Tuaregs have no mosque, and that their religious memorials are only marked on the ground by lines of stones. Hence, the Musulman prayer, repeated frequently in the same place, and near the hermitage, might give rise to an unfortunate legend.

distance between the Musulman tribes and Catholic France. Brother Charles expected a great deal of good from it.

He had already obtained a favourable reply from his sister and other relations, who agreed to receive the young Tuareg in their houses. The African missionaries were told of the scheme, and also promised to offer hospitality to the two travellers at Maison Carrée. Other letters were posted to France, asking his friends for the same favours or for introductions. It was touching to see Father de Foucauld, so hard upon himself, doing his best to arrange and settle everything, so that Uksem's journey might be as pleasant and friendly, and as little tiresome as possible. Would not the fate of many souls depend, at least to some extent, on the recollections of our civilization that this young barbarian would bring back? Such a journey " is the means of overthrowing a host of errors at a single stroke, of opening men's eyes, of bringing about a several months' *tête-à-tête* with a chosen soul. It goes without saying, there is to be no paying of visits to museums or curiosities; he must be made to partake of the sweetness and affectionate atmosphere of family life in Christian society, and be given a glimpse of what Christian life is, and be shown how religion impregnates the whole of life."

Among these letters there is one which I want to give almost entirely. In it Charles de Foucauld forcibly set forth ideas lightly touched on elsewhere. It is addressed to his friend the Duc de Fitz-James, and dated *December* 11, 1912.

It begins thus: "I won't fail to tell you when I am coming to Marseilles; I shall be so delighted to see you again!" He then says that the journey is put off to the month of May, 1913. Uksem will hardly be ready to start before then, and, besides, "I do not wish to show him France in snow, cold, and north wind, without verdure and leaves; it would even have been very imprudent to expose the Saharan's chest to our cold and damp winter. So I have decided to go to France only this summer. With my young companion, I shall land at Marseilles about the first fortnight in May. . . ."

We French have two essential duties to fulfil in Africa : "The first thing is the administration and civilization of our North-West African Empire. Algeria, Morocco, Tunis, the Sahara, and the Sudan form an immense and magnificent empire in one lump, having this unity for the first time. . . . How are we to attach this empire to us? By civilizing it, by working to raise its inhabitants morally and intellectually as much as possible. The inhabitants of our African Empire are very varied: some, the Berbers, may rapidly become like us; others, Arabs, are slower in progress; the negroes are very different from each other; but all are capable of progress.

"The second thing is the *evangelization* of our colonies. . . . Now, what are we doing for the evangelization of our North-West African Empire? One might say, nothing. In Algeria, Tunis, and the Sahara, the only priests engaged in the evangelization of the natives are the White Fathers; they are, according to their 1910-1911 report, fifty-six in North Africa, eleven in the Sahara. A drop of water. I can well understand that the White Fathers, seeing the evangelization of the Musulmans to be slow and difficult, have turned aside their efforts and sent the great majority of their missionaries into Equatorial Africa, where they are working wonders, and affecting conversions as rapid as they are numerous, and winning heaven for a host of souls. Here they would have saved few, there they save many: so I can understand their going there. It is nevertheless true that Algeria, Tunis, and Morocco (where there are only chaplains at the consulates) are entirely neglected. . . . This is a situation which French Christians ought to remedy. It will be a work of time, demanding self-sacrifice, character, and constancy. We want good priests in fair quantity (not to preach: they would be received as Turks coming to preach Mahomet would be received in Breton villages, or much worse with the help of barbarism), but to establish contact, to make themselves loved, to inspire esteem, trust, and friendship; then we should want good lay Christians of both sexes to fulfil the same rôle, to enter into still closer contact, to go where the priest hardly can— above all, to Musulmans' homes, to give an example of Christian virtue, to show the Christian life, family, and spirit: then we want good nuns to take care of the sick and to bring up the children, mingling much with the population, dispersed by twos or threes wherever there are priests and Christians. . . . That being done, conversions, at the end either of twenty-five, fifty, or a hundred years, will come of themselves, as fruit ripens, according to the spread of education. . . . But if these unfortunate Musulmans know no priest, see, as self-styled Christians, only unjust and tyrannical speculators giving an example of vice, how can they be converted? How can they but hate our holy religion? How are they not to become more and more hostile to us? . . .

"After drawing your attention to these two very important points, let me add a word: whether it be to administer and civilize our African empire, or to evangelize it, we must first get to know its population. But we know very little of it. That is partly due to Musulman customs, but that is an obstacle which can be overcome; this deplorable fact remains, that we are alarmingly ignorant of our native African population. I have hardly quitted North Africa for the last thirty-two years (except during the ten years, from 1890 to 1900, which I spent in Turkey in Asia, Armenia, and the Holy Land); I have seen nobody, neither officer, nor missionary, nor colonist or any other person who knows enough of the natives; as for myself, I have a fair knowledge of my little corner of Tuaregs, but a very superficial acquaintance with the rest. . . . There is a vice which must be remedied; our administrators, officers, and missionaries must have a much *closer contact* with the populations, *long residence* in the same stations (with promotion on the spot for administrators and officers), that they may know and instruct their Superiors correctly, and that the latter may get to know through them. . . ."

The diary goes on, mentioning the events which take place around the hermitage. There were great and small happenings. The great one was the arrival of General Bailloud at the beginning of 1913, and the perfect success of the experiment with which he was entrusted. He was to secure the setting up of wireless communications between Tamanrasset and Paris. Attempts were made, and, to the satisfaction of Father de Foucauld, who clearly foresaw all the coming mechanical improvements, the capital of Ahaggar could " talk " without difficulty with the Eiffel Tower.

A little later a flight of storks passed over the hermitage, going from north to south.

On March 9, General Bailloud, wishing to thank the inhabitants for the good reception he had met with, sent a female camel for the poor. Charles de Foucauld had it killed, and the meat distributed to all the unfortunate without exception, to all the wives of the *harratins*, to the artisans, to the shepherds, to the married women, to the widows, and to the cast-off.

"On the morning of the 18th a thick damp fog and light south wind; it is the signal of spring. A man from In-Salah crosses the country. He tells me that the outer yard of my house yonder is buried under the sand, and that the rest of the house is threatened." Not a word of regret, not a syllable comes from the owner; he will go and see.

At last, after long delay, the most important of the caravans which set out yearly in September to go and fetch millet, returned to Tamanrasset. It was time : the population was beginning to suffer. Among the caravan chiefs was Uksem, the fiancé, the candidate chosen for the journey to France.

"I shall only be in Paris on May 25," wrote Brother Charles to a friend. "Pray for my little Uksem; he is going to be married to a flame of his childhood. It has long been settled; he is nearly twenty-two; Mlle. Kaubeshisheka is eighteen. They are very near relations, and have been brought up together. She is very intelligent and has plenty of determination."

Uksem's marriage took place at the beginning of April, and on the 28th Father de Foucauld jotted in his diary: "Set out for France at 6 o'clock in the morning with Uksem. The night before, his mother came to the hermitage and said : 'Say to your sister : Take great care of my child; I entrust him to you.'"

To avoid the expense of a guide they travelled by the mail which took the Fort Motylinski despatches to In-Salah. The travellers were at Maison Carrée on June 8. They only stopped two days in this house and country where Brother Charles had so many friends. Nevertheless, he saw some of them, and even pushed on to Birmandréis, where the White Sisters had their chief foundation. Those acquainted with monasteries know that a traveller, if he is a Christian, rarely visits these houses without being invited to relate what is happening to Jesus Christ and His servants in the countries where he has been. Thus was it with Brother Charles in the house where the old nuns, back from the missions of the great lakes and Kabylia, train novices to go joyfully and live in the bush, catechize the negroes, bring up the cast-off children, attend the sick, comfort many sorts of wretchedness, and keep quite pure in centres which are not so. Brother Charles was asked to explain what he had done and what he wished to do in Beni-Abbes and Hoggar. He spoke in a white room to nuns dressed in white, listening closely to every word, whether lofty or entertaining, and bowing at the name of their Master, Jesus. He was not eloquent, but the life he described was eloquent. In finishing, it occurred to him to say : "Which of you, Sisters, would sacrifice herself for the Tuaregs?" Silently, all arose with one motion.

We must, however, believe that the hour had not yet come. Brother Charles returned to Maison Carrée to find

Uksem. On the 10th they embarked on the *Timgad,* and the poor marabout, accustomed to the standard of deck passengers, now took first-class tickets to give pleasure to the infidel about to visit Christian countries; on the 13th he made a pilgrimage to Sainte-Baume; on the 15th, Mgr. Bonnet, Bishop of Viviers, received Father de Foucauld, a priest of his diocese, and Uksem — two very different examples of civilization — in his house set high on the ramparts of the old town, in the shadow of the cathedral. And from this summit, a place of prayer and mistral, the Tuareg, for whom rivers were but names and beds of sand and stone among pastures, perceived the full, strong, confined Rhone which came from the North between cultivated and quite green banks, which struggles and eddies and foams and, swirling with all its waters, passes out through the gates of Provence.

He was merry and in good health. Everybody fêted him. He understood a few words of French. He ate everything except fish and pork.

From Viviers they continued the journey by Lyons, where Father de Foucauld and Uksem became the guests of Colonel Laperrine; then they went into Burgundy. There they stopped for a few hours in a little valley with a canal in it and watered by a quick-flowing river, between two chains of wooded hills. If you cross, as the crow flies, a high undulating plateau to the north covered with wood and heaths, you land in the country of famous and rich slopes, where the villages are named Vougeot, Nuits, Musigny, Chambertin. But the Ouche flows through more shade; a peaceful and humble recess of our pasture and tillage land. You leave the railway at Gissey. Over a mile off, adjoining the market-town of Barbirey, there is an ancient manor with two wings and covered with tiles, where M. de Blic lives. This time it was only an introduction. Uksem, received by the brother-in-law, sister, nephews and nieces of his protector and friend, began to see what a French and Christian family, a country-house and day in the countryside were like. He gazed with astonishment at the courtyard before the castle full of plants and flowers, the terrace behind, the meadow which falls away to the stream, and then rises by steep slopes to the hills, and above all at the extreme beauty and vigour of the trees planted in the hollow of the park: plane-trees, sycamores, firs, elms, all their branches and leaves new to him. Then they took leave, promising to stay at Barbirey, on their return, for at least a week.

One after the other, Father de Foucauld's relations lent themselves to the plan he had made and received Uksem. First there was the Marquis de Foucauld at his castle of Bridoire, in Périgord. They still remember vividly more than one touching incident of that visit. "I remember," said one of the witnesses lately—" I remember the winsome youth and his admiration of the Father, and the Father's kindness to him. I see them both on all-fours in the smoking-room, cutting out on the floor with a carving-knife the trousers to be sewn by the young Tuareg during his leisure. I also see him, standing every night on the chapel steps, not daring to go in, through respect, his large eyes wet with tears during the household prayers."

After the visit to the head of the family, they went, also in Périgord, to Count Louis de Foucauld, at the Château de la Renaudie, then to Viscountess de Bondy, in villeggiatura at Saint-Jean-de-Luz. Then, passing through Paris, the Father returned to Barbirey about July 20. Uksem's "apprenticeship to the French way of life" was carried on in the gaiety of a numerous and united family. The Tuareg learned to knit, so as to give lessons to the women of his tribe later on; he quickly became dexterous, whilst his guide, the marabout, got tangled up in the needles and stitches. Uksem rode a bicycle on the road to Autun, and, in order to help him to do this well, the Tuareg *gandourah* was transformed into zouave's breeches with the help of a few safety-pins. "Teach him French," the Father said to his nephew Edouard; "in return for your lessons, when you come to see me in Africa, he will teach you to ride a *mehari,* in which he is a past master." In the evening they chatted, Mlles. de Blic sang songs by Botrel at the piano; they played at hunt-the-slipper and other traditional games. Uksem understood everything and laughed at the right moment. The experiment appeared to be successful. The Father showed no singularity in this family life. He was Charles at his sister Marie's. He ate what was served; he said his long prayers at night when he was sure that Uksem, "his child," was asleep. Worn out and aged by penance, and always hard upon himself, he seemed to have only one ambition—not to keep any of these young people from fully enjoying the holidays. One Sunday he was asked:

"Will you go to Vespers?"

"It is not obligatory."

"But the people will be surprised if they don't see you there."

"Then I shall go."

He was mainly engaged in civilizing Uksem, but he also promised himself to make known to a chosen few the pious association for the conversion of infidels who are French subjects. This affair was to take him to Champagne and Lorraine; he disclosed his plan to General Laperrine, to whose house he went on leaving Barbirey, and whose guests Uksem and he were. Laperrine, promoted to be a general since the preceding June 22, commanded the Sixth Brigade of Dragoons at Lyons. Happy at seeing his friend de Foucauld again, he said to him: "Your Tuareg only knows his Ahaggar mountains; you must show him the Alps and go to Switzerland; I shall be one of the party." He was so much so that his fine silhouette is seen in the corner of several photographs which represent Uksem beaming with admiration at the sea of ice, or climbing some peak of Mont Blanc. The travellers spent August 3 at Chamounix, the 4th at Lucerne, the 6th at Belfort. After the Swiss excursion there was a second stop at Barbirey—the longest; it lasted a fortnight. The young Tuareg, taken about everywhere, everywhere spoiled, was getting broken in. When he left Burgundy and took the train for Paris, he received from one of Father de Foucauld's friends a present with which he was delighted: a fowling-piece. He had to go out shooting at once and fire off his gun, and this letter was sent to one of M. de Blic's sons; it was written in *tifinar* and translated by Uncle Charles: "This is me, Uksem, who says: I greet Édouard warmly; I love thee very much; the time seems long without thee. I killed a partridge, a hare, and a squirrel. I embrace thee."

Some other visits, notably one to Berry, took up the last weeks. On September 25, Father de Foucauld, going down towards Marseilles, stopped at Viviers and spent the day with his dear bishop, Mgr. Bonnet, who authorized, " in the diocese, the little association (the confraternity), and encouraged it with a letter." Three days later, the travellers, finishing a journey of three months and a half in France, embarked for Africa, and Charles de Foucauld wrote to his sister: " Unless in exceptional circumstances, a missionary does not spend so long a time of rest with his relatives. In Uksem's voyage, God provided such an exceptional circumstance. I thank Him for it with my whole heart. . . . You also I thank, as well as Raymond and your children, for the pleasant weeks you made me spend, and for your extreme kindness to Uksem, kindness which does so much good to his soul; I quite understand that his joy at meeting his own relations again is tempered very much by his grief at leaving those who received him so well in France. The apostolate of kindness is the best of all."

These holidays—the only ones that Brother Charles believed he had the right to take during his career as a Christian—enabled him to see at leisure nearly all his family or friends once more. These were farewells; perhaps he thought so. To several among them, and also to some pious souls—met here and there and at once recognized, eternal relations that God shows in an instant—he spoke of the association he so much wanted to promote, the association blessed by the Bishop of Viviers: and not only did they enter into the spirit of this higher charity which is ever ready to pray for or to put its spiritual treasures at the disposal of fresh misfortune, but some men of good-will apparently were quite glad to devote themselves to the salvation of "our Musulman brothers" in other ways. He may have been mistaken as to the time: he believed that a few laymen would soon become "missionaries *à la* Priscilla,*"* as he said, and come to Africa to prepare by their example, by the care they gave to the sick and poor, for the evangelization of the Berbers and Arabs, which is the great duty of France. Then he wrote a very singular note to one of his relations, with this heading: " What does a Frenchwoman require to do good among the Tuaregs?"

" 1. The will to live among them long enough to know their language (which is not difficult), and to be known by them, because you can only do good when you know and are known.

" 2. Much patience and gentleness: the Tuaregs cannot make fine distinctions; they cannot tell a person's quality, and pass quickly from barbarous behaviour to exaggerated familiarity.

" 3. An elementary knowledge of medicine—above all, of the complaints of young women and little children—so as to be able to attend to the sick without a doctor and dispensary.

" 4. Ability to vaccinate, and the wherewithal for vaccination.

" 5. Ability to bring up children abandoned by their mother at birth.

" 6. Ability to impart the rudiments of hygiene.

" 7. Ability to wash in the simplest way, to iron a little (but not to starch), to cook a little, so as to teach it.

" 8. Ability, both for yourself as well as to teach by

example, to give the orders required for the laying out of a kitchen garden, a poultry-yard, and a stable containing a few goats. Goats are abundant in the country, but they don't know how to feed them on clover or garden herbs; there are hens, but of too small a kind, and they don't know how to protect them by wire-netting from birds of prey; a few vegetables are cultivated, but without the necessary care, also their yield is very poor, whilst the soil and climate of Ahaggar would grow nearly all the vegetables and fruits of France, and of as good a quality as at Algiers.

"It would be well, but it is not indispensable, to know when and how to shear sheep and goats, how to spin their wool and hair, how common fabrics are made with the wool and hair thus spun; a few days spent with the White Sisters of Laghuat or Ghardaïa would do for learning all this. It would be an excellent thing to take with one a native woman of mature age, expert in such labours, and accustomed to do them for the White Sisters.

"The Tuaregs have many goats and sheep, but they do not shear them, and let their hair and wool go to waste. None of them can weave.

"It would also be well to be able to knit and crochet, so as to teach the women if need be. The women sew very well, prepare skins very well, and, with a great deal of cleverness and delicacy, do a lot of various leather-work. They look upon it as beneath them to spin, weave, knit, etc. Being extremely conservative, they are most antagonistic to all new work.

"N.B.—One of the things which it is most necessary to teach the Tuareg women, is personal cleanliness. They never wash themselves, and hardly ever wash their clothes; they cover their hair with butter, have no fleas, for fleas do not exist in the country, but they have an abundance of other parasites. They say it makes them ill to wash; there is some truth in this in the case of those who only wash themselves in the open air without wiping themselves; they must be taught to use a towel, and to do their toilet privately. A Frenchwoman in the Tuareg country will do well to have a good supply of Marseilles soap and very common towels, in order to give some to the women.

"The Tuaregs are gay and childlike; if one wishes to know them quickly and be known by them, one must attract them. A gramophone, without great compositions, but with lively and gay tunes and songs, peals of laughter, animal cries, dance music, etc., is a means of attraction.

It is the same with pictures: in that line nothing equals photographs viewed through a stereoscope; not photographs of buildings, nor landscapes, but those of persons, animals, and animated scenes: the photographs they like best are those of their compatriots, taken in their own country. Bring a verascope, take plenty of photographs of Tuareg groups, and show them; and you will get numerous visitors. A collection of coloured postcards representing persons and animals is also a good thing.

"There is no lack of women who come and ask for a remedy to blacken the few white hairs which begin to show on their heads: bottles of *jet-black* dye might well find a place in the stock of drugs: this would be a charity and a way of winning faithful friends.

"Several thousand sewing-needles of all sizes (very fine for the young, more or less coarse for the grown-ups and old women), and one or two thousand safety-pins a year, to give to the women, are very useful things to have.

"There is no need to establish a hospital, but a simple dispensary, with a place to bring up the children cast off at birth, and a 'turning-box' with a bell in order to take them in discreetly."

The return journey had to be made slowly for two reasons: the extreme heat that the travellers met with as soon as they had left the seaside; then the lean condition of the saddle- and pack-camels, which during their absence had had little care; so much so that though the departure from Maison Carrée took place at the end of September, the Father and his companion only came in sight of the hermitage on November 22.

At the request of Uksem they had passed through Timmimun. Brother Charles had not seen the oasis for seven years, and was astounded at the progress made: "A great increase of commerce with the North and South, an increase of the native industry of woollen materials, the taking in hand and training of the population, the increase and decoration of the buildings: a well-kept native infirmary; a school kept by a French teacher, helped by an Arab monitor; the school has about eighty pupils."

On November 22 they entered the Tamanrasset valley before daybreak.

"I wished to get here before daylight," the Father explained to M. de Blic, "to get off the camel quietly without a crowd of people, and to have the whole day to put a little order into my hermitage, which has been uninhabited for seven months. Uksem was neither ill nor downcast for a minute during the whole journey; he did not cease to be as nice as possible; he found all his people here in good health. How many times has he spoken to me of you, Marie and your sons, of Barbirey and its fine verdure! He has acquired a taste for French, and makes great efforts not to forget what he knows. He teaches a few words to some of his relations, who go into ecstasies on hearing him speak to me in my language; and he is going, I hope, to begin giving lessons in knitting and crochet; he is recruiting pupils. This journey has had an effect which I see already beginning: it increases the trust they have in me, and consequently in all the French."

A few days later he wrote again: "Poor Uksem spent only twenty days here. He has just set out again for six months, he is going 750 miles away from here towards Tahua right in the Sudan, to superintend the grazing of the family camels. During his first year of marriage he will have spent forty days with his wife. . . . When shall we win his soul altogether? He, his father, his father-in-law, his mother and others, are souls of goodwill; but to cease believing what one has always believed, what one has always seen believed around one, what is believed by all whom one loves and respects—this is difficult."

In the first months of 1914, the visits of Uksem's father and sisters were almost daily, and in a letter to the Duc de Fitz-James, Brother Charles says that since his return to Tamanrasset he has seen Frenchmen four times, officers or non-commissioned officers.

Officers passing through quiet Ahaggar, now less opposed to the tastes of civilized folks, were a joy to Father de Foucauld. He made their visits an opportunity for a fête both of the natives and themselves. Nowhere does he tell of the "entertaining gatherings" which were held, not round the hermitage, but somewhat to the east, before the door of the "guest-house." Fortunately the young officers often took notes of their impressions, and two diaries of the road have been handed to me.

On January 20, 1914, Commandant Meynier, Doctor Vermale (Assistant-Surgeon), and M. Lefranc (editor of the *Temps*) arrived at Tamanrasset, where they spent three days.

"The great interest of Tamanrasset," says Doctor Vermale,[1] "is the presence of Father de Foucauld. Yesterday evening we had tea at his hermitage, and he takes all

---

[1] Manuscript notes.

his meals with us. He has a wonderfully intelligent head. By his kindness, his sanctity and learning, he has won a great reputation among the population. I am promising myself to spend some interesting days with him. ... I was obliged to interrupt my written talk to go and lunch with Father de Foucauld, then to the grand fête of rejoicing given in our honour. It has quite a character of its own on account of the presence of women of the Dag-Rali tribe, which is now close to Tamanrasset. In our *zeriba*, they squat down in their most beautiful clothes; they are tall, and many of them pretty. Pre-eminent among them is the celebrated Dassine, the wife of Aflan, formerly renowned for her beauty, and retaining the very fine eyes of her glorious youth, and much wit and distinction. Gifts were distributed to them, then there was a prodigiously successful phonographic performance; the men's songs slightly puzzled them but interested them very much, because the Tuareg never sings before women. Then a great doll lottery was got up, whilst outside the negroes gave themselves up to wild dances. All this lasted three hours."

My second witness is Lieutenant L——, whom I had the pleasure of seeing at Algiers. The detachment commanded by Captain de Saint-Léger and Lieutenant L—— and entrusted with a mission to Hoggar in June, 1914, was composed, in addition to the officers, of ten *mehari* mounted men of the Saharan Company of Tidikelt, and Father de Foucauld's collaborator and friend of the French, M'ahmed Ben Messis. It set out from In-Salah on June 13 and entered on the high Tamanrasset plateau on the morning of July 1.

"At a few miles from the village we halted for a short space to do our toilet. For we are going to make our entry into the 'capital' of Ahaggar, in which is the residence of the *amenokal* Musa ag Amastane, where there are numerous Tuareg nobles, and where, above all, is one of the greatest propagators of French influence in the Sahara—the one who, by his example and persuasion, has been able to contribute in a large measure in rallying to our cause the Tuareg people hitherto reputed to be the most impervious to all notions of civilization. This is Father de Foucauld, who is as learned as he is modest, and he never feared exile in the midst of the Sahara at a stormy period.

"At first view, Tamanrasset appears more important than the other centres already visited. Hardly any more *zeribas* are seen; they have disappeared to make room for numerous houses, like those that are built in the Tidikelt *ksurs*. These buildings give Tamanrasset the aspect of a little agricultural village, of a fairly important productive centre.

"Some of these houses have even a European form, ornamented with terraces and galleries; the prettiest is certainly that of the *amenokal* Musa Ag Amastane, who has set up his residence in Tamanrasset, and who even possesses a very well cultivated garden. This house which we visited at the invitation of Akhamuk, Musa's *khoja*, is situated a little apart; it serves as a point of support to other little buildings in which Musa's family live, Tuaregs nobles of the Kel-Rela, and particularly the celebrated Dassine, Musa's cousin, reputed in days of yore to be the most beautiful of Ahaggar women.

"It is thanks to the Father de Foucauld that Tamanrasset is in a relatively flourishing condition; it was his advice and example which led numerous Tuaregs to work the generous soil which gives them a livelihood. Among them the Dag-Rali and their chief Uksem are very especially interested in agricultural work, and their perseverance is to-day bearing its fruits. The Dag-Rali were essentially a nomad tribe; the Kel-Rela *imrad* of Tuareg nobles, it was decimated at the time of the battle of Tit in 1902. It is beginning to rise again; the young boys have become men who, under the energetic influence of their chief Uksem, have almost entirely renounced the nomad life, the long fruitless rounds in the desert, to become agriculturists."

During Captain de Saint-Léger's and Lieutenant L——'s stay at Tamanrasset there was a gathering of the notables in front of the guest-house. On the stone bench placed along the wall and which looks towards the west, the Captain was seated; he had Father de Foucauld on his right and Lieutenant L—— on his left. . . . Before him, forming a half-circle, were the *amenokal* Musa ag Amastane, his *khoja* Akhammuk, the guide and interpreter Ben Messis, the poetess Dassine, and a good number of men and women whose tents formed brown molehills on the stony and burnt plain. What amusement do you think Father de Foucauld, their old friend, was offering them? A reading of La Fontaine's fables! He had handed an illustrated copy of the fables to the Captain, who presided at the meeting. M. de Saint-Léger began by translating the verses into Arabic, and commented on them. Ben Messis translated the Arabic into Tuareg, and he had not finished speaking when bursts of laughter arose on all sides. Talks began between members of the audience; those who understood best explained *The Lion and the Rat, The Frog who wanted to become as big as an Ox,* the *Milkmaid and the Milk-jug,* to the others. They came to the officer who had the volume on his knees, in order to see the pictures. After La Fontaine, an artist among artists who wrote for the simplest and most refined of men, had thus amused the assembly of Hoggar nomads, there was, as in Paris, " an hour's music."

Fête-days were followed by ordinary days, days of overwork. One can judge of the undiminished ardour of the scholar and the piety of the monk by these simple lines which I take from his diary:

"*May* 8, 1914.—Began to make a fair copy of the *whole* Tuareg-French dictionary."

"*Same date.*—Received permission this evening, and put the reserved Host in the tabernacle."

"*July* 31.—This evening reached page 385 of the dictionary."

"*August* 31.—Reached page 550."

Suddenly the great news reaches Hoggar: war is declared between Germany and France. The diary shows material proof of the emotion it caused; nothing but notes in telegraphic style. I copy a few, which tell of the first arrangements made by the young French officers in the Sahara, and the immediate attacks upon the natives friendly to us.

"*September 3rd,* 5 *a.m.*—Express to hand from Fort Motylinski, telling me that Germany has declared war on France, invaded Belgium, attacked Liége. M. de La Roche (commander of the station) starts on the 4th or 5th for Adrar, with all his band. He orders Afegzag to muster a *gum,* and Musa to come with at least twenty men, into Ahaggar.[1]

"Saw Afegzag; he orders 10 Dag-Rali, 10 Iklam, 10 Aguh-n-Tabli, 10 Aït-Lohen, 10 Kel-Tazulet, to muster immediately; personally, he sets out this evening for Motylinski, where he will be to-morrow morning.

---

[1] The *amenokal* was far away, in the Tassili of Hoggar, near Tin-Zauaten (to the south-west of Hoggar); he had only a very small number of his people with him.

"*September* 7.—M. de La Roche and Corporal Garnier arrive at 9 a.m. M. de La Roche will set out to-morrow for Adrar."

"*September* 9.—Received 1,500 cartridges of 1874 for Musa."

"*September* 10.—Courier from In-Salah; letter from de Saint-Léger and official news. I take note of it, and send at once to Fort Motylinski."[1]

"*September* 11.—Noon post to hand. Captain de Saint-Léger orders M. de La Roche to remain at Ahaggar with his whole force. I forward the order by express. Bad news; we are retreating all along the frontier, before superior forces. We cannot help Belgium. The Germans occupy Brussels."

"*September* 24.—Received news on September 11 from In-Salah and on 3rd from Paris. Always falling back; Government sits at Bordeaux."

"*September* 30.—This evening page 700 of the dictionary."

"*October* 12.—Victory! a great victory, apparently decisive! The Germans had driven our army of the north back to the Marne, even beyond the Marne. . . . Then from September 8 to 12, a general battle which lasted five days took place on the whole course of the Marne. . . ."[2]

Four days later a letter from Musa, written from Tin-Zaouaten and brought by a *mehari* rider, said that he was nearly carried off by a party of Uled-Jerir, which surrounded their camp with thorn branches and fired copper bullets. Warned by the messenger's sister who had escaped from their hands, the *amenokal* had set out in the night for the nearest Kel-Ahaggar encampment. He had only six men with him. He left two of them as rear-guard, and sent on one in advance to tell his men to come and meet him. So he was saved. His opponents entered Tin-Zauaten, raided 400 camels, made ten prisoners, and then went away. But towards the middle of December, Musa started in pursuit of them. He caught them up and attacked them, twenty to twenty, on this side of Bir-

---

[1] Captain de Saint-Léger at that time commanded the Saharan Company of In-Salah.
[2] Letter to Sergeant Garnier, of the Saharan Company of Tidikelt.

Zemile, killed seven of their men, carried off all the captured camels and *meharis*, and left his enemies to die of thirst in the desert.

The attempt against Musa was only the precursor of more serious events and more direct attacks. Armed bands, recruited in Tripoli, would no doubt soon try to enter into our territories; emissaries would be launched across the Sahara preaching the holy war against us, and none of our friendly tribes who were faithful would escape temptation. From the first day Charles de Foucauld foresaw it. What would he do? Would he shut himself up in the fortified post of Motylinski, as he was invited to do? Not for a moment did he think of it. His immediate duty was to stay where he was and to live just as he was living; he had a smile for all, he gave to all as he had done, and suffered a great sorrow without anyone seeing it.

"The Tuaregs do not know Germany even by name. . . . You know what it costs me to be so far away from our soldiers and the frontier; but my duty is evidently to remain here, to help to keep the population calm. I shall not leave Tamanrasset until the peace. . . . Every nine days a special messenger, carrying official despatches, will be sent to us. The official despatches take twenty-five days to come from Paris, the letters and papers forty; the latest letter to hand from Paris is yours of August 4, the last official despatches (which come by telegraph as far as El-Golea) are of August 20. Nothing is changed outwardly in my peaceful and regular life, *because the natives must not see any show of excitement or of an unusual state of things.* . . ."[1]

However, this man, ever haunted by the thought of the best, wanted to be confirmed in the resolution he had formed of staying at Ahaggar. No doubt his duty clearly seemed to be there, where none could replace him. But some friend or soldier might think otherwise. The hermit therefore wrote to General Laperrine, who was "prudent" and in the first line of battle, and also knew about things African. He asked: "Should I not do more good at the front as chaplain or stretcher-bearer? If you don't tell me to come, I shall wait here till peace comes; if you tell me to come, I shall set out on the spot, and speedily."[2] By return of post, two months later, he got this reply: "Wait."

The question was settled provisionally. I say provision-

---
[1] Letters of September 13 and October 5, 1914.
[2] Letter of December 14.

ally, because a year later Charles de Foucauld heard that priests were fighting, and, supposing that a dispensation might have been granted, he asked again. "And shall I not be one of them? If only I might serve!"

The correspondence between the two great Saharans, the monk and the soldier, began at the beginning of the war and went on till one of them disappeared. I have been through forty-one of Father de Foucauld's letters to his friend, from December, 1914, up to November 16, 1916, and which the General had carefully classified. They are quite military. They tell all he knows of the friendly and hostile tribes and their movements, of intrigues entered into by the Senussi, who were closely linked with the Turks of Tripoli and with the Germans; of sudden attacks and the whole of the news of the desert. When opportunity offered, he took the side of his clients, the nomads, who complained of certain delays or excesses of the administration. His decisions were always clear and firm. When the danger of a rising or an attack became pressing, he said: "This is what I should do." And no doubt in more than one case his advice was followed by Laperrine, who, from afar, exercised his right of counsel in our African matters. In any case, the great chief was warned.

Letters addressed to others during this war period gave expression above all to his inner life. They were often very fine in their patriotic tone, their invariable and resolute hope, their note of authority, also in the secret and repressed anxiety they sometimes suggest. He said: "As soon as the post comes in, I count the days until the next one." I think that by selecting passages from these letters and arranging them in order of date, I shall give a picture of the two last years of Père de Foucauld's life, free from repetition, and better than the most careful summary would be.

"*September* 15, 1914.—In spirit and prayer I am at the frontier."

"*October* 21, 1914.—This is the war for Europe's independence of Germany. And the way in which the war is carried on shows how necessary it was, how great was Germany's power, and how it was time to break the yoke before she became still more formidable; it shows by what barbarians Europe was half enslaved, and near becoming completely so, and how necessary it is once for all to deprive of force a nation which uses it so badly and in such an immoral and dangerous way for others. It is Germany and Austria that wanted war, and it is they who deserved to have it made against them, and who, I hope, will receive a blow that will make them unable to do any harm for centuries."

"*December* 7, 1914.—The Tripoli disturbance has not crossed the frontier. We cannot thank God enough for the numberless favours that He has bestowed on the eldest daughter of His Church; not the least is the fidelity of our colonies. . . .

"The confidence of the Tuaregs in me keeps on increasing. The work of the slow preparation for the Gospel is pursued. May the Almighty soon make the hour strike for you to send workers into this part of your field. . . ."[1]

"*February* 20, 1915.—The south of Tripoli is disturbed; Saint-Léger and 200 or 300 soldiers are on the frontier, to prevent bands in revolt against the Italians from breaking into our territory. Only one French adjutant and six or seven native soldiers remain at Fort Motylinski. This adjutant is a capital fellow. We often write to each other, but we rarely see one another; being alone, he cannot leave his post, and I, having a great deal to do, cannot move from here without serious reason. I have not been to Fort Motylinski for two years."

"*February* 21, 1915.—Like you, I find that the work (to pray for the conversion of our colonial infidels) is more indispensable than ever, now that so many of our infidel subjects give their blood for us. The loyalty and courage with which our subjects serve us show everyone that more must be done for them than we have done in the past. The first duty is the one we know—the salvation of souls; but everything is bound up together, and many things which don't properly involve the action of priests and monks are very important for the good of souls: their education, their good civil administration, their close contact with honest French people, for some their settling down and an increase of material welfare. Also I should like our 'union,' which ought before everything to urge each of us to unite ourselves to our Lord and to be filled with His spirit, living according to His will and grace, also to urge each one to do, according to his conditions and means, all that he can for the salvation of the infidels of our colonies."

"*March* 12, 1915.—Like you, I hope that from the great evil of this war will go forth a great blessing to souls—a

[1] Letter to Mgr. Livinhac, Superior-General of the White Fathers.

blessing in France, where the sight of death will inspire serious thoughts, and where the accomplishment of duty in the greatest sacrifices will uplift souls and purify them, bringing them nearer to Him who is the uncreated good, and make them more fit to see the truth and stronger to live in conformity with it;—a blessing to our Allies, who in coming nearer to us come nearer to Catholicism, and whose souls, like ours, are purified by sacrifice—a blessing to our infidel subjects, who, fighting in crowds on our soil, learn to know us and get nearer to us, and whose loyal devotion will stir up the French to work for them more than in the past, and govern them better than in the past."

"*April* 15, 1915.—Saint-Léger leaves In-Salah, and takes command of another Saharan company, that of Twat. . . . He is replaced by another friend, also very much liked, Captain Duclos, whom I knew there as lieutenant, an officer of great worth and fine character. . . . I constantly see Uksem. Marie asks me if he knits: he knits wonderfully, and all the young people in his encampment and village have begun to knit and crochet under his directions; knitted socks, and crocheted vests and caps. That took a long time, but since his return, thanks to one of his sisters-in-law who set about it with a great deal of good-will, it started, and everybody is beginning it."

"*July* 15, 1916.—*St. Henry.*—A happy feast to you, my dear Laperrine, I am thinking of you, and praying very much for you to-day. . . .

"The Tuaregs here remember you, speak of you, and love you as if you had left the Sahara yesterday.

"I am well; in spite of the drought and locusts, the gardens in Tamanrasset are increasing; there is not a single *zareba* now left; there are only houses, several of which have chimneys. Some *harratins* are beginning to learn a little French; they come of their own accord and ask me, nearly every evening, how such or such a word is said. Nearly all the Dag-Rali women in the vicinity of Tamanrasset and a certain number of *harratins* know how to knit socks, caps, and vests, to the great joy of the old and of not a few of the young people. . . ."

"*August* 2, 1915.—My dear Laperrine, thanks for your letter of June 14, which came last night. I am delighted to know that you are well. May God bless you and protect France! I lead my ordinary life in a great apparent calmness, but in spirit I am at the front with you and your soldiers. After the abridged Tuareg-French dictionary, and the dictionary of proper names, now the larger Tuareg-French dictionary is finished and ready to be printed. I have just begun copying poetry for the press. ... It seems strange at so grave a time to be spending my days copying out pieces of verse!

"The *Echo de Paris* tells me of the enemy having killed Father Rivet, a Jesuit, professor at the Roman College, who in 1893 resigned his commission in the Chasseurs Alpins. ... It seems to me that he must at least be forty-five, and he must have served, not as a conscript, but as a volunteer: the paper says that he was made lieutenant to the legion. ... I did not think a priest was allowed by the laws of the Church to enlist, although he is obliged to go to the regiment when he is called up. There may have been recent pontifical decisions with which I am not acquainted. None could know better than Father Rivet, a professor of canon law.[1] Should the laws of the Church permit me to enlist, would it be better for me to do so? If so, how am I to set about enlisting and getting sent to the front (for it is much better to be here than in a depôt or an office). Between the little unit that I am and zero, there is very little difference, but there are times when everybody ought to come forward. ... Reply without delay; by the same post I am writing to ask whether the Church authorizes anyone in my position to enlist."

"*August* 2, 1915.—A young negro who knows Ghardaïa, the Fathers and Sisters, told me a few days ago: '*When the Sisters come here I shall put my wife with them, so that she may learn to weave, and I shall ask to be their gardener.*' ... The time is near when the Sisters will be received by the natives with great gratitude, above all by the settled cultivators. ... Will God arrange things in such a way as to bring the White Fathers and the White Sisters here?"

"*September* 7, 1915.—To-morrow will be the feast of the nativity of the Blessed Virgin, ten years since my Tamanrasset hermitage was built and I have said Mass

[1] The information which reached Father de Foucauld was not correct. Father Rivet, a professor of canon law at Rome, was mobilized because his class was called up; he had obeyed, but to show his respect for the ecclesiastical law which forbids Churchmen to shed blood, he had decided in attacks, as an officer could do, to go against the enemy with only a stick in his hand.

in it. I owe much thanksgiving and gratitude to God for all the graces He has bestowed on me here."

"*October* 13, 1915.—Thank you, my dear Laperrine, for your letter of August 24, and for the very pretty tricolour badge, ' the hope and salvation of France,' you have sent me; it reached me safely, it is in front of me on my table, a souvenir of you in this great year."

"*November* 19, 1915.—The courier from Azjer has not yet come in. But I hear this : the Dehibat post of Tunis is attacked by the Senussi, commanded by officers in khaki uniforms, with field-glasses and revolvers (Germans, no doubt). General Moinier has sent reinforcements. The situation is serious on all the Tunis-Tripoli frontier."[1]

"*January,* 1916.—Never have I felt as much as now the happiness of being French; we both know that there are many unhappy things in France; but in the present war she is defending the world and future generations against the moral barbarism of Germany.

"For the first time I really understand the Crusades; the present war, like the preceding Crusades, will have the result of preventing our descendants from becoming barbarians. It is a blessing that cannot be too dearly paid for."[2]

"*March* 6, 1916.—Uksem is still far away, they have no more need of him to learn to crochet and knit; all the young women and girls and the greater part of the children, and not a few men in the neighbourhood, know how to do it; your parcel of wool and cotton has provided work for many fingers. . . .

"They are at present actively working at a road for motors between Wargla and In-Salah.

"Besides this, in a year we shall have a wireless station at Motylinski. Militarily and administratively, this progress is very favourable, and politically too; these works show the natives that nothing is changed in France, and that France carries on the war without difficulty or uneasiness."

---

[1] Letter to General Laperrine. Here I notice two things : the first that the General used to write to his friend *by every mail.* In the second place, that these mails reached Tamanrasset every eighteenth day, bringing news forty or sixty days old ; but from the middle of 1916 they became a little more frequent, and a mail arrived every fortnight. Official telegrams took about twenty-two days to reach Tamanrasset.
[2] Letter to General Mazel.

"*April* 10, 1916.—My dear Laperrine, it appears that when you went with Musa to Fihrun's, on coming back from Niamey, Fihrun proposed to Musa to assassinate you with your escort. As Musa refused, Fihrun reproached him with having no courage. Musa answered him: ' Thou followest thy way, I mine; in a few years from now, we shall see which of the two is the better.' I heard this from Uksem, chief of the *Dag*-Rali; I believe it is true, and my gratitude and affection for Musa is greatly increased."

On April 11 there was another letter to the General. The French fort of Janet, on the Tripoli frontier, was surrounded at the beginning of March by more than 1,000 Senussi armed with a cannon and mitrailleuses. Behind the ramparts there were only fifty men, commanded by Quartermaster Lapierre. It is rumoured in the desert that the little garrison held out as long as it could, and that, after eighteen days' siege, the outworks being destroyed, the soldiers nearly all wounded, the only well filled up, the non-commissioned officer in command had the fort blown up. "The Senussi have the road free to come here," adds Father de Foucauld. "By this word 'here' I do not mean Tamanrasset, where I am alone, but Fort Motylinski, the capital of the country, which is thirty miles from Tamanrasset. If my advice is followed, we shall all come through if attacked. I have advised a retreat with all the munitions and stores to an impregnable place well supplied with water in the mountains, where we can hold out indefinitely and against which cannon is useless. If they do not follow my advice and are attacked, God knows what will happen. . . . But I think that they will follow my advice; I shall do everything in my power to get them to do so. Don't be uneasy if you are without a letter for some time; it may happen that our messengers will be intercepted without any misfortune having happened to us for all that. I am in daily correspondence with the commander of Fort Motylinski, Sub-Lieutenant Constant. If I think it useful, I shall go and pay him short visits; if he is attacked I shall join him. The population is all right. . . . We are in the hands of God; nothing happens except what He permits."

A clear-sighted decision and worthy of Charles de Foucauld. Not to leave Tamanrasset, nor the poor *harratins,* for the insufficient reason that there may, from one moment to another, be an incursion attempted by the Senussi; but if the soldiers of Fort Motylinski are the first to be attacked, to join them. In either case, to be at the danger-point. While awaiting probable events to seek a place in the mountains, easy to fortify and defend, even against cannon; also while waiting, to make no change in his habits, "to keep confident and smiling." It is not only in France we see that Frenchmen kept smiling; they did so in the Sahara, and that without getting the order of the day.

The very next day Charles made the journey from Tamanrasset to Fort Motylinski, to choose the defensive position to which the little garrison of the *borj* would retire in case of attack. He had pointed out four of them, and he knew every stone in the country.[1] With Sub-Lieutenant Constant he discovered a fifth only a few miles from Motylinski, and he reminded the General, the other great Saharan, of it thus : " Those narrow gorges, where the Tarhauhaut valley is buried; those gorges at the entrance of which there is a thick forest of *berdis* (that is to say, reeds), and then running water for over two miles between the very steep sides. It has been agreed that Constant will put the *berdi* in a state of defence, and a part of the gorges downstream, by means of trenches and firing shelters, and transport stores and munitions, and set a guard there, and betake himself there on the first alarm. Fortunately, Constant has at this moment four other Frenchmen—two good quartermasters, a corporal of the Engineer Corps, and a private soldier—and thirty native soldiers, one of whom is the excellent non-commissioned officer Belaïd. With this number of rifles thus surrounded, and the strong position chosen, he can defend himself advantageously against very numerous enemies, and cannon has no power over him."[2]

Charles de Foucauld's absence only lasted forty-eight hours. He returned to his post without garrison or defence; to the hermitage. The news of the taking of Janet had already spread. The messenger, like all the desert messengers, was questioned, and, like a rural postman, he told what he knew. The chief of the tribe of the *D*ag-Rali *imrad* at once hastened to the marabout's. Musa's representative followed him there. He was first of all upset, but a few words from Chief Uksem, and Father de Foucauld's tranquil countenance restored his confidence. The three men took counsel together and made

---
[1] These details and many others—in a word, the whole preparation for the defence—are given in a letter of April 9 to Commander Meynier.
[2] Letter to General Laperrine, April 27, 1916.

some preparations; it was agreed, for instance, that vedette posts should be established in five places, so that Tamanrasset and Motylinski might be informed of the enemy's approach.

By degrees more exact accounts of the taking of Janet reached the valley. No, Quartermaster Lapierre did not blow up the fort. After a fine defence of twenty-one days, having no more stores, no longer able to get to the well of the dismantled redoubt, he made a sortie, on the night of March 24. His little troop wandered about the desert for three days, hoping to meet some French detachment. After that it was surrounded by the Fellagas and captured. The quartermaster was ordered to pronounce the form of abjuration; he refused. Nevertheless, he was not killed, but led into captivity, first into the Janet oasis, then to Rhât, afterwards to Fezzan. The story was more truthful, but danger was no less great on that account. The officers of our posts and Father de Foucauld expected that the tribes in revolt, proud of having captured a fortress from the French, and excited by agitators from Tripoli, were preparing fresh attacks.

"*May* 15.—Complete victory is indispensable, otherwise everything would have to be begun over again in a few years, and probably under less favourable conditions, for God has visibly protected us. The resistance of Belgium, the alliance of England and Russia, the coming in of Italy, the fidelity of our colonies and the English colonies, are, among others, among many others, exceptional graces on which one cannot reckon. These graces ought to give us every hope, for God has without doubt bestowed them on us because He wills us to conquer and protect the world against the inundation of German paganism which threatened it; what would become of our Latin nations, if victorious Germany imposed Germanic education on them? What liberty would remain to the Church, if the German Emperor had triumphed? The Allies, wishing it or not, knowing it or not, carry on a real crusade. They are fighting not only for the freedom of the world, but for the freedom of the Church and the upholding of Christian morals in the world.[1]

"*May* 30, 1916.—The Saint-Cyr commissions of my time are serving the fatherland well: Mazel, d'Urbal, and Pétain are among them. My seniors, too: Maud'huy, Serrail, Driant."

[1] Letter to M. de Blic.

"*Whit-Monday*.[1]—Every year the month of June brings in the anniversary of my ordination, and renews and increases my gratitude to you who adopted me and made me a priest of Jesus Christ. With my whole heart I pray for you. More than fifteen years ago you accepted me as a son, and I also pray for your beloved diocese of Viviers.

"In body I am here, where I shall remain till peace comes, believing I am more useful here than elsewhere; but how often my spirit is in France at the front, where the struggle must be at this moment more ardent than ever, and behind the lines, where so many families are weeping for their most beloved, or are in mortal anxiety.

"Around me, the native population is calm and faithful; its attitude is excellent.

"I still greatly desire to see the confraternity started in France for the conversion of the French colonies, the scheme of which you were good enough to approve. During this Whitsuntide I think more than ever of the fifty millions of native infidels in our colonies. May the Holy Ghost set up His reign in their souls, and may the French, who ask for this help to defend their own temporal fatherland, help them to obtain the eternal fatherland!"

The threats were too serious for the military authorities not to think of protecting Father de Foucauld and the Tuaregs or their servants, who were friendly to us and inhabited Tamanrasset. At the beginning of 1916, on the plans and under the direction of the Father, they had begun the construction of a small fort. The hermit changed his abode on June 23. He thus went from the left to the right bank of the Wady Tamanrasset, and was nearer the village houses. We shall see that all precautions had been taken to enable the little fortress to stand a siege.

It formed a square measuring about twenty feet on the sides; surrounded by a ditch two yards deep. At the angles it was strengthened by four bastions provided with embrasures, the terrace of which was reached by a staircase. The walls, in *toubes,* were two yards thick at the base, and over sixteen feet high. There was no opening outside, except a very low door. The danger lay there; the door might be forced; the enemy might slip into the place by surprise. This had been guarded against as much as possible. The first door prevented a man from entering upright; he had to stoop; besides, it did not give direct admission to the fort, but to a brick corridor, so narrow

[1] Letter to Mgr. Bonnet, Bishop of Viviers.

that only one man could pass; and it was closed by a second low door. Then, just opposite the outside opening, and to prevent attacks with stones or pikes, they had built a solid small wall on the platform, very close to the façade, so that it was impossible to fire from outside at a person in front of the entrance door. Furthermore, the latter was also defended by two bastions at the angles. A cross made of two tamarisk branches was planted on the top of the wall over the door. Lastly, for crossing the ditch there remained a ridge of earth ending to the left of the small protection wall. The inside was arranged so as to receive a considerable band of refugees and combatants.

Lieutenant L——, who was then staying at Tamanrasset, thus describes the various parts of the fortified hermitage :[1]

"In the centre of the yard, about thirteen feet square, was a well about twenty feet deep, covered with a thick door strengthened by plates of sheet-iron. Plenty of water. All around, pretty spacious rooms, all of them rectangular.

"One was used by the Father as a chapel; another reserved for passing guests; another was used to store provisions, cotton stuffs, etc., which the Father reserved for the Tuaregs; lastly, a fourth constituted the Father's private apartment: it was at once bedroom, study, and dining-room, all on the same footing and giving their true meaning to the words as used by Father de Foucauld.

"The study alone deserved its name: books everywhere, manuscripts scattered over the little table, made out of packing-cases, that served as a bureau.

"Thus built, the little fort is impregnable against a band armed with rifles; to scale it is almost impossible, and two men, or even one man armed with grenades, would be enough for its defence."

"*June* 16, 1916.—The Senussi danger appears to be turned aside for the moment. Our Janet fort on the Tripoli frontier was taken by the Senussi on March 24, and retaken by our troops on May 16: our soldiers pursued the flying enemy. As long as the Italians have not retaken all the south of Tripoli, which they have evacuated, our Tripoli frontier will be threatened, and a serious watch will be necessary: let us hope it will be kept up. They are distant countries; when the authorities who reside at Algiers are spoken to, they only half believe what they are told,

---

[1] The building was only finished on October 15.

only grant half what is asked for, and consent to take the necessary measures only after an accident has happened."

"*July* 16, 1916.—Such isolated missionaries as I am are very few. Their rôle is to prepare the way, so that the missions which replace them will find a friendly and trustful population, souls somewhat prepared for Christianity, and, if possible, a few Christians. You have partly set forth their duties in your article in the *Echo de Paris:* ' The greatest service.'[1] We must get ourselves accepted by the Musulmans, become their sure friends, to whom they come when in doubt or trouble; on whose affection, wisdom, and justice they can absolutely rely. It is only when we arrive at this point that we shall come to do good to their souls.

"Therefore my life consists in having the greatest possible intercourse with those who surround me, and in rendering all the services I can. As soon as intimacy is established, I speak, always or nearly always, in a *tête-à-tête,* of our good God, and briefly giving each man what he can bear: avoidance of sin, a perfect act of love, a perfect act of contrition, the two great commandments of the love of God and of our neighbour, examination of conscience, meditation on the last things, the creature's duty of thinking of God, etc., giving to each according to his strength, and going on slowly and prudently.

"There are very few isolated missionaries fulfilling this pioneer work; I wish there were many of them : every parish priest in Algeria, Tunis, or Morocco, every military chaplain, every pious catholic layman, could be one. The Government forbids the secular clergy to carry on anti-Musulman propaganda; but it is not a question of open and more or less noisy propaganda; friendly intercourse with many natives, tending to induce Musulmans slowly, gently, and silently to come closer to Christians and become their friends. This nobody can be forbidden to do. Every parish priest in our colonies could exert himself to train his male and female parishioners to be Priscillas and Aquilas. There is quite a loving and discreet propaganda to be carried on among the infidel natives—a propaganda which requires as great kindness, love and prudence, as when we wish to bring a relation who has lost the Faith back to God. . . .

" Let us hope that when we have won the war our colonies will make fresh progress. What a beautiful mission for our younger sons of France, to go and colonize the African

---

[1] Letter to Réne Bazin.

territories of the mother-country, not to get rich, but to make France beloved, to make souls French, and above all to obtain eternal salvation for them.

"I think that if the Musulmans of our colonial empire of North Africa are not converted gradually and gently, a national movement like that of Turkey will come about; an intellectual élite will be formed in the large towns, educated à la Française, but having neither the French mind nor heart, an élite which will have lost all the faith of Islam, but which will keep the label in order to be able to use it to influence the masses. On the other hand, the crowd of nomads and countrymen will remain ignorant, estranged from us, firmly Mahometan, incited to hatred and contempt of the French by their religion, their marabouts, and by their contact with the French (representatives of authority, colonists, merchants)—contacts which too often are not apt to make them love us. National or barbarian feeling will therefore become worked up in the educated élite; when it finds an opportunity—for instance, at a time of France's difficulties at home or abroad—it will make use of Islam as a lever to rouse the ignorant mass, and seek to create an independent Musulman African Empire.

"The French North-West African Empire—Algeria, Morocco, Tunis, French Western Africa, etc.—has a population of thirty millions; it will, thanks to peace, have double in fifty years. It will then be in full material progress, rich, intersected with railways, inhabited by people trained to the use of arms, the élite of which will have received its education in our schools. If we have not been able to make these people French, they will drive us out. The only means of making them French is for them to become Christians."[1]

"*August* 31, 1916.—From here to In-Salah the motor-road is finished or very nearly finished. The first motor that comes here will be a joy to me : it puts a finish to our taking possession of the country. This road should be carried on to the Sudan : it is only four hundred and forty miles from here to Agades, the first Sudan post—the same distance as from here to In-Salah : four months' work.[2] This would be an enormous advantage for administration and defence, and an enormous economy.

[1] The paragraph is the repetition, almost word for word, of a passage in a letter written in 1912 to the Duc de Fitz-James. His longer experience only strengthened the conviction of the witness.
[2] The first motor reached In-Salah on August 11.

"*September* 1, 1916.[1]—The corner of the Sahara from which I write to you, my dear Mazel, is still calm. However, we are on the *qui vive,* on account of the increasing agitation of the Senussi in Tripoli; our Tuaregs here are faithful, but we might be attacked by the Tripolitans. I have transformed my hermitage into a little fort; there is nothing new under the sun. When I see my embrasures I think of the fortified convents and churches of the tenth century. How old things come back, and how what we thought had disappeared is for ever reappearing! They have given me six cases of cartridges and thirty Gras rifles, which remind me of our youth. . . .

"I am pleased that you have our brave Laperrine under your orders; I hope that you will long have him. It is to him we owe the peace of the Algerian Sahara: the wisdom and vigour of his acts, and the incomparable memory he left behind, are the cause of the fidelity of these reputedly troublesome populations.

"Enclosed is the translation of a prayer of the ninth century, which has probably been said and sung more than once in Rheims Cathedral :

"' Almighty and eternal God, who hast established the empire of the Franks to do Thy holy will in the world, and to be the glory and rampart of Thy holy Church, let Thy heavenly light shine everywhere and always upon the praying sons of the Franks, so that they may see what they should do to extend Thy kingdom in the world, and that they may ever increase in charity and valour, to fulfil what Thy light hath shown them.'"

"*September* 15, 1916.—Unfortunately, the news from the Tripoli frontier is bad. . . . Without having suffered a check, our troops are falling back before the Senussi: they are not now on the frontier, but a long way this side of it; after recapturing Janet, they have evacuated it; they have evacuated some other points. This retreat before a few hundred rifles is lamentable. There must be (how far up I don't know) some serious error in the command. It is clear that if we fall back without any fighting the Senussi will advance. If the method is not promptly changed, they will get here some day. I regret worrying you again, but dear truth wills that I should tell you this."

"*September* 24, 1916.—A few days ago we had a great alarm. News came that we were to be attacked; but the

---

[1] To General Mazel, commanding the Fifth Army.

news was false; nothing turned up, and yesterday's news shows that, on the contrary, the situation is very good. The alarm only served to prove the fidelity of the population; far from looking like going over to the enemy, they gathered round the officer in command of the neighbouring fort, and round me, ready to defend the fort and the hermitage. This fidelity was very pleasing, and I am very grateful to these poor people, who might have taken refuge in the mountains where they had nothing to fear, and who preferred to shut themselves up in the neighbouring fort and my hermitage, although they knew the enemy had cannon and bombardment was certain.

"*Same Period.*—By the crusade that He gets the eldest daughter of His Church to carry on, God provides the opportunity and grace for innumerable acts of virtue : acts of devotion, self-forgetfulness, charity, resignation, mercy; the sacrifice of life, happiness, and all that is dear; acts of love of God. No doubt there is also evil; evil will be mixed with good up to the end of the world; but for the two years that the war has lasted, an amount of heroic acts of virtue have been accomplished and a number of sacrifices offered to God in union with that of His Son, such as are usually produced only in a great number of years. Here is a total of merits and immolations which purify and raise France, and bring her nearer to God. I have great hope that she will come out, not only victorious, but better, much better, from this crusade."[1]

"*October* 1, 1916.—I look upon the long months during which the war detains me in the Sahara as a time of retreat, during which I pray and reflect, asking Jesus to make known to me the final shape to be given to our confraternity."

"*October* 15, 1916.—Musa, who is three hundred and seventy-five miles from here, hearing that the neighbouring fort was to be attacked, at once sent all the men he had with him that he could dispose of—about eighty—by forced marches, to help us to defend ourselves. . . . Since the beginning of the war Musa could not be better than he has unceasingly been. The condition of the people who surround me is enough to make one weep. They are so surrounded by evil and error! It is difficult for them to lead even a naturally good life! There are good natures,

[1] Letter to Colonel P. Leroy.

but in the environment in which they are, and with their ignorance, how can they be saved?"

"*October* 31, 1916.—In Azjer there has been only one military event since my last letter. About September 20, a big revictualling convoy, led by Duclos, from Flatters to Polignac, was attacked on the way at Wady Ehen by three hundred Senussi commanded by an ex-corporal of the Tidikelt Company, for several years in revolt. The Senussi were defeated with serious losses; all the loads of the convoy arrived safely at Polignac. On our side there were some killed and wounded; amongst the killed, an excellent adjutant, Lenoir, had a bullet through his heart: he was carried to Polignac and buried there. The defeated Senussi retired in haste in the direction of Admer.

"Did I tell you that about forty days ago a little *rezzu* (twenty men) of Kel-Azjer operated on the Tefedest (Eastern Slope) at Amrah? We were pretty long without any accurate details of it: I have just received some. It only raided a hundred of the Kel-Inrar camels and rapidly fell back. Up to the present there have been no other enemy *rezzus* against Ahaggar, and, if things go all right in Azjer, there will be none.

"A rather big Senussi *rezzu* operated in the north of Aïr; instead of raiding, they told the people to 'move and come and settle down altogether at Fezzan with us, and we shall do you no harm; if you refuse we shall raid you.' Some Kel-Aïr accepted and followed them in revolt; the Sudan tirailleurs of Agades overtook them, beat the Senussi, and brought back the revolters. Some Kel-Ahaggar, who happened to be on the way of the Senussi's *rezzu*, pretended to accept their terms and followed them for a day or two; then at night, eluding their watch, set out by forced marches towards Adrar and escaped them."[1]

"*November* 16, 1916.—How good God is to hide the future from us! What a torture life would be were it less unknown to us! and how good He is to make so clearly known to us the heaven hereafter which will follow our earthly time of trial!"

The writer of these lines had only two weeks to live. He did not know it, but he was ready to receive death any day from the hands of those for whom he had so much prayed, walking so far over the sand and pebbles, suffering so

[1] Letter to General Laperrine.

severely from thirst and heat, working so many days and nights, in so much solitude, and for whom, in short, he had toiled so hard with body and mind. The following letters express his last thoughts; his resolution appears in them as well as his charity. These letters, among others, were found in the small fort at Tamanrasset after his assassination: they must have been given on December 1, 1916, to the *méhari* rider arriving from Motylinski, and going on to In-Salah, after stopping at the hermitage.

"*November 28, 1916 (to the Prioress of the Poor Clares of Nazareth, who had fled to Malta).*—France, in spite of appearances, is still the France of Charlemagne, St. Louis, and Jeanne d'Arc; the old soul of the nation lives on in our generation: the saints of France are always praying for her; the gifts of God are without repentance, and the people of Saint-Rémi and Clovis are still the people of Christ. . . . In choosing France for the birthplace of the devotion to the Sacred Heart and the apparitions of Lourdes, our Lord has clearly shown that He keeps France's rank of the first-born for her.

"I can regularly say Holy Mass every day. I have another happiness: that of having the reserved Sacrament in my little chapel. I am always by myself. Some Frenchmen come to see me from time to time: every thirty or forty days I see one of them on his way.

"We live in days when the soul strongly feels the need of prayer. In the tempest which is blowing over Europe we feel the nothingness of the creature, and turn to the Creator. In the bark tossed about by the billows we turn to the divine Master, and implore Him who can give victory with a word, and restore a great and durable peace. We raise our hands to heaven as Moses did during the battle of his people, and where man is powerless we pray to Him who is almighty. Before the Blessed Sacrament we feel so clearly in the presence of real Being, when all that is created appears so plainly bordering upon nothingness!

"Pray very much, most Reverend Mother, for the poor infidels who surround me and for their poor missionary. With you, I pray for France."

December 1, 1916.—A reply to an officer, a military interpreter of the army of the East, who had written from Monastir of his decision to go into a regiment of colonial infantry, and asked Father de Foucauld for a prayer:

"Very dear Brother in Jesus,

"I have this morning received your letters of October 3 and 9, moved by the thought of the greater dangers that you are perhaps going to meet, that you probably are already incurring. You have done quite right in asking to join the troops. We must never hesitate to ask for posts in which danger, sacrifice, and devotion are greatest: let us leave honour to any who desire it, but let us always ask for danger and toil. As Christians we should give an example of self-sacrifice and devotion. It is a principle to which we must be faithful all our life, in simplicity, without asking ourselves whether pride does not enter into our conduct: it is our duty, let us do it, and ask the well-beloved Spouse of our soul that we may do it in all humility, in all love of God and our neighbour. . . .

"Don't be anxious about your home. Trust yourself and it to God, and walk in peace. If God preserves your life, which with my whole heart I ask Him to do, your home will be more blessed because, sacrificing yourself more, you will be more united to Jesus, and will have a more supernatural life. If you die, God will keep your wife and son without you, as He would have kept them through you. Offer your life to God through the hands of our Mother, the most Blessed Virgin, in union with the sacrifice of our Lord Jesus Christ, and with all the intentions of His Heart, and walk in peace. Be sure that God will give you the best lot for His own glory, the best for your soul, the best for the souls of others, since that is all you ask of Him, since you will fully and without any reservation all that He wills for you.

"Our corner of the Sahara is peaceful. I pray for you with my whole heart, and at the same time for your home.

"This will reach you about Christmas and the 1st of January. Look for me quite near you on those two days. A happy and holy New Year to you; many holy New Years, if it be God's will; and then heaven! God guard you and protect France! May Jesus, Mary and Joseph between them guard you in all your life on earth, at the hour of death, and in eternity.

"I embrace you, as I love you in the Heart of Jesus.
"Ch. de Foucauld."

Father de Foucauld was certain he would be attacked, and he had long desired to die for his lost sheep. He continued to live alone and in peace. Not a shadow of uneasiness dimmed the joyful expression of his face. He even spoke to his friends of plans far ahead, because we are made for constant rebirth and fresh starts, and we always arrange our lives for a longer time than we have to live.

In the middle of 1915 he had finished the Tuareg-French dictionary; on October 28, 1916, the diary says: "Finished the Tuareg poems." The hermit had resolved to return to France as soon as he had heard of victory, and to remain there as many months as would be necessary to plant firmly the Confraternity of Prayer for the infidels in a generous land: then to return to Ahaggar and give himself up more completely and directly to the religious apostolate, to preparing the way of Christ, now that the tools of conversion were ready, the methods tried, and that he had perceived the first blades of the coming harvest.

God had only made him for sowing. Charles de Foucauld never saw the victory; he never saw France again; he went among the good servants whom God receives and thanks, because they have saved their souls and taken care of the souls of others.

In order to understand better the causes that led to the death of Father de Foucauld, we must recapitulate the political and military situation of the Eastern Sahara at this time. To the south of Tripoli, in Fezzan, Si Mohamed Labed, the Senussi religious chief, had his headquarters, and had assembled in his camp our enemies the Azjer Tuaregs. Senussi, Azjers, outlawed partisans, whom the Hoggars called by the common name of *Fellagas,* occupied Rhât, in Tripoli, a place abandoned by the Italians, where they found stores, material, and munitions of war. At some distance from Rhât, and in our own possessions, Janet, taken by the Fellagas, retaken by us, had been finally evacuated, on account of the insurmountable difficulty of re-victualling. A little more to the north Fort Polignac was also evacuated. A band of rebels operating on the Sudan region besieged Agades, under the command of Rhaussen. Except for a few tents scattered about the Hoggar mountains, most of the encampments depending on Musa ag Amastane were in this same region with the flocks. The *mehari* men of Fort Motylinski followed and protected them. The garrison of the Fort, thus reduced, was not very mobile, and incapable of helping Father de Foucauld and his *harratins.*

On December 1, a Friday, at nightfall, the Father was alone at home, and the door was bolted. His servant was in the village, as well as two *mehari* riders of the Motylinski post, who had come on service business, and were waiting for the night to regain the fort.

Now, a score of Fellagas were, at that moment, near Tamanrasset, and were seeking to seize the marabout whom they would have kept as a hostage, and to plunder the fortlet in which they knew there were arms and provisions. As the country was denuded of troops, they were almost sure of succeeding. Nevertheless, for their *coup de main*, they recruited some Tuareg nomads and also some *harratins*, even among those whom the Father took care of, helped and treated as brothers, and, in particular, an Amsel husbandman called El Madani. The people of the *rezzu* were armed with Italian repeating rifles (for five shots); all their auxiliaries were not armed. Together, some on foot, others on camels, advanced to within two hundred yards of the fortlet, made their camels crouch under the garden wall, and silently surrounded the dwelling of the "marabout of the *Rumis*." There were about forty of them. But they had to have a member of the Father's household with them to get the door opened. El Madani, knowing the habits and the password of his benefactor, approached the fortlet door and knocked. Soon the Father came and asked, as his custom was, who was there, and what he wanted. "It is the postman from Motylinski," was the reply. As it was, indeed, the day on which the mail went through, the Father opened the door and put out his hand. His hand was seized and firmly held. Immediately some Tuaregs, hidden close by, sprang forward and pulled the priest out of the little fort, and, with cries of victory, bound his hands behind his back and left him on the platform, between the door and the small wall that masked it, in the care of one of the men of the band, armed with a rifle. Father de Foucauld knelt down and remained motionless; he was praying.

Here I set down and combine the evidence of Paul, the negro servant, and that of another *harratin*, as they were recorded in two official reports, and I shall complete them from statements in various records.[1]

"On *December* 1, after having served the marabout's dinner, I went to my *zariba*, about five hundred yards from there. It was about 7 o'clock, and dark.

"A short time afterwards, when I had myself finished my

[1] Report of Captain de La Roche, commanding that portion of Hoggar, to the Colonel Commanding, December 6, 1916: the report of Captain Depommier, of September 11, 1917; the account of the assassination given to the Comtesse de Foucauld in May, 1917, by Captain de La Roche; information gathered at Hoggar by Lieutenant Proust; information gathered by Sub-Lieutenant Réjot, of the Agurai post, near Meknes, in January, 1918; various personal letters.

meal, two armed Tuaregs sprang into the *zariba* and said to me: 'Are you Paul, the marabout's servant? Why do you hide? Come and see with your own eyes what is happening: follow us!' I replied that I was not hiding, and that what was happening was God's will.

"On arriving near the marabout's house, I perceived the latter seated, his back to the wall, on the right of the door, his hands bound behind his back, looking straight in front of him. We did not exchange a single word. I crouched down as ordered, on the left of the door. Numerous Tuaregs surrounded the marabout; they were speaking and gesticulating, congratulating and blessing the *hartani* El Madani, who had drawn the marabout into the trap, foretelling a life of delights for him in the other world as a reward for his work. Some other Tuaregs were in the house, going in and coming out, carrying various things found in the interior—rifles, munitions, stores, *chegga* (cloth), etc. Those who surrounded the marabout pressed him with the following questions: 'When does the convoy come? Where is it? What is it bringing? Are there any soldiers in the *bled*? Where are they? Have they set out? Where are the Motylinski soldiers?' The marabout remained impassible, he did not utter a word. The same questions were then put to me, as well as to another *hartani*, who was passing in the wady and caught in the meantime.

"The whole did not last half an hour.

"The house was surrounded by sentinels. At this moment one of the sentinels gave the alarm, shouting: 'Here are the Arabs! Here are the Arabs (the soldiers of Motylinski).' At these cries, the Tuaregs, with the exception of three, two of whom remained in front of me and the other standing on guard near the marabout, went towards the place whence the cries came. A lively fusillade broke out. The Tuareg who was near the marabout brought the muzzle of his rifle close to the head of the latter and fired. The marabout neither moved nor cried. I did not think he was wounded: it was only a few minutes afterwards that I saw the blood flow, and that the marabout's body slipped slowly down upon its side. He was dead."[1]

---

[1] In Captain de La Roche's report there is a slight variation; Paul expressed himself thus: "The *hartani* (whom they were questioning) said that there were two soldiers in the *bled*, who were to leave Tamanrasset that same evening for Tarhauhaut, and that they had perhaps already set out. He had no sooner said that, than the soldiers came on their camels; they were coming to greet the marabout. The enemies entered the trenches which surround the Father's house, and all fired

"The Tuaregs were not long in returning, after having killed the two soldiers who, on their way through Tamanrasset were coming, as usual, to greet the marabout before taking the road back to Motylinski. They entirely stripped the marabout of all his effects, and threw him into the ditch which surrounds the house. They then discussed what they were going to do with the body, and whether they were going to kill me or not, *en kafer* (unbeliever) like my master. On the intervention of the *bled harratins* and their chief, who, at the noise of the firing, had run up, I was spared and set at liberty. As to the marabout, some wished to carry him off and hide him, others wanted to tie him to a tree which was not far from the house in the wady, and let him become the prey of the dogs of the Tuareg Chikkat of the *Dag*-Rali tribe, whom they knew to be the marabout's personal friend.[1]

"Lastly, other Tuaregs, who took no interest in the question, and found enough in the victuals discovered in the house to satisfy their desires, put an end to the discussion, compelling everyone to look after his own share of the booty.

"The marabout's body was momentarily forgotten. The assassins spent the night in eating and drinking. Next morning the discussion was renewed without a final solution being reached, and the marabout's body was abandoned without being mutilated.

"In the morning the Tuaregs were able to surprise and kill one more isolated soldier, who knew nothing of the drama, and came from Motylinski and was going to the marabout's with the mail from In-Salah.

"They left Tamanrasset about noon, carrying off their plunder. The *harratins* then buried the marabout and soldiers. That evening I set out to go and inform the station at Fort Motylinski, where I arrived at noon on December 3."[2]

---

together. Bu Aïsha fell at once; Bujema Ben Brahim tried to run away, but he had hardly gone sixty yards when he fell.

"The marabout, at the moment the *mehari* riders appeared, made an intuitive movement, foreseeing the fate that was reserved for them. Then . . ."

[1] "Father de Foucauld had indeed a great affection for Chikkat and his son Uksem, whom he made one of his legatees; I cannot say that such noble feelings were reciprocated. In fact, Uksem participated very actively in the rebellious movement that broke out in February among the Hoggar, two months after the assassination of Father de Foucauld." (Note by Captain Depommier.)

[2] A different reading of the same evidence, according to Captain de La Roche's report: "They ate Ben Aïsha's camel and slept there. In

Captain Depommier added the following observations to Paul's account:

"What was the object of the assassins? What feelings governed them?

"Among the primary feelings impelling the assassins, we must certainly put fanaticism, ' War on the Roumis.' For a long time, the propaganda of the Holy War had been active in the district; many of its propagators came from the east from amongst the Senussi, and had gained to their cause the Aït-Lohen, a Hoggar tribe bordering on the Azjer region. Father de Foucauld knew all about this. (Father de Foucauld himself had knowledge of a plot for his assassination hatched in September by the *hartanis* of Amsel. Papers found after his death by Captain de La Roche prove it. Father de Foucauld never mentioned this to anybody.) However, that was probably not the only cause of the assassins' conduct.

"Why did they attack Father de Foucauld alone and a priest, who had won, by a thousand acts of charity and kindness, the sympathy, if not the gratitude, of many of those who came to him? Must we see in this only the work of fanatics, and think that the latter disregarded the precepts of the Koran, which recommends the sparing of priests?

"Another cause of the crime appears much simpler. It is this. Few things were hidden at Father de Foucauld's, and everybody knew he had rifles, carbines, and munitions in store; it was a question of appropriating these arms; perhaps they might also find a big sum of money in the house of this generous benefactor. Lastly, the band were not unaware that the Motylinski garrison had been reduced to a few men, and could do nothing against them.

"But then, why did the robbers assassinate Father de Foucauld when the arms had been captured and the house was in their possession? Some of the rumours brought in might lead us to believe that it was only a matter of chance, of circumstances. Father de Foucauld's guard would not have received the order to kill him; on the contrary, Ebeh, according to the instructions received from Si-Labed, his chief, would have recommended his being kept a prisoner,

---

the morning they were preparing to go away when Kuider ben Lakhal, who was bringing the mail, arrived. The enemy took up positions, some in the ditch, others on the terrace; they fired at him, but he was not hit. Suddenly his camel *baraqued* (knelt down), they then threw themselves on Kuider and held his hands and legs. One of them shot him from behind in the head. They tore up the sack and all the papers in the mail."

" The Tuaregs were not long in returning, after having killed the two soldiers who, on their way through Tamanrasset were coming, as usual, to greet the marabout before taking the road back to Motylinski. They entirely stripped the marabout of all his effects, and threw him into the ditch which surrounds the house. They then discussed what they were going to do with the body, and whether they were going to kill me or not, *en kafer* (unbeliever) like my master. On the intervention of the *bled harratins* and their chief, who, at the noise of the firing, had run up, I was spared and set at liberty. As to the marabout, some wished to carry him off and hide him, others wanted to tie him to a tree which was not far from the house in the wady, and let him become the prey of the dogs of the Tuareg Chikkat of the *Dag-Rali* tribe, whom they knew to be the marabout's personal friend.[1]

" Lastly, other Tuaregs, who took no interest in the question, and found enough in the victuals discovered in the house to satisfy their desires, put an end to the discussion, compelling everyone to look after his own share of the booty.

" The marabout's body was momentarily forgotten. The assassins spent the night in eating and drinking. Next morning the discussion was renewed without a final solution being reached, and the marabout's body was abandoned without being mutilated.

" In the morning the Tuaregs were able to surprise and kill one more isolated soldier, who knew nothing of the drama, and came from Motylinski and was going to the marabout's with the mail from In-Salah.

" They left Tamanrasset about noon, carrying off their plunder. The *harratins* then buried the marabout and soldiers. That evening I set out to go and inform the station at Fort Motylinski, where I arrived at noon on December 3."[2]

---

together. Bu Aïsha fell at once; Bujema Ben Brahim tried to run away, but he had hardly gone sixty yards when he fell.

"The marabout, at the moment the *mehari* riders appeared, made an intuitive movement, foreseeing the fate that was reserved for them. Then . . ."

[1] " Father de Foucauld had indeed a great affection for Chikkat and his son Uksem, whom he made one of his legatees; I cannot say that such noble feelings were reciprocated. In fact, Uksem participated very actively in the rebellious movement that broke out in February among the Hoggar, two months after the assassination of Father de Foucauld." (Note by Captain Depommier.)

[2] A different reading of the same evidence, according to Captain de La Roche's report: " They ate Ben Aïsha's camel and slept there. In

Captain Depommier added the following observations to Paul's account :

" What was the object of the assassins ? What feelings governed them ?

" Among the primary feelings impelling the assassins, we must certainly put fanaticism, ' War on the Roumis.' For a long time, the propaganda of the Holy War had been active in the district; many of its propagators came from the east from amongst the Senussi, and had gained to their cause the Aït-Lohen, a Hoggar tribe bordering on the Azjer region. Father de Foucauld knew all about this. (Father de Foucauld himself had knowledge of a plot for his assassination hatched in September by the *hartanis* of Amsel. Papers found after his death by Captain de La Roche prove it. Father de Foucauld never mentioned this to anybody.) However, that was probably not the only cause of the assassins' conduct.

" Why did they attack Father de Foucauld alone and a priest, who had won, by a thousand acts of charity and kindness, the sympathy, if not the gratitude, of many of those who came to him ? Must we see in this only the work of fanatics, and think that the latter disregarded the precepts of the Koran, which recommends the sparing of priests ?

" Another cause of the crime appears much simpler. It is this. Few things were hidden at Father de Foucauld's, and everybody knew he had rifles, carbines, and munitions in store; it was a question of appropriating these arms; perhaps they might also find a big sum of money in the house of this generous benefactor. Lastly, the band were not unaware that the Motylinski garrison had been reduced to a few men, and could do nothing against them.

" But then, why did the robbers assassinate Father de Foucauld when the arms had been captured and the house was in their possession ? Some of the rumours brought in might lead us to believe that it was only a matter of chance, of circumstances. Father de Foucauld's guard would not have received the order to kill him ; on the contrary, Ebeh, according to the instructions received from Si-Labed, his chief, would have recommended his being kept a prisoner,

---

the morning they were preparing to go away when Kuider ben Lakhal, who was bringing the mail, arrived. The enemy took up positions, some in the ditch, others on the terrace ; they fired at him, but he was not hit. Suddenly his camel *baraqued* (knelt down), they then threw themselves on Kuider and held his hands and legs. One of them shot him from behind in the head. They tore up the sack and all the papers in the mail."

"Turkey, incited by Germany, wished to make the Tuaregs in the first place, then all the desert tribes, revolt against us. The agents of the policy saw very quickly that their object could not be attained if Father de Foucauld remained in the midst of the Northern Tuaregs, whence his influence radiated. They decided to seize him and keep him as a hostage, but their resolution was not, according to the General, to put him to death. A band was launched towards Tamanrasset, etc."

In fact, it seems quite probable that, as the Holy War was being preached in the whole of French Africa, the chief of the band who seized Father de Foucauld wished to get rid of the principal cause which prevented the defection of the Hoggar Tuaregs—that is to say, the great and dominating influence of the beloved hermit of Tamanrasset. If it is contended that this chief was too poor a creature to allow himself to be led by considerations of a general character, and that the allurement of gain suffices to explain his aggression and the ruffianly act of his troop, it is very easy to admit that the principal chiefs of the insurrection made use of these bandits of a second order, and associated them with vaster plans. We must think that the Musulman world obeys very well-informed chiefs, capable of very broad designs.

I ought to make several other remarks on this last act of life, death, for which our whole life prepares us, if we will. Father de Foucauld, since his conversion, never for one day stopped thinking of that hour after which there are no others, and which is the supreme opportunity offered for our repentance and acquisition of merit. He died on the first Friday of December, the day consecrated to the Sacred Heart, and in the manner that he wished, having always desired a violent death dealt in hatred of the Christian name, accepted with love for the salvation of the infidels of his land of election—Africa. Betrayed and bound, he refused to reply to the insults as well as to the questions of those who surrounded him, and said not a word again, imitating in that his divine model: *Jesus autem tacebat.* May it be maintained that he died a martyr, in the exact sense of that word, according to Catholic doctrine? Of this I shall say what I know.

Two weeks after the assassination, when the information gathered was brought to In-Salah, the rumour went about that the assassins had ordered Father de Foucauld to apostatize and recite the *shehada*—that is to say, the form of Musulman prayer—and that he had refused: a letter addressed to M. de Blic, to announce his brother-in-law's death, is the proof. Neither Captain de La Roche's report nor that of Captain Depommier mentions it. But that Father de Foucauld, during that half-hour of bad treatment and insults which he endured before being killed, was called upon to abjure, is very probable for two reasons : first, as a Saharan officer writes to me, because the contrary would be the exception with Musulmans who never separate death from the *shehada;* in the second place, because the conversation reported by the negro Paul was repeated by him in 1921. I heard, indeed, that when questioned again on the subject of the murder, Father de Foucauld's servant replied: "In my presence, the enemy simply asked: 'Where is the convoy? Where are the people?' After de Foucauld's death, I heard them say between themselves : *' He was asked to say the* shehada, *but he replied:* "*I am going to die." This last sentence was said by the Aït-Lohen, whose names I do not know.*"

To-day it appears, therefore, probable that, according to custom, Father de Foucauld was called upon to abjure. It appears certain that the assassination did not immediately follow his refusal: the arrival of the Motylinski *mehari* riders was the determining cause of his death. The first idea was to make Father de Foucauld a prisoner; an opportunity of killing him was offered, and he was killed for fear that he might escape or be delivered. However, hatred of Christians cannot be considered as unconnected with this drama, and the domestic Paul is of this opinion, since, in his evidence, he says that he also was threatened with death, *as an unbeliever.*

It must also be remarked that Father de Foucauld, having built the fortlet so that the poor people of the village might be sheltered with him, never would abandon them, and that it was therefore through his obstinate charity that he died.

When the people of the *rezzu* had retired in the direction of Debnat (west of Fort Motylinski) the victims' bodies did not remain long abandoned. The *harratins,* being no longer afraid, approached and interred the victims in the ditch of the little fort, a few yards from the place where Father de Foucauld fell. His body was not freed from the bonds by which his arms were bound, but after having deposited it in the ditch, the *harratins,* who knew the Christians put their dead into coffins, placed stones, sheets of paper, and fragments of wooden cases around the body. Then they walled up the door of the fortlet.

The first thing the commander of the Hoggar district did

was to set off in pursuit of the band of Fellagas. The *rezzu* was "hooked" on December 17, and lost several men.[1] It was only on December 21 that Captain de La Roche was able to go to Tamanrasset. He came accompanied by a sergeant and a soldier. Immediately on his arrival he went and examined the graves, and had the layer of earth which covered the bodies made thicker; he planted a cross on the Father's grave; and then had military honours paid to those who had died for France. Only then did the officer enter the fortified hermitage.

"The inside of the *kasba* had been pillaged; the bandits carried off everything of any value. The remainder was thrown into disorder, torn and partly burned. The whole library and all the papers were scattered about the room which served as chapel and room. Here are the various things found:

"Articles of worship and devotion and pious books; the four volumes of the dictionary and the two volumes of poetry could be reconstructed in their entirety; stationery, a colonial helmet, a camp-table, a camp-bed, a big thermometer; a certain number of letters written by the Father on December 1, sealed and stamped, etc."[2]

Among the "articles of worship" and the "articles of devotion" found in the fortlet, there was the Father's rosary; the Stations of the Cross made of little boards on which he had drawn, with the pen and very finely, scenes of the Passion; a wooden cross, with a very finely drawn representation of the body of Christ. In stirring up with his foot the ground on which all sorts of things had been thrown, the young officer found in the sand a small monstrance in which the Host appeared to be still enclosed. He picked it up respectfully, wiped it, and enveloped it in a linen cloth. "I was very worried," he relates later, "for I felt it was not for me thus to carry the good God."

When the time arrived to leave Tamanrasset, he took the little monstrance, put it in front of him on the saddle of his *mehari*, and thus did the thirty miles

[1] Later on, in February, 1918, a detachment of Saharan troops, operating against the rebels, found in a camp at 188 miles to the east of Tamanrasset, sandals, kitchen utensils, scissors, and different things belonging to Father de Foucauld. In the fight seven men of the camp were killed. (Note of Sub-Lieutenant Béjot, of the Aguraï station.)
[2] Report of December 27, 1916, to the Lieutenant-Colonel commanding the oasis territory in the Azjer country. Communicated by the Governor-General of Algeria.

which separate Tamanrasset from Fort Motylinski. This was the first procession of the Blessed Sacrament in the Sahara. When he arrived at the station his embarrassment was great. On the way M. de La Roche remembered a conversation that he had had one day with Father de Foucauld. When he said to him : " You have permission to keep the Blessed Sacrament; but, if a misfortune happened to you, what should be done?" the Father replied : " There are two answers : make a perfect act of contrition, and administer communion to yourself, or send the consecrated Host to the White Fathers by post." He could not make up his mind to do the second. Having called a non-commissioned officer of the post, an old ecclesiastical student who was a fervent Christian, M. de La Roche held counsel with him. They thought it best for one of them to give himself communion. The officer "put on white gloves he had never worn" to open the cover of the monstrance and assure himself that he was not mistaken that the Host was there. It was there all right, just as the priest had consecrated and adored it. The two young men asked one another : " Will you receive it, or shall I ?" Then the non-commissioned officer knelt down and made his communion.[1]

Of the numerous expressions of respect and admiration which were addressed to Father de Foucauld's family, I shall only publish the letter of the chief of the Hoggar Tuaregs, and those of the Bishop of Viviers.

Letter of Musa ag Amastane to Madame de Blic.

" Praise to the one God.

" To her Ladyship our friend Marie, the sister of Charles our marabout, whom traitors and deceivers, people of Azjer assassinated, from Tebeul Musa ag Amastane, *amenokal* of Hoggar.

" Much greeting to our aforesaid friend Marie! As soon as I heard of the death of our friend, your brother Charles, my eyes closed; all is dark to me : I wept and I shed many tears, and I am in great mourning. His death is a great grief to me.

"I am far from where the thieving traitors and deceivers killed him; that is to say, they killed him in Ahaggar; and I am in Adrar, but, if it please God, we shall kill those who

---

[1] Statement made by Captain de La Roche to the Comtesse de Foucauld, May, 1917 ; statement also made at Maison Carrée, and letter to M. de Blic, December 27, 1916.

killed the marabout, until we have taken our vengeance to the full.

"Say good-day for me to your daughters, your husband, and all your friends, and tell them : Charles the marabout has died not only for you, but for us all. May God have mercy on him, and may we meet him in paradise!

"*The* 20 *of Safar*, 1335 (*December* 13, 1916).
"*Translated at Fort Motylinski, December* 25, 1916."[1]

Letter of Mgr. Bonnet, Bishop of Viviers, to Madame de Blic.

"Episcopal Residence, Viviers,
"*January* 17, 1917.

"Madame,
"The sorrow which afflicts you, touches me too painfully for me to keep from uniting my legitimate and profound regrets to yours.

"I feel most acutely your loss in the person of the Reverend Father de Foucauld. In my long life I have known few more loving, sensitive, generous, and ardent souls than his. God had so entered into him, that his whole being overflowed with light and charity.

"You know better than I do what hold the great and holy love of Church, country, and family had on his heart and how great was his ardour; you know how heroic was his zeal for the salvation of souls: his departure for heaven will be an irreparable misfortune for the countries whose return to the Faith he so skilfully and courageously prepared, unless the blood which has just watered them be for them a sowing of Christian seed.

---

[1] The *amenokal* of Hoggar died at the end of 1920, and his last words were to recommend the people of Hoggar to be faithful to France. Thus he bore in mind Father de Foucauld's advice. The Father called him "my best friend among the Tuaregs." The letter which informed me of this event first told of Musa's illness, the cause of which was not known. On December 22, he rested more calmly than before, and his near relations left him with the hope that he would soon be cured ; but on December 23, at one in the morning, he asked to say his prayers, and repeated several times : "Follow the good road of the French," and expired in the presence of his two negroes, Othman and Ilbak. On December 23, at 7, the burial took place before the whole population in tears.

"Musa Ag Amastane was Commander of the Legion of Honour, and military honours were paid him by the Saharan detachment commanded by an officer.

"Immediately after the ceremony, the nobles, *imrad* chiefs and notables went to the commander of the station and swore to follow Musa's counsels and to remain faithful to the French Government."

"I should not be comforted in the misfortune which strikes you if I did not consider that your dear and venerated martyr is more living than ever, that he has ceased to suffer, but does not cease to love us; that he is nearer God, more powerful over His Heart, and that he may make Him merciful to our afflicted Church, to wounded France, to my diocese that petitions him, to his family which mourns him.

"With, etc. . . .

"J. M. Frédéric,
"*Bishop of Viviers.*"

The same year, thanking Madame de Blic for the memento he had received, Mgr. Bonnet wrote this second letter, dated All Saints' Day:

"Episcopal Residence, Viviers,
"*November* 1, 1917.

"The precious picture could not have reached me more opportunely than on the day when my thoughts turn to him in ardent memory and fervent prayer amongst the immense legion of saints that the Church proposes for our especial remembrance to-day. The public veneration that I give him along with others, I offer every day in the secret of my soul: I owe him so much! He so often prayed effectively for my diocese and me during his life, and I must be silent about all the favours he has granted me since he is nearer God."[1]

In December, 1917, the Father's great friend, General Laperrine, passed through Hoggar. A few weeks later he wrote to Madame de Blic from Timbuctoo:

"I called at Tamanrasset on December 9. I considered that the last wishes of your brother, saying that he wished to be buried where he fell, had been taken too literally, and he was left in the provisory grave made by his servant Paul, in the ditch of the house, a ditch which risked being flooded with water at the first rains.

"On my return from Motylinski, on December 15, I had him exhumed and interred on the top of the hill on which his *borj* is, and about 200 yards to the west of this one (the hill is a simple undulation of the ground, but isolated in the middle of the plain, and is seen from very far). The

[1] Mgr. Bonnet, whom I questioned at Viviers on the subject of Father de Foucauld, thus summed up his judgment: " He was a great character, a great man, and a great saint."

three native soldiers killed at the same time as he, two of whom were the involuntary cause of his death through trying to deliver him, are buried at his feet. The very simple grave, without any inscription, is surmounted by a black wooden cross, but larger and stouter than the one which was on the grave in the ditch. Moreover, from its position, it is seen from a long way off.

"M. Lutaud, Governor-General of Algeria, got a sum voted to erect a monument to him at Tamanrasset; in order to do this without slighting his last wishes, I intend to leave the grave as it is, but about five yards off, on the ridge of the same undulation of the ground, I mean to put up a large cross of Hoggar granite, a kind of mission cross, a cross which will be seen from a great distance.

"Your brother was, as it were, mummified when we exhumed him, and could still be recognized. The translation was very moving."

In another letter, addressed to Father Voillard, of the White Fathers, the General said:[1] "The ball entered behind the right ear and came out through the left eye. He was buried in the position in which he was killed; kneeling, his elbows tied behind his back. We were obliged to inter him in that position, so as not to break his limbs : we simply wrapped him in a shroud."

Whilst the last burial was being carried out by his friend, the General was very much affected; he was astonished that the body was without any break and the face so recognizable, while what remained of the Arabs buried near him was only a little dust. One of the native soldiers then said to him : "Why are you astonished that he is thus preserved, General? It is not astonishing, since he was a great marabout."

These words were reported to me by a witness who heard them.

When he thus gave Charles de Foucauld a final resting-place, and placed it under the sign of the cross, which alone explains the life and death of the hermit, the General did not suspect that he was marking the place of his own tomb. We know that this other great servant of his country, a conqueror who spared bloodshed to friends and foes, after having so many times, at the head of his *mehari* riders, crossed the Sahara which he had pacified, was led to attempt crossing his kingdom by way of the air in February, 1920. The aeroplane, which started from Tamanrasset and was to carry him in a few hours as far as Senegal, got lost among

[1] Letter of December 15, 1917.

the fogs and fell in the desert. Wounded in the fall, having suffered without complaining for many days, exhausted by hunger and thirst, Laperrine died in the Anesberakka region on March 6, and his body, wrapped in the linen of the aeroplane, was put on the back of a camel, and again took the road to Tamanrasset. He was buried near his friend; Father de Foucauld took him in on his way.

What has become of the hermitages inhabited by Father de Foucauld in various parts of the Sahara? I tried to find out, and some evidence has reached me.

The " Fraternity " at Beni-Abbes was put under the custody of the French officers of the Arab Office. It is used as a shelter for poor nomads who cross the plateau. No doubt the chapel has lost its priest, who each morning bade Christ to come down to where He was more unknown than in Bethlehem. But the altar remains; the canvases on which Jesus, Mary, and Saints are represented, hang on the walls; the thick close columns continue to support date-wood joists and the roof of leaves and earth which the rain had once got through. They have kept on the gardener Hajj ben Ahmed, who receives his wages regularly from France. Some vegetables grow in the garden, and the palm grove has prospered.

At In-Salah, nothing is left. The *pied-à-terre* of the traveller is covered with the sand, which at present threatens the enclosure walls, and will break them down at the first simoom.

I have also bad news of the Kudiat cabin. Some day we shall certainly hear of the Father's observatory being destroyed; in the month of March, 1920, it was very much damaged by field-mice, which swarm up there.

The Tamanrasset fortlet has held out. France occupies and repairs it. It is used as lodgings for the lieutenant and a shelter for the bureaus of the detachment of the Saharan Company. The soldiers cultivate the garden; they have even sown flowers in it, which one of my friends, a traveller, saw blooming in February, 1920.

We may hope that these relics of earth and stone will not disappear too quickly. But the memory of the man who did not seek, like the rest of men, a convenient house, defended against cold, heat, and the passer-by, will continue and increase. The name of de Foucauld will be cited among those of the servants of God; he will be exalted in Christian communities which will not fail to rise up in the heart of Islam. Kabyles, Arabs, blacks, Hindoos, their souls opened to the truth, and seeing what a price was paid for their ransom, will remember the apostles who worked for them in poverty, obscurity, and extreme indigence of consolation. May the new missionaries hasten on the work of evangelization prepared by Cardinal Lavigerie, by the White Fathers, by the great brotherly monk Charles de Foucauld, sent to Africa as a sign of mercy, and as the messenger of the salvation which is to be hers.

Lord Jesus Christ, who art with us, be with the host of peoples and tribes that depend on us. Sole remedy of death, Living God, bring to Thyself the souls of the Musulmans so long left in error. And, for that, first touch some essentially missionary hearts in France, a still undependable mother with too little affection for her millions of African and Asiatic children. Thy servant Charles de Foucauld has shown the way; he endured their pride, their hardness, sometimes their treachery; he implored Thee so much for them; he was a monk without a monastery, a master without disciples, a penitent and a solitary, ever hoping for a time he was not to see. He died at his work. For his sake, have pity on them! Give part of Thy riches to the poor of Islam, and forgive the nations of the baptized their inveterate love of money.

APPENDIX

ASSOCIATION

For the Growth of the Missionary Spirit;
especially in our French Colonies.[1]

TO found this Association was one of the constant thoughts of Father de Foucauld. "After the peace," he wrote to one of his friends,[2] "I shall do all in my power for the final establishment of our Union, going where necessary and remaining in France as long as necessary. May the will of Jesus Christ be done in this and in all things."

The rules of this Union, drawn up in 1909, were abridged and simplified in 1913 and 1916. They are inspired by two essential ideas. The first is that at present a vigorous effort of evangelization of the infidels must be made, and that there is great negligence among Christians with respect to this primary duty, notably among us French people, who have not yet worked at the evangelization "of our Musulman brothers, who are French subjects." The second, which gives the Association its distinctive character, is that this hard work will not be accomplished if we only try to get alms and prayers. We must also ask the greatest possible number of Catholics to bear the Infidels always in mind, to have a "missionary spirit." *They will get it by a seriously Christian life* which will maintain this thought and make it pass into action. The means to arrive at this sincere, profound, and active Christianity, is to bind ourselves to the observance of a rule, and organize ourselves into an Association.

The thought of Father de Foucauld embraced all infidels. Consequently, according to him, each mother-country should be called on to constitute a similar Union for its own colonial infidels, who could not ordinarily attain to the knowledge of the true religion except through the Christian peoples upon whom they depend.

There is hardly a broader, more fraternal, or a more urgent idea. Approved first in 1909 by Mgr. Bonnet,

[1] I asked for this note from one of the men who were the friends of Father de Foucauld and talked with him about the Association.
[2] Letter to M. l'Abbé Laurain, All Saints' Day, 1916.

Bishop of Viviers, and by Mgr. Livinhac, Superior-General of the White Fathers, then by Cardinal Amette in 1919, the Association has received the individual and collective adhesion of persons or communities. As soon as it is known it will, no doubt, attract many hearts.[1] It is worthy to succeed from its breadth and generosity, from the very help with which it furnishes the clergy and faithful in setting forth a rule of life, a discipline, directed towards the apostolate under all its forms. It is the one legacy, the last word of Father de Foucauld to his friends.

[1] The President of the Association is His Grace Mgr. Le Roy, Archbishop of Caria, Superior-General of the Fathers of the Holy Ghost. Apply for admission or information to the Secretary of the Association Foucauld, 30, Rue Lhommond, Paris, V.

Lightning Source UK Ltd.
Milton Keynes UK
UKHW02f1821211018
330942UK00006B/98/P